Discrimination, Vulnerab Consumers and Financial Inclusion

This book addresses the questions of discrimination, vulnerable consumers, and financial inclusion in light of the emerging legal, socioeconomic, and technological challenges. New technologies – such as artificial intelligence-driven consumer credit risk assessment and Fintech platforms, the changing nature of vulnerability due to the ongoing COVID-19 pandemic, as well as the sophistication of digital technologies, which help circumvent legal barriers and protections – necessitate the continuous study of the existing legal frameworks and measures that are capable of tackling these challenges.

Organized in two major parts, the first addresses, from multiple national angles, the idea of a human rights approach to consumer law, in order to replace the mantra of economic efficiency that characterizes financial services with those of human dignity and freedom from discrimination and from debt-induced servitude. The second tackles the challenges posed by increased usage of technology in connection with financial services, which tends to solve, but also creates, additional issues for consumers in general, and for vulnerable groups in particular.

Cătălin-Gabriel Stănescu is Assistant Professor at the Centre for Market and Economic Law, University of Copenhagen.

Asress Adimi Gikay is Lecturer at Brunel University London with his research focusing on Artificial Intelligence, Law and Ethics.

Routledge Research in Finance and Banking Law

Housing and financial stability
Mortgage Lending and Macroprudential Policy in the US and UK
Alan Howard Brener

Conceptualizing the Regulatory Thicket
China's Financial Markets After the Global Financial Crisis
Shen Wei

Banking Bailout Law
A comparative study of the United States, United Kingdom, and the European Union
Virag Blazsek

Public-Private Partnerships in Emerging Economies
Augustine Edobor Arimoro

International Investment Protection within Europe
The EU's Assertion of Control
Julien Berger

Regulation and the Global Financial Crisis
Impact, Regulatory Responses, and Beyond
Daniel Cash and Robert Goddard

Discrimination, Vulnerable Consumers and Financial Inclusion
Fair Access to Financial Services and the Law
Edited by Cătălin-Gabriel Stănescu and Asress Adimi Gikay

Discrimination, Vulnerable Consumers and Financial Inclusion

Fair Access to Financial Services and the Law

Edited by Cătălin-Gabriel Stănescu and Asress Adimi Gikay

Routledge
Taylor & Francis Group

LONDON AND NEW YORK

First published 2021
by Routledge
2 Park Square, Milton Park, Abingdon, Oxon OX14 4RN

and by Routledge
52 Vanderbilt Avenue, New York, NY 10017

Routledge is an imprint of the Taylor & Francis Group, an informa business

British Library Cataloguing-in-Publication Data
A catalogue record for this book is available from the British Library

Library of Congress Cataloging-in-Publication Data
Names: Stanescu, Catalin-Gabriel, 1980- editor. | Gikay, Asress Adimi, 1984- editor.
Title: Discrimination, vulnerable consumers, and financial inclusion: fair access to financial services and the law / edited by Cătălin Gabriel Stănescu and Asress Adimi Gikay.
Description: Milton Park, Abingdon, Oxon; New York, NY: Routledge, 2021. | Includes bibliographical references and index.
Identifiers: LCCN 2020032994 (print) | LCCN 2020032995 (ebook) | ISBN 9780367511111 (hardback) | ISBN 9781003055075 (ebook)
Subjects: LCSH: Discrimination—Law and legislation. | Consumer protection—Law and legislation. | Credit—Law and legislation. | Financial services—Law and legislation. | Consumption (Economics)—Social aspects. | Low-income consumers. | Legal assistance to the poor.
Classification: LCC K3242.D575 2021 (print) | LCC K3242 (ebook) | DDC 343.07/25—dc23
LC record available at lccn.loc.gov/2020032994
LC ebook record available at lccn.loc.gov/2020032995

ISBN: 978-0-367-51111-1 (hbk)
ISBN: 978-1-003-05507-5 (ebk)

Typeset in Galliard
by MPS Limited, Dehradun

Contents

Acknowledgments

This book is the outcome of an international conference entitled "**Fair and Non-Discriminatory Access to Financial Services**" that took place at the Faculty of Law, University of Copenhagen, Denmark, in September 2019. The aim of the conference was to analyze recent trends and challenges posed by technological advancements and discriminatory practices against vulnerable consumer groups in accessing financial services in a number of international jurisdictions.

We would like to thank all those who answered the call and actively participated in the two days of presentations and discussions in Copenhagen and made both the event and this book possible.

Our appreciation goes to the **Carlsberg Foundation** and the **Dreyer Fund** for their generous financial support, their commitment to high-quality academic research, and their flexibility and responsiveness. Without them, it would have been impossible to organize the conference, bring together the participants from all around the world, record all presentations, interview all participants, and make them available for the wider public.

We express our gratitude to Professor **Caroline Heide-Jørgensen**, Head of the Center for Market and Economic Law (Faculty of Law University of Copenhagen) and Professor **Henrik Palmer Olsen**, Associate Dean for Research (Faculty of Law, University of Copenhagen) for their steady support and for endorsing, promoting, and hosting the conference.

Credit is also due to the amazing staff at the University of Copenhagen, who helped finance, organize, and run the conference: **Malene Vinberg Johansen, Cecilie Petersen, Michelle Goncalves Kjærulff**, and **Sharon O'Carroll Khan**.

Last, but not least, a special acknowledgment goes to **Siobhan Poole** and **Chloe James**, from Routledge, for their support and assistance in turning this book into a reality.

We hope the book will prove interesting and that it will facilitate the exchange of ideas and understanding, foster meaningful discussions, and lead to inspired solutions for the benefit of all vulnerable consumers.

Contributors

Cătălin-Gabriel Stănescu is Assistant Professor at the Centre for Market and Economic Law, University of Copenhagen. Cătălin became a member of the National Union of Romanian Bar Associations in 2006 and worked both in private practice and as in-house counsel for two major multinational corporations. In 2015, he obtained a doctorate (summa cum laude) in International Business Law (Central European University) with a thesis entitled "Self-Help, Private Debt Collection and the Concomitant Risks – A Comparative Analysis" (Springer, 2015). Since 2016, he joined the Faculty of Law, University of Copenhagen, teaching and researching in commercial and consumer law. Cătălin obtained a Marie Curie Individual Fellowship in 2018 and is currently conducting his research project on the need to harmonize regulation concerning abusive debt collection practices in the European Union. His other research interests concern consumer finance, digitization of financial services, fair and nondiscriminatory access to credit, consumer vulnerability, and economic inequality.

Dr. Asress Adimi Gikay is Lecturer at Brunel University London with his research focusing on Artificial Intelligence, Law and Ethics. In 2020, he completed his PhD (with Honor) in Individual Person and Legal Protections at Sant'Anna School of Advanced Studies (Pisa, Italy) with a thesis on the Regulation of Automated Consumer Credit Scoring in the EU and the US. He also earned a Doctorate Degree in Juridical Sciences (summa cum laude) at Central European University (CEU) in 2016 specializing in comparative secured transactions law. He holds an LLM in International Business Law (CEU) and an LLM in Comparative Law, Economic and Finance (IUC-Torino). He obtained his LLB with distinction from Addis Ababa University Faculty of Law in 2008.

Dr. Asress Adimi Gikay has published several articles in peer-reviewed journals on topics ranging from secured transaction law reform to the regulation of blockchain and cryptocurrencies including in the *Journal of Civil Law Studies*, *Case Western Reserve Journal of Law, Technology & the Internet*, *Tilburg Law Review*, and *Mizan Law Review*. He has also authored monographs published on the *International Encyclopedia of Laws* and a book titled *Competition Law in Ethiopia* published by Kluwer Law International.

Joanne Atkinson is Principal Lecturer in Law at the University of Portsmouth. Joanne qualified as a solicitor in England and Wales in 1999 and spent time working both in private practice and in-house for a global financial services corporation. She joined the University of Portsmouth in 2011, teaching corporate and commercial law in a variety of undergraduate and postgraduate courses. Joanne is the University's LLM course director and uses her experience in legal practice to enhance and enliven students' experience. Her research interests focus on consumer credit regulation and fair access to credit. Since 2019, Joanne has been a contributing editor of Goode's *Consumer Credit Law and Practice*.

Martha Buit holds an LLM (cum laude) in Legal Research with a focus on private law from the University of Groningen and is currently a PhD researcher at the Groningen Centre for European Financial Services Law. Her research concerns lending-based crowdfunding and how this alternative financing structure can be adequately regulated. In particular, the project focuses on achieving a balance between the protection of consumers and small and medium-sized enterprises and enabling the further innovation and growth of LB-crowdfunding.

Williams C. Iheme obtained his doctor of juridical science degree (SJD) in 2016 from Central European University, and his book titled *Towards Reforming the Legal Framework for Secured Transactions in Nigeria* (Springer, 2016) heralded a major law reform in Nigeria's secured transactions law in 2017. He was Visiting Research Scholar at the Cornell Law School in 2015. He is currently Associate Professor at the Jindal Global Law School and recurrent Visiting Professor at the Strathmore Law School. Before joining academia full time, he was practicing law for some years at top commercial law firms in Lagos where clients consulted him for his authoritative advice on contracts, corporate insolvency, secured transactions, etc. Apart from consumer protection law, his other research interests include corporate governance, insolvency, arbitration, international trade, and secured transactions.

MA Kailiang is a law PhD candidate sponsored by China Scholarship Council at the University of Paris-Sud/University of Paris-Saclay and Visiting Scholar in the Law School at the University of Copenhagen. He graduated from China University of Political Science and Law with a master's degree in Economic Law. His PhD dissertation focused on researching shareholder protection regimes in financial holding companies. He has published several papers on Internet finance regulation and reform of state-owned enterprises both in Chinese and English. Also, he participated in research programs supported by the National Social Science Fund of China and China University of Political Science and Law. Moreover, he has participated in several international conferences where he served as a speaker and contributed papers. He currently acts as the associate director of the Association of China Scholarship Council Fellows in Parisian Region and a member of the France-Chinese Association for Economic Law.

Chrystin Ondersma is Professor of Law at Rutgers Law School in New Jersey. She teaches in the fields of bankruptcy, commercial law, and consumer credit, and her recent scholarship focuses on the human rights implications of predatory lending, over-indebtedness, and insolvency systems. Prior to joining Rutgers, she worked in the Business Finance and Restructuring Department at Weil, Gotshal & Manges LLP in New York and clerked for the Hon. Michael Daly Hawkins of the U.S. Court of Appeals for the Ninth Circuit. She graduated magna cum laude from Harvard Law School, where she also worked as an executive editor of the *Harvard Civil Rights-Civil Liberties Law Review* and as a teaching assistant to then Professor Elizabeth Warren.

Dr. Holly Powley is Lecturer in Law at the University of Bristol. Her research interests lie in banking law and banking regulation. Holly holds an LLM in Commercial Law (Bristol) and completed her PhD in June 2016 (Bristol). Her dissertation is entitled "Reforming the Structure of Banking Regulation in the United Kingdom: Strengthening the Framework to Guard Against Communication Failures." Holly's research focuses on banking conduct and culture, considering both the impact of biases on decision-making processes within banks as well as the current legal framework for dealing with questions of banking standards and conduct. Holly is currently finalizing a project assessing the role of alternative dispute resolution in the financial advice context. Holly is an Associate Editor of *Brill Research Perspectives in International Banking and Securities Law*.

Sabrina Rochemont is a contributing volunteer member of the Cashless Society Working Party, formed in late 2016 and hosted by the Institute and Faculty of Actuaries (IFOA). The IFOA is a royal chartered, not-for-profit professional body that oversees actuaries' education, qualifications, and professional development worldwide. Sabrina joined the Working Party as a lay member. Her background lies in the professional management of corporate information technology services, specialized in change management. The Working Party research delivers a neutral, analytical assessment of developments to comprehend benefits, risks, and issues of a cashless society at the global level, in the public interest. It provides insights into specialist economic topics and identifies opportunities to learn from international experiences and to adapt public policy. It also provides insights into stakeholder interests that underpin entrenched positions on the transition in progress.

Emeritus Professor Keith Stanton studied law at Oxford and has taught at Bristol since 1973. He was appointed Professor of Law in 1994. He was Head of the Department of Law from 1992 to 1997 and of the School of Law from 2005 to 2009. He has served on the Executive Committees of the

Committee of Heads of University Law Schools and the Society of Legal Scholars. He was President of the Society of Legal Scholars in 2011–2012. His main research interests lie in the law of tort, particularly in relation to professional and statutory liabilities, and in banking law and regulation. His current research on the law of tort considers judicial methodology in tort cases, reform of the personal injury litigation system, and political aspects of tort reform. On banking law, he is currently researching the regulation of the banking and finance industry by the Financial Conduct Authority. He is co-editor of *The Common Law World Review* and a member of the editorial boards of *The Tort Law Review* and *The Journal of Professional Negligence*.

Prof. Tibor Tajti (Thaythy) is Professor of Law (since 2002), Chair of the International Business Law Program (since 2015), and former Director of the Doctoral Program (2007–2015) of the Legal Studies Department of Central European University. The courses he teaches as part of the master's program include comparative bankruptcy and secured transactions law, the regulatory environment of business, law for small and mid-scale start-up enterprises, the legal aspects of corporate finance, capital markets, and securities regulation. He also teaches insolvency law at the China-European Union School of Law, Beijing. His primary fields of expertise include bankruptcy and secured transactions law, corporate governance, corporate finance, and securities (financial) regulations. Each of these areas is approached from the perspectives of comparative law and the law-growth nexus. The latter focuses on selected legal tools whereby development can be boosted to fit the fast-changing and technology-dependent 21st century.

Eliza Varney is Senior Lecturer in Law at Keele University, United Kingdom. She holds a Doctorate in Law from the University of Hull, United Kingdom. Eliza's research is in disability equality, focusing on the compatibility of English contract law with the values pursued by the UN Convention on the Rights of Persons with Disabilities (CRPD), in particular the protection of human dignity. Eliza has also conducted research on disability equality and access to information and communication technologies (ICTs) and the implementation of the CRPD. Her publications include the monograph *Disability and Information Technology* (Cambridge University Press, 2013); book chapters, including contributions on Articles 21 and 49 CRPD in Ilias Bantekas, Michael Ashley Stein, and Dimitris Anastasiou (eds.) *The UN Convention on the Rights of Persons with Disabilities: A Commentary* (Oxford University Press, 2018); and articles in *Legal Studies, Northern Ireland Legal Quarterly, Communications Law, Utilities Law Review*, and *Zeitschrift fur Rechtssoziologie* ORCID: 0000-0002-0906-9210.

Introduction

Discrimination, Vulnerable Consumers and Financial

Stănescu and Gikay

This book addresses the questions of discrimination, vulnerable consumers, and financial inclusion in light of the emerging legal, socioeconomic, and technological challenges. New technologies – such as artificial intelligence-driven consumer credit risk assessment and Fintech platforms, the changing nature of vulnerability due to the ongoing Covid-19 pandemic, as well as the sophistication of digital technologies, which help circumvent legal barriers and protections –necessitate the continuous study of the existing legal frameworks and measures capable of tackling these challenges.

The contributions in this book were presented at the International Conference entitled "Fair and Non-Discriminatory Access to Financial Services," which was organized by the Centre for Market and Economic Law (Faculty of Law, University of Copenhagen) in Copenhagen on 26–27 September 2019.[1] They are premised on the failure of the existing market and consumer protection paradigms, and focus on the effects of the increased levels of social inequality, rapid technological advancement, widespread use of digitization, and consequences of a global pandemic[2] on the lives of consumers in general and vulnerable consumers in particular.

The introductory chapter discusses the difficulties around defining *vulnerability*, the application of the human rights principle of "non-discrimination" to financial services, financial inclusion, and potential regulatory and political solutions. It also provides the readers with an overview of each contribution in the book.

Financial services, contractual autonomy and consumer protection

The main driving force for the provision of financial services is profit. Financial institutions operate in the private law sphere, based on the notion of freedom of

---

1 For details, video presentations, and podcasts, visit https://jura.ku.dk/english/cme/calender/2019/access-to-financial-services/, accessed 30.06.2020.
2 While the chapters do not primarily focus on the Covid-19 pandemic, its coinciding with the editing process has allowed some of the contributors to address the effect of the pandemic on consumer vulnerability.

contract. Thus, it is assumed that if the parties freely entered into an agreement, it is binding. Nevertheless, contractual autonomy raises several issues. First, reasoning purely with the logic of profit or contractual autonomy, financial institutions can invoke business reasons to refuse entering into agreements with certain consumers.[3] Second, they may resort to commercial practices or impose terms that are not ethically or legally acceptable. Thus, contractual autonomy and business practices must be regulated and confined to the principles of fairness and non-discrimination.

In no other field is consumer protection more important than in financial services. The consumer's life may hinge on being granted credit. Financing education, a home, purchase of motor vehicle, and many other important aspects of the consumer's life in the modern world depend highly on accessing credit.[4] Those who are able to obtain credit have a better chance of improving their personal lives, whereas those who cannot access financing may enter a cycle of poverty and economic inequality. As the 2008 credit crunch and the ongoing Covid-19 crisis have emphasized, consumers are the most exposed category to vagaries of the market, de- and self-regulation of financial institutions, change in employment status, or temporary loss of income.

In many developing countries,[5] large segments of the population lack access to financial services, which is considered the main cause for the persistence of poverty, income inequality, and slow economic development.[6] The measures

3 According to an information sheet of the European Union (EU), banks are free to set limits to lending to nonresidents or to residents who work in another EU country, even if they are not allowed to discriminate between EU citizens on the basis of nationality. See https://europa.eu/youreurope/citizens/consumers/financial-products-and-services/consumer-credits-and-loans/index_en.htm, last updated 27.01.2020, accessed 30.06.2020. Similar wording, stating that banks cannot discriminate between EU citizens in granting mortgages *solely* on the basis of nationality, is to be found on an information sheet about mortgage loans (emphasis added). See https://europa.eu/youreurope/citizens/consumers/financial-products-and-services/mortgages/index_en.htm, last updated 09.03.2020, accessed 30.06.020. Two aspects are easily noticeable. First, credit discrimination appears to be allowed if it is not based only on nationality. Second, in the absence of clear anti-discrimination rules in accessing financial services, it is difficult to estimate the chances of consumers in proving and obtaining redress.
4 Jessica Mai, "7 ways your credit score can affect your life," *The Guardian* (May 5, 2016) https://www.businessinsider.com/how-your-credit-score-can-impact-your-life-2016-5?IR=T accessed 27.02.2019.
5 The phenomenon is also known in developed countries, as emphasized by data coming from the US, UK, or Australia. See Drew M. Anderson, Alexander Strand, and J. Michael Collins, "The Impact of Electronic Payments for Vulnerable Consumers: Evidence from Social Security" (Malden, USA) [Wiley Periodicals, Inc.] 52 *Journal of Consumer Affairs* 35: 42 and Therese Wilson, "Supporting Social Enterprises to Support Vulnerable Consumers: The Example of Community Development Finance Institutions and Financial Exclusion" (Boston) [Springer US] 35 *Journal of Consumer Policy* 197:198–199.
6 Thorsten Beck, Asli Demirgüç-Kunt, and Patrick Honohan, "Access to Financial Services" [World Bank] *World Bank Research Observer*, 120. See also Consumer Financial Protection Bureau – Empowering low income and economically vulnerable consumers. Report on a National Convening, November 2013, 25–29, available at: https://files.consumerfinance.gov/f/201311_cfpb_report_empowering-economically-vulnerable-consumers.pdf, accessed 30.06.2020.

implemented around the world had various degrees of success,[7] which shows that there is no single, global panacea to the issue of financial inclusion.[8] Nevertheless, the solution is ultimately a political one, because governments and legislators play the most important role in building an inclusive financial system,[9] especially, but not exclusively,[10] through prudential regulation of both traditional (banks) and fringe financial institutions (payday lenders).[11]

In the last decade, policies that encourage financial institutions to provide service to those that might be left out ("the unbanked")[12] were put in place. In the age of digitization, technology-based financial services are regarded as the beacon of financial inclusion,[13] despite concerns that they also foster vulnerability[14] or have a limited positive impact on vulnerable consumers.[15]

Thus, whether financial inclusion and fair access to financial services are real or myths must be critically examined.

Discrimination and financial services

Financial institutions engage in various discriminatory practices including differential treatment of consumers based on race, nationality, gender, physical or psychological disability, health conditions, and other similar factors.[16]

---

7 Ibid, 119; Jerry Buckland, *Building Financial Resilience Do Credit and Finance Schemes Serve or Impoverish Vulnerable People?* (1st ed. Springer International Publishing, 2018), 21–23; Wilson, 201–207.

8 Buckland, p. 19. According to Buckland's definition of financial inclusion, it is "a reformist process driven primarily by the state and inter-state actors that seeks to bring vulnerable people into the formal banking system to foster their financial well-being and, again, to stimulate economic growth, enhance national security, and reduce the funding of criminal activity."

9 Beck, Demirgüç-Kunt, and Honohan, 136; Buckland, 237; Wilson, 200–201.

10 Buckland, 196–198, 200–211.

11 Ibid, 191–194, 198–200.

12 Ibid, 19. According to Buckland, financial inclusion is primarily concerned with groups that have previously been excluded from formal banking (i.e., newcomers, indigenous peoples, income- and asset-poor people, rural and remote people, or unemployed people), and its main goals are to improve access to basic financial services such as bank accounts and basic credit, or saving products for the unbanked.

13 Douglas Arner, Ross Buckley, and Dirk Zetzsche, "Sustainability, FinTech and Financial Inclusion" (Dordrecht) [Springer Nature B.V.] 21 *European Business Organization Law Review* 7:7–35.

14 For instance, the increasing reliance on contactless payment is resulting in banks removing ATM machines from certain areas in the UK, which led to elderly people, who heavily rely on cash payments being left behind. Rupert Jones, "Cashless Britain: Over-55s and Low Earners at Risk of Being Left Behind" (*The Guardian*, March 23, 2019) https://www.theguardian.com/money/2019/mar/23/cashless-britain-over-55s-and-low-earners-at-risk-of-being-left-behind accessed 03.07.2020.

15 Buckland, 55–59; Anderson, Strand, and Collins, 54.

16 George Benston, "Consumer Protection as Justification for Regulating Financial-Services Firms and Products'"(Boston) [Kluwer Academic Publishers] 17 *Journal of Financial Services Research* 277:295.

Existing empirical evidence and research

In the aftermath of the 2008 financial crisis, it was revealed that in the US, between 2004 and 2008, "highly qualified prime retail and wholesale applicants for Wells Fargo residential mortgage loans were more than four times as likely to receive a subprime loan if they were African-American and more than three times as likely if they were Hispanic than if they were white."[17] "Conversely, during the same time period, borrowers with less favorable credit qualifications were more likely to receive prime loans if they were white than borrowers who were African-American or Hispanic."[18]

In recent years, consumers have been able to bring successful lawsuits against banks in the US for discriminatory practices, based on anti-credit discrimination legislation.[19] In *United States vs. Deposit Guaranty National Bank*, the defendant bank engaged in discriminatory lending practices. The court found that "loan officers had broad discretion to make override decisions, known as judgmental overrides, for credit-scored loan applications – that is, decisions to deny credit to applicants who scored at or above the stated cutoff score for loan approval ('high side overrides') and to grant credit to applicants who scored below that cutoff score ('low side overrides')."[20] As a result, African-American loan applicants were three times more likely to be rejected compared to white applicants.[21] The court entered a settlement order, which, among others, required the defendant to establish a $3 million compensation trust fund for the victims of its discriminatory lending practices.[22]

Wells Fargo Bank similarly engaged in discriminatory lending practices in mortgage loans, by placing African-American and Hispanic-American borrowers into subprime loans, "with adverse terms and conditions such as high interest rates, excessive fees, pre-payment penalties, and unavoidable future payment hikes, when similarly qualified Non-Hispanic white ("white") bor-

17 *United States of America vs. Wells Fargo Bank*, U.S. District Court of Columbia Case 1:12-cv-01150 Document 1 (filed 07/12/12), https://www.justice.gov/sites/default/files/crt/legacy/2012/07/12/wellsfargocomp.pdf accessed 25.04.2019.
18 Ibid.
19 Credit discrimination is seen to generate lost opportunities and denial of essential services, pushing vulnerable categories of consumers toward predatory lenders. In response, the US implemented the Equal Credit Opportunity Act, the Fair Housing Act, and the Civil Rights Act. Deanne Loonin, *Credit Discrimination* [Chi Chi Wu (ed.), 4th ed., National Consumer Law Center, 2005), 1–4.
20 *United States of America vs. Deposit Guaranty National Bank a division of First American National Bank*, U.S. District Court for Southern District of Mississippi Jackson Division, Settlement (1999), https://www.justice.gov/crt/housing-and-civil-enforcement-cases-documents-119 accessed 25.04.2019.
21 Ibid.
22 Ibid.

rowers received prime loans."[23] The scheme involved discrimination of African-American and Hispanic-American loan applicants in some cases with higher credit scores than white applicants.[24] Wells Fargo settled the case for $175 million.[25]

In 2016, the Consumer Financial Protection Bureau (CFPB) and the Department of Justice (DOJ) secured a settlement of $10.6 million for discriminatory lending through redlining from BancorpSouth.[26] The story is the same. BancorpSouth engaged in discriminatory mortgage loan practices, among others by providing loans to Caucasian Americans with credit scores of about 622, while denying them to African-Americans with credit scores of 625 and, according to the allegation, with higher income and better credit history.[27]

In the EU, empirical research and personal experiences also indicate the presence of financial discrimination fostered by the absence of sector-specific anti-credit discrimination legislation such as the one adopted in the United States. In Denmark, one of the authors was offered usual credit terms during preliminary talks with a bank agent, including a 20% down payment for a mortgage, but the terms worsened (and the requested down payment jumped to 40%) once he presented his passport and revealed being an EU expat.

A study in general access to financial services revealed an alarming level of discrimination based on ethnic origin in the financial industry in the EU Member States.[28] Under this study, a group of researchers sent banking related inquires to 1,281 banks in seven EU Member States, using dummy emails with "domestic

---

23 *United States of America vs. Wells Fargo Bank*, U.S. District Court of Columbia Case 1:12-cv-01150 Document 1 (filed 07/12/12), https://www.justice.gov/sites/default/files/crt/legacy/2012/07/12/wellsfargocomp.pdf accessed 25.04.2019.

24 Ibid. "For example, between 2004 and 2008, highly qualified prime retail and wholesale applicants for Wells Fargo residential mortgage loans were more than four times as likely to receive a subprime loan if they were African-American and more than three times as likely if they were Hispanic than if they were white. Conversely, during the same time period, borrowers with less favorable credit qualifications were more likely to receive prime loans if they were white than borrowers who were African-American or Hispanic."

25 U.S. Department of Justice, "Justice Department Reaches Settlement with Wells Fargo Resulting in More Than $175 Million in Relief for Homeowners to Resolve Fair Lending Claims," Press Release (July 12, 2012), https://www.justice.gov/opa/pr/justice-department-reaches-settlement-wells-fargo-resulting-more-175-million-relief accessed 25.04.2019.

26 U.S. Department of Justice, "Justice Department and Consumer Financial Protection Bureau Reach Settlement with BancorpSouth Bank to Resolve Allegations of Mortgage Lending Discrimination," Press Release (June 29, 2016), https://www.justice.gov/opa/pr/justice-department-and-consumer-financial-protection-bureau-reach-settlement-bancorpsouth accessed 10.02.2020.

27 *US and CFPB vs. BancoSouth*, U.S. District Court for the Northern District of Mississippi, Aberdeen Division, Case: 1:16-cv-00118-GHD-DAS (2016), Complaint, Para 101.

28 Stefan Matthias and others, "Ethnical Discrimination in Europe: Field Evidence from the Finance Industry" [Public Library of Science (PLoS)] 13 PloS one e0191959, 1–7.

names" and "Arabic names," arguing that a lower response rate, especially to the latter's investment and loan-related inquires, was the result of discrimination.[29]

In other research published in 2016 focusing on self-employed immigrants in Sweden, it was established that self-employed European immigrants and non-European immigrants are more likely to be denied loans or be charged higher interest rates compared to native applicants, with the situation being worse for non-European immigrants.[30] Controlling for different variables that could justify differential treatment, the researchers concluded that the difference in terms of accessing loan could only be explained by discrimination.[31]

Other empirical studies, conducted in Spain, found that local banks discriminate against vulnerable categories of consumers (mainly those with lower income, technological skills, or financial literacy),[32] while bank restructuring measures (such as closure of branches) may expose consumers to various levels of financial exclusion.[33] At the same time, consumers with severe illnesses and disabilities still have trouble accessing basic financial services in Hungary and Romania.[34]

An issue of interest is how discriminatory practices engaged in by private financial institutions such as banks are dealt with, in the context of the general understanding that businesses enjoy autonomy but are under obligation to provide fair and inclusive financial services. The two different approaches prevailing in the US and the EU in this regard are discussed below.

29 Ibid.
30 Lina Aldén and Mats Hammarstedt, "Discrimination in the Credit Market? Access to Financial Capital among Self-employed Immigrants," 69 *Kyklos* 3:3–31.
31 Ibid, 5. "We find clear evidence that self-employed immigrants of a non-European background subjectively perceive more discrimination by customers, suppliers, and banks compared to self-employed natives and self-employed European immigrants. Furthermore, self-employed immigrants apply for bank loans more frequently than do self-employed natives. Self-employed non-Europeans have a higher risk than self-employed natives of having their loan applications denied; if those loans are approved, they are charged higher interest rates than self-employed natives are. These results remain even when we control for a large number of variables and withstand different robustness checks. Therefore, we argue that, to some extent, discrimination in the credit market explains our results."
32 B. Fernández-Olit and others, "Banks and Financial Discrimination: What Can Be Learnt from the Spanish Experience?" 42 *Journal of Consumer Policy* 303: 319; Judith Clifton, Marcos Fernández-Gutiérrez, and Myriam García-Olalla, "Including Vulnerable Groups in Financial Services: Insights from Consumer satisfaction" [Routledge], 20 *Journal of Economic Policy Reform* 214: 214.
33 Joaquín Maudos, "Bank Restructuring and Access to Financial Services: The Spanish Case," 48 *Growth and Change* 963:964, 987–988. The author claims that the expansion of online banking mitigates the adverse effects of branch downsizings; however, use of the Internet in financial services is confirmed to be lower with vulnerable segments of consumers (elderly, lower education, and lower-income groups).
34 Dan Popa-Cazul nevăzătorului căruia o bancă a refuzat să-i deschidă un cont nu e singular. Ce spun nevăzătorii,comunitatea bancară și asociațiile de protecție a consumatorilor, 23.01.2020, available at: https://economie.hotnews.ro/stiri-finante_banci-23617862-cazul-nevazatorului-caruia-banca-refuzat-deschida-cont-nu-singular-vezi-spun-nevazatorii-dar-reprezentantii-comunitatii-bancare.htm, accessed 25.06.2020.

Diverse approaches to tackling discrimination in the US and the EU

A brief overview of anti-discrimination laws in the US and the EU shows how legal systems deal with discrimination in financial services. While in the US, there is sector-specific legislation concerning equal access to credit, in the EU, only general anti-discrimination laws apply to discrimination in financial services.

In the US, the Equal Credit Opportunity Act (ECOA) prohibits discrimination on the grounds of race, color, religion, national origin, and sex.[35] The Fair Credit Report Act (FCRA) and the Fair Housing Act (in case of mortgages) further supplement the ECOA.[36]

Whilst the ECOA seems to cover sufficiently discrimination based on known factors such as race and religion, it does not specifically address discriminations based on various proxies, such as Zip code.

Nevertheless, it has been applied to cases of discrimination that excluded minority neighborhoods under the practice of redlining.[37] By redlining, financial institutions exclude certain areas from providing financial services based on age, racial composition, or other similar factors due to the presumption that the area in question is economically not viable.[38] In one case, the DOJ and the CFPB fined Hudson City Savings Bank $32.25 million for excluding majority Black and Hispanic counties in New York through redlining.[39]

Implemented in the 1980s, the US law on anti-discrimination in consumer financial services was not designed to deal with the recent challenges presented by modern technology. In this regard, the US has not implemented a specific law addressing the phenomena of artificial intelligence-driven credit scoring. At a state level, California enacted the first comprehensive privacy law in use when it implemented the California Consumer Privacy Act (CCPA) of 2018.[40] So far, the assumption is that the ECOA is capable of being adapted to tackling

---

35 Equal Credit Opportunity Act of 1974 (15 U.S.C. § 1691 et seq.), § 701, "(a) It shall be unlawful for any creditor to discriminate against any applicant, with respect to any aspect of a credit transaction (1) on the basis of race, color, religion, national origin, sex or marital status, or age (provided the applicant has the capacity to contract); (2) because all or part of the applicant's income derives from any public assistance program; or (3) because the applicant has in good faith exercised any right under the Consumer Credit Protection Act."
36 The Fair Housing Act, 42 U.S.C. 3601 et seq.
37 Alex Gano, "Disparate Impact and Mortgage Lending: A Beginner's Guide" (Chicago) [American Bar Association] 26 *Journal of Affordable Housing & Community Development Law* 1100:1137.
38 Edward W. Larkin, "Redlining: Remedies for Victims of Urban Disinvestment" (New York, etc.) [Fordham University School of Law, etc.] 5 *Fordham Urban Law Journal* 83:84.
39 Press Release, U.S. Department of Justice, "Justice Department and Consumer Financial Protection Bureau Reach Settlement with Hudson City Bank to Resolve Allegations of Mortgage Lending Discrimination" (September 24, 2015) https://www.justice.gov/opa/pr/justice-department-and-consumer-financial-protection-bureau-reach-settlement-hudson-city accessed 01.03.2019.
40 California Consumer Privacy Act (CCPA) A.B. 375.

potential issues emerging from automated decisions that might have discriminatory effect. In addition, the FCRA contains provisions aimed at ensuring that Credit Reporting Agencies provide accurate information about the consumer, including credit scoring, to financial institutions.[41] However, this act does not have provisions dedicated to artificial intelligence-driven credit scoring. Whether these legal instruments are sufficient to tackle technology-based challenges is debatable (Ondersma, Chapter 1).

In the EU, there is no community level specific anti-discrimination law for consumer financial services. A proposal to extend anti-discrimination law beyond employment in a form of a directive was first made in 2008.[42] It was never adopted due to the resistance of several Member States.[43] The proposal was based on the realization that "while non-discrimination is recognized to be one of the fundamental values of the EU, in practice the level of legal protection to secure these values differs between Member States and between discrimination grounds."[44]

Today, general anti-discrimination law governs discrimination in financial services in the EU. By far, the most comprehensive legal regime enshrining non-discrimination rules is the Charter of Fundamental Rights of the European Union (CFREU), which is effective in all EU Member States.[45] The Consumer Credit Directive (CCD) embraces the CFREU's provisions on anti-discrimination through cross-reference.[46] The charter prohibits discrimination on the grounds of sex, ethnicity, religion, color, and many other factors.[47] The

---

41 15 USC § 1681a(c)(6), § 1681g(c), § 1681g(f), § 1681b(B)(IV), and 15 U.S.C. § 1681e(b).
42 The Commission Proposal for a Council Directive on implementing the principle of equal treatment between persons irrespective of religion or belief, disability, age or sexual orientation, COM(2008) 426 final, Brussels, 2.7.2008 https://eur-lex.europa.eu/legal-content/EN/TXT/PDF/?uri=CELEX:52008PC0426&from=EN accessed 10.02.2020.
43 Krystyna Romanivna Bakhtina, "Extending Protection against Age Discrimination Outside the Area of Employment" (2018), 24 *European Journal of Current Legal Issues* 1:9.
44 Ibid, 5.
45 Equality and Human Rights Commission, "What Is the Charter of Fundamental Rights of the European Union?" https://www.equalityhumanrights.com/en/what-are-human-rights/how-are-your-rights-protected/what-charter-fundamental-rights-european-union accessed 10.02.2020.
46 Directive 2008/48/EC on credit agreements for consumers (The Consumer Credit Directive), Recital 45: "This Directive respects fundamental rights and observes the principles recognized in particular by the Charter of Fundamental Rights of the European Union. In particular, this Directive seeks to ensure full respect for the rules on protection of personal data, the right to property, nondiscrimination, protection of family and professional life, and consumer protection pursuant to the Charter of Fundamental Rights of the European Union."
47 Charter of the Fundamental Rights of the European Union (CFREU), (2000/C 364/01), Art. 21(1): "Any discrimination based on any ground such as sex, race, color, ethnic or social origin, genetic features, language, religion or belief, political or any other opinion, membership of a national minority, property, birth, disability, age or sexual orientation shall be prohibited."

CFREU can be invoked in the context of discrimination in the provision of financial services as it has specific provisions that reiterate the need to ensure a high level of consumer protection;[48] provide for the legal, economic, and social protection of the family;[49] and guarantee the consumer the right to access services of general economic interest.[50] These provisions are interpreted to provide consumer protection in financial services.[51]

In case of automated decisions made by financial institutions, in line with the spirit of the charter, the General Data Protection Regulation (GDPR) prohibits processing of a special category of personal data that reveals, among others, the ethnic, racial, and sexual orientation of the data subject.[52] Processing these categories of data is prohibited as it is assumed that it does not achieve a legitimate purpose (unless exceptions are provided) than to unfairly target the individual or infringe upon the persons' fundamental rights and freedoms.[53] The rule prohibiting processing of special categories of data has several exceptions, including the consent of the data subject, protecting the vital interest of the data subject, for establishing legal claims or defenses, and data made public by the data subject, to mention the most important ones.[54] Notwithstanding these exceptions, the rule does supplement the prohibition of discrimination on the ground of sensitive factors.

While the legal regimes in the US and the EU seem to indicate two diverse approaches, other legal systems might have their own approach. China appears to be highly influenced by its prevailing political system and relies on sector-specific regulatory measures coupled with active judicial interpretation of contract law (Kailiang, Chapter 3). Notwithstanding all the above, adequate solutions are yet to be found (Ondersma, Chapter 1; Varney, Chapter 2; Kailiang, Chapter 3; and Stanescu, Chapter 8). All the examples mentioned have as a common denominator vulnerable consumers. In the next section, we turn our attention to defining who these vulnerable consumers are.

Vulnerable consumers

Consumer vulnerability is ventured in academic and legal literature across the globe for the past three decades. However, the term still lacks a precise, global meaning. The situation is not different in the EU. Although the concept is

48 CFREU, Article 38.
49 Ibid, Article 33.
50 Ibid, Article 36.
51 Iris Benöhr, *EU Consumer Law and Human Rights* (Oxford University Press 2013), 123 et seq.
52 GDPR, Article 1.
53 Voigt Paul and Bussche Axel von dem (eds.), *The EU General Data Protection Regulation (GDPR): A Practical Guide* (Springer 2017), 110.
54 GDPR, Article 9 (2)-(4).

specifically used in EU legislation[55] and it causes sympathy and concern, Member States attach different understandings and weight to it in policymaking.[56]

Consumer vulnerability in times of crisis

Generally, minors, people with physical or intellectual deficiencies, and the elderly (especially if affected by various medical conditions) are listed as vulnerable categories in need of extra protection.[57] Whether people with low income qualify as vulnerable continues to be a controversial matter,[58] although in our opinion, this view has to change after the Covid-19 pandemic (Ondersma, Chapter 1, Powley and Stanton, Chapter 9).

Conceptualizing vulnerable consumers

The most comprehensive European study on consumer vulnerability is a 2016 report financed by the EU Commission that examined the incidence of vulnerability in 30 European countries.[59] Among others, the study delivered an overview of how the concept of consumer vulnerability was addressed in the relevant literature. Given the extensive bibliography employed by the study, in the following lines we will only sum up its findings.

The study acknowledges the lack of a single and common definition of consumer vulnerability and takes note of various local interpretations of the concept. The communality appears to lay in the *ex-ante* assessment of potentially negative outcomes vis-à-vis consumer well-being. In other words, it is an assessment of risk, not of an actual outcome.[60] Vulnerability is divided into two broad categories, the first stemming from personal characteristics of the consumer[61] the second considering the transactional situation in which consumers may find

55 Directive 2005/29/EC concerning unfair business-to-consumer commercial practices in the internal market [Unfair Commercial Practices Directive (UCPD)].
56 Norbert Reich, *Vulnerable Consumers in EU Law* [Dorota Leczykiewicz and Stephen Weatherill (eds.), Hart Publishing Ltd 2016), 141; Peter Cartwright, "Understanding and Protecting Vulnerable Financial Consumers" (New York) [Springer, US] 38 *Journal of Consumer Policy* 119:120–121.
57 Clifton, Fernández-Gutiérrez, and García-Olalla, 217–218.
58 Reich, 139.
59 "Consumer Vulnerability across Key Markets in the European Union," Final Report, January 2016 (Consumer Vulnerability Report), available at: https://ec.europa.eu/info/sites/info/files/consumers-approved-report_en.pdf, accessed 25.06.2020.
60 Ibid, 42.
61 A good example here is the approach taken by the Unfair Commercial Practices Directive (UCPD), which stated that vulnerability may arise from consumers' mental or physical infirmity, age, or credulity, which suggests an emphasis on personal characteristics. However, the UCPD recognized that these factors are not the sole sources or manifestations of vulnerability, which left room for other factors as well.

themselves.[62] The report mentions further that vulnerability is not necessarily a static, but rather a dynamic or temporal condition,[63] as consumers move in and out of vulnerability or may be vulnerable in connection with some transactions but not others.[64] Nevertheless, vulnerability remains lasting for some consumer groups, due to their enduring personal characteristics.[65]

These findings are reinforced by the empirical studies mentioned above and recent research in the field,[66] and similar observations are being made in Australia,[67] China,[68] and the US.[69] Vulnerability can arise from the economic marginalization of the consumer, which may be caused by a variety of factors such as sudden unemployment or illness, social status, education level, income levels, gender, immigration status, sexual orientation, race, or ethnicity. Some of these factors can affect consumers temporarily or regionally (e.g., unemployment, illness, social status, education level, and financial literacy), while others are more insurmountable (e.g., race, ethnicity, age, and disability), which suggests that, depending on the circumstances, any consumer can become vulnerable at some point. This means that the concept of consumer vulnerability offers sufficient flexibility to cover categories that come from beyond the confinements of general consumer law such as consumer-investors in connection to financial fraud generated by pyramid and Ponzi-schemes (Tajti, Chapter 10).

All these aspects should be considered[70] when searching for solutions to consumer vulnerability in financial services.[71]

---

62 Consumer Vulnerability Report, 42–43; Julie Robson, Jillian Dawes Farquhar, and Christopher Hindle, "Working Up a Debt: Students as Vulnerable Consumers" [Routledge] 27 *Journal of Marketing for Higher Education: Contemporary Thought in Higher Education Marketing* 274:276.

63 Ibid, 286. The UK-focused study found that in certain situations students are recognized as vulnerable consumers regarding financial matters, particularly with reference to indebtedness.

64 Ibid, 44.

65 Ibid, 39.

66 Iain Ramsay, *Changing Policy Paradigms of EU Consumer Credit and Debt Regulation* [Dorota Leczykiewicz and Stephen Weatherill (eds.), Hart Publishing Ltd, 2016], 173–174.

67 Linda Brennan, Zuleyka Zevallos, and Wayne Binney, "Vulnerable Consumers and Debt: Can Social Marketing Assist?" [Elsevier Ltd] 19 *Australasian Marketing Journal* 203:205.

68 Jeff Jianfeng Wang and Qian Tian, "Consumer Vulnerability and Marketplace Exclusion: A Case of Rural Migrants and Financial Services in China" (Los Angeles, CA) [SAGE Publications] 34 *Journal of Macromarketing* 45:46–47.

69 Consumer Financial Protection Bureau, "Empowering Low Income and Economically Vulnerable Consumers," 16–17, *supra* fn 3.

70 Clifton, Fernández-Gutiérrez, and García-Olalla, 215–217, 232; Buckland, 19.

71 Domurath already proposed making vulnerability the general normative standard in all consumer credit and mortgage law, suggesting that "consumers taking on credit and mortgage obligations should be regarded vulnerable and more regulatory invention should   be allowed with regard to the content of contracts between consumers and financial service providers, given the lack of freedom in consumer transactions, behavior evidence about the unfitness of the average consumer standard and the fact that the EU model of access justice appears to deprive consumers of possible higher protection standards in national legislation." Irina Domurath, "The Case for Vulnerability as the Normative Standard in European Consumer Credit and Mortgage Law – An

Typologies of consumer vulnerability

The Consumer Vulnerability Report also identified types of vulnerability and how they can be exploited in practice.

The first is *informational vulnerability*, in situations where service providers have superior information, as in the case of complex financial products or when lenders design credit products to take advantage of consumers' ignorance or bias.[72]

The second is *supply vulnerability*, in situations where consumers cannot participate in the market or have less choices, due to their characteristics, as in the case of expensive financial products.

The third is *redress vulnerability*, in situations where consumers face difficulties in obtaining redress due to costs, time, or process-related constraints.

The fourth is *pressure vulnerability*, in situations where decisions are not voluntary. Finally, there is *impact vulnerability*, in situations where certain consumer groups suffer greater losses in comparison to other consumers, as in the case of low-income consumers who suffer a large loss on a financial product, given that their lower income amplifies the impact of the loss.[73]

Discussing these typologies helps us understand their links with the drivers of vulnerability addressed above and also identify specific responses. The contributions in this book provide convincing examples and potential solutions for all of them, as mentioned in the following subsection.

A paradigm shift?

The EU legislative instruments targeted particular groups of vulnerable consumers in energy and financial services markets, but the overall treatment of vulnerable consumers is unsystematic.[74] Despite calls advocating for a paradigm shift from average to vulnerable consumers and a greater emphasis on the social role of consumer law,[75] the general benchmark remains the former, while the latter is only applicable in limited contexts.[76] Contrary to what one would expect in the digital age (characterized by rapid technological changes and increasingly complex products and services), the trend appears to be not an increased standard of protection, but the exact opposite: a transition from the originally "weak

Inquiry into the Paradigms of Consumer Law" [Verlag Österreich] 2 *Zeitschrift für Europäisches Unternehmens-und Verbraucherrecht* 124:133–135.
72 Ramsay, 174; Brennan, Zevallos, and Binney, 205; Cartwright, 121–122.
73 Consumer Vulnerability Report, 44–45; Cartwright, 122–124.
74 Dorota Leczykiewicz and Stephen Weatherill, *The Images of the Consumer in EU Law* [Dorota Leczykiewicz and Stephen Weatherill (eds.), Hart Publishing Ltd, 2016], 17.
75 Geraint G. Howells, Christian Twigg-Flesner, and Thomas Wilhelmsson (eds.), *Rethinking EU Consumer Law* [Routledge 2018], 7–8.
76 Leczykiewicz and Weatherill, 17.

consumer" through the "average consumer" toward a "responsible" one[77] with increased levels of depoliticization, deregulation,[78] and standardization.

The question is whether the recent events caused by the global pandemic justify the application of the average consumer standard and the laissez-faire attitude, taking into consideration not only the behavioral studies proving it to be a purely artificial construct with no support in reality, but also the exposure of large groups of consumers to market rationalities. The majority of our contributors argue that it does not, and reshifting consumer policy toward "protection of the weak" is the only way to move forward.

This is even more so in the case of financial services. It is a troublesome certainty that economically marginalized consumers always pay more and benefit the least from them.[79] The idea that such results are part and parcel of neoliberal legal order, designed for market economy and based on freedom of contract,[80] is now challenged by a stream of literature arguing in favor of political and regulatory measures to reduce social inequality and improve the global level of social justice. After all, if we bail out banks and other financial institutions when the mighty market fails, it makes little sense to let consumers face the brunt of market failures alone.[81]

Thus, many contributions suggest that the concept of consumer vulnerability and human rights-based approaches to consumer protection may play a significant role in redesigning our social constructs and economies (Ondersma, Chapter 1; Varney, Chapter 2; Iheme, Chapter 4; Rochemont, Chapter 5; and Powley and Stanton, Chapter 9).

Financial inclusion

Another important theme of this book is financial inclusion. Literature shows that financial inclusion is inadequately defined and differently understood by scholars.[82]

77 Hans W. Micklitz, *The Consumer: Marketised, Fragmentised, Constitutionalised* [Dorota Leczykiewicz and Stephen Weatherill (eds.), Hart Publishing Ltd, 2016], 32–33; Stănescu Cătălin Gabriel, "The Responsible Consumer in the Digital Age: On the Conceptual Shift from 'Average' to 'Responsible' Consumer and the Inadequacy of the 'Information Paradigm' in Consumer Financial Protection" [Ubiquity Press] 24 *Tilburg Law Review*, 56–58.
78 Micklitz, 33.
79 Reich, 144; Thomas Piketty (ed.), *Capital in the Twenty-First Century* [The Belknap Press of Harvard University Press, 2014].
80 Reich, 157.
81 Michael Hudson (ed.), *Killing the Host: How Financial Parasites and Debt Destroy the Global Economy* [ISLET-Verlag, 2015], 27, 279; Thomas Piketty (ed.), *Why Save the Bankers?: And Other Essays on Our Economic and Political Crisis* [Houghton-Mifflin Harcourt, 2016], 57–59.
82 Thereza Balliester Reis, "Scrutinizing Financial Inclusion: A Critical Review of Its Definitions" (July 2, 2020), 1–2, available at https://ssrn.com/abstract=3641338, accessed 06.07.2020.

The difficulty lies in establishing who is to be financially included, what are the elements of financial inclusion (loan, payment service, mortgage, insurance, etc.), and whose responsibility is it to promote financial inclusion.[83]

We adopt a broader definition according to which financial inclusion requires financial institutions to actively and responsibly provide financial services that are appropriate to the needs of different consumers including vulnerable ones.[84] There are many ways of enhancing financial inclusion including through government loan programs, microfinance, and digital payments systems. Essentially, financial inclusion aims to embrace the section of society, known as "the unbanked," in the financial system. The unbanked are consumers that have no access to financial services – mainly savings and checking accounts as well as loan services offered by traditional banks.[85]

In the digital age, one way in which financial institutions provide inclusive financial services is through digital technologies that assess consumer creditworthiness differently from traditional banks, using the so-called "alternative data" that allows them to evaluate the financial soundness of consumers who are otherwise not quantifiable according to the standards of traditional banks. Alternative financial institutions use artificial intelligence (algorithms) and big data to conduct their assessment, relying on data that are not used by traditional banks in what is known as alternative credit scoring.

In 2015, the CFPB estimated that 11% of American consumers are credit invisible.[86] According to a survey conducted by the Federal Deposit Insurance Corporation (FDIC) in 2017, about 8.4 million households representing roughly 20 million citizens (6% of households) were unbanked.[87] Although the overall figure in the EU in 2017 is relatively lower at 3.6%, the percentages of consumers with no access to financial services in different Member States vary.[88]

---

83 Ibid, 7–16.
84 "Financial inclusion is the process of ensuring access to appropriate financial products and services needed by vulnerable groups such as weaker sections and low income groups at an affordable cost in a fair and transparent manner by mainstream institutional players." Deepali Pant Joshi, "Financial Inclusion and Financial Literacy, BI OECD Seminar-Roundtable on the Updates on Financial Education and Inclusion Programs in India" (June 28, 2011), 1, available at https://www.oecd.org/finance/financial-education/48303408.pdf, accessed 09.02.2020.
85 Ebonya Washington, "The Impact of Banking and Fringe Banking Regulation on the Number of Unbanked Americans" [University of Wisconsin Press] 41 *The Journal of Human Resources* 106:107.
86 Kenneth P. Brevoort, Philipp Grimm, and Michelle Kambara, "Data Point: Credit Invisible" [CFPB Office of Research, 2015], https://files.consumerfinance.gov/f/201505_cfpb_data-point-credit-invisibles.pdf accessed 23.04.2018.
87 FDIC, "The 2017 National Survey of Unbanked and Underbanked Households," https://www.economicinclusion.gov/downloads/2017_FDIC_Unbanked_HH_Survey_Report.pdf accessed 09.02.2020.
88 A report published by the European Central Bank shows that in 2017, around 10% of households in Italy and Slovakia were unbanked and 25% of households in Greece reported not having

Limited amount of research shows that alternative credit scoring is financially inclusive (i.e., provides access to financial services to those that are considered un-scoreable, invisible, or credit unworthy,[89] or in other words unbankable). Primarily, artificial intelligence-driven scoring eases and reduces the cost of processing alternative data including "social media footprints, psychometrics, online behavior data, and telecommunications data, including top-up patterns (for prepaid customers), mobile money use, and even calling patterns and contacts."[90] Furthermore, by increasing the data point that can be used for scoring, artificial intelligence-driven scoring could increase accuracy in scoring and reduce the incidences of refusing to loan to a creditworthy consumer, which in turn ensures that credit is distributed efficiently.[91] The cumulative effect of this is provision of financial services to consumers that are considered unattractive to traditional banks.

Essentially, by increasing the type of data used to assess a consumer's creditworthiness, artificial intelligence-driven credit scoring allows financial institutions to embrace consumers that are otherwise ignored by financial institutions that use traditional credit scoring systems.[92] The traditional credit scoring system is considered exclusionary due to the limited amount of data points it utilizes, which could lead to lack of access to financial services and credit facilities for millions of consumers. The use of big data-driven credit scoring is said to be more pronounced in emerging markets where nontraditional data are being intensively used to score the consumer with no credit history.[93]

To the above, one can add the expansion of the concept of responsible lending, built around the assessment of consumers' creditworthiness.[94] Seen as

---

any financial accounts. See Miguel Ampudia, Michael Ehrmann, "Financial Inclusion: What's It Worth?" European Central Bank Working Paper Series No 1990/January 2017, https://www.ecb.europa.eu/pub/pdf/scpwps/ecbwp1990.en.pdf accessed 09.02.2020.

89 N. Henry and J. Morris, *Scaling Up Affordable Lending: Inclusive Credit Scoring January 2018* (2018), 10–12.

90 Disruptive Technologies in the Credit Information Sharing Industry: Developments and Implications, Fintech Note, No. 3, World Bank Group, 19.

91 Susan Wharton Gates, Vanessa Gail Perry, and Peter M. Zorn, "Automated Underwriting in Mortgage Lending: Good News for the Underserved?" [Taylor & Francis Group] 13 *Housing Policy Debate* 369. The authors conclude that automated loan underwriting predicts default more accurately than manual underwriting and that increased accuracy leads to higher loan approval rates.

92 Majid Bazarbash, *FinTech in Financial Inclusion: Machine Learning Applications in Assessing Credit Risk* (International Monetary Fund, 2019), 2.

93 Anamitra Deb, "How Disruptive Credit Scoring in the Emerging Markets Can Provide Formal Loans to Millions," OMIDYAR NETWORK (October 26, 2015), https://www.omidyar.com/blog/how-disruptive-credit-scoring-emerging-markets-can-provide-formal-loans-millions accessed 23.02.2018.

94 Article 8 of CCD and Article 18 of Directive 2014/17/EC on credit agreements for consumers relating to residential immovable property (Consumer Mortgage Directive).

an overly paternalistic measure to protect vulnerable consumers from over-indebtedness,[95] these mechanisms require and use a large amount of data relating to a borrower and the credit risk it poses.[96] Two major issues arise. On the one hand, the financial privacy of the consumer is sacrificed for the benefit of the financial industry, without an adequate balance of consumers' liberties, institutional guarantees, or interests.[97] On the other hand, the exclusive reliance on automated credit scoring is feared to divide consumer-debtors into good or bad, which exposes the latter category to the risk of financial exclusion from regular credit and becoming victim of unscrupulous money lenders.[98] Our contributors further endorse these worries (Atinkson, Chapter 6 and Buit, Chapter 7).

Digital financial services could also enhance financial inclusion through creation of alternative payment and money transfer systems, such as mobile payments. For instance, in Kenya, "about one million people (2% of the population) came out of the extreme poverty [...] a service that allows users to store monetary value on a mobile phone and send money to other users via text messages."[99] Whilst digitization of financial services might create opportunity for businesses to cater to the needs of underserved consumers in the developing world, it has also had an adverse effect in the developed world, among others, through the exclusion of vulnerable consumers, such as the elderly, from financial services (Rochemont, Chapter 5). ·

The vicious circle[100] created by rules, which, at least in theory, were meant to protect consumers combined with unrestricted discriminatory behavior of banks and financial institutions toward certain categories of consumers, translates into more expensive financial products, lower-quality banking services, increased levels of overindebtedness,[101] financial exclusion, and economic marginalization[102] of the

95 Karen Fairweather, Paul O'Shea Paul, and Grantham Ross, *Credit, Consumers and the Law: After the Global Storm* [Taylor & Francis, 2016), 4–7.
96 Vanessa Mak, "What Is Responsible Lending? The EU Consumer Mortgage Credit Directive in the UK and the Netherlands," 38 *Journal of Consumer Policy* 411.
97 Hans W. Micklitz, Jules Stuyck, and Evelyne Terryn, *Cases, Materials and Text on Consumer Law* (1st ed., Hart Publishing 2010), 379; Federico Ferretti, "The Regulation of Consumer Credit Information Systems: Is the EU Missing a Chance?" (Alphen aan den Rijn, The Netherlands) [Kluwer Law International] 34 *Legal Issues of Economic Integration* 115:124.
98 Micklitz, Stuyck, and Terryn, 378–379.
99 Luigi Ferrata, "Digital Financial Inclusion – An Engine for 'Leaving No One Behind'" (Zagreb) [Institute of Public Finance] 43 *Public Sector Economics,* 445, 453.
100 Micklitz, Stuyck, and Terryn, 379.
101 Olha Cherednychenko and Jesse Meindertsma, "Irresponsible Lending in the Post-Crisis Era: Is the EU Consumer Credit Directive Fit for Its Purpose?" (New York) [Springer, US] 42 *Journal of Consumer Policy* 483, 490–491; Clifton, Fernández-Gutiérrez, and García-Olalla, 231; Wilson, 199–200; Buckland, 61, 237.
102 Beck, Demirgüç-Kunt, and Honohan, 121. See also Center for Responsible Lending, Consumer Federation of America, National Consumer Law Center – Comments to the Consumer Financial Protection Bureau Proposed Rule on Payday, Vehicle Title and Certain High-Cost Installment Loans, (October 7, 2016), 22–27, available at: https://consumerfed.org/wp-content/uploads/2016/10/10-7-16-Payday-Rule_Comment.pdf, accessed 30.06.2020.

most vulnerable. It is, thus, important to reopen the question of consumer vulnerability in light of the new realities.

The contributions

This book's themes are organized in two major parts. The first addresses, from multiple national angles, the idea of a human rights approach to consumer law, in order to replace the mantra of economic efficiency that characterizes financial services with those of human dignity, freedom from discrimination, and freedom from debt-induced servitude. The second tackles the challenges posed by increased usage of technology in connection to financial services, which tends to solve but also to create additional issues for consumers in general and for vulnerable groups in particular.

We would like to advise the reader that most chapters conveniently combine more than one theme of the book. For instance, while financial technology is considered beneficial in terms of enhancing financial inclusion in developing regions, it has the effect of exposing consumers to vulnerability in developed regions specially by excluding the elderly from fair access to financial services (Rochemont, Chapter 5).

Part I: human rights-centered and fair access to financial services: discrimination and financial inclusion

Ondersma (Chapter 1) argues that although credit discrimination is prohibited in the US, it remains a pervasive reality, given that vulnerable consumer groups are still unable to access credit on decent terms and are subjected to discrimination with regard to debt collection, debt relief systems, and insolvency regimes. In her opinion, while these problems are significant, the fundamental issue remains poverty and the absence of adequate social safety nets. She proposes a human rights approach and advocates for spending energy, time, resources, and political capital on measures aimed at eliminating poverty and creating a strong social security system, rather than providing more access to credit, which could only foster a debt spiral.

Varney (Chapter 2) also advocates for protection of human dignity, although from a contractual perspective. She argues that freedom of contract is not absolute and should not be permitted to act as a defense where financial services providers refuse to contract with vulnerable consumers or impose unfair terms on them, taking advantage of their precarious situation. Varney claims that states should opt for a positive interpretation of freedom of contract, shaped to ensure protection of equality and human dignity, which would enable them to condemn and refuse enforcement of transactions that harm social values, rather than the currently prevailing negative interpretation, which is confined to non-intervention by states in contractual relationships. Her contribution focuses on the role of positive interpretation of freedom of contract in enhancing non-discriminatory financial services to disabled persons.

Kailiang (Chapter 3) discusses discrimination against HIV patients in mainland China regarding insurance products. He argues that although China has a legal regime to protect insurance consumers, two problems are still present. First, the legal framework lacks a clear understanding of what constitutes reasonable discrimination in insurance contracts. Second, by using the principles of contractual freedom, the rules regarding discrimination against the insured can be circumvented.

Iheme (Chapter 4) takes the view that basic education, seen as a human right, is the long-term solution especially for developing countries. Without basic education, there can be no subsequent financial education and digital literacy as the consumers will not be able to carefully navigate through the myriad information and become able to make the right choices for their well-being. His chapter also ensures a smooth transition to the second part of the book, which delves into the impact of technology on financial services and consumer vulnerability, by arguing that the increased use of Fintech and digital financial services further heightens the rate of Internet fraud, theft of personal data, and consumer manipulation.

Rochemont (Chapter 5) underlines that without digital and financial education, vulnerable consumers remain likely to be abused by financial institutions. Thus, to bring them safely into the formal economy, cooperation between public and private sectors is needed, to design consumer financial protection rules centered on the financial industry's duty of care. Rochemont's contribution highlights that although developing countries have managed to overcome weak banking infrastructures by resorting to cashless alternatives, these have also raised significant challenges of vulnerability related to cyber security and privacy. She also highlights the role of financial technology in exposing vulnerable consumers to financial exclusion in the developed regions, a concern that policymakers and legislators should address in embracing technology-based financial services.

Part II: consumer vulnerability: the role of financial technology and changing socioeconomic contexts

Atkinson (Chapter 6) examines artificial intelligence-driven credit scoring and argues that if credit providers are able to cherry-pick the most profitable customers using sophisticated machine learning techniques, this may work directly against financial inclusion. Furthermore, it is not clear how lenders use the information concerning consumer's nationality, ethnic profile, religion, age, or any other protected characteristics under national legislation assessing creditworthiness poses clear risks of discrimination. In her opinion, this risk stems from the lack of transparency in the automated assessment process, which makes it difficult to prevent biases.

Buit (Chapter 7) shows that the regulatory framework regarding creditworthiness assessment in the Netherlands, rather than enhancing consumer access to credit, indicates further restrictions. Moreover, the application of consumer credit-related rules to peer-to-peer lending platforms leads to the exclusion of vulnerable consumers from these financing options as well, leaving them no alternative but predatory lending.

Stanescu (Chapter 8) analyzes the impact of digitization of nonjudicial debt collection on consumer-debtor protections, using as an example the federal Fair Debt Collection Practices Act (FDCPA) in the US. By using specific examples from patent applications concerning debt collection software, the chapter shows how technological innovation is used by the debt collection industry to circumvent the law and bypass the statutory protections of the FDCPA.

Powley and Stanton (Chapter 9) address the question of consumer vulnerability and the scope of the UK consumer protection agenda. This topic is a challenging one. Banks are private institutions conducting an essential public function: providing access to the payments system. This highlights the inherent tension between, on the one hand, the financial industry's obligation to provide access to core services and the duty of care owed to its customers and, on the other hand, the acknowledgement of business autonomy. In other words, any regulation must ensure consumer protection without subjecting firms to disproportionate and burdensome obligations. Their contribution shows that during the recent pandemic, the consumer's financial well-being appears to have taken priority over the financial institutions' profit, suggesting that in the eyes of the Financial Conduct Authority, retail banks conduct an essential social function and should not exploit consumers who need to access financial services.

Tajti (Chapter 10) breaks from the mainstream approach, which confines vulnerability to consumer law, and offers a multi-jurisdictionally focused contribution on the dire position of vulnerable consumers of collapsed pyramid and Ponzi schemes. He advocates for an extension of the vulnerable consumer concept to consumer-investors and criticizes the usual stigma attached to consumer groups that become victims of fraudulent schemes. His arguments revolve around the magnitude of the problem and the sheer number of vulnerable consumers harmed by fallen schemes; the trust shock reverberating through the financial and legal systems, which affects several generations; the resulting financial exclusion of hundreds of thousands of consumers; the negative impact on the banking and economic systems; the emergence of systemic risks that tend to repeat and spread; and the security and sociopsychological risks, ranging from depression to physical illness and violent rebellions. Based on an in-depth discussion of all the above, Tajti concludes that all consumers deserve the healing hands of the system when victims of fraudulent financial schemes.

Conclusion

While the overall themes have been touched upon already in academic literature, these contributions bring new evidence regarding the challenges faced by vulnerable consumers when accessing financial services. Given the rapid expansion of technology, the increased complexity of digital financial services and products, the widespread discrimination, the reduction of banking premises and of human interaction, as well as the economic uncertainties caused by unexpected events, such as financial crises or pandemics, the life of consumers is not going to get any easier, unless legislators recognize the risks and do something about them.

Although the chapters of this book took aim at vulnerability, financial inclusion, technological innovation, and human rights approaches to consumer law from various angles, in multiple jurisdictions spread over four continents, the common conclusion is that we need a more courageous, proactive, and socially inclusive consumer policy.

Bibliography

Aldén L. and Hammarstedt M., 'Discrimination in the Credit Market? Access to Financial Capital among Self-employed Immigrants' (2016) *69 Kyklos* 3.

Anderson D.M., Strand A. and Collins J.M., 'The Impact of Electronic Payments for Vulnerable Consumers: Evidence from Social Security' (2018) *52* (1) *Journal of Consumer Affairs* 35.

Arner D., Buckley R. and Zetzsche D., 'Sustainability, FinTech and Financial Inclusion' (2020) *21 European Business Organization Law Review* 7. (Dordrecht) [Springer Nature B.V.]

Bazarbash M., *FinTech in financial inclusion: machine learning applications in assessing credit risk* (International Monetary Fund 2019).

Beck T., Demirgüç-Kunt A. and Honohan P., 'Access to Financial Services' (2009) *World Bank Research Observer*. (World Bank).

Benöhr I., *EU consumer law and human rights* (Oxford University Press 2013).

Benston G., 'Consumer Protection as Justification for Regulating Financial-Services Firms and Products' (2000) *17 Journal of Financial Services Research* 277. (Boston) [Kluwer Academic Publishers].

Brennan L., Zevallos Z. and Binney W., 'Vulnerable consumers and debt: Can social marketing assist?' (2011) *19 Australasian Marketing Journal (AMJ)* 203. [Elsevier Ltd].

Buckland J., *Building Financial Resilience Do Credit and Finance Schemes Serve or Impoverish Vulnerable People?* (1st ed. 2018. edn, Springer International Publishing 2018).

Cartwright P., 'Understanding and Protecting Vulnerable Financial Consumers' (2015) *38 Journal of Consumer Policy* 119. (New York) [Springer US].

Cătălin Gabriel S., 'The Responsible Consumer in the Digital Age: On the Conceptual Shift from 'Average' to 'Responsible' Consumer and the Inadequacy of the 'Information Paradigm' in Consumer Financial Protection' (2019) *24 Tilburg Law Review*. [Ubiquity Press].

Cherednychenko O. and Meindertsma J., 'Irresponsible Lending in the Post-Crisis Era: Is the EU Consumer Credit Directive Fit for Its Purpose?' (2019) *42 Journal of Consumer Policy* 483. (New York) [Springer US].

Clifton J., Fernández-Gutiérrez M. and García-Olalla M., 'Including vulnerable groups in financial services: insights from consumer satisfaction' (2017) *20 Journal of Economic Policy Reform* 214. [Routledge].

Domurath I., 'The Case for Vulnerability as the Normative Standard in European Consumer Credit and Mortgage Law – An Inquiry into the Paradigms of Consumer Law' (2013) *2 Zeitschrift für Europäisches Unternehmens- und Verbraucherrecht* 124. [Verlag Österreich].

Fernández-Olit B. and others, 'Banks and Financial Discrimination: What Can Be Learnt from the Spanish Experience?' (2019) *42 Journal of Consumer Policy* 303.

Ferrata L., 'Digital financial inclusion – an engine for "leaving no one behind"' (2015) *43 Public Sector Economics* 445. (Zagreb) [Institute of Public Finance].

Ferretti F., 'The Regulation of Consumer Credit Information Systems: Is the EU Missing a Chance?' (2007) *34 Legal Issues of Economic Integration* 115. (Alphen aan den Rijn, The Netherlands) [Kluwer Law International].

Gano A., 'Disparate Impact and Mortgage Lending: A Beginner's Guide' (2018) *26 Journal of Affordable Housing & Community Development Law* 1100. (Chicago) [American Bar Association].

Gates S.W., Perry V.G. and Zorn P.M., 'Automated underwriting in mortgage lending: Good news for the underserved?' (2002) *13 Housing Policy Debate* 369. [Taylor & Francis Group].

Henry N. and Morris J., *Scaling Up Affordable Lending: Inclusive Credit Scoring, Technical Report* (January 2018) https://www.researchgate.net/publication/342010616.

Howells Geraint, Twigg-Flesner Christian and Wilhelmsson Thomas, *Rethinking EU consumer law* (Howells G.G., Twigg-Flesner C. and Wilhelmsson T. eds, Routledge 2018).

Hudson M., *Killing the host: how financial parasites and debt destroy the global economy* (Hudson M. ed, ISLET-Verlag 2015).

Karen F., Paul O.S. and Ross G., *Credit, Consumers and the Law: After the global storm* (Taylor and Francis 2016).

Larkin E.W., 'Redlining: Remedies for Victims of Urban Disinvestment' (1976) *5 Fordham Urban Law Journal* 83. (New York, etc.) [Fordham University School of Law, etc.].

Leczykiewicz D. and Weatherill S., *The Images of the Consumer in EU Law* (Leczykiewicz D. and Weatherill S. eds, Hart Publishing Ltd 2016).

Loonin D., *Credit discrimination* (Wu C.C. ed, 4th ed. edn, National Consumer Law Center 2005).

Mak V., 'What is Responsible Lending? The EU Consumer Mortgage Credit Directive in the UK and the Netherlands' (2015) *38 Journal of Consumer Policy* 411.

Matthias S. and others, 'Ethnical discrimination in Europe: Field evidence from the finance industry' [2018] *13 PloS one e019* 1959. [Public Library of Science (PLoS)].

Maudos J., 'Bank Restructuring and Access to Financial Services: The Spanish Case' (2017) *48 Growth and Change* 963.

Micklitz H-W, *The Consumer: Marketised, Fragmentised, Constitutionalised* (Leczykiewicz D. and Weatherill S. eds, Hart Publishing Ltd 2016).

Micklitz H-W, Stuyck J. and Terryn E., *Cases, Materials and Text on Consumer Law* (1st edn, Hart Publishing 2010).

Paul V. and Axel von dem B., *The EU General Data Protection Regulation (GDPR): a practical guide* (Voigt P. and Bussche Avd eds, Springer 2017).

Piketty T., *Capital in the twenty-first century* (Piketty T. ed, The Belknap Press of Harvard University Press 2014).

Piketty Thomas, *Why save the bankers?: and other essays on our economic and political crisis* (Piketty T. ed, Houghton Mifflin Harcourt 2016).

Ramsay I., *Changing Policy Paradigms of EU Consumer Credit and Debt Regulation* (Leczykiewicz D. and Weatherill S. eds, Hart Publishing Ltd 2016).

Reich N., *Vulnerable Consumers in EU Law* (Leczykiewicz D. and Weatherill S. eds, Hart Publishing Ltd 2016).

Robson J., Farquhar J.D. and Hindle C., 'Working up a debt: students as vulnerable consumers' (2017) *27 Journal of Marketing for Higher Education: Contemporary Thought in Higher Education Marketing* 274. [Routledge].

Wang J.J. and Tian Q., 'Consumer Vulnerability and Marketplace Exclusion: A Case of Rural Migrants and Financial Services in China' (2014) *34 Journal of Macromarketing* 45. (Los Angeles, CA) [SAGE Publications].

Washington E., 'The Impact of Banking and Fringe Banking Regulation on the Number of Unbanked Americans' (2006) *41 The Journal of Human Resources* 106. [University of Wisconsin Press].

Wilson T., 'Supporting Social Enterprises to Support Vulnerable Consumers: The Example of Community Development Finance Institutions and Financial Exclusion' (2012) *35 Journal of Consumer Policy* 197. (Boston) [Springer US].

Part I

1 Tackling issues in consumer credit

The role of human rights

Chrystin Ondersma[*]

As inequality soars around the globe and racism, sexism, heterosexism, and xenophobia persist, questions arise regarding the role of economic policy, including credit policy, and the role of human rights in redressing injustice concerns. The Covid-19 pandemic – in particular in the United States – has laid bare the risks of a society operating in a state of pervasive overindebtedness, without robust health care access, without housing rights, and without employment protections. When households can hardly make ends meet and are already overindebted, and when no safety net is in place to protect against hardship, both the economic consequences and the human rights consequences are dire.

In my previous works, I advocated for a human rights approach to consumer credit by presenting a framework that prioritizes a basic level of human dignity for all rather than wealth maximization.[1]

This essay revisits the human rights issues that arise in the consumer credit context and considers how we can best redress these issues. In doing so, I highlight pitfalls that are important to avoid, whether the discussion is centered on human rights bodies, European Union Member States, other governmental bodies, or any individual or organization working to further human rights.

Although credit discrimination based on race and gender is prohibited,[2] it is nevertheless a pervasive reality in the United States.[3] In the United States, white cisgender men often have access to credit on decent terms, absent a

---

[*] Professor of Law and Judge Morris Stern Scholar, Rutgers Law School. This essay is adapted from my keynote address, "The Role of Human Rights in Tackling Issues in Consumer Credit," given at International Conference on Fair and Non-discriminatory Access to Credit, Faculty of Law, University of Copenhagen (September 26, 2019).

[1] Chrystin Ondersma, "Consumer Financial Protection and Human Rights" (2017), 50 *Cornell International Law Journal* 543; Chrystin Ondersma, "A Human Rights Approach to Consumer Credit" (2015), 90 *Tulane Law Review* 373; Chrystin Ondersma, "A Human Rights Framework for Debt Relief" (2014), 36 *University of Pennsylvania Journal of International Law* 269.

[2] Equal Credit Opportunity Act of 1974.

[3] See Sterling (n4), Debruyn (n7), and Rice (n11).

problematic credit history. The same is not true for women, transgender individuals, immigrants, and people of color. Even with strong financial credentials and credit scores, individuals in these categories, especially Black and Latinx debtors, are often denied loans or are offered loans with far less favorable terms. Black and Latinx individuals are: (1) routinely required to provide additional financial information before receiving a loan;[4] (2) less likely to receive assistance with completing the loan application (such as help filling out forms);[5] and (3) more likely to be denied a loan than white individuals with equivalent financials.[6] Black and Latinx individuals are more than twice as likely to be denied a home mortgage, taking into consideration their income, loan amount, and neighborhood.[7] Black and Latinx debtors are charged thousands of dollars more to finance a car and likely to be charged more for the car itself.[8] Such individuals are also more likely to be pressured to buy add-on products like service contracts.[9] However, attempts to negotiate for better terms did not change this result.[10] As of 2019, more than 60% of nonwhite applicants received more unfavorable terms on automobile loans than white applicants with equivalent credit histories.[11] Women pay more for mortgages than men with similar credit profiles,[12] and Black and Latinx women are offered the worst terms.[13] In 2013, 39% of women were denied mortgage refinancing.[14] Black and Latinx debtors are also more likely to be "targeted with risky financial

4 Sterling A. Bone, Glenn L. Christensen, and Jerome D. Williams, "Rejected, Shackled, and Alone: The Impact of Systemic Restricted Choice on Minority Consumers' Construction of Self" (2014), 41 *Journal of Consumer Research* 451, 455.

5 Ibid.

6 Ibid.

7 Jason Debruyn, "Blacks and Latinos Denied Mortgages at Rate Double Whites" (*WUNC*, 15 February 2018), www.wunc.org/post/blacks-and-latinos-denied-mortgages-rates-double-whites, accessed 25 May 2020.

8 John W. Van Last, "Examining Discrimination in the Automobile Loan and Insurance Industries" (*U.S. House Committee on Financial Services*, 1 May 2019), https://financialservices.house.gov/uploadedfiles/hhrg-116-ba09-wstate-vanalstj-20190501.pdf, accessed 25 May 2020.

9 Ibid.

10 Ibid.

11 Lisa Rice, "Missing Credit: How the U.S. Credit System Restricts Access to Consumers of Color" (*National Fair Housing Alliance*, 26 February 2019), https://financialservices.house.gov/uploadedfiles/hhrg-116-ba00-wstate-ricel-20190226.pdf, accessed 25 May 2020.

12 Chris Matthews, "Study Finds Women Are Charged Higher Rates for Mortgages" (*Fortune*, 8 September 2016), https://fortune.com/2016/09/08/study-finds-women-are-charged-higher-rates-for-mortgages/, accessed 25 May 2020.

13 Ibid.

14 Allen Abraham, "Credit Discrimination Based on Gender: The Need to Expand the Rights of a Spousal Guarantor Under the Equal Credit Opportunity Act" (2016), 10 *Brooklyn Journal of Corporate, Financial & Commercial Law* 473, 491 (citing Lisa Prevost, "Investigating Sex Discrimination" (*New York Times*, 21 February 2013), www.nytimes.com/2013/02/24/realestate/investigating-sex-discrimination-by-lenders.html?, accessed 25 May 2020.

products,"[15] such as high-interest predatory loans.[16] This unequal access to fair credit terms violates the individual's human right to be free from discrimination.[17]

Predatory lending also raises human rights concerns beyond discrimination. In some cases, the loan and collection procedure can be considered a taking of the debtor's property without due process. Examples include situations where an item is procured by fraud and where an individual's ability to challenge the terms of the loan is thwarted by mandatory arbitration.[18] In some cases, individuals are arrested or threatened with arrest for failure to pay debts even though they cannot afford to pay. Every year, thousands of individuals are arrested and jailed for failure to pay debts, while millions more often go without food or essential medicine in order to pay the debt to avoid arrest.[19] This practice of imprisoning individuals for failure to pay a debt violates both human rights obligations and U.S. constitutional law.[20]

Human rights issues, such as discrimination, can also arise in the context of debt relief systems and insolvency regimes. For example, in the United States, Black and Latinx debtors are disproportionately pushed into repayment and often never receive debt relief.[21] Instead, these individuals face extended periods of servitude to creditors with repayment plans that do not permit debtors to meet their basic needs.

---

15 Chrystin Ondersma, "Small Debts, Big Burdens" (2019) 103 *Minnesota Law Review* 2211, 2216 (citing Susan Burhouse and others, "2013 FDIC National Survey of Unbanked and Underbanked Households," (*FCIC,* October 2014), www.fdic.gov/householdsurvey/2013execsumm.pdf, accessed 25 May 2020.

16 Brentin Mock, "Redlining Is Alive and Well – and Evolving"(*CityLab*, 28 September 2015), www.citylab.com/equity/2015/09/redlining-is-alive-and-welland-evolving/407497/, accessed 25 May 2020.

17 UN General Assembly, "International Covenant on Civil and Political Rights" (1967), 999 United Nations Treaty Service 171, https://treaties.un.org/doc/Treaties/1976/03/19760323%2006-17%20AM/Ch_IV_04.pdf, accessed 25 May 2020 (ICCPR).

18 Predatory lending may also interfere with individuals' ability to meet their basic needs.

19 Americal Civil Liberties Union, "A Pound of Flesh: The Criminalization of Private Debt" (*ACLU,* 2018), 4, 35, www.aclu.org/sites/default/files/field_document/022318-debtreport_0.pdf, accessed 25 May 2020 (ACLU Report).

20 For example, a disabled woman in Texas – whose only income was exempt social security disability income – was arrested for failure to appear in a case involving a $1,500 loan for truck driving school that had ballooned to $13,000 over the years with income and fees. *ACLU Report* at 47. Three U.S. marshals came to her home while she was asleep and shackled her feet and waist after she dressed and put on her prosthetic leg. Ibid. In a Maryland case, an elderly married couple (ages 78 and 83) were jailed for failing to appear in court where they owed $2,342.76 to their homeowner's association. Ibid, 8. The couple was never even served with notice to appear at the order to show cause for a hearing. Ibid. While in jail, the husband "began vomiting blood and became non-responsive," and had to be transferred for emergency treatment. Ibid. A man in Indiana, who owed $4,023.88 due to an auto loan deficiency, was placed under arrest in front of his four young kids and jailed for two nights after being strip searched and sprayed for lice. Ibid, 55. The man asserted that he was never aware of the lawsuit. Ibid.

21 Consumer bankruptcy attorneys often push African-Americans disproportionately to use a specific type of bankruptcy that requires greater repayment of debt without receiving total forgiveness of their debt. Jean Braucher, Dov Cohen, and Robert M. Lawless, "Race, Attorney Influence, and Bankruptcy Chapter Choice," (2012), 9 *Journal of Empirical Legal Studies* 393, 393–394.

The poor are disproportionately affected by predatory lending, oppressive collection tactics, threats of arrest, and debt relief regimes. Of course, access to fair credit and fair insolvency systems are also important for middle-class individuals and families. Everyone should have access to fair credit and fair insolvency systems whether trying to build wealth, start or expand a business on a level playing field, or access fair credit in the event of an emergency, such as a family breakup, job loss, or other crises that resulted in unmanageable debt.

It is important to recognize, though, that while predatory lending, abusive debt collection practices, and lack of access to debt relief are significant problems, they may not be the most fundamental problems within poor communities. The fundamental problems are often poverty and the lack of a sufficient safety net. When income is not sufficient to meet basic needs, and the social safety net does not extend the necessary coverage to enable a person to meet his or her basic needs, the result is often insecurity with respect to housing, food, and health care. When emergencies arise, low-income individuals and families must often turn to credit to keep the lights on, keep the refrigerator working, make rent payments, obtain food, and secure medical care.[22]

Senator Bernie Sanders of Vermont, a long-term independent and democratic socialist voice in the federal government, has long called for health care to be recognized as a human right and successfully coalesced a movement to bring this idea into the American mainstream during the 2016 Democratic presidential primaries.[23] While a popular sentiment, there has been significant pushback to the idea that health care is a right to all Americans.

These burdens fall hardest on Black and Latinx individuals who, as a result of persistent and systematic racism that they face, are more than twice as likely as white individuals to be poor.[24] Black and Latinx debtors are less likely to have savings available to cover emergency expenses.[25] Controlling for income, there are twice as many debt collection lawsuits in Black communities than in white communities.[26]

22 Ondersma (n 15), 2215.
23 Sydney Ember, "Bernie Sanders Went to Canada, and a Dream of 'Medicare for All' Flourished" (*New York Times*, 9 September 2019), www.nytimes.com/2019/09/09/us/politics/bernie-sanders-health-care.html, accessed 25 May 2020; Richard M. Salsman, "Memo to the Supreme Court: Health Care Is Not a Right" (*Forbes*, 3 April 2012), https://www.forbes.com/sites/richardsalsman/2012/04/03/memo-to-the-supreme-court-health-care-is-not-a-right/#4cc5a90d34f9, accessed 25 May 2020.
24 American Civil Liberties Union (n 19), 10.
25 Ibid (citing Pew Charitable Trusts, "What Resources Do Families Have for Financial Emergencies?" (*PEW trusts*, 2015), www.pewtrusts.org/-/media/assets/2015/11/emergencysavingsreportnov2015.pdf, accessed 25 May 2020) (stating that if "the bottom 25 percent of … white households" liquidated all financial assets, they would have $3,000 on average, whereas a quarter of African-American families "would have less than $5 if they liquidated all of their financial assets").
26 Ibid, 11 (citing Paul Kiel and Annie Waldman, "The Color of Debt: How Collection Suits Squeeze Black Neighborhoods" (*ProPublica*, 8 October 2015), www.propublica.org/article/debt-collection-lawsuits-squeeze-black-neighborhoods, accessed 25 May 2020.

Because we have limited time, resources, energy, and political capital, it is the duty of state and federal representatives and regulators to choose where to devote this capital. In doing so, we must decide how to best incentivize these decision makers to act. Under a human rights approach to consumer credit, how do we select which regulatory and policy changes to prioritize? From economists' perspective, time and political capital should be devoted to the causes that provide the most resources to the general public, even if the added resources are automatically allocated to the communities that already have unfettered access to such resources. Under this analysis, the focus might be on expanding access to credit for the middle class, or on harmonizing credit principles so that the system works more efficiently. From a human rights standpoint, by contrast, the priority is not wealth maximization, but ensuring that everyone's human rights are protected. This allows us to ask a series of questions, including: (1) Does everyone have a standard of living consistent with human dignity?; (2)Does everyone have access to food, shelter, medical care, and education?; and (3) Is everyone free from discrimination?

One key pitfall to avoid from a human rights standpoint is the mistake of allowing economic efficiency to trump concerns about human dignity; rights to be free from discrimination and debt-induced servitude; and rights to adequate health care, housing, and food consistent with a life of human dignity. It is a mistake to emphasize harmonization and efficiency over human rights. There is already tremendous pressure generated by wealthy corporations and individuals to focus on economic efficiency and wealth maximization and substantial resources deployed to that end. By contrast, the priority from a human rights standpoint should be a fundamental floor of dignity and protection to which all individuals are entitled. This means that *even if* a given proposal does *not* maximize economic efficiency, the proposal may still be necessary, from a human rights standpoint, to ensure that more individuals can live lives of dignity that are free from abuse.

That is not to say that human rights principles are inconsistent with wealth maximization and efficiency. In fact, complying with human rights principles is consistent with long-term wealth maximization in that financial products that are safe and non-discriminatory have lower default rates; also, if individuals are trapped in debt spirals they have no resources to contribute to the real economy (such as home purchases and other consumer spending). Nevertheless, human rights require a different focus in terms of political capital since wealth maximization should not be a primary focus for those concerned about protecting human rights.

But those concerned about human rights should not waste energy defending policies designed to protect human rights on efficiency grounds. Of course, if such interference has human rights consequences, then it is properly the domain of human rights, but the focus must be on achieving policies that best protect human rights for the most people. For example, from a human rights standpoint, a policy that allowed everyone to achieve an adequate standard of living would be better than a policy that increased the total wealth without enabling everyone to meet basic needs.

The focus on economic efficiency, or the seep of efficiency concerns into human rights concerns, is particularly problematic when combined with an increased focus on harmonization. With respect to changes in the European Union, harmonization legislation was passed under efficiency goals.[27] Article 169(2)(b) allows consumer protection independent of market rationales, but it has hardly been used.[28] Further, the consumer credit directive[29] explicitly made harmonization paramount, purportedly in the interest of the consumer. This may have been a good faith effort to prevent a race to the bottom. However, harmonization landed more on the side of permissiveness, with a focus on disclosure and transparency, rather than truly preventing abusive terms.[30] Consequently, Member States endeavoring to create robust consumer protection have faced challenges, as more restrictive consumer protection laws may be deemed incompatible with harmonization principles that prioritize intrastate trade governed by uniform rules.

This leads to an inquiry into what happens when efficiency and harmonization are prioritized. The United States can serve as a cautionary tale. Many states have usury laws designed to cap the interest rates that lenders may charge. Credit card companies, however, aimed to charge higher interest rates and argued that they could use the maximum interest rates permitted in the states in which they were domiciled, which were the states without usury caps. The Supreme Court agreed.[31] As a result, U.S. consumers, even in states with usury caps, are not fully protected from usurious interest.[32]

27 The Treaty on the Functioning of the European Union [2012] OJ C326/01.
28 Iris Benohr, *EU Consumer Law and Human Rights* (Oxford University Press, 2013) 27–33.
29 Consumer Credit Directive 87/102/EEC of 22 December 1986 for the approximation of the laws, regulations, and administrative provisions of the Member States concerning consumer credit [1987] OJ L42/48.
30 Catalin Gabriel Stănescu, "The Responsible Consumer in the Digital Age: On the Conceptual Shift from 'Average' to 'Responsible' Consumer and the Inadequacy of the 'Information Paradigm' in Consumer Financial Protection" (2019) 24 *Tilburg Law Review* 49, http://doi.org/10.5334/tilr.143, accessed 25 May 2020 (citing Article 114, Para 3 of TFEU: "The Commission [...] concerning [...] consumer protection, will take as a base a high level of protection, taking account in particular of any new development based on scientific facts" with those of Article 169, Para 1 of TFEU: "In order to promote the interests of consumers and to ensure a high level of consumer protection, the Union shall contribute to protecting the [...] economic interests of consumers, *as well as* to promoting their right to information, education and to organize themselves in order to safeguard their interests").
31 *Marquette Nat'l Bank vs. First of Omaha Serv. Corp.* [1978] 439 US. 299, 313–15. There, the Court held that the plain meaning of 2 U.S.C. § 85, which authorizes a national banking association "to charge on any loan" interest at the rate allowed by the laws of the state "where the bank is located," referred to the location of incorporation of the bank rather than the location at which the credit card offer was made. The Court dismissed the argument that the holding would impair states' abilities to enact usury caps, reasoning: "This impairment, however, has always been implicit in the structure of the National Bank Act, since citizens of one State were free to visit a neighboring State to receive credit at foreign interest rates." Ibid, 318–319.
32 For example, a man named Kevin lost his job and racked up $7,000 in credit card charges, but Kevin's credit card accrued a 25% interest and additional attorney's fees. Chrystin

The second and closely related pitfall that should be avoided is diverting resources, energy, and time away from protecting or expanding the social safety net and toward expanding credit access.

In the United States in the 1960s, a family of three could achieve a life of adequate standard of living consistent with human dignity on a minimum wage job.[33] The minimum wage has not kept pace with inflation, however, and today is insufficient to keep a two-person family above the poverty level. The social safety net has since eroded, labor laws and antitrust laws have been weakened, and tax policy has changed dramatically so that those at the top are no longer contributing to the allocation of resources.

Increasing access to credit per se should not be a human rights goal. It can be an economic goal, although it is often overrated as an economic goal, but the role of human rights in the consumer credit context is to protect human rights – again, rights to be free from discrimination and debt-induced servitude and rights to an adequate standard of living consistent with human dignity.

For middle-class individuals, entrepreneurs, and businesses, avoiding discrimination in consumer credit access and ensuring fair terms is not only critical, but is also certainly a human rights concern. For the impoverished, ensuring access to basic needs without requiring the poor to instinctively turn to credit is the best way to avoid most of the problems discussed herein. In many cases, the erosion of the social safety net is what makes it necessary for individuals and families to turn to credit. In other words, it is more important, from a human rights standpoint, to fight against the erosion of the social safety net than to expand credit access. That is not to say that both cannot be accomplished consistently with human rights; it is just to identify priorities given limited political capital, resources, and energy.

As Abbye Atkinson argues, credit can never be a solution to poverty, unless a person in the future will have more than they have in the present. Otherwise, individuals would face ever deepening debt:

> Credit as meaningful social provision for low-income borrowers implies an expectation that notwithstanding their present condition, low-income borrowers will be *better* off in the future and able to repay their debts without hardship. This is an unduly optimistic expectation given … that decades of data suggest that low-income Americans can consistently expect to be in worse economic shape as time passes. Credit is fundamentally

Ondersma, "A Human Rights Approach to Consumer Credit" (2015), 90 *Tulane Law Review* 373, 375. When Kevin obtained employment, Capital One garnished 25% from Kevin's wages, or roughly $500 from each paycheck, until Kevin repaid a total of $6,000. Ibid. However, even after paying the $6,000, Kevin still had a balance of $10,000. Ibid.

33 David Cooper, "The Minimum Wage Used To Be Enough To Keep Workers Out Of Poverty – It's Not Anymore" (*Economic Policy Institute*, 4 December 2013), www.epi.org/publication/minimum-wage-workers-poverty-anymore-raising/, accessed 25 May 2020.

incompatible with the entrenched intergenerational poverty that plagues low-income Americans.[34]

Without a social safety net, individuals facing job loss, medical emergencies, or other crises often have no choice but to turn to credit. In 2016, an estimated 70 million Americans had a debt go into collection, with "one-in-four consumers report[ing] feeling threatened by a debt collector."[35] The same year saw nearly one in five individuals have medical bills in collection.[36] One in three American families have $0 in savings, and 41% of families reported that they would be unable to come up with $2,000 to cover an emergency expense in 2018.[37] According to a 2017 survey from the Bureau of Labor Statistics, the poorest 10% of the country spends 35% of their family income on health care, while the richest 10% spends only 3.5% of their family income on health care.[38] Additionally, because the government does not sufficiently subsidize higher education, there was over $1.5 trillion of outstanding student debt as of 2018. Graduating students in 2018 had an average of nearly $30,000 in student debt, and 11.5% of student loans were over 90 days delinquent.[39] Individuals and families have turned to credit to cover emergencies, to cover medical bills, and to pay for school. When they are inescapably mired in debt, they may turn to bankruptcy (although this process is still difficult even in the United States, especially for the poorest debtors).[40]

34 Abbye Atkinson, "Rethinking Credit as Social Provision" (2019) 71 *Stanford Law Review* 1093, 1098–1099 [citing Lawrence Mishel, Elise Gould, and Josh Bivens, "Wage Stagnation in Nine Charts" (*Economic Policy Institute*, 6 January 2015), https://termadiary.org/wp-content/uploads/2017/05/wage-stagnation-in-nine-charts.pdf, accessed 25 May 2020 (showing income growth and stagnation for low- and middle-wage workers)]. Moreover, the Bureau of Labor Statistics reports that most low-income workers consistently experience "periods of unemployment, involuntary part-time employment, and low earnings" that "hinder [their] ability to earn an income above the poverty threshold." "A Profile of the Working Poor, 2016" (*U.S. Bureau of Labor Statistics*, July 2018), www.bls.gov/opub/reports/working-poor/2016/home.htm, accessed 25 May 2020 (BLS Report).
35 "CFPB Survey Finds Over One-in-Four Consumers Contacted by Debt Collectors Feel Threatened" (*Consumer Financial Protection Bureau*, 12 January 2017), www.consumerfinance.gov/about-us/newsroom/cfpb-survey-finds-over-one-four-consumers-contacted-debt-collectors-feel-threatened/, accessed 25 May 2020.
36 Breno Braga, Signe-Mary McKernan, and Caleb Quakenbush, "Debt in America: An Interactive Map" (*Urban Institute*, 17 December 2017), https://apps.urban.org/features/debt-interactive-map/?type=overall&variable=pct_debt_collections, accessed 25 May 2020.
37 American Civil Liberties Union (n 19), 10.
38 "How Much of Americans' Paychecks Go to Health Care, harted" (*Advisory Board*, 2 May 2019), www.advisory.com/daily-briefing/2019/05/02/health-care-costs, accessed 25 May 2020.
39 "A Look at the Shocking Student Loan Debt Statistics for 2019" (*Student Loan Hero*, 4 February 2019), https://studentloanhero.com/student-loan-debt-statistics/, accessed 25 May 2020.
40 In a previous paper, I argue that the United States, in light of a weak social safety net, should aim to make access to bankruptcy easier because having access to bankruptcy should be an important human rights goal. Ondersma (n 11), 2247–2248.

Some would suggest that we should focus on ensuring that individuals are able to access credit in emergency situations, but Atkinson explains why this is not a viable solution. As Atkinson states, such individuals will never be able to repay. A better solution from a human rights perspective is that the government provide emergency funds for the poor to cover expenses like this. Some cities now do this, including New York City.[41]

A relatively small grant can make a tremendous difference for families and individuals struggling to overcome emergencies. On average, individuals that have a debt in collections only owe around $1,300.[42] For nonmedical debt, the median is $366, and for medical debt, the median is $207.[43] Only 2.8% of nonelderly individuals experienced family medical expenses over $10,000, and only 14% experienced medical expenses over $5,000 (43% experienced medical debt in excess of $2,000).[44] If individuals could access funding to cover these emergencies, rather than turning to credit, this would help low-income individuals and families avoid debt-induced spirals.

In the wake of Covid-19, the government has had to scramble to provide aid[45] so that the millions of Americans suddenly without work are able to meet their basic needs – whether this relief is sufficient remains in serious doubt.[46] A system with better employment protections, robust health care access, and housing and food guarantees would likely have mitigated the damage. As it stands, millions of Americans now face severe debt for emergency Covid-19 treatment[47] and will need debt relief.

This work focused on consumer credit and debt relief in a human rights context because it is often not possible for the poor to survive without credit. Thus, it is not possible to meet human rights principles in the United States under the current economic system without access to debt relief. As a result, much of my work focused on reducing predatory lending and increasing access to

41 "One Shot Deal" (*NYC 311*), https://portal.311.nyc.gov/article/?kanumber=KA-01104, accessed 25 May 2020.
42 American Civil Liberties Union (n 19), 9.
43 Ibid.
44 Melissa Jacoby, "The Debtor-Patient Revisited" (2007), 51 *St. Louis University Law Journal* 207, 309–310 (citing Didem Bernard and Jessica Banthin, "Out-of-Pocket Expenditures on Health Care and Insurance Premiums Among the Non-Elderly Population, 2003" (*Agency for Healthcare Research and Quality*, March 2006), https://meps.ahrq.gov/data_files/publications/st122/stat122.shtml, accessed 25 May 2020.
45 Coronavirus Aid, Relief, and Economic Security Act of 2020.
46 Jordain Carney, "Sanders Calls for $2,000 Monthly Payments, Suspending Some Bills Amid Pandemic" (*The Hill*, 3 April 2020), https://thehill.com/homenews/senate/491051-sanders-calls-for-2000-monthly-payments-suspending-some-bills-amid-pandemic, accessed 25 May 2020.
47 Megan Leonhardt, "Uninsured Americans Could Be Facing Nearly $75,000 in Medical Bills if Hospitalized for Coronavirus" (*CNBC*, 1 April 2020), www.cnbc.com/2020/04/01/covid-19-hospital-bills-could-cost-uninsured-americans-up-to-75000.html, accessed 25 May 2020.

debt relief. But a more direct route to human rights goals includes a focus on expanding housing, food, education, and medical access for the poor, as well as radically overhauling our labor laws, antitrust laws, and tax policy.

Those concerned about human rights should indeed fight for a financial system that is fair and works for everyone – to root out predatory lending, end discriminatory lending, and fight to make sure debt relief is fair and accessible. Certainly, countries must continue to work to combat credit discrimination, which is an issue even in European Union Member States with strong social safety nets.[48] But those in countries with robust social safety nets should also not neglect the fight to preserve and expand these safety nets. Those in countries without robust social safety nets should focus more on building this protection than on expanding credit access. We should also fight for strong labor laws, antitrust laws, and other laws designed to help achieve a system that again makes it possible for families to meet an adequate standard of living on a minimum wage. We should resist pressure to spend more time fighting for increased access to credit than ensuring that more people can live lives consistent with human dignity. And we should resist pressure to spend more time making sure markets work efficiently than ensuring that markets do not deprive individuals of their human rights.

48 For example, one study found that individuals with Arabic names were less likely to be offered credit than individuals with domestic names. Matthias Stefan and others, "Ethnical Discrimination in Europe: Field Evidence from the Finance Industry" (2018) 13(1) PLoS ONE, https://journals.plos.org/plosone/article?id=10.1371/journal.pone.0191959, accessed 25 May 2020.

2 Beyond negative interpretations of freedom of contract

The interplay between private law and human rights in light of the UN *convention on the rights of persons with disabilities*

Eliza Varney[*]

Introduction

The contractual realm is one into which parties step voluntarily.[1] It is a sphere where they can exercise the freedom to choose their contracting partners and the terms of their agreement.[2] At the same time, it is also a space where individuals, including people with disabilities, can encounter barriers such as inaccessible environments, facilities and information, as well as negative attitudes from service providers.[3] Such barriers have the potential to harm these contracting parties, creating an environment in which people are vulnerable[4] (a term rooted in the Latin verb '*vulnerare*', meaning 'to wound').[5] In the relation between a person with a disability and a service provider such as a bank, such harm could take several forms, arising at various stages of the contracting process.[6] It could

[*] Senior Lecturer in Law, Keele University, e.varney@keele.ac.uk, ORCID: 0000-0002-0906-9210. I would like to thank Mike Varney, Abi Pearson, Catalin Gabriel Stanescu and Asress Adimi Gikay for constructive comments. Any errors are my own.

1 Dori Kimel, 'Neutrality, Autonomy, and Freedom of Contract' (2001) 21 OJLS 473.
2 John Cartwright, *Formation and Variation of Contract* (2nd edn, Sweet & Maxwell 2018), 1–06.
3 Michael Oliver, *The Politics of Disablement* (Palgrave Macmillan 1990); Colin Barnes, 'Theories of Disability and the Origins of the Oppression of Disabled People in Western Society' in Len Barton (ed) *Disability and Society: Emerging Issues and Insights* (Longman 1996); Stanley Herr, Lawrence Gostin and Harold Hongju Koh (eds) (2003) *The Human Rights of Persons with Intellectual Disabilities: Different but Equal* (OUP 2003); Lucy Series and Anna Nilsson, 'Article 12 CRPD: Equal Recognition before the Law' in Ilias Bantekas, Michael Ashley Stein and Dimitris Anastasiou (eds) *The UN Convention on the Rights of Persons with Disabilities: A Commentary* (OUP 2018), 380–381.
4 Andrea Fejős, 'Social Justice in EU Financial Consumer Law' (2019) 24 *Tilburg Law Review* 68, at 69.
5 Charles Talbut Onions (ed), *The Oxford Dictionary of English Etymology* (1st edn, OUP 1996); Jonathan Herring, *Vulnerable Adults and the Law* (OUP 2016), 6.
6 Yvette Maker and others, 'From Safety Nets to Support Networks: Beyond 'Vulnerability' in Protection for Consumers with Cognitive Disabilities' (2018) 41 UNSWLJ 818.

include the bank's refusal to accept the individual as a customer due to his or her disability,[7] the bank's failure to provide the person with appropriate and accessible information regarding the risk of standing as surety for a loan taken by a family member,[8] or the bank's inclusion of unfair terms in a standard form contract provided to the consumer on a 'take it or leave it' basis.[9] In such contexts that place the individual in a vulnerable position, there is a clear imbalance between the parties, and addressing this imbalance requires a multi-layered approach and a combination of public and private law measures.[10] It requires, *inter alia*, provisions for combating discrimination and promoting equality in access to goods and services.[11] It also necessitates an effective legal framework where private law provides a safety net,[12] including in the form of vitiating factors that would enable individuals to seek to invalidate contracts entered into, among other reasons, as a result of incapacity or undue pressure[13] (as long as these defences can be invoked by anyone and disability and incapacity are not conceptually equated).[14] Also necessary is a framework for regulating unfair terms, including in standard form contracts.[15] Among other reasons, which include concerns for people's economic interests, such endeavours are rooted in wider social values, including the need to protect equality and human dignity.[16] In this context, a focus on safeguarding human dignity could be understood as the need to ensure that no one is disadvantaged due to their subjective characteristics[17] and that every human being is treated

---

7 See, for example, National Council for Combating Discrimination (NCCD), Romania, Press Release, 22 January 2020 (concerning a fine imposed by the NCCD on a bank which refused to accept as a customer a person with a visual disability who could not access the information provided solely in print format). See https://cncd.ro/2020-01-22-comunicat-de-presa-referitor-la-hotararile-adoptate-de-colegiul-director-al-cncd-in-sedinta-din-data-de-22-01-2020 (*in Romanian*) accessed 25 April 2020.
8 Fiona Burns, 'The Elderly and Undue Influence Inter Vivos' (2003) 23 LS 251.
9 Fejős, above n 4, 74; Friedrich Kessler, 'Contracts of Adhesion: Some Thoughts about Freedom of Contract' (1943) 43 *Colum.L.Rev.* 629, at 632.
10 Hugh Collins, *Regulating Contracts* (OUP 1999), 361.
11 Yvette Maker and others, 'Ensuring Equality for Persons with Cognitive Disabilities in Consumer Contracting: An International Human Rights Law Perspective' (2018) 19 *Melbourne Journal of International Law* 178.
12 Maker and others, above n 6, 831.
13 Peter MacDonald Eggers, *Vitiation of Contractual Consent* (Routledge 2016); Nelson Enonchong, *Duress, Undue Influence and Unconscionable Dealing* (3rd edn, Sweet & Maxwell 2018).
14 Michael Bach, 'The Right to Legal Capacity under the UN Convention on the Rights of Persons with Disabilities: Key Concepts and Directions for Law Reform', Toronto, Institute for Research and Development on Inclusion and Society (IRIS 2009), 5.
15 Richard Lawson, *Exclusion Clauses and Unfair Contract Terms* (12th edn, Sweet & Maxwell 2017).
16 Sinai Deutch, 'Are Consumer Rights Human Rights?' (1994) 32 Osgoode Hall L.J. 537, at 537.
17 Zoe Apostolopoulou, 'Equal Treatment of People with Disabilities in the EC: What does "Equal" mean?' (2004) *Jean Monnet Working Paper* 09/04 https://jeanmonnetprogram.org/archive/papers/04/040901.html accessed 25 April 2020.

with respect.[18] Vulnerability should not be associated with belonging to a particular group or having a particular medical condition, but should be rooted in the context of the transaction examined (e.g., questioning whether service providers made available appropriate and accessible information to enable the individual to make an informed decision).[19]

To resist measures that protect vulnerable parties in the contractual sphere, powerful players such as service providers may attempt to bring to their aid foundational concepts such as freedom of contract, construed narrowly to oppose state intervention in the contractual sphere.[20] This chapter challenges interpretations of freedom of contract that would support such endeavours. The discussion opposes negative interpretations of this concept confined to nonintervention by the state and limited to a narrow perception of individuals as economic actors in pursuit of self-interest, in favour of positive interpretations of freedom of contract, which embrace wider social values such as equality and dignity.[21]

Part 1 explores the way in which the UN Committee on the Rights of Persons with Disabilities (CRPD Committee) did not allow the concept of freedom of contract to be used as a shield against intervention in the pursuit of equality objectives. In *Nyusti vs. Hungary* (*Nyusti*),[22] the CRPD Committee confirmed that the human rights of persons with disabilities to enjoy equal access to services (such as financial services) prevail over the claims of private parties (in this case, a bank whose view was endorsed by the Hungarian government) to resist 'interference with freedom of contract'.[23] The bank had relied on the problematic view that any requirement to make its automatic teller machines (ATMs) accessible to persons with visual disabilities constituted an infringement of their freedom of contract, and that its customers with visual disabilities, who could not access these services, knew what they agreed to when they entered into the contract with the bank.[24] Despite the merits of the decision in *Nyusti*, which found Hungary to be in breach of its obligations under the CRPD[25] to ensure, *inter alia*, that private parties providing services to the public 'take into account all aspects of accessibility for persons with disabilities',[26] the CRPD Committee failed to engage with the wider question of the interplay between human

---

18 Denise Réaume, 'Discrimination and Dignity' (2003) 63 La.L.Rev. 645.
19 Herring, above n 5, 6.
20 Philip Shuchman, 'Consumer Credit by Adhesion Contracts' (1962) 35 Temp.L.Q. 125.
21 Hugh Collins, 'The Impact of Human Rights Law on Contract Law in Europe' Cambridge Legal Studies Research Paper 13/2011, at 5.
22 *Nyusti and Takács vs. Hungary*, CRPD/C/9/D/1/2010, 11 March 2010. See Oliver Lewis, '*Nyusti and Takacs v Hungary*: Decision of the UN Committee on the Rights of Persons with Disabilities' (2013) 4 E.H.R.L.R. 419.
23 *Nyusti and Takács vs. Hungary*, above n 22, paragraphs 2.13 and 2.16.
24 ibid, paragraph 2.12.
25 G.A. Res. 61/611, 13 December 2006, A/61/611, 15 IHRR 255.
26 Article 9(2)(b) CRPD; *Nyusti and Takács vs. Hungary*, above n 22, paragraph 9.4.

rights and private law, or to challenge such negative interpretations of freedom of contract.

These issues are not confined to one isolated incident or to one particular jurisdiction.[27] Barriers encountered by persons with disabilities in the contractual sphere continue to remain prevalent[28] and are likely to increase, given the rise in the number of people with disabilities (including people developing mental health conditions such as dementia).[29] Such barriers have a negative impact on the extent to which people with disabilities can exercise their right to full and equal enjoyment of all human rights and fundamental freedom,[30] including the right to independent living,[31] and to the protection of their human dignity.[32] Moreover, service providers continue to resist calls for equality on the basis of paternalistic perceptions of disability, cost-related considerations and negative interpretations of freedom of contract,[33] while state actors appear to be more inclined to listen to industry voices than the views put forward by people with disabilities.[34] In seeking to challenge negative interpretations of freedom of contract and to promote a positive understanding of this concept based on the values promoted by the CRPD, this discussion aims to pick up what the CRPD Committee left unaddressed in *Nyusti* and subsequent decisions.[35] It explores key messages implicit within the framework of the CRPD about the rights of persons with disabilities in the contractual sphere and the need to recognise the primacy of consumers' social values over the economic concerns of market players.

Part 2 examines interpretations of freedom of contract in a domestic context. Whilst a larger-scale project could focus on a comparative approach across a range of jurisdictions and could assess the multilayered approach for addressing vulnerability at various stages of the contracting process (including precontractual negotiations, contract formations and factors that may vitiate consent, contract

27 See, for example, UN Department of Economic and Social Affairs (UNDESA), *The Report on the World Social Situation 2018: Promoting Inclusion through Social Protection*, ST/ESA/366, 8 November 2018, 72; NCCD, above n 7; P. J. Mathew Martin and Manukonda Rabindranath, 'Digital Inclusion for Access to Information: A Study on Banking and Financial Institutions in India' (2017) *SAGE Open* 1; Anwuli Irene Ofuani, 'The Right to Economic Empowerment of Persons with Disabilities in Nigeria: How Enabled?' (2011) 11 AHRLJ 639, at 640.
28 Eimear O'Brien, 'Are you treating your Vulnerable Customers Fairly?' (2017) 6 CRJ 10.
29 Alzheimer's Society, *Dementia UK: Update*, 2014; World Health Organisation and the World Bank, *Summary World Report on Disability*, WHO/NMH/VIP/11.01, 2011, 8.
30 UN Convention on the Rights of Persons with Disabilities, Article 1.
31 ibid, Article 19.
32 ibid, Article 1.
33 *Nyusti and Takács vs. Hungary*, above n 22, paragraphs 2.13, 2.14 and 2.16. See also NCCD, above n 7; Maker and others, above n 6, 824.
34 Paul Hirst, 'Ownership and Democracy' (1998) 69 Pol.Q. 354; Anthony Ogus, *Regulation, Legal Form and Economic Theory* (Hart 2004), 22.
35 See *Bacher vs. Austria*, CRPD/C/19/D/26/2014, 6 April 2018.

terms and the consequences of breach),[36] the limited scope of this chapter is confined to English contract law and is focused on three vitiating factors: incapacity, unconscionability and undue influence. Issues such as equality and non-discrimination in accessing services or the regulation of unfair contract terms tend to reflect a more visible interplay between public and private spheres of regulation.[37] Such visibility has been less apparent with regard to vitiating factors, where the focus seems to be on allowing only a limited degree of intervention, rooted in procedural considerations.[38] Another reason why vitiating factors provide an interesting focus for this study is because this middle layer of the multilayered approach mentioned above relies to a great extent on case law,[39] leading to questions about the way in which courts interpret foundational concepts such as freedom of contract.

Throughout this discussion, reference is made to the contracting parties as A (referring to the individual seeking to rely on arguments of vulnerability created by the context of the transaction) and B (referring to the other party, who could be another individual or a service provider such as a bank, and who, in order to resist attempts to invalidate the contract, is seeking to rely on a strict interpretation of freedom of contract). Whilst reference to the parties as A and B may seem too abstract, this is designed to simplify the discussion of technical points of law and to enhance the central message that this chapter aims to put forward. The key message of this discussion is that when we talk about vulnerable parties in the contractual sphere and the measures to safeguard the interests of these parties, we should not see these measures as the state 'interfering' with freedom of contract. Rather than looking at the realm of contract law as a single sphere, rooted in economic values, focused on facilitating interactions between private parties, where the state is not allowed to step in, this realm should be envisaged as resting on two concentric spheres. In the inner, economic sphere, parties can pursue their self-interest based on a noninterventionist approach, but certain triggers could cause the transaction to step out of this inner sphere into the outer, social sphere where the state could seek to address issues such as vulnerability. Such triggers may be caused by vitiating factors leading to grossly imbalanced contacts that harm A's dignity. They may also include situations where B refuses to contract with A because of A's disability, or where B contracts with A based on grossly imbalanced and unfair terms in a standard form contract, which could also harm A's dignity.

---

36 See, for example, EU-level provisions for regulating unfair contract terms under Council Directive 93/13/EEC on Unfair Terms in Consumer Contracts [1993] OJ L95/29, as amended by Directive (EU) 2019/2161 of the European Parliament and of the Council as regards the better enforcement and modernisation of union consumer protection rules [2019] OJ L328/7. See discussion in Simon Whittaker, 'Consumer Contracts' in Hugh Beale and others (eds), *Chitty on Contracts* (33rd edn, Sweet & Maxwell 2018), 38–218.

37 Collins, above n 10, 361.

38 Hugh Collins, *The Law of Contract* (4th edn, Butterworths 2003), 270–271.

39 See, however, the Mental Capacity Act 2005, ss 2, 3, 15–19 and Part 2 (regarding contracts where an individual's property is under the court's control).

Freedom of contract should never be used to condone B's harmful behaviour or to attempt to bring transactions behind the closed doors of a private realm not open to scrutiny.[40] Instead, this foundational concept of private law should be shaped by positive values that reflect both the economic and social dimensions of contract law, and the interplay between private law and human rights.[41] This positive interpretation of freedom of contract is closer to the values pursued by the CRPD, such as equality and the protection of human dignity. Whilst the CRPD has no binding force in the United Kingdom (as this instrument was signed and ratified, but not incorporated into domestic law),[42] the Convention has persuasive authority[43] and, therefore, its values should not be overlooked.

I The CRPD: a benchmark for a positive interpretation of freedom of contract?

When examining the CRPD with the contractual sphere in mind, the Convention appears, at first instance, to be relatively silent. There is no equivalent provision to Article 15(2) of the UN Convention on the Elimination of all Forms of Discrimination against Women (CEDAW),[44] which makes explicit reference to the equal right to conclude contracts and the equal right and equal opportunities to exercise legal capacity.[45] While Article 12 of the CRPD reaffirms the equal right of persons with disabilities to recognition as persons before the law[46] and to enjoy legal capacity 'in all aspects of life',[47] there is no explicit call on States Parties to provide persons with disabilities with equal opportunities to exercise legal capacity. There is also no explicit reference to equality in the contractual sphere, although this is implicit,[48] including in the call on States Parties to take all appropriate measures to ensure the equal right of persons with disabilities to 'control their own financial affairs' and 'have equal access to bank loans, mortgages and other forms of financial credit'.[49]

---

40 Hugh Collins, 'The Vanishing Freedom to Choose a Contractual Partner' (2012) 76 LCP 71, at 72.

41 Deutch, above n 16, 554; Collins, above n 40, 73.

42 See, for example, *In the Matter of Various Lasting Powers of Attorney* [2019] EWCOP 40, at 62.

43 See, for example, *AH vs. West London Mental Health Trust* [2011] UKUT 74, at 16–17; *Burnip vs. Birmingham City Council* [2013] PTSR 117, at 22; *P vs. Cheshire West and Chester Council* [2014] UKSC 19, at 36.

44 GA Res 34/180, 18 December 1979, A/34/46, 1249 UNTS 13.

45 UN Convention on the Elimination of All Forms of Discrimination against Women, Article 15(2). See Jo Lynn Southard, 'Protection of Women's Human Rights under the Convention on the Elimination of All Forms of Discrimination against Women' (1996) 8 Pace Int'l L.Rev. 1, at 37.

46 UN Convention on the Rights of Persons with Disabilities, Article 12(1). See Bach, above n 14, 2.

47 UN Convention on the Rights of Persons with Disabilities, Article 12(2).

48 ibid, Article 12(1) and (2).

49 ibid, Article 12(5).

The CRPD acknowledges that some persons with disabilities may require support in exercising legal capacity[50] and that safeguards must be put in place to ensure that 'measures relating to the exercise of legal capacity' are, *inter alia*, free of undue influence,[51] although the Convention is unclear on the extent to which the right to exercise legal capacity can be restricted (if at all) and on the link between the concepts of legal, mental and contractual capacity.[52]

The guidance offered by the CRPD Committee on how to interpret the Convention in the contractual sphere is also limited. In its General Comment 1,[53] other than two references to Article 15 CEDAW,[54] the CRPD Committee refers only once to the equal right to exercise legal capacity by entering into contracts. This reference is part of its discussion on the provision of support to exercise legal capacity.[55] The Committee calls on public and private actors, including banks and other financial institutions, to provide information in accessible formats in order to enable persons with disabilities to perform legal acts required to conclude contracts,[56] but provides no further guidance on how this should operate in practice. With regard to the concepts of legal and mental capacity, the Committee rightly distinguishes the concept of universal legal capacity (the ability to hold and exercise rights and duties)[57] from mental capacity (the decision-making skills which may be influenced by external factors and vary from person to person).[58] Yet, it insists that legal standing (to hold rights) and legal agency (to exercise rights) cannot be separated[59] and adopts an absolute stance on mental capacity assessments based on functional tests focused on an individual's ability to, *inter alia*, process information, finding these to be incompatible with Article 12 CRPD.[60]

---

50 ibid, Article 12(3).
51 ibid, Article 12(4).
52 Peter Bartlett, 'The United Nations Convention on the Rights of Persons with Disabilities and Mental Health Law' (2012) 75 MLR 752, at 768; John Dawson, 'A Realistic Approach to Assessing Mental Health Laws' Compliance with the UNCRPD' (2015) 40 Int'l J.L.& Psychiatry 70; Robert Dinerstein, 'Implementing Legal Capacity under Article 12 of the UN Convention on the Rights of Persons with Disabilities: The Difficult Road from Guardianship to Supported Decision-Making' (2012) 19 *Human Rights Brief* 8; Amita Dhanda, 'Legal Capacity in the Disability Rights Convention: Stranglehold of the Past or Lodestar for the Future?' (2007) 34 Syracuse J.Int'l L.& Com. 429.
53 CRPD Committee, General Comment No. 1: Article 12 (Equal Recognition before the Law), 19 May 2014, UN Doc. CRPD/C/GC/1.
54 ibid, paragraphs 6 and 35.
55 ibid, paragraph 17, with reference to Article 12(3) CRPD.
56 ibid.
57 ibid, paragraph 13.
58 ibid. See Anna Arstein-Kerslake and Eilionóir Flynn, 'The General Comment on Article 12 of the Convention on the Rights of Persons with Disabilities: A Roadmap for Equality Before the Law' (2016) 20 I.J.H.R. 471, at 474.
59 CRPD Committee, General Comment No. 1, paragraph 14.
60 ibid, paragraph 15. See Sascha Callaghan and Christopher Ryan, 'An Evolving Revolution: Evaluating Australia's Compliance with the Convention on the Rights of Persons with Disabilities in Mental Health Law' (2016) 39 UNSWLJ 596, at 604.

The Committee also fails to consider the issue of contractual capacity involving a party who may act outside a framework of support to enter into a grossly imbalanced transaction to their detriment, whilst lacking the mental capacity to understand the consequences of the transaction. While the starting point should always be a pre-sumption of contractual capacity and a focus on support to exercise capacity[61] (e.g., accessible information, informal or formal support arrangements),[62] the exercise of universal legal capacity could be facilitated by a legal framework where parties can rely, when appropriate, on defences such as contractual incapacity,[63] but where disability and incapacity are never conceptually equated.[64]

If an intervention may amount to indirect discrimination on the basis of disability, this may be objectively justified only if it pursues a legitimate aim.[65] Such legitimate aim may be to protect the dignity[66] of a party (A) in a situation of financial risk,[67] as a result of entering into a grossly asymmetrical contract while being in a vulnerable position where the other party (B) decided to proceed with the transaction without ensuring that A received appropriate independent legal advice regarding the transaction, despite having (actual or constructive) knowledge of A's condition.[68] A's vulner-ability may derive from the fact that their consent was affected by vitiating factors such as incapacity, unconscionability or undue influence. Intervention should also be permitted only on an objective basis that moves beyond A's medical condition to include environmental factors such as the circumstances of the transaction (e.g., whether A entered into a grossly imbalanced contract in the absence of accessible independent advice) and

---

61 UN Convention on the Rights of Persons with Disabilities, Article 12(3). See Eilionóir Flynn and Anna Arstein-Kerslake, 'Legislating Personhood: Realising the Right to Support in Exercising Legal Capacity' (2014) 10 Int. J.L.C. 81, at 131.

62 CRPD Committee, General Comment No. 1, paragraph 17. See Lucy Series, 'Relationships, Autonomy and Legal Capacity: Mental Capacity and Support Paradigms' (2015) 40 Int'l J.L.& Psychiatry 80, at 85; Piers Gooding, Anna Arstein-Kerslake and Eilionóir Flynn, 'Assistive Technology as Support for the Exercise of Legal Capacity' (2015) 29 *International Review of Law, Computers and Technology* 245, at 251; Tina Minkowitz, 'Abolishing Mental Health Laws to Comply with the Convention on the Rights of Persons with Disabilities' in Bernadette McSherry and Penelope Weller (eds), *Rethinking Rights-Based Mental Health Laws* (Hart 2010), 160; Eilionóir Flynn, 'Mental (in)Capacity or Legal Capacity: A Human Rights Analysis of the Proposed Fusion of Mental Health and Mental Capacity Law in Northern Ireland' (2013) 64 NILQ 485, at 498.

63 Eliza Varney, 'Redefining Contractual Capacity? The UN Convention on the Rights of Persons with Disabilities and the Incapacity Defence in English Contract Law' (2017) 37 LS 493.

64 Bach, above n 14, 21.

65 Wayne Martin and others, 'Achieving CRPD Compliance. Is the Mental Capacity Act of England and Wales Compatible with the UN Convention on the Rights of Persons with Disabilities? If Not, What Next? An Essex Autonomy Project Position Paper', Report sub-mitted to the UK Ministry of Justice, 22 September 2014, 30.

66 UN Convention on the Rights of Persons with Disabilities, Article 3(a).

67 ibid, Article 11.

68 Martin and others, above n 65, 30.

only if it constitutes a reasonable means to achieve a legitimate aim.[69] Regrettably, the CRPD Committee provided no guidance on how vitiating factors in contract law, such as incapacity, unconscionability and undue influence, could act as a safety net in such circumstances.

The jurisprudence of the CRPD Committee illustrates further missed opportunities to provide guidance on how concepts such as contractual capacity and freedom of contract should be interpreted in light of the Convention. *Nyusti*[70] highlighted States Parties' obligations to take 'all appropriate measures' to eliminate discrimination on the basis of disability by private parties such as banks[71] and ensure that such private parties offering services to the public 'take into account all aspects of accessibility'.[72] Despite the merits of this decision, the CRPD Committee failed to engage explicitly with the issue of freedom of contract or to challenge the negative interpretation of this concept put forward by the private bank and endorsed by the State to resist intervention in the pursuit of equality objectives. In seeking to justify its refusal to provide accessible ATMs and enable its customers with visual disabilities to use these facilities independently, the bank stressed that independent use of ATMs would increase banking security risks for these customers, 'due to their special situation',[73] reflecting a paternalistic perception of people with disabilities as objects of care, rather than as subjects of rights.[74] Overlooking the security risks faced by anyone who has to rely on others to access their bank account[75] and the infringement on human dignity associated with inaccessible services,[76] the bank insisted that the availability of accessible ATMs would motivate people with visual disabilities to use these facilities 'without help', endangering their 'personal safety'.[77] The bank also approached the issue of equal access to financial services from a solely economic perspective focused on the cost of inclusion (rather than the wider social costs of exclusion),[78] insisting that the provision of accessible ATMs would impose on it 'an unexpected financial burden'.[79]

The bank's approach was also problematic in their interpretation of freedom of contract based on a negative, noninterventionist approach (rather than a positive

---

69 ibid.

70 *Nyusti and Takács vs. Hungary,* above n 22.

71 ibid, paragraph 9.4; UN Convention on the Rights of Persons with Disabilities, Article 4(1)(e).

72 *Nyusti and Takács vs. Hungary,* above n 22, paragraph 9.4; UN Convention on the Rights of Persons with Disabilities, Article 9(2)(b).

73 *Nyusti and Takács vs. Hungary,* above n 22, paragraph 2.5.

74 Heiner Bielefeldt, 'New Inspiration for the Human Rights Debate: The Convention on the Rights of Persons with Disabilities' (2007) 52 NQHR 397.

75 Anna Lawson, 'Accessibility Obligations in the UN *Convention on the Rights of Persons with Disabilities: Nyusti and Takacs vs. Hungary*', (2014) 30 SAJHR 380.

76 *Nyusti and Takács vs. Hungary,* above n 22, paragraph 2.12.

77 ibid, paragraph 2.12.

78 Interview with Guido Gybels, RNID (now Action on Hearing Loss), 17 August 2009.

79 *Nyusti and Takács vs. Hungary,* above n 22, paragraph 2.5.

approach that justifies intervention to protect social values such as equality and dignity),[80] as it stressed that an obligation to provide accessible services would amount to interference into the parties' contractual relations and infringe their freedom of contract.[81] Perhaps even more concerning is the positive reception of these arguments in Hungary's highest courts, as both the Court of Appeal and the Supreme Court agreed with the cost-based vision of accessibility and negative interpretation of freedom of contract put forward by the bank.[82] This position was ultimately challenged before the CRPD Committee, which, in a judgement that engaged more with accessibility arguments than with the issue of freedom of contract, found Hungary to be in breach of its obligations under Article 9(2)(b) CRPD to ensure that private entities offering facilities and services open to the public consider all accessibility aspects for persons with disabilities.[83]

While the applicants in *Nyusti* were ultimately successful in their claim under Article 9(2)(b) CRPD,[84] they did not provide sufficient justifications to enable the CRPD Committee to consider their claim under Article 12(5) CRPD, concerning the equal right of persons with disabilities to control their financial affairs.[85] Nevertheless, their successful claim should have provided the Committee with more scope to engage with the wider issue of asymmetrical power in contracts involving individuals and private entities such as banks. The Committee should have challenged a narrow, market individualist[86] understanding of freedom of contract that assumes that parties are free to pursue their own interest in the contractual sphere, placing insufficient weight on the inequality of bargaining power illustrated in the asymmetrical relation between individuals and banks, and on the proliferation of standard form contracts based on a 'take it or leave it basis'.[87] The CRPD Committee should have also contested negative visions of freedom of contract based on nonintervention by the state, in favour of a positive understanding of this concept where intervention is permitted if required to pursue wider social values such as the protection of equality and dignity.[88]

In the contractual sphere, the CRPD Committee's decision in *Nyusti*[89] is more significant for what can be read between the lines, rather than for what was stated explicitly. Implicit in this decision is the recognition that Convention rights permeate not just the public domain, but also the private sphere, affecting the contractual

80 Collins, above n 21, 5.
81 *Nyusti and Takács vs. Hungary*, above n 22, paragraphs 2.5 and 2.12.
82 ibid, paragraphs 2.13–2.16.
83 UN Convention on the Rights of Persons with Disabilities, Article 9(2)(b); *Nyusti and Takács vs. Hungary*, above n 22, paragraphs 10 and 9.4.
84 *Nyusti and Takács vs. Hungary*, above n 22, paragraph 9.4.
85 ibid, paragraph 8.3.
86 John Adams and Roger Brownsword, Understanding Contract Law (5th edn, Sweet & Maxwell 2007), 194.
87 Kessler, above, n 9, 632; Andrew Burgess, 'Consumer Adhesion Contracts and Unfair Terms: A Critique of Current Theory and a Suggestion' (1986) 15 Anglo-Am.L.R. 255.
88 Collins, above n 21, 5.
89 *Nyusti and Takács vs. Hungary*, above n 22.

relationships between parties. The Committee endorsed, albeit implicitly, the perception that the contractual relation of the applicants (who were consumers with disabilities) with the bank was not confined to the economic sphere and, therefore, should not be rooted in a noninterventionist stance. Instead, the contractual relationship was located within a wider, social sphere, where intervention may be justified in the pursuit of equality objectives. A further significant aspect of the CRPD Committee's decision in *Nyusti*[90] is the implicit recognition that in a process of balancing dignity and freedom of contract, the protection of human dignity is ranked as a higher value that justifies interference with freedom of contract.

The framework of values advanced by the CRPD rests on a rights-based understanding of disability, moving away from a focus on the medical condition of individuals[91] and building on the social model of disability, concerned with addressing the social barriers faced by persons with disabilities when accessing a particular context.[92] In the contractual realm, barriers such as the unavailability of accessible information may lead to asymmetry in the parties' bargaining positions,[93] enhancing consumer vulnerability.[94] Furthermore, barriers such as inaccessible services and facilities may produce isolation, dependence on others[95] or lack of confidence to approach service providers or to decline unwanted offers of services.[96] The CRPD recognises the need to adapt society to accommodate the full spectrum of abilities,[97] including in its general principles a call for accessibility,[98] 'full and effective participation and inclusion in society'[99] and 'respect for difference and acceptance of persons with disabilities as part of human diversity and humanity'.[100] In addition, the States Parties' general obligations

---

90 ibid.
91 UN Convention on the Rights of Persons with Disabilities, Preamble, paragraph (e) and Article 1. See Colin Barnes and Michael Oliver, 'Disability Rights: Rhetoric and Reality in the United Kingdom' (1995) 10 *Disability and Society* 111.
92 Rannveig Traustadóttir, 'Disability Studies, the Social Model and Legal Developments' in Oddný Arnardóttir and Gerard Quinn (eds) *The UN Convention on the Rights of Persons with Disabilities – European and Scandinavian Perspectives, International Studies in Human Rights, Vol. 100* (Brill 2009), 1; Sarah Fraser Butlin, 'The UN Convention on the Rights of Persons with Disabilities: Does the Equality Act 2010 Measure up to UK International Commitments?' (2011) 40 ILJ 428.
93 Michael Trebilcock and Steven Elliott, 'The Scope and Limits of Legal Paternalism: Altruism and Coercion in Family Financial Arrangements' in Peter Benson (ed), *The Theory of Contract Law: New Essays* (CUP 2001), 62.
94 Carol Kaufman-Scarborough, 'Social Exclusion: A Perspective on Consumers with Disabilities' in Susan Dunnett, Kathy Hamilton and Maria Piacentini (eds) *Vulnerable Consumers: Conditions, Contexts, Characteristic* (Routledge 2015) 157.
95 WHO and the World Bank, above n 29, 11.
96 Maker and others, above n 11, 192.
97 Anna Lawson, 'The United Nations Convention on the Rights of Persons with Disabilities: New Era or False Dawn?' (2007) 34 Syracuse J.Int'l L.& Com. 563, at 573.
98 UN Convention on the Rights of Persons with Disabilities, Article 3(f).
99 ibid, Article 3(c).
100 ibid, Article 3(d).

under the Convention include a call to 'take all appropriate measures to eliminate discrimination on the basis of disability' by private enterprises,[101] while the CRPD provisions on accessibility call on States Parties to ensure, *inter alia*, that such requirements are considered by private entities offering services to the public.[102] These obligations contribute toward meeting the Convention's overall purpose to promote 'the full and equal enjoyment of all human rights and fundamental freedoms by all persons with disabilities' and 'respect for their inherent dignity',[103] reflecting a perception of persons with disabilities as citizens with full entitlements in society.[104]

In meeting these objectives, an important role can be played by a vision of contract law that perceives people not only as economic actors in pursuit of self-interest, but also as participants in the wider social sphere,[105] and which aims to protect citizenship values such as equality, dignity, autonomy and inclusion.[106] Furthermore, the concept of autonomy should be interpreted broadly to include relational autonomy, recognising our interdependence.[107] Based on this perspective, contract law is not confined to a unidimensional role to enable transactions in the economic realm but reflects a multidimensional role that permeates the economic and social spheres, as it facilitates transactions and connects people into mutual relations.[108] In this vision, concepts such as freedom of contract should not be restricted to a narrow, negative interpretation concerned with resisting state intervention, and should, instead, be interpreted broadly to consider social values alongside economic concerns.

II English contract law: a framework rooted in a negative interpretation of freedom of contract?

The CRPD sparked the need to reexamine legal concepts, including freedom of contract, in light of the values pursued by the Convention.[109] The United

---

101 ibid, Article 4(1)(e). See also Article 5.
102 ibid, Article 9(2)(b). See CRPD Committee, 'General Comment No. 2: Article 9 (Accessibility)', 22 May 2014, UN Doc. CRPD/C/GC/2. See also UN Convention on the Rights of Persons with Disabilities, Article 21(c).
103 UN Convention on the Rights of Persons with Disabilities, Article 1. See Réaume, above, n 18, 51; Sandra Fredman, 'Equality: A New Generation?' (2001) 30 ILJ 145, at 155.
104 Deirdre Smith, 'Who Says You're Disabled? The Role of Medical Evidence in the ADA Definition of Disability' (2007) 82 Tul.L.Rev. 1, 71; Halvor Hanisch, 'Recognising Disability', in Jerome Bickenbach, Franziska Felder and Barbara Schmitz (eds) *Disability and the Good Human Life* (CUP 2014), 124.
105 Giovanna Procacci, 'Poor Citizens: Social Citizenship versus Individualisation of Welfare' in Colin Crouch, Klau Eder and Damian Tambini (eds) *Citizenship, Markets and the State* (OUP 2001), 63; Cass Sunstein, *After the Rights Revolution: Reconceiving the Regulatory State* (HUP 1990), 58.
106 UN Convention on the Rights of Persons with Disabilities, Article 3.
107 Amita Dhanda, 'Constructing a New Human Rights Lexicon: Convention on the Rights of Persons with Disabilities' (2008) 5 Sur: Int'l J Hum Rts 43, at 49.
108 Gunther Teubner, 'Contracting Worlds: The Many Autonomies of Private Law' (2000) 9 *Social and Legal Studies* 399, at 400.
109 UN Convention on the Rights of Persons with Disabilities, Article 4.

Kingdom ratified the CRPD in 2009 and, whilst this instrument has not been incorporated into national law and is of limited direct assistance in domestic courts,[110] its relevance cannot be ignored. Through its ratification, the United Kingdom undertook that 'wherever possible, its laws will conform to the norms and values' enshrined in the Convention.[111] This section emphasises that CRPD values could (and should) inform a positive interpretation of the concept of freedom of contract in English contract law.

Freedom of contract is a foundational concept of English contract law, emphasising that parties are free to choose whether to enter into a contract, who to contract with and under which terms.[112] However, this freedom is not absolute, and courts may decline to enforce contracts affected, *inter alia*, by vitiating factors such as incapacity, unconscionability or undue influence.[113] This may be perceived as 'interference' with freedom of contract, leading to questions about the extent to which the state should be allowed to intervene. An interpretation of freedom of contract focused on negative liberty (defined as freedom from state control)[114] would seek to resist such interference, limiting it to procedural factors (e.g., vitiation of consent) and unconcerned with substantive considerations (e.g., whether the parties entered into a grossly asymmetrical contract). This vision is not concerned with who the parties are (e.g., whether there is a gross imbalance in their bargaining power)[115] and reflects a narrow conception of autonomy, perceiving the parties as economic actors in pursuit of their individual interests.[116] An alternative vision of freedom of contract is to focus on positive values such as promoting respect for human dignity, where the state would refuse to enforce transactions that harm such values.[117] This would reflect a broad, relational conception of autonomy, focused on the interdependence between human beings,[118] where contract law facilitates transactions that connect people into mutual relations within a wider social sphere.[119]

In English contract law, the prevalent vision appears to be a narrow understanding of freedom of contract, focused on limited intervention confined to procedural grounds and generally unconcerned with imbalance in the contracting parties' bargaining power. This point is illustrated with reference to the current legal framework on contractual incapacity (focused on the common law

---

110 *R (on the application of NM) vs. Islington LBC* [2012] EWHC 414, [98]; *R (on the application of MA) vs. Secretary of State for Work and Pensions* [2013] EWHC 2213, [80]; *Hainsworth vs. Ministry of Defence* [2014] EWCA Civ 763, [30].
111 *AH vs. West London Mental Health Trust* [2011] UKUT 74, [16], per Carnwath LJ.
112 Adams and Brownsword, above n 86, 194.
113 Gareth Spark, *Vitiation of Contracts: International Contractual Principles and English Law* (CUP 2013).
114 Collins, above n 21, 5.
115 Adams and Brownsword, above n 86, 194.
116 Collins, above n 21, 5.
117 ibid.
118 ibid, 6.
119 Teubner, above n 108, 400.

approach), undue influence and unconscionability. Whilst the discussion in the previous section focused on a case involving contracting parties affected by inaccessible services[120] and the present section will look at cases where parties seek to avoid a contract affected by vitiating factors, the common thread of the discussion is the wider question whether the concept of 'freedom of contract' can be used to resist interventions in pursuit of substantive fairness and social objectives such as the protection of human dignity.

The doctrines of incapacity, undue influence and unconscionability have the potential to assist vulnerable contracting parties, including parties whose capacity to understand the implications of a transaction has been affected by mental health conditions such as dementia. Whilst English contract law starts from a *prima facie* presumption of contractual capacity for all adults, a party (A) may seek to set aside a contract on grounds of incapacity, with reference to the test under the Mental Capacity Act (MCA) of 2005[121] (for contracts for necessary goods and services),[122] or the common law test (for all other contracts).[123] Based on a time and issue specific approach, these tests consider that A lacked the mental capacity to enter into a contract if, at the time of the transaction, he was unable to make a decision for himself regarding the transaction, due to 'an impairment of, or a disturbance in the functioning of the mind or brain' (under the MCA 2005 test),[124] or because he was 'so insane' that he 'did not know what he was doing' (under the common law test).[125] If A is unable to rebut the *prima facie* presumption of contractual capacity under these tests, he may seek to render the transaction voidable by relying on the equitable doctrines of undue influence and unconscionability. This may be the case if his weakness has been exploited by the other contracting party (B) (in the case of unconscionability),[126] or if A and B were in a relationship of trust and confidence and B took unfair advantage of his influence over A (in the case of undue influence).[127] The latter doctrine may also have relevance in tripartite situations where A acts as surety for a debtor in support of the latter's loan from a bank, and the bank had constructive notice of undue influence, as the surety and the debtor were in a

---

120 *Nyusti and Takács vs. Hungary,* above n 22.

121 Mental Capacity Act 2005, ss 2(1) and 3(1). See Simon Whittaker, 'Personal Incapacity' in Hugh Beale and others (eds), *Chitty on Contracts* (33rd ed, Sweet & Maxwell 2018), 9-092. See, for example, *A London Borough vs. G* [2014] EWHC 485 (COP) concerning capacity to make decisions regarding, *inter alia*, financial affairs.

122 Mental Capacity Act 2005, s 7. See Whittaker, above n 121, 9-097.

123 *Imperial Loan vs. Stone* [1892] 1 QB 599; *Re Beany* [1978] 1 WLR 770. See Whittaker, above n 121, 9-089.

124 Mental Capacity Act 2005, ss 2(1) and 3(1).

125 *Imperial Loan vs. Stone,* above n 123, at [601], per Lord Esher.

126 *Fry vs. Lane* (1888) 40 ChD 312; *Cresswell vs. Potter* [1978] 1 WLR 255; *Alec Lobb vs. Total Oil* [1985] 1 WLR 173.

127 *Allcard vs. Skinner* (1887) 36 ChD 145; *Barclays Bank vs. O'Brien* [1994] 1 AC 180; *Royal Bank of Scotland Plc vs. Etridge (No. 2)* [2001] UKHL 44.

noncommercial relation.[128] The doctrines of unconscionability and undue influence have a role to play even where A's *prima facie* presumption of contractual capacity can be rebutted under the MCA 2005 test or the common law test, as contracts where A's property is not under the court's control,[129] or where B had no knowledge of A's mental incapacity,[130] remain valid, unless they can be rendered voidable on the basis of vitiating factors such as undue influence or unconscionability.

The extent to which these doctrines can assist vulnerable contracting parties can, however, be affected negatively by a range of factors. First, the scope of these doctrines can be confined by a narrow interpretation of their relevant triggers. If A seeks to rely on the incapacity defence for contracts governed by the common law (which are outside the control of the court[131] and do not involve the purchase of necessary goods and services),[132] A needs to show both his mental incapacity and B's knowledge of his condition.[133] This can be a very high threshold if courts interpret the knowledge requirement to be confined to actual knowledge, or if any acceptance of constructive knowledge in this definition[134] is limited to situations where A's incapacity is apparent,[135] rather than where B ought to have known about A's incapacity due to the circumstances of the transaction.[136] Concerns regarding narrow triggers for intervention can be raised also with regard to the doctrines of undue influence and unconscionability. To rely on these doctrines, A needs to show both his vulnerability (e.g., mental impairment resulting from a medical condition, in the case of unconscionability,[137] or impaired consent resulting from B's pressure, in the case of undue influence)[138] and B's unacceptable conduct (e.g., overt persuasion or failure to protect from a relationship of influence and a transaction that calls for an explanation for undue influence,[139] or exploitation of weakness, knowingly taking advantage of A to enter into a contract disadvantageous for A, in the case of unconscionability).[140] In

---

128 *Barclays Bank vs. O'Brien*, above n 127, 196; *RBS vs. Etridge*, above n 127, [87]. See Hugh Beale, 'Duress and Undue Influence' in Hugh Beale and others (eds), *Chitty on Contracts* (33rd edn, Sweet & Maxwell 2018), 8-117.

129 Mental Capacity Act 2005, ss 2, 3, 15–19 and Part 2. See Whittaker, above n 121, 9-092.

130 *Imperial Loan vs. Stone*, above n 123; *Hart vs. O'Connor* [1985] AC 1000. See Edwin Peel, *Treitel on the Law of Contract* (14th edn, Sweet & Maxwell 2015), 12–054.

131 Mental Capacity Act 2005, s 15.

132 ibid, s 7.

133 *Imperial Loan vs. Stone*, above n 123, 601.

134 *Dunhill vs. Burgin* [2014] UKSC 18, at [25].

135 Whittaker, above n 121, para 9-081.

136 Varney, above n 63.

137 *Boustany vs. Pigott* (1995) 69 P & CR 298. See Beale, above n 128, 8-134.

138 *RBS vs. Etridge*, above n 127, [9]. See also *Wright vs. Carter* [1903] 1 Ch 27; *CIBC Mortgages vs. Pitt* [1994] 1 AC 200; See Herring, above n 5OUP, 243.

139 *RBS vs. Etridge*, above n 127, [6-8]; *Hammond vs. Osborn* [2002] EWCA Civ 885. See Herring, above n 5, 244–245.

140 *Boustany vs. Pigott*, above n 137; *Fineland Investments vs. Pritchard* [2011] EWHC 113. See Spark, above n 113, 286; Andrew Burrows, *A Restatement of the English Law of Contract* (2nd edn, OUP 2016), 41.

cases of unconscionability, a narrow focus on B's unacceptable conduct confined to 'deliberate' exploitations of A's weakness (rather than on B's passive unacceptable conduct to proceed with the contract despite the circumstances of the transactions) would appear to allow B to 'take advantage of [A]'s vulnerable state, short of actively manipulating' A.[141] Similar concerns could be raised in cases of undue influence, given questions of whether the scope of this doctrine includes B's passive unacceptable conduct to proceed with the transaction despite having knowledge of A's vulnerability, and whether such knowledge is confined to actual knowledge.[142]

Second, the current framework appears focused on limited intervention with the parties' freedom of contract, confined to procedural grounds. For example, B could seek to resist challenges based on undue influence or unconscionability by stressing that A exercised his free will when entering into the contract[143] (even where this is grossly imbalanced), after having received independent legal advice.[144] This narrow approach is driven by concerns to uphold the security of transactions[145] (making it harder for A to be released from their contractual obligations on the basis of vitiating factors), facilitate commercial convenience[146] (enabling B to point to the independent legal advice received by A) and ensure certainty[147] (as procedural factors appear to be easier to assess than substantive considerations). Nevertheless, this approach risks leaving vulnerable parties with insufficient protection of their economic interests (e.g., as a result of entering into a grossly imbalanced transaction, to their detriment) and social interests (e.g., due to the harm to their human dignity and the wider social implications of allowing such grossly imbalanced contracts with vulnerable parties to be enforceable). Furthermore, insufficient weight is placed on whether the independent legal advice was appropriate and accessible to A,[148] and whether it addressed both economic and social considerations.

Third, the current framework appears to be unconcerned with who the contracting parties are.[149] It seeks to provide a 'middle course' that protects the

141 Herring, above n 5, 251.
142 Beale, above n 128, 8-059.
143 *Inche Noriah vs. Shaik Allie bin Omar* [1929] AC 127, 135; See Beale, above n 128, 8-099; Marcus Moore, 'Why Does Lord Denning's Lead Balloon Intrigue Us Still? The Prospects of Finding a Unifying Principle for Duress, Undue Influence and Unconscionability', (2018) 134(Apr) LQR 257, at 273.
144 *RBS vs. Etridge*, above n 127, [20]; *Morley vs. Loughnan* [1893] 1 Ch. 736, at 752; See Beale, above n 128, 8-099; Mindy Chen-Wishart, 'Undue Influence: Beyond Impaired Consent and Wrongdoing towards a Relational Analysis' in A Burrows and Lord Rodger of Earlsferry (eds) *Mapping the Law: Essays in Memory of Peter Birks* (OUP 2006), 221; Peter Millett, 'Equity's Place in the Law of Commerce', (1998) 114 LQR 214, at 220.
145 Adams and Brownsword, above n 86, 192.
146 Herring, above n 5, 249.
147 Adams and Brownsword, above n 86, 189.
148 Trebilcock and Elliott, above n 93, 79.
149 Adams and Brownsword, above n 86, 194.

interests of both parties,[150] assuming that they approached the transaction from balanced bargaining positions.[151] Once again, this provides insufficient protection to vulnerable contracting parties. In cases where A seeks to rely on the incapacity defence, the requirement to show B's knowledge of incapacity as a condition for rendering the contract voidable may protect B's interests but places insufficient weight on A's lack of consent,[152] resulting in an imbalanced approach.[153] Similarly, in cases where A seeks to render a contract voidable on grounds of undue influence, any assumption of a balanced bargaining position distorts subsequent assessments of whether access to independent legal advice redressed this alleged balance. Furthermore, attempts to 'balance' the interests of parties such as individuals and banks overlook the gross asymmetry in these parties' bargaining positions and access to resources.[154] Moreover, such approaches neglect the structural inequalities that may affect the contracting parties[155] and the social context within which the transactions take place.[156]

Fourth, this framework illustrates a narrow conception of autonomy, perceiving contracting parties solely as individuals in pursuit of their self-interests within the economic sphere. It appears to be unconcerned with issues of relational autonomy, which focus on the connection between the parties within a wider social context[157] and on the values that should govern these parties' relationships, including social values based on interdependence and mutuality.[158]

At the root of all these concerns is a narrow interpretation of freedom of contract, where the state can intervene only in narrowly defined circumstances shaped by procedural factors and where contract law has a unidimensional role limited to enforcing agreements.[159] Intervention, when permitted as part of procedural mechanisms, is confined to the economic realm and is not understood to be transcending economic and social spheres. Such a framework overlooks the role of the state as a central pivot in enforcing (or refusing to enforce, where appropriate) the contractual relations between the parties.[160]

---

150 Peter Watts, 'Contracts made by Agents on Behalf of Principals with Latent Mental Incapacity: The Common Law Position' (2015) 74 CLJ 140, at 145.
151 Herring, above n 5, 228 and 257.
152 Henry Goudy, 'Contracts by Lunatics' (1901) 17 LQR 147, at 150.
153 A Hudson, 'Mental Incapacity Revisited' (1986) *The Conveyancer and Property Lawyer* 178, at 181.
154 Rosemary Auchmuty, 'Men Behaving Badly: An Analysis of English Undue Influence Cases' (2002) 11 *Social and Legal Studies* 257, at 271.
155 ibid, 266.
156 Alison Diduck, '*Royal Bank of Scotland Plc vs. Etridge* (No 2): Commentary' in Rosemary Hunter, Clare McGlynn, Erika Rackley (eds) *Feminist Judgments, from Theory to Practice* (Hart 2010), 152.
157 Dhanda, above n 52, 49.
158 Herring, above n 5, 228.
159 ibid, 225.
160 Seana Shiffrin, 'Paternalism, Unconscionability Doctrine and Accommodation' (2000) 29 Phil.& Pub.Aff. 205, at 227.

There is, however, an alternative vision of freedom of contract and of the state's role in the contractual sphere. This vision understands the role of contract law as multidimensional, transcending economic and social spheres[161] and actively enforcing positive values such as the protection of human dignity.[162] Rather than perceiving the protection of vulnerable contracting parties on grounds of incapacity, undue influence or unconscionability, as an 'interference' with freedom of contract due to procedural concerns, this could be understood as a circumstance where the state refuses to enforce grossly imbalanced contacts[163] which have stepped out of an inner, noninterventionist sphere of contract law (concerned with economic values), into a wider sphere (shaped by social concerns).

The contractual realm cannot be seen solely through an economic lens. Given the reference in this discussion to the interplay between economic and social concerns in contractual relations, we need to focus on the economic and social dimensions of our contracting world.[164] This contractual realm could be perceived as being based on two concentric spheres: an inner sphere rooted in economic values and an outer sphere shaped by social considerations. The inner economic sphere relies on a noninterventionist approach where parties are free to choose whether to contract, who to contract with and under which terms.[165] Parties may enter into imbalanced transactions and be held to their bargains, provided that these constitute an exercise of their free will, unconstrained by vitiating factors.[166]

There are, however, circumstances where the transaction steps out of this inner economic sphere into the outer social sphere of contract law. These could include grossly imbalanced contracts where A lacked the mental capacity to understand the transaction and B had knowledge of the incapacity[167] (interpreted broadly to include constructive knowledge-based circumstances),[168] or where A entered into the transaction as a result of B's undue influence[169] or B's exploitation of A's weakness[170] (interpreted broadly to include passive unacceptable conduct where B went ahead with the grossly asymmetrical contract despite having actual or constructive knowledge of A's vulnerability).[171] Such transactions would not be enforced not because the state 'interfered' with freedom of contract, but because these have stepped out from the inner economic sphere into the outer social sphere of contract, where the state does not give its agreement to enforce such contracts,

161 Teubner, above n 108, 400.
162 Collins, above n 21, 5.
163 Mindy Chen-Wishart, 'Undue Influence: Vindicating Relationships of Influence' (2006) 59 C.L.P. 321.
164 Teubner, above n 108, 400.
165 Adams and Brownsword, above n 86, 192.
166 Herring, above n 5, 226.
167 *Imperial Loan*, above n 123; *Hart vs. O'Connor*, above n 130; *Dunhill vs. Burgin*, above n 134.
168 Varney, above n 63.
169 *RBS vs. Etridge*, above n 127.
170 *Fry vs. Lane*, above n 126.
171 See discussion in Beale, above n 128, 8-059.

due to their harm to values such as human dignity.[172] Under this approach, the contractual relation between A and B could be visualised as a lever on a balance scale, with the parties at each end of the scale and the state in the middle, as the fulcrum. Factors such as incapacity, unconscionability or undue influence could be seen to act as a weight pressing A down into a danger zone of gross imbalance (bringing the transaction within the outer social sphere), and the state could refuse to enforce such a transaction[173] unless B can point toward a counter-weight (such as the presence of appropriate and accessible independent legal advice that addresses both economic and social concerns)[174] to redress any gross imbalance and lift A back into the noninterventionist economic sphere.

This vision would address the challenges highlighted previously with reference to a narrow interpretation of freedom of contract. First, it would rely on a broad interpretation of the relevant triggers for incapacity, unconscionability and undue influence, to include B's constructive knowledge of A's incapacity or vulnerability based on the circumstances of the transaction and to also include B's passive unacceptable conduct by going ahead with a grossly imbalanced transaction despite having such constructive knowledge. Second, as a factor for assessing whether B ought to have known about A's mental incapacity or vulnerability, this framework could consider either procedural factors alone or a combination of substantive and procedural factors (e.g., a grossly imbalanced contract where A received no independent legal advice).[175] Yet, this framework should not go as far as advocating intervention on the basis of substantive factors alone,[176] as the scope of such an assessment would be too uncertain. Instead, concerns for the substantive fairness of the transaction could be seen as a trigger for raising procedural protections. Third, this vision would show concern for who the contracting parties are (e.g., assessing whether any independent legal advice received was appropriate and accessible) and would not assume that parties started from a balanced position, as such assumptions tend to favour the stronger party.[177] Fourth, by focusing on the relation between the parties and the rules that should govern these relations within a wider social context,[178] this framework would demonstrate concern with issues of relational autonomy, including values such as interdependence and mutuality.[179] Finally, by adopting a broad, positive interpretation of freedom of contract that includes social values, this vision would recognise the interconnected economic and social spheres of

---

172 Shiffrin, above n 160, 227–228.
173 ibid, 239.
174 Trebilcock and Elliott, above n 93, 79.
175 *York Glass vs. Jubb* (1925) 134 LT 36, [1925] All ER 285 at [292]; *Dunhill vs. Burgin,* above n 134, at [25]. See Whittaker, above n 121, para 9-082.
176 *Archer vs. Cutler* [1980] 1 NZLR 386.
177 Herring, above n 5, 228–229.
178 Chen-Wishart, above n 147.
179 Herring, above n 5, 228.

contract law[180] and the contribution that private law can play in securing social objectives such as the protection of equality and human dignity.[181]

The relevance of this vision is not confined solely to vitiating factors affecting contractual relations. As discussed at the start of this chapter, vulnerability can arise at various stages of the contracting process. Consequently, addressing gross imbalances between the parties, which have the potential to harm human dignity, requires a multilayered approach combining public and private law measures.[182] This section focused on vitiating factors, which could be seen as the middle layer of this multilayered approach. Nevertheless, in addition to an effective framework regarding vitiating factors, which can act as a safety net, enabling individuals to invalidate grossly imbalanced transactions,[183] the protection of social values in the contractual sphere also requires, *inter alia*, provisions for combating discrimination and promoting equality in the access to goods and services,[184] as well as provisions for regulating unfair terms, including in standard form contracts for the provision of services.[185]

These contexts raise issues of gross imbalance in the bargaining strength of individuals, when compared with service providers.[186] Yet, whenever service providers refuse to contract with an individual because of his or her disability, or whenever these market players impose unfair terms on a 'take it or leave it' basis, leaving the individual with a choice between accepting these unfavourable terms or having no access to the service,[187] such unfavourable circumstances transcend the noninterventionist, economic sphere of contracting, stepping into a wider, social sphere. In this social dimension, service providers cannot hide behind narrow interpretations of freedom of contract that seek to resist state interference. If the relation between A (an individual) and B (a service provider) is envisaged as a lever on a balance scale, with the state in the middle as the fulcrum and the parties at each end of the scale, B's refusal to contract with A because of A's disability or B's imposition of unfair contract terms in a standard form contract would press A down into the danger zone of gross imbalance, controlled by the social dimension of the contractual realm. Equality legislation[188] and measures to control unfair

---

180 Teubner, above n 108, 400.
181 Collins, above n 21, 1-2.
182 Collins, above n 10, 361.
183 Maker and others, above n 6, 831.
184 Bob Hepple, *Equality: The Legal Framework* (2nd edn, Hart 2014), 135.
185 Nicholas Wilson, 'Freedom of Contract and Adhesion Contracts' (1965) 14 *International and Comparative Law Quarterly* 172, at 174.
186 Fejős, above n 4, 74.
187 Kessler, above, n 9, 632; Stephanie Drotar, 'Breaking "Too Darn Bad": Restoring the Balance Between Freedom of Contract and Consumer Protection' (2014) 59 N.Y.L.Sch.L.Rev. 603, at 604–605.
188 See, for example, the Equality Act 2010, Part 10 (ss 142–148) (contracts). See Simon Whittaker, 'Introduction' in Hugh Beale and others (eds), *Chitty on Contracts* (33rd edn, Sweet & Maxwell 2018), 1-038.

contract terms[189] operate in this social dimension of the contractual sphere, illustrating the interplay between public and private law.[190]

The state may condemn the behaviour of service providers as discriminatory,[191] it may refuse to enforce some transactions because of their harm to human dignity[192] or it may declare that certain contract terms are unenforceable.[193] Visualising this as a framework where the gross imbalance of power between A and B has caused the relation between these parties to '*step out*' from the inner economic sphere into the outer social sphere, rather than as a framework where the state '*interferes with*' freedom of contract, is more than just a change of semantics. It is also a change of focus, moving away from finding vulnerability on the basis of A's medical condition, and concentrating instead on the context of the transaction (e.g., whether A entered into a grossly imbalanced transaction in the absence of accessible independent advice). Furthermore, rather than justifying aspects of this regulatory framework on the basis of social values, whilst explaining other aspects as attempts to redress market failures,[194] this vision recognises the common thread of protecting both economic and wider social values (such as equality and dignity) within the contractual sphere. Moreover, by adopting a positive interpretation of freedom of contract that embraces these values, this foundational concept of contract law can no longer be listed by service providers as a justification for resisting equality endeavours.[195]

Conclusion

Measures to protect a party's dignity in the contractual framework (whether through equality provisions, measures to regulate unfair contract terms or refusal to enforce transactions affected by vitiating factors such as incapacity, unconscionability and undue influence) should not be seen as 'interference' with freedom of contract. Instead, they should be perceived as instances where the transaction between the parties stepped out of an inner, noninterventionist sphere, into a wider sphere of contract law informed by social considerations. As freedom of contract is not absolute,[196] it is important that the boundaries of this concept are shaped by positive values such as the protection of equality and human dignity, reflecting a broad, relational conception of autonomy which

---

189 See, for example, the *Consumer Rights Act* 2015, Part II (in particular ss 61–71) (unfair terms). See Michael Bridge (ed), *Benjamin's Sale of Goods* (10th edn, Sweet & Maxwell 2019), 14-138.
190 Collins, above n 10, 361.
191 Whittaker, above n 188, 1-038.
192 Shiffrin, above n 160, 227.
193 See, for example, Consumer Rights Act 2015, s 65(1), 'bar on exclusion or restriction of negligence liability' causing death or personal injury. See Whittaker, above n 36, 38-409.
194 Collins, above n 10, 59.
195 Lawson, above n 74, 388.
196 Whittaker, above n 188, 1-036; Patrick Atiyah, *The Rise and Fall of Freedom of Contract* (Clarendon Press 1979); Peter Benson, 'The Unity of Contract Law' in Peter Benson (ed), *The Theory of Contract Law: New Essays* (CUP 2008), 185.

recognises the interdependence between people and where contract law has a multidimensional role that permeates social and economic spheres. Under this approach, contract law is brought closer to the vision of equality advanced by the CRPD, informing our understanding of the correlation between abstract concepts and real people.

3 Anti-discrimination efforts for insurance consumers

Legislation and practice in Mainland China

Ma Kailiang

1 Introduction

Since Chinese[1] accession to the World Trade Organization (WTO), many foreign insurance companies have entered the Chinese market, and, at the same time, Chinese insurance companies are gradually entering the international market. The governance rules for insurance companies are also being brought into line with international standards. Although the insurance sector has developed rapidly, it also has many problems.[2] In particular, there is a lack of systematic protection for insurance consumers in the Chinese legal system. In fact, Chinese regulators have only been working on regulations for insurance consumers since 2015.[3] Although the existing insurance law stipulates that the rights and interests of consumers should be protected, the level and objectives of this protection are not clear. In the process of law enforcement, many loopholes appear, and some insurance companies are happy to benefit from them, using unclear legal provisions to deceive consumers and infringe their rights and interests. Since the necessary rules of insurance law mainly come from provisions in the insurance contract, the contract is also the primary evidence and the basis on which consumers make claims during the litigation process. From the perspective of legal theory, there is a close relationship between legal rules and legal principles. Legal principles tend to be more deterministic than legal rules when the matters under regulation are more complex or when the economic interests

1 This contribution was presented at the 'Surpass IRN – Fair and non-discriminatory access to financial services' conference, which was organized by the Centre for Market and Economic Law, Faculty of Law, University of Copenhagen in 2019. I am grateful to everyone who reviewed this article and commented on it. I would also like to thank the China Scholarship Council for the support of my research. I am responsible for any errors in the text.
2 Ken Wailer, 'Insurance Sector Following WTO Accession' (ANU Press, December 2012) http://press-files.anu.edu.au/downloads/press/p214211/pdf/10.-Insurance-sector-following-WTO-accession-Ken-Waller.pdf accessed 10 October 2019.
3 Yishun Ren, '"保险消费者"概念质疑 — 以"保险相对人"概念取代"保险消费者"的合理性 (The Concept Questions and Judicial Problems of "Insurance Consumer" – And the Rationality to Replace the Concept of "Insurance Consumer" with "Insurer Counterparty")' [2015] 法学论坛 (Legal Forum) 92.

involved are more diverse.[4] However, Chinese legislation on insurance consumers lacks both detailed legal provisions and specific legal principles. As a result, when the interests of Chinese insurance consumers are infringed, it is difficult for the current law to give comprehensive protection.

Consumers are subject to discriminatory practices in the purchase of commercial insurance, but sometimes the laws do not work well to reduce the impact of this behavior, which means that the number of relevant cases has not decreased.[5] As for the situation in China, search results from the Chinese Judicial Case Academy of the Supreme People's Court show that there are not many relevant judicial cases. The most famous example is a case from 2008, in which a Chinese insurance consumer brought an action because the insurance company included AIDS in a clause in the insurance contract that exempted it from accepting claims, and therefore an AIDS patient could not get compensation from the insurance company.[6] Although the judge in the case ruled against the insurance consumer, the case prompted the Chinese insurance industry to improve its insurance products and services. The most direct evidence of this is that the Insurance Association of China revised its 'Demonstration of Part of the Personal Insurance Product Terms' shortly after the judgment was given, and an insurance consumer can no longer be denied compensation from an insurance company because he or she was HIV positive.[7] This is regarded as a classic case of discrimination against Chinese insurance consumers. Therefore, although Chinese insurance consumer rights protection is still not systematic enough, the relevant legal system is continually being revised and improved through legal practice.

2 The concept of an insurance consumer in Mainland China

In the context of the Chinese legal system, before studying the system for the protection of insurance consumers, it is important to define what consumers and insurance consumers are. This must be set within the legal framework.[8] According to information provided by the Chinese Judicial Case Academy of the Supreme People's Court, although there are very few cases in which insurance

4 John Braithwaite, 'Rules and Principles: A Theory of Legal Certainty' [2002] Australian Journal of Legal Philosophy 73.
5 Daniel Schwarcz, 'Towards a Civil Rights Approach to Insurance Anti-Discrimination Law' [2019] DePaul Law Review 2.
6 Junrong Liu, Qiang Zhang, and Xiaomei Zhai, 当代生命伦理的争鸣与探讨 (*Dang Dai Sheng Ming Lun Li de Zheng Lun Yu Tan Tao*) [中央编译出版社 (Central Compilation & Translation Press) 2010].
7 Insurance Association of China, '人身保险产品条款部分条目示范写法 (Demonstration of Part of the Personal Insurance Product Terms)' (*Insurance Association of China*, 10 July 2009) http://www.iachina.cn/art/2009/7/10/art_22_9900.html accessed 25 October 2019.
8 Yunge Wu, '关于法律保护职业打假之反思 (Reflections on the Legal Protection of Professional Anti-counterfeiting)' (bjgy.chinacourt, 28 November 2017) http://bjgy.chinacourt.gov.cn/article/detail/2017/11/id/3088414.shtml accessed 25 October 2019.

consumers in China have brought actions for discrimination, the interests of insurance consumers are being damaged for other reasons. For example, according to information published by the China Banking and Insurance Regulatory Commission, some insurance companies will infringe consumers' right to know,[9] fair trade rights,[10] and options[11] by deceiving them and concealing important matters concerning insurance contracts. Regulators are focusing on investigating and punishing these violations by insurance companies. However, there are many discussions in legal academia in China about the legal basis that should be used by regulators when handling insurance consumer cases. The core problem is that there are no specific provisions to define insurance consumers in Chinese current laws, but the term 'insurance consumers' has been widely used in the regulations as the basis for monitoring insurance companies. Therefore, when the interests of insurance consumers are damaged, whether because of discrimination or for other reasons, and the legislators want to protect them better, the legislators should clarify the concepts of 'consumers' and 'insurance consumers'.

2.1 Consumers

The definition of 'consumer' is mainly regulated in Chinese Consumer Protection Law. According to the definition given in the Consumer Protection Law, consumers can only be natural persons, and the purpose for which they are purchasing goods or services is mainly for daily consumption.[12] The term 'insurance consumer' does not have a clear definition in the Chinese legal system. Up to now, no normative legal document in China, including the China Insurance Law, has defined the concept of 'insurance consumer' or even mentioned this term. Consumers therefore naturally think that the idea of 'insurance consumers' is subordinate to that of 'consumers'.[13]

Therefore the analysis and understanding of the concept of 'insurance consumers' should start with the idea of 'consumers'. In a transaction, the consumer is one party, and the other party is the operator of the business.[14] Consumption, in modern Chinese, refers to the consumption of material wealth for production or living.[15] Based on this, consumers can be understood as subjects who consume material wealth. The legal sense of 'consumer' is broad and complex.

9 Chinese Consumer Protection Law (CCPL), Article 8.
10 Ibid, 10.
11 Ibid, 9.
12 Ibid, 2.
13 Shiyang Wen and Qingrong Fan, '"保险消费者"概念辨析 (An Analysis of the Concept of "Insurance Consumer")' [2017] 现代法学 (Modern Law Science) 86.
14 Kristie Thomas, 'Analysing the Notion of "Consumer" in Chinese Consumer Protection Law' [2018] The Chinese Journal of Comparative Law 305.
15 Ren (n 3) 91.

According to Chinese Consumer Protection Law,[16] the purpose for which a consumer purchases goods or services should be their daily consumption.[17] However, in modern China, consumption includes both daily consumption and production consumption. The consumption described in Chinese Consumer Protection Law is only daily consumption. Production consumption, on the other hand, refers to the behavior and processes by which people use the various factors of production and engage in labor production.[18] Therefore, the legal meaning is much narrower than the understanding of the general public. The legal definition of consumers can be understood in two ways. First, one can look at the purpose of the transaction: the purchasing behavior of consumers is only to satisfy their consumption needs for daily life and does not include consumption for production. Second, with regard to the characteristics of consumers, consumers are limited to natural persons and cannot be legal persons or other organizations.[19]

2.2 Insurance consumers

In recent years, although insurance consumers were not discriminated against in these cases, they were cheated by insurance company salesmen and suffered losses. From a macro perspective, even though there are only a few cases in which there was discrimination against insurance consumers, in order to protect the interests of insurance consumers fully and comprehensively, legislators should clarify the term 'insurance consumer' as soon as possible. When frauds occur, Chinese Consumer Protection Law does not adequately protect the interests of insurance consumers.[20] Although many insurance consumers expect insurance companies to pay damages in accordance with the punitive damages system[21] stipulated in Chinese Consumer Protection Law, which would be very expensive for insurance companies, there is great uncertainty in the actual implementation of this system.[22]

16 CCPL, Article 2.
17 Thomas (n 14) 295.
18 Baidu Baike, '生产消费 (Production Consumption)' [2014] https://baike.baidu.com/item/生产消费 accessed 31 May 2020.
19 Qingkai Gao, '消费者概念：登场机制与规范构造 (Conception of "Consumer"-Entry Mechanism and Regulatory Structure)' [2019] 法学 (Law Science) 160.
20 Shuxian Chen, '论"保险消费者"概念的科学性 (On the Scientific Nature of the Concept of "Insurance Consumer")' [2016] 现代经济信息 (Modern Economic Information) 293.
21 According to Article 55 of Chinese Consumer Protection Law, when a business operator commits fraud when providing goods or services, it must pay compensation for the losses the consumer has suffered, in accordance with the consumer's requirements. The amount of compensation is three times the purchase price of the goods or the cost of receiving the service. The operator must also return the purchase price to the consumer.
22 Xuhong Guo, '论保险消费的特殊性与保险消费者权益保护 (On the Particularity of Insurance Consumption and the Protection of Insurance Consumers' Rights and Interests)' 中国保险报 *(China Banking and Insurance News)* (Beijing, 14 December 2018) 3.

The Insurance Consumer Rights Protection Bureau of the China Insurance Regulatory Commission[23] has defined 'insurance consumers' as natural persons, legal persons, and other organizations that take steps to establish contractual insurance relationships with legitimate insurance operators, to purchase insurance products, and to accept insurance services.[24] This definition has certain limitations. It limits the concept of 'insurance consumers' to those entering into contractual insurance relationships, but it does not emphasize the purpose of the transactions. Since there is no special law to protect insurance consumers, consumers who buy insurance have to apply under Chinese Consumer Protection Law to protect their rights and interests.[25] However, if an insurance consumer makes a claim under Chinese Consumer Protection Law, he or she must satisfy the definition of a consumer and must be consuming for the sake of living. How, therefore, can insurance consumers protect their rights if they have bought an investment insurance product? If this concept is followed, then there are loopholes in application of the law. Some Chinese scholars therefore believe that the transaction purposes of insurance consumers should not be limited to consuming for their daily needs and should be specifically stipulated when the concept of insurance consumers is defined in the future.[26]

Moreover, if insurance consumers are fully covered by Chinese Consumer Protection Law, there is no reason to include legal persons and other social organizations within the definition of 'insurance consumers', because, under Chinese law, it is not clear whether 'consumers' include legal persons. According to local government regulations in Shanxi Province in China, consumers can only be natural persons, while in Jiangxi Province consumers can be legal persons.[27] On this issue, the Chinese legal system is therefore vague. This means that if a legal person or social organization is damaged as the result of purchasing an insurance product, the legal protection given to it at this time is imperfect. Despite the lack of legal basis, the term 'insurance consumer' is widely used in legal texts and judicial decisions.[28] If 'insurance consumer' is a sub-concept of 'consumer', then the consumption should be consumption for daily life, but, in practice, some insurance products are used for investment. For these situations,

---

23 This has now been reformed and was renamed the China Banking and Insurance Regulatory Commission in 2018.
24 The Insurance Consumer Rights Protection Bureau of the China Insurance Regulatory Commission, 'Thoughts on the Issue of Insurance Consumers' Rights and Interests' [2012] Insurance Studies 31.
25 CCPL, Article 28.
26 Chen (n 20) 293.
27 Shunwu Xiao, '论消费者权益保护法的谦抑性 (On the Modesty of Consumer Protection Law)' [2019] 法商研究 (Studies in Law and Business) 152.
28 For example, in 2017, a Chinese citizen sued the Guangdong Insurance Regulatory Bureau in an administrative lawsuit. In the judgment of the Guangdong Higher People's Court, which is the final judgment, the expression 'insurance consumers' was used. This case was recommended by the Supreme People's Court of China, because it is a typical case in which the interests of consumers are protected.

how should we understand 'consumers'? There are two main points of view. First, purchasers of such insurance products are not consumers, because they are investors. Second, they should instead be considered as consumers, because this situation combines consumption and investment.[29]

With the continuous development of the Chinese economy, the conflicts between insurance companies and insurance consumers will not stop if the corresponding judicial system is not improved. As Chinese citizens become more aware of the rule of law, discrimination may be on the decline, but lawsuits brought by insurance consumers for other reasons will still regularly be heard in the courts. If a consumer proves that the insurer has engaged in misleading sales behavior, and punitive damages are proposed, then can the court make a judgment under Chinese Consumer Protection Law to protect the legitimate rights and interests of the insurance consumer?[30] This is not only a major challenge in legal theory, but also a thorny judicial problem that needs to be studied in depth.

However, from the current state of the law, the author believes that researchers should consider the issue of consumer protection from a macro perspective, that is to say, they should fully consider the relationship between consumer protection and other relevant laws that would be involved in protecting consumer rights. Chinese Consumer Protection Law does not explicitly state that consumers who have purchased investment-based insurance products can be protected. However, Chinese Consumer Protection Law stipulates that operators, including those providing financial services, should disclose relevant information about goods or services to consumers.[31] This means that an insurance consumer can be subject to Chinese Consumer Protection Law, provided that the consumer is engaged in consumption, not investment. If an insurance consumer's transactions include both investment and consumption, it is sufficient to subject his or her consumption to separate regulation under Chinese Consumer Protection Law, while investment behavior can be monitored under Chinese Insurance Law. Similarly, when discussing whether a trader is an insurance consumer, the researcher must also consider whether his or her trading behavior is a daily consumption, rather than an investment, in light of Chinese Consumer Protection Law, which needs to be specifically analyzed in the context of a specific insurance contract.

3 Anti-discrimination legislation to protect insurance consumers in Mainland China

In the Chinese legal regime for the protection of insurance consumers, the relevant legal provisions can be divided into two types: those giving direct

---

29 Wentao Hu, '保险消费者概念的法律厘定 (The Legal Definition of Insurance Consumer Concept)' [2017] 华侨大学学报(哲学社会科学版) [Journal of Huaqiao University (Philosophy & Social Sciences)] 109.
30 Guo (n 22) 2.
31 CCPL, Article 28.

protection and those giving indirect protection. Detailed arguments will be discussed below. In a law that directly protects consumers, the legal provisions are directly related to insurance, while a law giving indirect consumer protection contains statutory provisions that do not directly involve insurance. Such indirect protection can play a role in protecting insurance consumers in specific situations.

3.1 Laws directly protecting insurance consumers

In 2014, the China Insurance Regulatory Commission[32] issued its 'Opinions on Strengthening the Protection of Insurance Consumers' Rights and Interests',[33] which is a direct regulation for insurance consumers. In the context of Chinese law, guidelines issued by regulators are binding. Although this regulation does not clarify the concept of an insurance consumer, it frames the design of the protection for insurance consumers in China for the future. Specifically, it is based on the premise of perfecting the system and creating a sound mechanism for protection, focusing on the implementation of preventive protection and the safeguarding of the transaction process. At the same time, the regulation strengthens the primary responsibilities of insurance companies and implements transparent supervision, thereby increasing investigation and punishment and enhancing oversight and assessment.[34] The regulation also addresses consumer education,[35] promotes the integrity of the industry,[36] strives to solve the outstanding problems that affect the immediate interests of consumers,[37] endeavors to improve consumers' insurance knowledge and rights protection capabilities,[38] and effectively protects the legitimate rights and interests of insurance consumers.[39]

In recent years, despite the lack of legal interpretation of the definition of an insurance consumer, there has been positive progress in relation to the legal system surrounding such consumers. Consumer protection in insurance

---

32 In 2018, this body was reformed and renamed the China Banking and Insurance Regulatory Commission.

33 The original text is in Chinese and the English translation is from the Peking University Center for Legal Information. It is a binding legal document in the Chinese legal system. According to Article III (4) of the Opinions on Strengthening the Protection of Insurance Consumers' Rights and Interests, financial institutions should respect the personal dignity and national customs of financial consumers and must not discriminate against financial consumers on the basis of differences in gender, age, race, ethnicity, or nationality. This regulation is related to the anti-discrimination regulation for insurance consumers.

34 Opinions on Strengthening the Protection of Insurance Consumers' Rights and Interests (OSPICRI), V.

35 Ibid, VI.

36 Ibid, VIII.

37 Ibid, IV.

38 Ibid, VIII.

39 OSPICRI, IX.

contracts has been strengthened from different angles. This is mainly reflected in the aspects discussed below. In terms of sales management, Chinese lawmakers in 2013 standardized the identification and law enforcement requirements for misleading behavior in personal insurance sales, brought in effective punishments for misleading sales behavior, and protected the legitimate rights and interests of an applicant, insured, or beneficiary.[40] In addition, in 2012, Chinese insurance regulatory authorities organized and carried out a unified online questionnaire survey on the misleading effect of sales to solicit public comments.[41] Since 2017, after obtaining the consent of the consumer, the insurance company must clearly prompt the policyholder for all relevant important information, and the entire transaction will be recorded on video for later verification.[42]

In terms of claims management, the insurance regulatory authorities have, since 2016, required the insurance companies to establish a system for the return visits of customers, a complaints handling mechanism, and a dispute mediation mechanism; to announce to the public how to make claims and complaints; and to accept social supervision. A dispute about the settlement of a claim should be addressed through mediation.[43] In terms of small insurance claims, the Insurance Association of China played a leading role in 2015 in improving the construction of an information platform and assisting in the monitoring and disclosure of information about small insurance claims.[44]

In terms of service evaluation, a Chinese insurance regulatory body set up the insurance company service evaluation committee in 2015. This committee has formulated a service evaluation work plan, determined an evaluation index system and scoring rules, and examined the service evaluation results.[45] This shows that Chinese regulatory authorities do pay attention to the interests of insurance consumers.

In terms of complaint management, in 2020 the Chinese government has improved the system for handling, supervision, inspection, notification of assessment, and accountability of consumer complaints. This will unblock consumer complaint channels for the industry and insurance companies, urge insurance companies to handle complaints seriously, and encourage insurance companies to take timely regulatory measures in respect of complaints.[46]

In terms of dispute mediation, in 2016, Chinese regulators focused on promoting local insurance industry associations to strengthen the

---

40 Guidelines for the Determination of Misleading Sales of Personal Insurance, Article 1.
41 Methods for Misleading Evaluation of the Integrated Management of Personal Insurance Industry (Trial), Article 5.
42 Interim Measures for the Retrospective Administration of Insurance Sales Practices, Article II.
43 Guidelines for the Management of Auto Insurance Claim Settlements, I.
44 Guidelines for Small-Sum Insurance Claim Settlement Services (for Trial Implementation), II.
45 Measures for Evaluating the Services of Insurance Companies (for Trial Implementation), Article 3.
46 Measures for the Administration of the Handling of Banking and Insurance Consumer Complaints (MAHBICC), Article 5.

construction and management of the operation of dispute mediation institutions. Local governments must actively promote the establishment of diversified insurance dispute resolution mechanisms including mediation, arbitration, and litigation.[47]

It should be noted that, as a result of the development of Internet finance in China, online insurance experienced explosive growth between 2012 and 2015, and the future development potential of the Chinese online insurance industry is enormous.[48] Chinese insurance regulators therefore specifically formulated laws[49] in 2015 to regulate the operation of online insurance companies and protect the rights of online insurance consumers. These laws clearly state that insurance institutions should ensure that insurance consumers enjoy high-quality insurance services and have their basic rights protected. This means that if an online insurance company has discriminated against an insurance consumer, the insurance consumer can complain.[50]

In addition, in the most direct and specific part of the legal system at present, the State Council of China, in response to the issue of discrimination against insurance consumers, has taken active steps to protect the rights and interests of financial consumers.[51] According to this, financial institutions should respect the personal dignity and national customs of consumers and must not discriminate on the basis of differences in the gender, age, race, ethnicity, or nationality of financial consumers.[52] This is also known as the right to respect for commercial consumers and can be found in Chinese Consumer Protection Law.

Moreover, in the existing legal system, insurance regulatory laws[53] in China stipulate that insurance companies should formulate insurance clauses and insurance rates fairly and reasonably and must not damage the legitimate rights and interests of policyholders, insured persons, and beneficiaries.[54] In the event of a dispute over the terms of the insurance contract, the terms are to be interpreted to give a reasonable understanding.

---

47 Opinions of the Supreme People's Court and the China Insurance Regulatory Commission on Comprehensively Advancing the Building of the Mechanism Linking Litigation with Mediation for Insurance Disputes, IV.
48 Iresearch Inc., '2019年中国互联网保险行业研究报告 (2019 China Internet Insurance Industry Research Report)' (*Iresearch*, June 2019) http://report.iresearch.cn/report_pdf.aspx?id=3392 accessed 29 April 2020.
49 Interim Measures for the Supervision of the Internet Insurance Business (IMSIIB), Article 1.
50 Ibid, 2.
51 Daye Trust Co. Ltd., '金融消费者权益保护工作报告(2018年度) [Financial Consumer Rights Protection Work Report (2018)]' (*Daye Trust Co. Ltd.*, 10 May 2019) http://www.dytrustee.com/uploadfiles/file/20190510/20190510195755_0545.pdf accessed 28 April 2020.
52 Guiding Opinions of the General Office of the State Council on Strengthening the Protection of Financial Consumers' Rights and Interests, III (4).
53 Chinese Insurance Law (CIL).
54 CIL, Article 30.

3.2 Laws on indirect protection of insurance consumers

In the process of protecting insurance consumers, in addition to the laws directly related to insurance that have specific application, we can invoke other laws and regulations that relate to discrimination against insurance consumers in particular situations.

First, there are the rules on consumer protection. Because of the lack of a clear definition of 'insurance consumer', the regulation of insurance consumers has always been governed by Chinese Consumer Protection Law. According to the newly revised version of Chinese Consumer Protection Law, the personal dignity and national customs of consumers should be respected.[55] Therefore, if an insurance consumer believes he or she is being discriminated against, then he or she can protect rights under this clause.

Second, there is the law on cash payments. In 2018, the People's Bank of China took steps to require financial institutions including insurance companies not to use discriminatory measures by refusing to accept cash payments. If an organization or individual refuses to accept cash or adopts discriminatory measures to exclude cash, this will be considered as a violation of Chinese financial regulation laws. Branches of the People's Bank of China and other relevant regulatory authorities will then take disciplinary measures under the law.[56]

Third is the legal system regarding prices. Price discrimination is a typical kind of discrimination against consumers,[57] and there are many cases of this type in the Chinese judicial case system. It should be noted that although the current judicial case database[58] in China does not include jurisprudence in which insurance consumers have initiated lawsuits as the result of price discrimination, it does not mean this situation will not occur in the future. According to the Chinese legal system for prices, under the same transaction conditions, operators cannot discriminate against other suppliers of similar goods or services on prices when providing the same goods or services.[59] If a consumer encounters price discrimination when accepting insurance services, he or she can use the Chinese price law as a legal basis for an action.[60]

Fourth, there is Chinese civil law system. China is currently in the process of formulating a Civil Code. To date, the General Provisions of the Chinese Civil Law are in effect and are generally binding, while specific provisions are

55 CCPL, Article 14.
56 Announcement No. 10 [2018] of the People's Bank of China 'Announcement on Cracking Down on the Act of Refusing to Accept Cash Payment', Article 2.
57 Lars Stole, 'Price Discrimination and Competition' [2017] Handbook of Industrial Organization 2249.
58 itslaw.com, '价格歧视 (Price Discrimination)' (*itslaw*, 29 October 2019) https://www.itslaw.com/bj accessed 30 October 2019.
59 Price Law of the People's Republic of China (PLPRC), Article 14.
60 Ibid, 2.

still under study.[61] According to the relevant regulations, the personal dignity of natural persons is protected by the law.[62] This means that citizens are exempt from discrimination when it comes to civil and commercial conduct. This, of course, is binding for insurance activities. In addition, personal rights will be introduced separately during the formulation of the Civil Code, which means that the personal dignity of Chinese citizens will be highly protected in the future.

In short, whether we consider the direct or indirect legal rules, these cannot adequately summarize the Chinese regulatory system in the field of insurance consumers. However, the above represent the primary regulatory documents. In practice, for various different reasons, a variety of legal norms may be involved, such as administrative law, criminal law, procedural law, etc., and these need to be considered in the specific circumstances for detailed analysis.

4 Judicial practice relating to the protection of insurance consumers in Mainland China against discrimination

In addition to the basic legal system and concepts, this chapter introduces Chinese judicial practice in the protection of insurance consumers against discrimination. The author found only one publicly available case relating to discrimination against an insurance consumer. The incident occurred in 2008. It is highly relevant for the topic of this chapter, even though the final outcome of the case was negative because of the practice of the Chinese insurance industry at that time. The judge who presided over the case did not discuss the issue of discrimination directly, but explained the decision from the perspective of the contract.[63] Despite its negative outcome, this case prompted legal reforms and led to the removal of AIDS from exemption clauses in Chinese insurance contracts.

4.1 Case details

According to China Central Television,[64] which is the authoritative news outlet in China, in February 2008, Mr Li, an HIV carrier from Yunnan Province, purchased an insurance product from a major insurance company, PingAn Life Insurance Company. Such insurance products are mainly used in case of accidental injuries.

---

61 Zhengyan Luo, '《民法典草案》人格权编的宪法学省思 (Constitutional Thoughts on the Personal Rights of Draft Chinese Civil Code)' [2020] 浙江社会科学 (Zhejiang Social Sciences) 42.
62 General Provisions of the Civil Law of the People's Republic of China, Article 109.
63 CCTV.com, '艾滋感染者告保险公司歧视,一审驳回原告诉讼请求 (HIV-infected Person Sued an Insurance Company for Discrimination, and the Court of First Instance Dismissed the Plaintiff's Lawsuit)' (*CCTV.com*, 10 October 2009) http://news.cctv.com/law/20090710/105196.shtml accessed 28 October 2019.
64 Ibid.

However, after completing the procedure to purchase the insurance product, Mr Li found that the exemption clause in the insurance contract stipulated that the insurance company would not pay out if the insured person was infected with HIV. Mr Li believed that, although he had purchased commercial insurance, he would not be able to get compensation from the insurance company even if there was an accident in the future, since he had AIDS. He therefore wanted to surrender and terminate the insurance contract, but the insurance company salesman did not agree. This meant that Mr Li did not have a legal right in the purchased insurance from the beginning to the end, nor could he reduce his losses by changing the coverage and surrendering the policy. He believed that the insurance company's insurance clauses discriminated against AIDS patients. After securing legal support, he took the insurance company to court and asked the court to order that the clause was invalid. In his complaint, he wrote that, by equating AIDS or HIV infection with war, military operations, riots, armed rebellion, and nuclear radiation as one of the exemptions, the insurance company was discriminating against AIDS patients and people living with HIV, thus violating Chinese regulations on infectious diseases[65] and AIDS.[66] Mr Li's representative stated that, according to the relevant provisions,[67] AIDS is a class B infectious disease, while plague and cholera belong to the more severe class A. However, under the insurance contract, if the consumer was infected with a more serious class A disease, he could still claim, but if he was infected with the more minor class B disease of AIDS, he would be refused compensation. This means that only AIDS patients are not covered by the insurance company, which is clearly discriminatory.

The insurance company, in its defense, stated that it believed that the risk for AIDS patients could not be calculated and was not easy to estimate. An AIDS patient does not only face HIV, but also needs to undergo the detection and treatment of a series of complications caused by HIV. For insurance companies, these symptoms are unpredictable and costly. Commercial insurance companies are themselves pursuing a profit and must control the risk of claims being made, keeping them within an affordable range. Moreover, the AIDS-related exemption clause described in the case was common practice in the Chinese insurance industry at the time, and the defendant was not alone among commercial insurance companies in taking such measures.[68]

---

65 Law of the People's Republic of China on the Prevention and Treatment of Infectious Diseases (2004 Revision) (PTID 2004), Article 16. This law was amended in 2013 and is also Article 16 of the revised law.

66 Regulation on the Prevention and Treatment of HIV/AIDS, Article 3. This regulation was amended in 2019, and the provision remains Article 3 of the revised version.

67 Law of the People's Republic of China on the Prevention and Treatment of Infectious Disease, Article 3. According to their severity, infectious diseases are divided into three grades: A, B, and C, with A being the most serious.

68 Legaldaily, '昆明艾滋病人诉保险公司歧视案—审败诉，不予理赔成行规 (Kunming AIDS v. Insurance Company Discrimination Case Lost at First Instance)' (PKULAW, 10 July 2009) http://pkulaw.cn/(S(pvgj1x45wuwnwm5555df4e55))/fulltext_form.aspx?Gid=24463& Db=news&EncodingName=big5 accessed 25 October 2019.

The Basic Level People's Court[69] in Yunnan Province accepted the defendant's case and dismissed the plaintiff's claim, after analyzing the positions of the two parties. At the time, the judge who presided over the case decided that the plaintiff could not directly prove that the insurance company would be exempted from liability under the accident insurance purchased by him. Even if the insured had had an accident, it could not be proved that the insurance company would be exempt from liability. Therefore, the court rejected the plaintiff's claim. The insured refused to accept the judgment and appealed to the Intermediate People's Court. However, his appeal was eventually dismissed.[70]

In addition to taking legal measures, Mr Li wrote an open letter to the Chinese insurance industry regulator. In the letter, he stated that he suffered unreasonable treatment as an ordinary AIDS insured in the process of purchasing commercial insurance. He said the insurance company's accident insurance contract terms showed institutional discrimination against patients with AIDS, severely harming the feelings of AIDS patients and violating the relevant provisions prohibiting discrimination against HIV carriers and AIDS patients. The regulator responded that it would strengthen its supervision of the products.[71]

In February 2009, a year after the incident, China revised its Insurance Law.[72] The provisions of insurance contracts have had a significant impact on the product management system for personal insurance.[73] In July 2009, the Insurance Association of China also issued updated guidelines[74] on the terms of insurance contracts for life insurance products, noting that HIV/AIDS cannot be used as a reason for insurance companies to waive their insurance obligations and liabilities.[75] This was a great victory for insurance consumers!

4.2 Reflections on the case

The law is continuously being developed and improved so that it is more in line with developments in society. However, to achieve this, it is necessary for

---

69 Donald C. Clarke, 'Empirical Research into the Chinese Judicial System' [2003] https://ssrn.com/abstract=412660 accessed 27 April 2020.

70 Global Commission on HIV and the Law, 'Regional Dialogue Submissions Asia-Pacific Regional Dialogue' [Global Commission on HIV and the Law, February 2011] https://hivlawcommission.org/wp-content/uploads/2017/06/COMPILED-SUBMISSIONS-APRD.pdf accessed 29 April 2020.

71 Clarke (n 69).

72 CIL, Articles 13 and 14.

73 Weidong Xu, '坚守合同公平正义理念的成功立法实践–试评2009年修订的《中华人民共和国保险法》(Successful Legislative Practice Adhering to the Concepts of Contract Fairness and Justice - A Trial Review of the Insurance Law of the People's Republic of China in 2009)' [2010] 法律适用 (Journal of Law Application) 4.

74 Demonstration of Part of the Personal Insurance Product Terms 2009.

75 Insurance Association of China (n 7).

consumers to participate and be actively engaged in defending their rights and promoting the development of society.

4.2.1 Development of law and society: integration and conflict

In Mr Li's case, the insurance company argued that it was industry practice to include AIDS in exemption clauses. In this regard, and because of the wide-ranging influence of the case, the media conducted investigations in the same year and found that 24 Chinese insurance companies included AIDS and HIV infections in exemption clauses in their accident insurance products.[76] Discriminatory practice was certainly common in China at the time.

Although the regulatory authorities had registered the insurance products of these insurance companies, the plaintiff's representative believed that the insurance company's registration was based on the situation in China in 1997. At that time, AIDS was very frightening in the country because of its medical consequences, and there were restrictions on public awareness. Thus, Chinese laws on AIDS patients were not sound. Nevertheless, with successful implementation of the law on infectious diseases and AIDS,[77] the Chinese public obtained a more objective understanding of AIDS. Regrettably, the insurance product filing system at that time was not updated. According to the China AIDS Response Progress Report, as of the end of 2007, about 700,000 people were living with HIV in China.[78] The market demand for insurance products was also growing, so, to some extent, the case reminded Chinese legislators that the current law should be updated in line with the social needs of the time. The renewal of laws often requires a certain amount of external force,[79] and, in many cases, this external force comes from the public.

4.2.2 Remedies for aggrieved consumers

In this case, although the plaintiff's action ultimately failed, he took his complaints to the administrative authorities to protect his rights. The lawsuit was unknown at the time, but Mr Li took various steps to appeal to the public to pay attention to the case. Eventually, the case became known throughout the country and was publicized by China's most famous media outlets. This caused public concern about AIDS patients and the disadvantages of the insurance industry. Finally,

---

76 Clarke (n 69).
77 This mainly refers to the Law of the People's Republic of China on the Prevention and Treatment of Infectious Diseases (2013 Amendment) and the Regulation on the Prevention and Treatment of HIV/AIDS (2019 Amendment).
78 Feng Pan, '中国艾滋病流行：挑战在继续 (Chinese AIDS Epidemic: The Challenge Continues)' [中国科学院 *(Chinese Academy of Science)*, 2 December 2008] http://www.cas.cn/xw/zjsd/200906/t20090608_647442.shtml accessed 27 October 2019.
79 Gunther Teubner, 'Global Bukowina: Legal Pluralism in the World-Society' [2009] https://papers.ssrn.com/sol3/papers.cfm?abstract_id=896478 accessed 26 April 2020.

regulators took steps to bring reform. Mr Li's methods to defend his rights were in line with the provisions of Chinese Consumer Protection Law. In fact, in the face of a consumer dispute, Chinese Consumer Protection Law proposes five solutions: negotiate with the business operator, request a consumer association or other mediation organization established by law to mediate, complain to the administrative authority, submit a request for arbitration to the arbitration institution, or bring an action in the people's court.[80]

Although the law does not stipulate the order in which these five methods should be implemented, from the perspective of the expense of resolving a dispute, the cost of the methods increases from one to the next. From the point of view of litigation, in particular, the large population means that the number of litigation cases in China is enormous, and the number of judges is still insufficient, so this has also formed a litigation problem that has been hotly debated in recent years.[81] According to the Chinese Judicial Case Academy of the Supreme People's Court, from 2014 onward, there has been an increase in the number of judicial precedents on consumer discrimination, which also poses a challenge to the judicial capacity of judges.[82] According to the China News Network, in 2008, 189,000 judges in Chinese courts concluded 9,839,000 cases, and, on average, each judge heard 52 cases that year. After China implemented the legal officer quota system,[83] during the first half of 2017, 120,000 judges in the Chinese courts settled 8,887,000 cases, and on average, each judge heard 74 cases in half a year; it was expected that each would hear more than 150 cases over the whole year.[84] Therefore, from the perspective of final dispute resolution, adopting multiple dispute resolution methods is also conducive to improving the efficiency of dispute resolution.

5 Challenges for insurance consumers wishing to make discrimination claims in Mainland China

Although China has established a legal system to protect insurance consumers, there are usually two problems in practice. First, defining insurance consumers

---

80 CCPL, Article 39.
81 Yeru Cao, '法官员额制改革进程中的几个逻辑问题 (Several Logical Problems in the Process of Reforming the Staffing System of Judges)' [2016] 金陵法律评论 (Jin Ling Law Review) 143.
82 On the website, the trend can be seen from the data by searching for 'consumer discrimination'.
83 The White Paper on the Judicial Reform of the Chinese Courts issued by the Supreme People's Court stated that the establishment of a legal officer quota system would ensure rigorous assessments to select the best judges to enter the posts and that they were equipped with judges' assistants, clerks, and other trial support personnel to ensure that 85% of human resources in courts were allocated to the front line.
84 Chinanews.com, '最高法：法官平均办案数量提升至2008年的近3倍 (Supreme People's Court: The Average Number of Cases Handled by Judges has Increased to Nearly Three Times that of 2008)' (*Chinanews.com*, 1 August 2017) https://news.china.com/domestic/945/20170801/31021791_1.html accessed 27 October 2019.

has become an important issue for future legal reform in China. Second, by using the contractual freedom and voluntary principles of insurance contracts, the issue of discrimination against the insured can be circumvented. The root cause of these problems is that China lacks a sound system to protect financial consumers. Therefore, Chinese insurance consumers are now facing enormous challenges in bringing discrimination claims.

5.1 Unclear legal definition of insurance consumer

In the current Chinese insurance legal system, although there is no clear definition of an insurance consumer, as mentioned above,[85] the term is frequently used in legal documents. To some extent, this leads to unclear rights and obligations for insurance consumers. When insurance consumers suffer discrimination, insurance companies have reasons with which to justify themselves. According to the Insurance Law,[86] insurance companies should abide by the principle of good faith when engaging in insurance activities, to protect the legitimate rights of consumers. This means that consumers should be able to complain to insurance companies or insurance salesmen. In real life, consumers can exercise this right. However, more specifically, what can consumers complain about? Chinese law[87] defines the behavior that can be the subject of a complaint and states that a consumer complaint refers to the making of a claim about civil rights and interests to the bank or insurance institution when the consumer has a dispute with the bank or insurance institution (or their employees) in respect of purchasing an insurance product or accepting insurance-related services. Is the definition of consumer here the same as the definition of consumer in Chinese Consumer Protection Law? The law does not explain this, and in practice this causes some confusion,[88] which is why it is important to clarify the concept of an insurance consumer. In the online insurance relationship, this point is also fully repeated. At present, there is a lack of insurance expertise among online insurance consumers in China. In particular, for insurance contracts signed using Internet technology, such as smart contracts, even if there is algorithmic discrimination, consumers cannot easily detect it.[89] The absence of a clear definition has caused online consumers to face great costs in defending their rights.

Also, from its characteristics, an insurance contract should be a contingent contract.[90] In the case of Mr Li, the insurance company signed an insurance

---

85 n 20.
86 CIL, Article 5.
87 MAHBICC, Article 2.
88 Ning Ma, '消费者保险立法的中国愿景 (Chinese Vision of Consumer Insurance Legislation)' [2019] 中外法学 (Peking University Law Journal) 685.
89 Yanchao Li, '我国互联网保险消费者权益保护的法律思考 (Legal Thinking on the Protection of Internet Insurance Consumers' Rights and Interests in China)' [2019] 保险职业学院学报 (Journal of Insurance Professional College) 15.
90 Guo (n 22) 2.

contract with him, so the insurance responsibility should be performed according to the requirements for a contingent contract. Even if an insurance contract is treated as a civil contract, it cannot violate the mandatory provisions of Chinese law prohibiting discrimination against consumers.[91] Specifically, insurance products are intangible products, and the insurer provides invisible protection by the transfer of risk from the insurance counterpart. At the time the insurance contract is agreed upon, the insured and the insurer are not sure whether an insured accident will occur during the insurance period. After the expiration of the insurance contract, the insured cannot request a refund if no insurance accident has occurred and no insurance claims have been paid. If we want to use the concept of an 'insurance consumer', then we should build on the specific study of the unique nature of insurance activities and the various legal relationships contained therein. At present, insurance counterparts are all treated as consumers, and exceptional protection is given in accordance with Chinese Consumer Protection Law, but it is inherently challenging to justify this. The concept mentioned above of an 'insurance consumer' is likely to cause sizeable theoretical confusion, legal problems, and academic controversy.[92]

5.2 Conflicts between legal interpretation and prevention of discrimination

Although the objective of 'insurance' protection can be seen as a public good, a social governance tool, or a large-scale product, insurance is first of all to be regarded as a private law contract.[93] The traditional insurance contract law has two main characteristics. First, the legislators at an early stage had a distrustful attitude toward insurance transactions, and these were considered to be speculative, similar to gambling.[94] This attitude can be seen in the doubts in the legislation about consumers. Second, insurance law is based on arbitrariness.[95] Historically, legislators tended to protect consumers through nonmandatory measures.[96] The main problem is that the cost of enforcing binding standards is too high, and it is easy to cause dissatisfaction among the parties. The arbitrary norm can provide the necessary protection to the insurer and avoid the

---

91 PTID 2004, Article 16.
92 Wen (n 13) 85.
93 Kenneth Abraham, 'Four Conceptions of Insurance' [2013] University of Pennsylvania Law Review 55.
94 Thomas Lee Hazen, 'Disparate Regulatory Schemes for Parallel Activities: Securities Regulation, Derivatives Regulation, Gambling, and Insurance' [2005] Annual Review of Banking and Financial Law 375.
95 Tianzhu Ma, '相对强制性规范——保险格式条款规制的特殊技术 (A Study on Relative Mandatory Norm in Insurance Law – A Unique Technique for Regulating Standard Insurance Clauses)' [2016] 保险研究 (Insurance Studies) 105.
96 Ma (n 88) 669.

drawbacks caused by mandatory rules. Autonomy then becomes one of the essential principles in trading.[97]

In Chinese law, policyholders include natural persons and legal persons.[98] Corporations mainly purchase insurance to diversify their business risks on a continuous basis, so they frequently engage in insurance transactions. Because they receive more support from external sources to determine whether their insurance purchase decisions are reasonable, they have more market information, and the adverse effects on them are small. However, with regard to natural persons, individual consumers often lack accurate market information and professional knowledge. When they are discriminated against, the costs of protecting their consumer rights are high.[99] Moreover, regarding the legal problem of the definition of consumer, when the law is not clear, the trial judge has a certain discretion.[100] China is not a common law country, and *stare decisis* is not the only basis for a judge's decision, which easily leads to different judgments in similar cases.[101] As mentioned above,[102] the regulations on whether consumers include legal persons are different in different local provinces in China. This also increases the difficulty and uncertainty for insurance consumers who are trying to fight discrimination through litigation.

This situation in the development of the rule of law is not unique to China. The Ministry of Finance of British Columbia in Canada has described a similar situation. For insurance contracts, the most crucial goal is to maintain and promote consumer protection; second, in the process of signing and implementing insurance contracts, both parties should minimize unnecessary government intervention and excessive regulation. In this way, on the one hand, the primary insurance needs of consumers can be met, and, on the other hand, insurance companies can continue to innovate in a competitive environment.[103] Therefore, in litigation cases, judges should give priority to protecting the interests of consumers when interpreting contracts.

---

 97 Li (n 89) 14.
 98 CIL, Article 10.
 99 Jing Mi, '对共享经济中消费者权益保护之反思 (Reflection on the Protection of Consumer Rights and Interests in the Sharing Economy)' [2020] 电子科技大学学报(社科版 [Journal of University of Electronic Science and Technology of China (Social Sciences Edition)] 5.
100 Yanping Liu, '民事审判中法官自由裁量权的规制 (Regulation of Judges' Discretion in Civil Trials)' [2018] 东南司法评论 (Southeast Justice Review) 8.
101 Yanyan Wang, '"同案不同判"的正当性探究 (The Legitimacy of "Different Sentences in Similar Cases")' [2019] 广西政法干部管理学院学报 (Journal of Guangxi Administrative Cadre Institute of Politics and Law) 30.
102 n 23.
103 The Ministry of Finance of British Columbia, Canada, 'Insurance Act Review Discussion Paper' (Government of British Columbia of Canada, March 2007) http://www.llbc.leg. bc.ca/public/PubDocs/bcdocs/408836/consultIAR.htm accessed 20 October 2019.

6 The legislative trends in insurance consumers' discrimination claims in Mainland China

Although China does not currently have a special insurance consumer law, there are clear legislative trends for the future. Two points are presently known. First, China has been drafting a Civil Code since 2014.[104] The policymakers want to establish a separate chapter on the right to personality.[105] On 28 May 2020, the Chinese Civil Code was voted on by the National People's Congress of China, it has been confirmed that it will come into force on 1 January 2021.[106] This reflects respect for people, which is equally applicable to insurance consumers. Second, starting from 1 March 2020, Chinese insurance consumers have had a specific legal basis[107] for complaining to insurance companies, and the details of the complaints system for insurance consumers have been clarified.

6.1 Personality rights in the Chinese Civil Code

In 2014, China decided to compile a Civil Code to make this public.[108] This is a systematic project, which has involved a large number of controversies, such as whether personality rights can be discussed in a separate chapter. This has now been confirmed, and a draft chapter on personality rights was published in 2019.[109] It will be implemented on January 1, 2021.[110]

---

104 People.cn, '十八届四中全会：加强市场法律制度建设，编纂民法典 (The Fourth Plenary Session of the Eighteenth Central Committee: Strengthening the Construction of the Market Legal System and Compiling the Civil Code)' [*People.cn*, 28 October 2014] http://politics.people.com.cn/n/2014/1028/c1001–25926258.html accessed 25 April 2020. At the Fourth Plenary Session of the Eighteenth Central Committee of the Communist Party of China, the Chinese government for the first time proposed a plan to compile a Civil Code.
105 Lixin Yang, '民法典人格权编专题研究 (Monographic Study on the Personality Rights of Civil Code)' [2019] 河南社会科学 (Henan Social Sciences) 25.
106 The National People's Congress of the People's Republic of China, '中华人民共和国主席令（第四十五号）(Order of the President of the People's Republic of China No. 45)' http://www.npc.gov.cn/npc/c30834/202005/498f8c85ef7c4e0da99c778922ac9abc.shtml accessed 31 May 2020.
107 MAHBICC, Article 1.
108 Shiguo Liu, '人格权独立成编回应人民法治需求 (Personality Rights should be Compiled Independently to Respond to the People's Demand for the Rule of Law)' 光明日报 *(Guangming Daily)* (Beijing, 8 October 2018).
109 The National People's Congress of the People's Republic of China, '民法典人格权编草案再次亮相 (The Draft of the Code of Personality Rights of the Civil Code Appears Again)' [*The National People's Congress of the People's Republic of China*, 21 April 2019] http://www.npc.gov.cn/zgrdw/npc/cwhhy/13jcwh/2019-04/21/content_2085547.htm accessed 29 April 2020.
110 The National People's Congress of the People's Republic of China (n 106).

From the perspective of comparative law, personality rights are treated as a separate chapter when they are mentioned in the Civil Code, because of the need for social development, and this is different from protection of personality rights in the French Civil Code and the German Civil Code.[111] Furthermore, Chinese Civil Code is being formulated in a critical era of technological change, and the protection of personality rights has become a fundamental issue in the Internet age. The forms of discrimination are more diverse, but there are still no rules on personality rights that can be used by judges in adjudicating disputes over personality rights. This is because, in the current Chinese legal system for protecting personality rights, the protection of personality rights is mainly based on legal principles, and there is a lack of specific legal rules for judicial practice.[112] Personality rights are related to the protection of personal dignity and individual rights, and this is reflected in the various departmental laws. As far as the law on the protection of consumer rights and the insurance law are concerned, each has independent provisions on personal dignity. After the concept of insurance consumers was proposed, the lack of uniform regulations on the idea made various conflicts in the application of the law appear. The provisions of the Civil Code on this issue would solve this conflict to a certain extent.

6.2 The bank and insurance consumer complaints system

In 2019, China began to study the complaint rule for insurance consumers. The rule[113] has now been effective since 1 March 2020, and is a generally binding and enforceable law. It specifically explains that an insurance consumer complaint occurs when a consumer has a dispute with a bank or insurance institution or its practitioners in relation to purchasing a bank or insurance product or accepting a bank or insurance-related service; such a consumer may make a claim in relation to his or her civil rights and interests with the bank or insurance institution.[114] In the case mentioned in this article, after Mr Li had lost his action in court, he filed a complaint with the insurance regulator. Therefore, the enactment of the rule is a precious step for the further protection of insurance consumers.

In more detail, the introduction of this system will refine the processes and basic principles for complaints from insurance consumers. In particular, it adheres to the principle that there should be a convenient and efficient way to resolve disputes among multiple dispute resolution methods. Besides, the process for complaints by insurance consumers will be refined. In the case of complaints, consumers will be required to submit the necessary materials, including basic

---

111 Liming Wang, '论人格权独立成编的理由 (Reasons for Personality Right to Be a Separate Part)' [2017] 法学评论 (Law Review) 8.
112 Weiwei Pang, '论人格权法独立成编的必要性——以既有规范为中心 (On the Necessity of Establishing Personality Rights as Independent Section: Focus on Existing Norms)' [2018] 中国政法大学学报 (Journal of CUPL) 205.
113 MAHBICC.
114 MAHBICC, Article 2.

information about the parties, the main claims, and factual evidence. The bank or insurance institution must respond within a limited time after receiving a complaint and resolve the related issues. The supervision and management systems of insurance companies will be further refined, especially in terms of their liability systems, with various measures relating to business operations, senior management personnel, institutional establishments, and administrative punishments.[115]

In addition, some scholars have proposed that a separate insurance consumer law should be developed. This idea is worthy of consideration, because Chinese society is gradually strengthening the protection of consumers. If an insurance consumer law is enacted, then it would be beneficial. Given the popularization of online insurance products, the supervision of these products is still in a disorderly state, and there is an urgent need to standardize and regulate the system thoroughly.[116] Although China has introduced a special law[117] for online insurance, the current technology in the insurance industry is developing quickly, especially with regard to smart contracts and blockchain technology, and it is very difficult to protect insurance consumers against discrimination through technical means.[118] The traditional consumer protection system cannot completely solve the problems in the trading of online insurance products. In this era of technological change, these need to wait for further developments.

7 Conclusion

Chinese insurance consumer protection is going through a critical period. Although the 2008 case warned Chinese society about the efforts being made by insurance consumers to combat discrimination, it also suggested that Chinese lawmakers should update the relevant legal system promptly in response to the changing times. However, perfection of a legal system is never instantaneous, and it never reaches an end.

As a country whose law is based primarily on the civil law model,[119] China has experienced a long process of development as a society ruled by law. At present, the legal interpretations and definitions for insurance consumer protection are still inadequate, and this has created some challenges for judicial practice. At the same time, Chinese legislators have established a series of direct and indirect legal systems to protect insurance consumers. With the development of society,

---

115 Administrative Measures on the Handling of Consumer Complaints in the Banking and Insurance Industry, Article 44.
116 Li (n 89) 13.
117 IMSIIB.
118 The Banker, '智能保险：金融与技术融合视野下的治理边界——金融科技法律政策观察 (Smart Insurance: Governance Boundary from the Perspective of the Fusion of Finance and Technology – Observation of Financial Technology Law and Policy)' [2018] https:// kuaibao.qq.com/s/20180518B1QBUY00?refer=spider accessed 30 April 2020.
119 Xianchu Zhang, 'The New Round of Civil Law Codification in China' [2016] University of Bologna Law Review 121.

Chinese insurance consumer protection will still encounter new problems. However, China will continue to pay more attention to the rights of insurance consumers in the future. We believe that China will soon establish a sound protection system for financial consumers.

Bibliography

Abraham K., 'Four Conceptions of Insurance' [2013] *University of Pennsylvania Law Review 55.*

Braithwaite J., 'Rules and Principles: A Theory of Legal Certainty' [2002] *Australian Journal of Legal Philosophy 73.*

Clarke D.C., *'Empirical Research into the Chinese Judicial System'* [2003] https://ssrn.com/abstract=412660 accessed 27 April 2020.

Gao Q.K., '消费者概念：登场机制与规范构造 (Conception of "Consumer"-Entry Mechanism and Regulatory Structure)' [2019] 法学 *(Law Science) 160.*

Guo X.H., 论保险消费的特殊性与保险消费者权益保护 *(On the Particularity of Insurance Consumption and the Protection of Insurance Consumers' Rights and Interests)'* 中国保险报 (China Banking and Insurance News) (Beijing, 14 December 2018) 3.

Hazen T.L., 'Disparate Regulatory Schemes for Parallel Activities: Securities Regulation, Derivatives Regulation, Gambling, and Insurance' [2005] *Annual Review of Banking and Financial Law 375.*

Hu W.T., '保险消费者概念的法律厘定 (The Legal Definition of Insurance Consumer Concept)' [2017] 华侨大学学报(哲学社会科学版) *(Journal of Huaqiao University (Philosophy & Social Sciences)) 109.*

Jing Mi, '对共享经济中消费者权益保护之反思 (Reflection on the Protection of Consumer Rights and Interests in the Sharing Economy)' [2020] 电子科技大学学报(社科版) *(Journal of University of Electronic Science and Technology of China (Social Sciences Edition)) 5.*

Liu J.R., Zhang Q. and Zhai X.M., 当代生命伦理的争鸣与探讨 *(Dang Dai Sheng Ming Lun Li de Zheng Lun Yu Tan Tao)* (中央编译出版社 (Central Compilation & Translation Press) 2010).

Liu Y.P., '民事审判中法官自由裁量权的规制 (Regulation of Judges' Discretion in Civil Trials)' [2018] 东南司法评论 *(Southeast Justice Review) 8.*

Luo Z.Y., '《民法典草案》人格权编的宪法学省思 (Constitutional Thoughts on the Personal Rights of Draft Chinese Civil Code)' [2020] 浙江社会科学 *(Zhejiang Social Sciences) 42.*

Ma N., '消费者保险立法的中国愿景 (Chinese Vision of Consumer Insurance Legislation)' [2019] 中外法学 *(Peking University Law Journal) 685.*

Pan F., 中国艾滋病流行：挑战在继续 *(Chinese AIDS Epidemic: The Challenge Continues)'* (中国科学院*(Chinese Academy of Science)*, 2 December 2008) http://www.cas.cn/xw/zjsd/200906/t20090608_647442.shtml accessed 27 October 2019.

Pang W.W., '论人格权法独立成编的必要性——以既有规范为中心 (On the Necessity of Establishing Personality Rights as Independent Section: Focus on Existing Norms)' [2018] 中国政法大学学报 *(Journal of CUPL) 205.*

Ren Y.S., '"保险消费者"概念质疑——以"保险相对人"概念取代"保险消费者"的合理性 (The Concept Questions and Judicial Problems of "Insurance Consumer" –

And the Rationality to Replace the Concept of "Insurance Consumer" with "Insurer Counterparty")' [2015] 法学论坛 *(Legal Forum)* 92.

Schwarcz D., 'Towards a Civil Rights Approach to Insurance Anti-Discrimination Law' [2019] *DePaul Law Review* 2.

Teubner G., *'Global Bukowina: Legal Pluralism in the World-Society'* [2009] https://papers.ssrn.com/sol3/papers.cfm?abstract_id=896478 accessed 26 April 2020.

Thomas K., 'Analysing the Notion of 'Consumer in Chinese Consumer Protection Law' [2018] *The Chinese Journal of Comparative Law* 305.

Tianzhu Ma, '相对强制性规范——保险格式条款规制的特殊技术 (A Study on Relative Mandatory Norm in Insurance Law – A Unique Technique for Regulating Standard Insurance Clauses)' [2016] 保险研究 *(Insurance Studies)* 105.

Wailer K., *'Insurance Sector Following WTO Accession'* (ANU Press, December 2012) http://press-files.anu.edu.au/downloads/press/p214211/pdf/10.-Insurance-sector-following-WTO-accession-Ken-Waller.pdf accessed 10 October 2019

Wang L.M., '论人格权独立成编的理由 (Reasons for Personality Right to Be a Separate Part)' [2017] 法学评论 *(Law Review)* 8.

Wen S.Y. and Fan Q.R., '"保险消费者"概念辨析 (An Analysis of the Concept of "Insurance Consumer")' [2017] 现代法学 *(Modern Law Science)* 86.

Xiao S.W., '论消费者权益保护法的谦抑性 (On the Modesty of Consumer Protection Law)' [2019] 法商研究 *(Studies in Law and Business)* 152.

Xu W.D., '坚守合同公平正义理念的成功立法实践-试评2009年修订的《中华人民共和国保险法》(Successful Legislative Practice Adhering to the Concepts of Contract Fairness and Justice - A Trial Review of the Insurance Law of the People's Republic of China in 2009)' [2010] 法律适用 *(Journal of Law Application)* 4.

Yang L.X., '民法典人格权编专题研究 (Monographic Study on the Personality Rights of Civil Code)' [2019] 河南社会科学 *(Henan Social Sciences)* 25.

Zhang X.C., 'The New Round of Civil Law Codification in China' [2016] *University of Bologna Law Review 121.*

4 Vulnerability, financial inclusion, and the heightened relevance of education in a credit crisis

Williams C. Iheme[*]

Part I: vulnerability of financial consumers

Introduction: credit use as the entry point of vulnerability

Credit is undeniably the lifeblood of modern economies.[1] Its use and the issues arising from it intersect with many aspects of commercial law, including consumer protection, which is the aspect of law that specifically protects consumers.[2] A wise use of credit in catering to one's basic needs and more could reasonably be linked to the user's success in life. Needless to say, if individuals have sufficient access to affordable credit, the economy in which they operate will generally do well.[3]

Thus, given the heightened importance of credit and its indispensability in the economic well-being of financial consumers, it is possible that in the absence of a sufficient regulatory framework and enforcement, these consumers would easily be subjected to the onerous and exploitative lending practices of financial institutions.[4] Indeed, if the terms of debt repayment were unilaterally

[*] LLB, LLM, SJD, Associate Professor of Law, Center for International Trade and Economic Laws, O.P. Jindal Global University. My thanks go to the organizers and participants of the International Conference "Surpass IRN - Fair and Non-Discriminatory Access to Financial Services", organized in 2019 by the Centre for Market and Economic Law, Faculty of Law, University of Copenhagen, where the initial draft of this work was presented. I am grateful to Dr. Cătălin G. Stanescu (University of Copenhagen) and Dr. Asress A. Gikay (Brunel University) for providing me with constructive feedback on the earlier drafts of this work. I am also grateful to Dr. Joseph Nwobike SAN for his authoritative perspectives on Nigerian law which benefitted the research. The author can be reached via email: wciheme@jgu.edu.in; williamsiheme@gmail.com
1 Henry Macleod, *Principles of Economical Philosophy* (2nd edn Longmans, Green, Reader & Dyer, 1872) 481; Kath Weston, 'Lifeblood, Liquidity, and Cash Transfusions: Beyond Metaphor in the Cultural Study of Finance' [2013] 19 JRAI, 24.
2 For more insight on 'vulnerable consumer,' see Rossella Incardona and Cristina Poncibò, 'The Average Consumer, the Unfair Commercial Practices Directive, and the Cognitive Revolution' [2007] 30 Journal of Consumer Policy, 28–29.
3 Lien-WenLiang, et al, 'The Impact of SMEs' Lending and Credit Guarantee on Bank Efficiency in South Korea' [2017] 7 Review of Development Finance 134, 134–135.
4 See Peter Cartwright, *Banks Consumers and Regulation* (Hart 2004) chap 6; William

stipulated, and more likely unconscionable and difficult to fulfill by consumers, their eventual default becomes the entry point of their vulnerability and losses.[5]

Yet, it is difficult to begrudge financial institutions for being excessively protective of their customers' money, especially if they were acting within the confines of the relevant prudential lending guidelines typically issued by central banks, the aim of which is to secure lending transactions and significantly reduce the avoidable risk of losing their customers' deposits. As more financial institutions obtain operational licenses to do business, the competition among them could increase and cause them to engage in financial innovations that might bear deceptive outlooks, including the creation and sale of shrouded products to financial consumers.[6]

Scholars and financial experts are in agreement that the packaging and sale of shrouded and deceptive products to financial consumers deepen consumers' vulnerability,[7] as default in repayment could lead to loss of collateral and financial savings.[8] Such a system creates a rising rate of indebtedness amongst consumers, negative domino effects, and a generally inspired loss of confidence in accessing credit.[9] Before the 2008 financial crisis, predatory and obscure lending practices were reported to be ongoing in many parts of the world, including the United States, where the credit crisis erupted,[10] following the excessive amount of credit

Whitford, 'The Functions of Disclosure Regulation in Consumer Transactions' [1973] Wisconsin Law Review 400.

5 Peter Cartwright, 'Conceptualising and Understanding Fairness: Lessons for and from Financial Services' in Mel Kenny J. Devenney and Lorna Fox O'Mahoney (eds.), *Unconscionability in European Private Financial Transactions* (CUP 2010).

6 ROFIEG, '30 Recommendations on Regulation, Innovation and Finance' (2019) Final Report to the European Commission, 23 https://ec.europa.eu/info/sites/info/files/business_economy_euro/banking_and_finance/documents/191113-report-expert-group-regulatory-obstacles-financial-innovation_en.pdf; Banque de France, 'The Dangers Linked to the Emergence of Virtual Currencies: The Example of Bitcoins' (2013) https://www.banquefrance.fr/sites/default/files/medias/documents/focus-10_2013-12-05_en.pdf accessed 23 May 2020.

7 In this chapter, the meaning of a 'vulnerable consumer' is as defined by the European Commission as 'a consumer, who, as a result of socio-demographic characteristics, behavioural characteristics, personal situation, or market environment: is at higher risk of experiencing negative outcomes in the market; has limited ability to maximise his/her wellbeing; has difficulty in obtaining or assimilating information; is less able to buy, choose or access suitable products; or is more susceptible to certain marketing practices.' See Vera Jourova, 'Understanding Consumer Vulnerability in the EU's Key Markets' (2016) https://ec.europa.eu/info/sites/info/files/consumer-vulnerability-factsheet_en.pdf accessed 24 May 2020.

8 Debra Ringold, 'Social Criticisms of Target Marketing: Process or Product' [1995] 38 American Behavioural Scientist 578, 584; Craig Smith and Elizabeth Cooper-Martin, 'Ethics and Target Marketing: The Role of Product Harm and Consumer Vulnerability' (1997) 61 Ethics and Target Marketing 1, 4.

9 Orkun Akseli, 'Vulnerability and Access to Low Credit' in James Devenney & M. Kenny (eds.), *Consumer Credit, Debt and Investment in Europe* (CUP 2012) 4.

10 Dell'Ariccia Giovanni, et al, 'Credit Booms and Lending Standards: Evidence from the

that was lent to customers who had no reasonable means of repaying in full.[11] The ensuing debts were then securitized and sold to unsuspecting investors. Similarly, subprime mortgage lending to mortgagors who were more susceptible to defaults on their mortgages helped to trigger the financial crisis.[12]

In a credit crisis (comparable to the Covid-19 pandemic), the typical response of many governments' central banks is to engage in quantitative easing, which is basically to inject credit into the economy through the banks as a way of helping them build up their financial reserves and be able to meet lending requests to borrowers toward economic recovery.[13] Another method currently being undertaken by central banks around the globe is to buy government bonds and the debts of certain companies that provide essential products and services.[14] This way, the positive impact will enable financial institutions to continue to lend credit at an affordable rate to consumers, whose spending gives a good boost to economic recovery.[15] Even though the idea of quantitative easing is to provide some cushioning effect on the economy through the injection of credit; this has to be controlled at some point in order to prevent inflation from occurring due to excessive credit flow in the system.[16] Inflation diminishes the value of money in consumers' savings accounts and generally increases the costs of basic necessities of life for vulnerable consumers.[17]

Part of the task of this chapter is to examine the various shades of vulnerability of financial consumers vis-à-vis access to credit and how they affect the realization of financial inclusion. In addition to discussing the meaning and effect of vulnerability of consumers, it will consider the likely impact of lack of access to credit on this demographic and the possible way forward through strategic reforms of credit and insolvency laws.[18]

Subprime Mortgage Market' (2012) 44 (2) Journal of Money, Credit and Banking, 367–84, 368.

11 Ibid, 372.

12 Steven Schwarcz, 'Understanding the Subprime Financial Crisis' (2009) 60 South Carolina Law Review, 549–572.

13 See 'Quantitative Easing: What Is It, Will It Work and What Are the Alternatives?' *The Guardian* (London, 7 October 2011) https://www.theguardian.com/business/2011/oct/07/quantitative-easing-what-is-it accessed 7 May 2020.

14 John Plender, 'The Seeds of the Next Debt Crisis,' *Financial Times* (London, 4 March 2020) https://www.ft.com/content/27cf0690-5c9d-11ea-b0ab-339c2307bcd4 accessed 5 May 2020; Eric Toussaint, 'The Economic Crisis and the Central Banks' (*Committee for the Abolition of Illegitimate Debt,* 25 March 2019) https://www.cadtm.org/The-Economic-Crisis-and-the-Central-Banks accessed 5 May 2020; Sujata Rao, 'As Central Banks Break the Junk Debt Barrier, Investors Will Follow,' *Reuters* (6 May 2020) https://in.reuters.com/article/us-health-coronavirus-ratings-analysis/as-central-banks-break-the-junk-debt-barrier-investors-will-follow-idINKBN22I1WW accessed 7 May 2020.

15 cf Plender (n 14).

16 Ibid.

17 For an expert discussion on the effects on inflation, see Thomas Piketty, *Capital in the 21st Century* (HUP 2014), Part Four.

18 Thomas Laryea, 'Approaches to Corporate Debt Restructuring in the Wake of Financial

Similarly, access to consumer credit is critically helpful in the consumer's effort to escape from poverty, especially in developing countries where individuals typically undertake the burden of providing themselves with most of the basic necessities of life,[19] and where the poor (especially in a credit crisis) are unattractive to the mainstream financial institutions that usually insist on real estate collateral that is hardly affordable by the consumers asking for loans.[20] In that case, to solve pressing problems, individuals turn to any available alternatives, even if riskier, such as pyramid and Ponzi schemes or other unregistered money lenders (payday lenders) that demand very high interest rates and aggressively enforce defaults, thereby deepening the consumers' vulnerability.[21]

Aim, questions, and structure

This chapter makes two principal claims. The first is that financial consumers are more vulnerable in a credit crisis because financial institutions reduce lending to them,[22] demand unaffordable collateral, or charge higher interest in order to cushion the underlying risks. This situation forces consumers to access credit from nontraditional, riskier lenders which consequently worsens their financial conditions. However, vulnerability of financial consumers in the circumstance can be significantly reduced if adequate and purposeful amendments in credit and insolvency laws are made. Second, it claims that an increased use of digital financial services by consumers can help achieve a high level of financial inclusion that will in large part tackle poverty. Nevertheless, for this to be achieved, digital financial users, especially in developing countries must be provided with a more heightened level of basic and financial education.

To buttress these claims, the chapter adopts a conceptual methodology that anchors on the textual analysis of black letter law, a functional approach to legal reasoning, and interpretation of the established principles of consumer protection law from multijurisdictional (mainly the United Kingdom and the United States) perspectives and how these legal phenomena interface positively with consumer vulnerability. The chapter's central inquiries are guided by a set of questions. The first question seeks to know the underlying benefits financial

---

Crises' (*IMF Staff Position Note*, 26 January 2010) 6 https://www.imf.org/external/pubs/ft/spn/2010/spn1002.pdf accessed 2 May 2020.

19 DIFB, 'Growth Building Jobs and Prosperity in Developing Countries' https://www.oecd.org/derec/unitedkingdom/40700982.pdf accessed 29 May 2020.

20 Paola Omede, 'A Tale of Two Markets: How Lower-end Borrowers Are Punished for Bank Regulatory Failures in Nigeria' (2019), J. Consumer Policy https://link.springer.com/article/10.1007/s10603-019-09439-8 accessed 7 May 2020.

21 Marianne Bertrand and Adair Morse, 'Information Disclosure, Cognitive Biases, and Payday Borrowing' (2011) 66 The Journal of Finance, 6, 1865-893, 1866.

22 Kevnin Wack, 'Credit Card Lenders Clamp Down to Mitigate Coronavirus Risk,' *American Banker* (29 May 2020) https://www.americanbanker.com/news/credit-card-lenders-clamp-down-to-mitigate-coronavirus-risk accessed 30 May 2020.

consumers enjoy from access to credit laws in a market economy and whether these laws in their current form could expose consumers to vulnerability in a credit crisis. Second, in a credit crisis, which necessitates restrictions in lending and a higher rate of default in repayment of consumer debts, what critical amendments in credit and insolvency laws could prevent or mitigate the ensuing vulnerability of consumers?

Third, if an increased use of digital finance leads to a higher rate of financial inclusion, and the latter is agreed to be an integral element in the cure for poverty, how will an increased level of education, especially in developing countries, help to achieve a type of financial inclusion that does not deepen the vulnerability of consumers? The argument undertaken in the third inquiry is not necessarily to advocate for a direct textual inclusion of the 'right to financial inclusion' into the various body of rights in the traditional instruments, but to use the functional approach to determine whether the benefits accruing from financial inclusion are similar to those obtainable from formal education, which is regarded as a sure means by which an individual can empower themselves and possibly escape from poverty.

The chapter has four parts. Part I deals with the vulnerability of consumers in general and the role of credit and insolvency law in a credit crisis toward mitigating or preventing consumer vulnerability. Part II deals with the increased use of digital financial services and its intersection with financial inclusion on the one hand and the underlying difficulties experienced by vulnerable consumers in their struggles to gain access to affordable credit, especially in a credit crisis, on the other hand. Part III discusses the heightened need for a bespoke consumer education by consumer protection regulators, as well as treatment of basic education as a positive right by governments, as a meaningful way of tackling vulnerability stemming from online and offline deceptions and fraud, financial scams, and harmful manipulation of consumers with fake information.[23] Part IV is the conclusion.

Vulnerability and access to low-cost credit

In a credit crisis (which could be triggered by the Covid-19 pandemic), financial institutions will generally reduce lending to consumers.[24] Alternatively, they will lend them at a very high interest rate or require them to furnish generally un-affordable collateral to mitigate the heightened risk of default. These onerous terms increase a consumer's rate of default and the possibility of becoming more vulnerable after loss of their collateral. Additionally, these consumers could easily be enticed by informal and low-credit lenders whose terms of credit could *prima*

---

23 Sam Smith, 'Online Transaction Fraud to More Than Double to $25BN by 2020,' *Jupiter Research* (Hampshire, 2 May 2016) https://www.juniperresearch.com/press/press-releases/online-transaction-fraud-to-more-than-double accessed 27 May 2020.
24 cf Wack (n 22).

facie be better than those offered by the traditional financial institutions. However, borrowing credit from such nontraditional, less or nonregulated lenders might not only cost the consumer more due to payment of a higher interest rate but also cause them to lose their collateral to aggressive debt collectors, using unorthodox mechanisms to recover debts.[25]

As one of the preventive responses to the forgoing issues, many countries around the globe have started to amend their insolvency laws to prevent insolvent liquidation against individuals and businesses on the basis of inability to repay debts.[26] In addition, these countries have created moratoriums on debt repayment. In response, some financial institutions will likely offer consumer credit to only those consumers in possession of good credit scores who are ready to furnish reliable guarantees and excess collateral so as to mitigate their heightened risk of default.[27] This situation will likely increase the existing level of consumer vulnerability.

However, it should be noted that if banks, in fear of the amplified level of default by financial consumers increase interest rates on credit, this could generally lead to a decreased amount of borrowing among financial consumers which invariably would weaken the possibility of a quick economic recovery that would typically benefit banks. It is also possible that desperate consumers wanting to satisfy pressing household demands might succumb to predatory lending practices, which force them to accumulate too much debt that eventually crushes their economic well-being and general ability to repay their debts.[28]

Similarly, if financial institutions highly reduce lending to financial consumers due to their generally weakened financial portfolios,[29] they might find out that the depositors' funds in their possession will become liabilities especially if they have to pay interest on deposits.[30] Thus, to stay afloat, banks could

25 Lauren Saunders, 'Fintech and Consumer Protection: A Snapshot,' *National Consumer Law Center* (March 2019). Author says that 'some nonbank lenders are using bank partnerships to avoid state licensing and interest rate laws and in order to make loans at rates as high as 160% APR that would otherwise be illegal.' https://www.nclc.org/images/pdf/cons-protection/rpt-fintech-and-consumer-protection-a-snapshot-march2019.pdf accessed 27 May 2020.

26 Taking a few examples: On 22 March 2020, the Australian government passed the Coronavirus Economic Response Package Omnibus Bill 2020 into law. https://treasury.gov.au/sites/default/files/2020-03/Fact_sheet-Providing_temporary_relief_for_financially_distressed_businesses.pdf On 28 March, measures to reform UK insolvency legislation were announced by the Department for Business Energy & Industrial Strategy aimed at supporting business. https://www.cliffordchance.com/content/dam/cliffordchance/briefings/2020/03/coronavirus-uk-insolvency-reforms-announced.pdf accessed 9 May 2020.

27 Scott Frame, et al, 'The Effect of Credit Scoring on Small-Business Lending' [2001] 33 Journal of Money, Credit and Banking 3, 813, 815.

28 cf Bertrand, et al (n 21) 1865–1866.

29 cf Wack (n 22).

30 Amitava Chakrabarty, 'Will Corona Crisis take a Toll on Savings Account Interest Rates?' *Financial Express* (29 March 2020) https://www.financialexpress.com/money/will-corona-crisis-take-a-toll-on-savings-account-interest-rates/1912747/ accessed 7 May 2020.

begin to charge interest on savings accounts as is already the case in the United States,[31] and some of the already impoverished customers might withdraw their funds and generally resort to keeping large amount of cash in their homes.[32] In places with little security, this could lead to a higher rate of home burglaries and thefts, with the large amount of cash at home being the attraction.[33]

Each country's government will have the responsibility of cushioning the negative impacts of the Covid-19 crisis by injecting funds into their economies, just as was done after the 2008 financial crisis, where for instance, the UK government injected about 37 billion pounds into the major banks in exchange for taking part in their management and limiting the bonuses that were paid to top executive staff.[34] In the Covid-19 circumstance, the UK government through the Financial Conduct Authority has provided a three-month moratorium for consumer debt repayments, which aims to provide relief to consumers and prevent their vulnerability.[35]

The main point in all of these interventions is that the market on its own cannot be expected to solve the economic effects of the Covid-19, because without the interventions of governments, financial consumers who are in need of credit to jumpstart themselves would fall into the snares of lenders, offering them onerous terms of credit that would worsen their vulnerable state and generally dim the possibility of any quick economic recovery.

31 Sarah Foster, 'Fed Drops Rates to Zero in Emergency Rate Cut Due to Coronavirus Effects,' *Bankrate* (15 March 2020) https://www.bankrate.com/banking/federal-reserve/fed-second-emergency-cut-zero-rates-coronavirus/ accessed 8 May 2020.

32 This view may not always be the case in a credit crisis, especially if the fear of unemployment and recession surpasses the effect of the reduced interest rate on savings. See Tejvan Pettinger, 'How Do Interest Rates Affect Savers and Saving Levels?' *The Economics* (1 July 2018) https://www.economicshelp.org/blog/102/interest-rates/effect-of-interest-rates-on-savers-and-economy/ accessed 7 May 2020.

33 A study on this issue was conducted in 50 countries. See William Pridemore, et al, 'Cashlessness and Street Crime: A Cross-national Study of Direct Deposit Payment and Robbery Rates' [2018] Justice Quarterly, 2 DOI: 10.1080/07418825.2018.1424923 accessed 11 May 2020.

34 Robert Peston, 'UK Banks Receive 37bn Bailout,' *BBC News* (London, 13 October 2008). The package contained '[e]ssential steps in helping the people and businesses of the country and supporting the economy as a whole.' http://news.bbc.co.uk/2/hi/business/7666570.stm accessed 4 May 2020.

35 'There will be a fast-track system for approval, but not everyone will be granted a payment holiday. The unpaid interest will still be recovered later, but individual credit ratings will not be affected.' Patrick Collinson, 'UK Banks Set out Details of Covid-19 Mortgage Holidays,' *The Guardian* (London, 17 March 2020) https://www.theguardian.com/money/2020/mar/17/uk-banks-set-out-details-of-covid-19-mortgage-holidays accessed 8 May 2020. For a critique of this intervention, see Asress Gikay, 'Does the UK Government's Measures on Consumer Default during Coronavirus Pandemic Leave Behind Those Who Should Benefit the Most?' (17 April 2020) http://www.asressgikay.org/2020/04/17/does-the-uk-governments-measures-on-consumer-default-during-coronavirus-pandemic-leave-behind-those-who-should-benefit-the-most/ accessed 23 May 2020.

The link between the exploitation of vulnerable financial consumers and credit crisis

One of the frequently cited causes for the 2008 crisis was the irresponsible and deceptive lending practices by U.S. financial institutions.[36] U.S. banks lent excessive amount of credit to vulnerable consumers with very poor credit scores.[37] The repeal of the Glass Steagall Act[38] which separated commercial and investment banking was partly responsible for the crisis.[39] However, its repeal and enactment of the Gramm-Leach-Bliley Act (the Financial Modernization Act of 1999), which made it possible to consolidate commercial and investment banks, resulted in the introduction of riskier lending practices of investment banks into commercial banks,[40] which eventually matured into the global financial crisis.[41]

Similarly, due to lack of adequate regulation at that time,[42] banks did not

---

36 'To sustain profits, vertically integrated financial institutions encouraged their originators to contract mortgages fraudulently. This, in turn, compelled MBS issuers and underwriters to misrepresent the quality of mortgage assets bundled into securities. As a result, the biggest and most integrated financial institutions were the most likely to commit predatory lending and securities fraud.' Neil Fligstein and Alex Roehrkasse, 'The Causes of Fraud in Financial Crises: Evidence from the Mortgage-Backed Securities Industry' [2016] 81 American Sociological Review, 617–643, 618.

37 Elizabeth Renuart, 'An Overview of the Predatory Mortgage Lending Process' [2004] 15 Housing Policy Debate 3, 467–502, 479.

38 This act was formally called the Banking Act of 1933.

39 'The Glass-Steagall Act was enacted in 1933 in response to banking crises in the 1920s and early 1930s. It imposed the separation of commercial and investment banking. In 1999, after decades of incremental changes to the operation of the legislation, as well as significant shifts in the structure of the financial services industry, Glass-Steagall was partially repealed by the Gramm-Leach-Bliley Act.' Oonagh McDonald, 'The Repeal of the Glass-Steagall Act,' *CATO Institute* (16 November 2016) https://www.cato.org/publications/policy-analysis/repeal-glass-steagall-act-myth-reality accessed 30 April 2020.

40 'The most important consequence of the repeal of Glass-Steagall was indirect—it lay in the way repeal changed an entire culture. Commercial banks are not supposed to be high-risk ventures; they are supposed to manage other people's money very conservatively. It is with this understanding that the government agrees to pick up the tab should they fail. Investment banks, on the other hand, have traditionally managed rich people's money—people who can take bigger risks in order to get bigger returns. When repeal of Glass-Steagall brought investment and commercial banks together, the investment-bank culture came out on top. There was a demand for the kind of high returns that could be obtained only through high leverage and big risk-taking.' See Joseph Stiglitz, 'Capitalist Fools,' *Vanity Fair* (January 2009) https://www.vanityfair.com/news/2009/01/stiglitz200901-2 accessed 25 April 2020.

41 Ibid.

42 'The Dodd-Frank Act, officially called the Dodd-Frank Wall Street Reform and Consumer Protection Act, is a legislation signed into law by President Barack Obama in 2010 in response to the financial crisis that became known as the Great Recession. Dodd-Frank put regulations on the financial industry and created programs to stop mortgage companies and lenders from taking advantage of consumers. The dense, complex law continues to be a hot topic in American politics: Supporters say it places much-needed restrictions on Wall Street, but critics charge Dodd-Frank burdens investors with too many rules that slow economic

strictly follow the relevant prudential guidelines as contained in the Basel II Convention, which require them to always match the size of their lending with their overall capital base so that the effect of mass repayment defaults will not pose an existential threat to the banking system.[43] The poor enforcement of this Basel II framework led to the lending of excess credit to subprime loan borrowers and mortgagors, and the resulting debts were securitized and sold without much concern to the underlying risks of securitization.[44] In the case of subprime mortgages, the excessive lending and default in obtaining adequate collateral were largely borne by the buyers of the securitized debts in the global financial market who had no adequate information on the true nature of what they were buying given that those securitized debts were marketed through special purpose entities.[45]

In the events leading to the 2008 crisis, vulnerability of financial consumers came from their trust and confidence in the regulators of the financial systems, to protect them from any excesses of the banks.[46] This legitimate expectation stemmed from the fact that most financial consumers lack concrete knowledge of finance and are not in any realistic position to afford the advisory opinions of lawyers and accountants prior to entering into financial agreements with banks.[47] The decline in the housing market and the consequent default of

growth.' See https://www.history.com/topics/21st-century/dodd-frank-act accessed 5 May 2020).

43 Kern Alexander, 'Global Financial Standards Setting, the G10 Committees and International Economic Law' (2009) 34 Brooklyn Journal of International Law, 861–881.

44 'By turning the cash flows from a pool of illiquid underlying assets (such as mortgages) into tradable bonds, securitization created liquidity—and that liquidity promised to make the financial system better diversified and more resilient. Instead of bankers having to hold onto and support every loan they originated until it matured or defaulted, securitization allowed risks to be stripped from the loans and disbursed beyond the traditional geographical areas in which a particular lender had been operating to investors in any country of the world. The gain from this innovation was the reduced cost of mortgages and more affordable home ownership for a range of marginally less-creditworthy individuals.' Gerard Caprio Jr., et al, 'The 2007 Meltdown in Structured Securitization: Searching for Lessons, Not Scapegoats' (2010) 25 *The World Bank Research Observer* 1, 125–155, 129. https://doi.org/10.1093/wbro/lkp029 accessed 2 May 2020.

45 Ibid, 141.

46 See the Basel II Framework on banking regulations which emphasizes minimum capital requirements, the supervisory review process, and market discipline. https://www.bis.org/publ/bcbs157.htm accessed 11 May 2020. '[B]asel II rests on three mutually reinforcing pillars: (1) minimum capital requirements; (2) supervisory review of banks' capital adequacy; (3) strengthened market discipline of capital adequacy.'

47 '[W]hile regulators and enforcers expect consumers to protect themselves with the data provided by disclosure requirements, consumers are still vulnerable to the craftiness of professionals offering financial services despite obvious risks posed.' Gabriel C. Stǎnescu, 'The Responsible Consumer in the Digital Age: On the Conceptual Shift from "average" to "responsible" Consumer and the Inadequacy of the "information Paradigm" in Consumer Financial Protection' (2019) 24 Tilburg Law Review 49 DOI: http://doi.org/10.5334/tilr.143 accessed 24 May 2020.

borrowers in repaying their loans and mortgages led many banks to repossess mortgaged houses.[48] The investors who purchased the securitized repayment defaults of the borrowers could not also be repaid upon the maturity of the securities, and this kept them in a vulnerable position as well.[49] Cumulatively, the domino effect attained a global height as banks could not repay their debt obligations to each other, and bigger banks reacted by reducing lending to financial consumers.[50]

Rating agencies were also accused of causing the crisis due to their insincere and nontransparent ratings.[51] Many financial consumers typically base their decisions on the basis of the information provided by rating agencies.[52] Therefore, financial investments in certain companies turned out to be bad decisions because the corporate assets were watered and not reflective of the true economic statuses of the companies.[53]

Thus, among other possible elements, the systemic race for excessive profits especially from vulnerable consumers who were charged high interest rates led to the crisis, and banks and financial institutions reacted by severely reducing lending to them.[54] This high level of restrictions invariably saw a rise in the

---

48 'But these mortgages had a much higher rate of repossession than conventional mortgages because they were adjustable rate mortgages (ARMs). The payments were fixed for two years, and then became both higher and dependent on the level of Fed interest rates, which also rose substantially. Consequently, a wave of repossessions is sweeping America as many of these mortgages reset to higher rates in the next two years. And it is likely that as many as two million families will be evicted from their homes as their cases make their way through the courts.' See 'The US Subprime Crisis in Graphics,' *BBC News* (London, 21 November 2007) http://news.bbc.co.uk/2/hi/business/7073131.stm accessed 11 May 2020.
49 Ibid.
50 Ibid.
51 Thomas Hurst, 'The Role of Credit Rating Agencies in the Current Worldwide Financial Crisis' [2009] 61 Company Lawyer, 61–64; Elliot Smith, 'Bringing Down Wall Street as Ratings Let Loose Subprime Scourge,' *Bloomberg* (24 September 2008) https://www.bloomberg.com/news/articles/2008-09-24/bringing-down-wall-street-as-ratings-let-loose-subprime-scourge accessed 6 May 2020.
52 Marwan Elkhoury, 'Credit Rating Agencies and Their Potential Impact on Developing Countries' [2009] UNCTAD Discussion Papers No. 186, 2. https://unctad.org/en/docs/osgdp20081_en.pdf; David Gillen, 'In Rating Agencies, Investors Still Trust' *New York Times* (4 June 2009) https://www.nytimes.com/2009/06/05/business/economy/05place.html (both websites were accessed 11 May 2020).
53 'The three main rating agencies, Moody's, Standard & Poor's, and Fitch, have been scorned and vilified for their bad performance in rating subprime securities. They gave AAA ratings to securities whose quality was far lower. Indeed, a significant proportion of subprime securities rated in years preceding the crash have been downgraded, often significantly; many of such securities have even defaulted.' Claire Hill, 'Why Did Rating Agencies Do Such a Bad Job Rating Subprime Securities?' [2010] 71 Uni. Pitt. L. Rev. 585, 585-7. https://scholarship.law.umn.edu/faculty_articles/80 accessed 9 May 2020.
54 Reacting to the effects of the financial crisis, Robert Peston, the BBC business editor, explained that 'all banks are having greater difficulties than normal getting funding from the market but as a specialist mortgage lender, no-one really wants to lend to Northern Rock.' http://news.bbc.co.uk/2/hi/business/6994099.stm accessed 1 May 2020.

demand for an excessive amount of collateral from consumers, and their general inability to satisfy the collateral requirement made them poorer and more vulnerable due to the increased level of temptation to access credit from rapacious and unregulated lenders.[55] In other words, the global economy is better off when consumers are not exploited to the point where a financial crisis becomes the outcome.

Covid-19 and the underlying insolvency law reforms and economic interventions around the globe

After the 2008 financial crisis, many countries made adjustments to support their financial systems so as to prevent a similar crisis from recurring. In the United Kingdom, the United States, and the European Union, many pieces of legislation were enacted in response to the crisis. As hinted earlier, financial institutions typically react to a financial crisis by reducing lending, especially to financial consumers and small businesses that may not be able to offer adequate collateral.[56] As Finch opined, in a credit crisis, banks generally become more inclined to over-secure their debts by creating floating charges[57] on their debtors' movable assets, fixed charges on their immovable assets, requirement of bank guarantees, and comprehensive insurance covers over the underlying collateral of the debtors in which the banks are named to be the first loss payees.[58] The high cost associated with the provision of this kind of collateral places financial consumers in a more vulnerable position, because they would have to spend more money to acquire insurance premiums and bank guarantees in order to be eligible for loans. In the process of acquiring credit to solve personal issues, they could offer to accept collateral that is in the last analysis worth more than the accessed loans.

It is the responsibility of each country's government to develop unique responses towards mitigating the effects of a credit crisis, which could result from the Covid-19 pandemic. For instance, after the early 1990's economic recession in the United Kingdom, the 2002 Enterprise Act amendment was enacted to save vulnerable businesses.[59] One principal amendment of this act was the

---

55　Thomas Hogan, 'What Caused the Post-Crisis Decline in Bank Lending?' [2019] Issue brief no. 01.10.19. Rice University's Baker Institute for Public Policy, Houston, Texas. https://www.bakerinstitute.org/media/files/files/97fc7f24/bi-brief-011019-cpf-banklending.pdf accessed 30 April 2020.

56　cf Wack (n 22).

57　*Spectrum Plus Ltd vs. National Westminster Bank plc* [2005] UKHL 41, [2005] 3 WLR 58, whereby the House of Lords clarified the nature of assets that are capable of being secured by a fixed charge.

58　Vanessa Finch, 'Corporate Rescue in a World of Debt' [2008] Journal of Business Law 756–777, 766; Daniel Prentice, 'Bargaining in the Shadow of the Enterprise Act 2002' [2004] European Business Organization Law Review 153–159.

59　For the legislative history of the Enterprise Act, see the Department of Trade and Industry, *Our Competitive Future: Building The Knowledge Driven Economy: Government's*

modification of the right of a floating charge holder to appoint an administrator instead of a receiver.[60] No doubt the banking community was quite unhappy about the amendment on floating charges because it whittled the control element of the security device, the self-help aspect that enabled a powerful lender's swift realization of assets from a financially troubled company, whose financial distress had crystallized the underlying floating charges.[61] Part of the immediate reaction of banks in the United Kingdom was to limit their acceptance of certain assets, for instance, inventories and equipment, for which the floating charge was used to create security over, with the material risk of being acquired by buyers.[62]

As the effect of Covid-19 unfolds, banks will likely be more cautious and risk averse in lending, and in the absence of any bespoke regulation on enforcement of defaults, like a total suspension of the right to initiate an insolvency process, they will likely be more interested in enforcing repayment defaults on loans than agreeing to restructure them especially where there is no real prospect of full repayment.[63] For financial consumers, one could expect to see a higher rate of default due to a generally harsher economic environment; thus, certain movable property of this vulnerable group might run the risk of higher unacceptance for lending or acceptance on the condition of a very high interest rate.

A few economic interventions from around the globe toward mitigating consumers' vulnerability

Many loan contracts entered into by consumers before the Covid-19 pandemic have default, acceleration, or termination clauses hinged on a consumer's inability to repay debt when due. Thus, default in timely repayment could lead to loss of collateral, a higher interest rate payment, being subjected to any deficient sum if the underlying collateral does not satisfy the full debt, etc. English law, for instance, provides a basis for this approach in the *Grupo Hotelero* case[64] in respect of material adverse clauses, which could be used by banks to trigger events of MAC clauses[65] in loan contracts and floating charges to enable them to

Competitiveness (White Paper, Cm 4176, 1998); The Insolvency Service, *A Review of Company Rescue and Business Reconstruction Mechanisms* (White Paper, 1 September 1999); Department of Trade and Industry, *Productivity and Enterprise, Insolvency – A Second Chance* (White Paper, Cm 5234, 2001).

60 S. 248 of the Enterprise Act and Schedule B1, Insolvency Act 1986.

61 Louise Gullifer, 'The Reforms of the Enterprise Act 2002 and the Floating Charge as a Security Device' (2008) 46 Can Bus LJ 399, 419.

62 Ibid, 403.

63 In the United States for instance, there have been a number of legislative responses toward protecting financial consumers. See 'Major Consumer Protections Announced in Response to COVID-19,' *National Consumer Law Center* (7 May 2020) https://library.nclc.org/major-consumer-protections-announced-response-covid-19 assessed 10 May 2020.

64 *Grupo Hotelero Urvasco SA vs. Carey Value Added SL* [2013] EWHC 1039.

65 Luca Gambini and Chiara Sannasardo, 'How to Survive to Financial Crisis, Political Changes

accelerate demand for repayments and crystallize charges, respectively.[66] To mitigate consumers' vulnerability, the UK government introduced a Covid-19 scheme which seeks to shoulder about 80% or up to £2,500 of the wages of every employee that is retained by their employer.[67] Likewise, Denmark has undertaken to pay 75% of salaries for employees in its private sector whose earnings were affected by the pandemic.[68] This no doubt reduces the vulnerable position of many employees who would have been laid off and defaulted on their debt repayment obligations, which would have made them more vulnerable to predatory or unsympathetic lenders' enforcements of debts.

Similarly, in Australia, close to 200 billion Australian dollars have been budgeted to offset the effects of the pandemic, together with the six-month repayment deferral on loans worth $100 million or more being owed by consumers to banks.[69] The United States has introduced a series of stimulus packages totaling more than 2 trillion U.S. dollars for households and businesses.[70] France and the United Kingdom have made available €345 billion and €383 billion, respectively, as stimulus packages.[71] Germany has mapped out €550 billion to tackle cash flow difficulties of households and businesses, which is regarded as the highest rescue package it has unveiled since the Second World War.[72] And Europe's economic rescue packages at the time of this writing are worth about €1.7 trillion. All these efforts have unarguably reduced consumers' financial vulnerability during the Covid-19 pandemic and should be replicated in other systems.

and Other Adverse Events: An Overview of MAC Clauses in Recent Transactions with an In-Depth Analysis of the Abbott Laboratories/Alere Inc. Case' (2018) 10 Bocconi Legal Papers 347.

66 Philp Rawlings, 'Avoiding the Obligation to Lend' [2012] JBL 89, 100–110; McCann Fitzgerald, 'COVID-19: Issues Under Loan Agreements,' *Lexology* (13 March 2020) https://www.lexology.com/library/detail.aspx?g=f9c16314-fa91-49f8-bc58-1e3a621d60d5 accessed 18 April 2020.

67 'Coronavirus: UK Government Unveils Aid for Self-Employed,' *BBC News* (London, 26 March 2020) https://www.bbc.com/news/uk-52053914 accessed 30 April 2020.

68 Sarah Johansson, 'Danish Government Will Pay 75% of Threatened Private Sector Salaries,' *Brussels Times* (15 March 2020) https://www.brusselstimes.com/all-news/eu-affairs/100505/danish-government-will-pay-75-of-threatened-private-sector-salaries/ accessed 13 May 2020.

69 Jessica Irvine, 'Where Will All the Money Come from to Fund the Stimulus?' *The Sydney Morning Herald* (3 April 2020) https://www.smh.com.au/business/the-economy/where-will-all-the-money-come-from-to-fund-the-stimulus-20200403-p54goi.html accessed 9 May 2020.

70 Jacob Pramuk, 'Senate Passes $2 Trillion Coronavirus Relief Bill—House Aims for Friday Vote,' *CNBC News* (25 March 2020) https://www.cnbc.com/2020/03/25/senate-passes-2-trillion-coronavirus-stimulus-package.html accessed 11 May 2020.

71 Juliette Garside, 'Europe's Economic Rescue Packages Worth Combined €1.7tn,' *The Guardian* (London, 19 March 2020) https://www.theguardian.com/world/2020/mar/19/europes-economic-rescue-packages-worth-combined-17tn accessed 12 June 2020.

72 Ibid.

Insolvency law reforms

Another common approach around the globe toward mitigating the vulnerability of financial consumers is the prevention of businesses from being liquidated on the basis of their inability to repay debts. Presumably, this benevolent reform will be reciprocated by businesses through postponed demand and enforcement of debts against financial consumers. A few examples globally will suffice. India has suspended the operation of the Insolvency and Bankruptcy Code (IBC) 2016 for a period of one year, and creditors cannot commence insolvency processes against their debtors.[73] Since most businesses in India are SMEs, many of them will be saved from being wound up by their creditors as a result of the amendment, and this will impact positively on some financial consumers who are debtors of these businesses. Similarly, temporary suspension of the IBC will encourage a stronger focus on debt restructuring using the Companies Act's Schemes of Arrangement.[74] If more businesses are saved through restructuring, the probability of a high monopolistic market will be reduced, and this will impact positively on households and vulnerable consumers in terms of competitive prices.

In Singapore, the Covid-19 (Temporary Measures) Act 2020[75] was enacted to provide relief to financially distressed individuals and temporarily prevents creditors from enforcing certain contractual claims.[76] Per the act, a government assessor will determine on a case-by-case basis whether a debtor deserves a temporary protection by considering whether the default was due to Covid-19 circumstances and the time in which the contract in question was executed.[77] If, for instance, the contract giving rise to the default was entered into after the enactment of the act or the cause of default is incapable of being reasonably linked to the pandemic, then such a debtor will not qualify for the temporary protection under the act.[78]

So far, approaches taken by countries appear uniform and converge around total or partial suspension on one hand and amendments of specific provisions of their insolvency statutes on the other hand. Also, there has been a uniform approach toward increasing the debt value for statutory demand by more than several

---

73 Mukesh Butani, 'IBC Suspension: Reforms That Can Fill the Gap,' *BloombergQuint* (26 May 2020) https://www.bloombergquint.com/opinion/ibc-suspension-filling-the-gap accessed 27 May 2020.

74 S. 230 of the Companies Act, 2013.

75 S.1 thereof states the provisions in the COVID-19 (Temporary Measures) Act relating to temporary relief from legal action for inability to perform certain contracts, as well as increased thresholds for bankruptcy and insolvency for financially distressed individuals and businesses, will commence on 20 April 2020. https://www.mlaw.gov.sg/news/press-releases/2020-04-20-covid-19-temporary-measures-act-provisions-relating-to-temporary-reliefs-to-commence-on-20-april-2020 accessed 11 May 2020.

76 Ibid, ss. 7 and 11 of the Act.

77 Ibid, s.3 protects contracts entered into on or before March 25 2020.

78 Ibid.

hundred percentages. Apart from India and Singapore,[79] Australia has undertaken an insolvency law reform by increasing the statutory demand debt value from 2,000 to 20,000 Australian dollars, with the demand period stretching from 21 days to six months.[80] Before the Covid-19 pandemic, most of the insolvency statutes that drew inspiration from the English Insolvency Act of 1986,[81] including that of India,[82] embody the concept of wrongful trading,[83] which ties closely with directors' fiduciary duties, one of which is loyalty toward achieving results that are not inimical to a company's creditors by deepening insolvency. Thus, directors, being presumably experts in the company's business, are required to exercise their discretion wisely and in good faith which ought to enable them know the best time to stop corporate trading so as not to further deteriorate creditors' assets.[84]

To establish wrongful trading, it has to be proved that directors unreasonably continued to trade after a company experienced insolvency and there was no reasonable prospect to trade out of insolvency.[85] In the context of Covid-19 where many companies are beginning to experience cash-flow difficulties, it would be ruinous to surrender every financially distressed company to an insolvency process on the basis of the pandemic events; this will lead to an increased number of job losses which will worsen consumers' vulnerable state. The forgoing approaches toward preventing too many closure of businesses are generally suitable for countries during the pandemic, as it will ensure that prices for consumer goods and services do not consequently rise astronomically.[86]

In relation to the African continent, the African Development Bank (ADB) Group has responded to Covid-19 through the creation of the Covid-19 Response Facility that aims to help member countries address the challenges of the pandemic. The ADB provides up to US$10 billion to governments and the private sector in addition to the $3 billion Fight Covid-19 Social Bond on the

79 Ibid, s.14 'increased the monetary threshold for personal bankruptcy from $15,000 to $60,000, and that for corporate insolvency from $10,000 to $100,000 (Singaporean Dollars). The time period to satisfy a statutory demand from creditors was increased from 21 days to six months.'

80 Herbert Smith Freehills LLP, 'COVID-19 Australia: Temporary Changes to Insolvency Laws - Australian Federal Government Addresses COVID-19 Financial Distress,' *Lexology* (22 March 2020) https://www.lexology.com/library/detail.aspx?g=33bbfb34-0f08-429b-9012-a1e47def423c accessed 30 April 2020.

81 S. 214 Insolvency Act of 1986.

82 S. 66 Insolvency and Bankruptcy Code of 2016, India.

83 Andrew Keay, 'Wrongful Trading and the Liability of Company Directors: A Theoretical Perspective' [2005] 25 Legal Stud 431.

84 Ibid, 433. However, directors could still be criminally liable in respect of 'fraudulent trading' under ss. 213 and 246ZA, transactions defrauding creditors under s. 423, and 'misfeasance' under s. 212.

85 cf Keay (n 83) 432.

86 Writankar Mukherjee, et al, 'Consumer Goods Fly Off the Shelves as Coronavirus Spreads in India,' *The Economic Times* (16 March 2020) https://economictimes.indiatimes.com/industry/cons-products/fmcg/consumer-goods-fly-off-the-shelves-as-coronavirus-spreads-in-india/articleshow/74644159.cms?from=mdr accessed 27 May 2020.

international capital market.[87] All these efforts invariably seek to improve the conditions of vulnerable consumers.

In Part II, the chapter argues that although use of digital finance and financial inclusion have been widely acknowledged as being integral to the cure of poverty, there are some inherent elements that give rise to consumer vulnerability, and therefore, must be adequately addressed in order to achieve a financial inclusion system (especially in developing countries) that is substantially compatible with consumer well-being.

Part II: financial inclusion

Digital finance as an integral element of financial inclusion

The increased use of the Internet in many countries in the wake of the 21st century has expanded the activities of financial systems around the globe to accommodate a significant number of people who would have otherwise been left out by the traditional banking system.[88] Apart from the Internet, the heightened use of mobile telephones (especially smartphones) in more than 80 countries[89] has led to the possibility of poor financial consumers using digital financial services to buy and sell goods and services.[90] Before the year 2000, most of these transactions were cash-based. However, the use of digital finance rests partially on the assumption that the users do have formal bank accounts and the required digital means to carry out transactions on their accounts. Especially in the developing countries, this assumption is very rebuttable.[91] Thus, more efforts need to be made to educate poor financial consumers, especially those living in rural areas, on the benefits of using digital finance and becoming properly included in the financial systems.[92]

In the traditional banking system, some services still require a consumer to make a physical appearance at their bank and do some paperwork and are often delayed if many customers are waiting to be served. This increases the cost of

---

87 ADBG, 'The African Development Bank Group's Covid-19 Rapid Response Facility' (21 April 2020) https://www.afdb.org/en/documents/african-development-bank-groups-covid-19-rapid-response-facility-crf accessed 10 May 2020.

88 Susan Johnson, 'Competing Visions of Financial Inclusion in Kenya: The Rift Revealed by Mobile Money Transfer' [2016] Canadian Journal of Development Studies 83, 91.

89 Kate Lauer and Timothy Lyman, 'Digital Financial Inclusion: Implications for Customers, Regulators, Supervisors, and Standard-Setting Bodies,' *CGAP Brief* (February 2015) https://www.cgap.org/sites/default/files/Brief-Digital-Financial-Inclusion-Feb-2015.pdf accessed 11 May 2020.

90 CGAP, 'Digital Financial Inclusion,' *Research and Analysis Publication* (March 2015) https://www.cgap.org/research/publication/digital-financial-inclusion accessed 11 May 2020.

91 Gloria Grandolini, 'Five Challenges Prevent Financial Access for People in Developing Countries,' *World Bank Blogs* (15 October 2015) https://blogs.worldbank.org/voices/five-challenges-prevent-financial-access-people-developing-countries accessed 12 May 2020.

92 Ibid.

banking as banks have to factor in the high costs of services including the operation and maintenance of several brick-and-mortar branches. However, with
the use of digital finance, transaction costs are much lower because bank customers could perform a range of services across many banks, using their mobile
phones. This heightened possibility to switch banks has also caused many banks
to strive harder to retain their customers by providing competitive financial
services.[93]

Another benefit is that digital financial inclusion helps to reduce the amount of
physical cash in circulation, which helps to reduce the rate of cash-motivated
robbery.[94] As noted by Pridemore, et al, the possibility of being paid through a
digital means boosts sales because buyers from around the globe can make
purchases online, which would never have been possible if cash was exclusively
required as a means of payment. In fact, in developing countries with poor security, businesses now witness lower rates of broad-day robbery because of the
lesser probability of possessing a large amount of cash at any given period during
the day.[95] However, it should be noted that digital financial services can achieve
inclusion of the traditionally excluded population if the cost of services is generally low and affordable.[96]

The meaning and effect of financial inclusion

Providing vulnerable consumers with sustainable financial services that bring
them into the formal economy has generally been accepted, especially by the
United Nations, to mean financial inclusion.[97] In traditional banking systems,
factors such as culture and religion prevent vulnerable consumers, especially
those living in rural areas, from being included in mainstream financial services.[98]
Thus, dismantling barriers that limit the possibility of financial inclusion has been
linked to better economic growth and opportunities for vulnerable consumers
who will be able to invest more in education, make better decisions, and launch
themselves out of poverty.[99] Also, if more vulnerable consumers are financially
included, it will increase the deposit base for banks, make more money

93 GPFI, 'Issues Paper: Digital Financial Inclusion and the Implications for Customers,
Regulators, Supervisors and Standard-Setting Bodies,' *GPFI* (31 October 2014) https://
www.gpfi.org/sites/gpfi/files/documents/Issues%20Paper%20for%20GPFI%20BIS
%20Conference%20on%20Digital%20Financial%20Inclusion.pdf accessed 12 May 2020.
94 Peterson Ozili, 'Impact of Digital Finance on Financial Inclusion and Stability' [2018] Borsa
Istanbul Review, 5. doi:10.1016/j.bir.2017.12.003 accessed 10 May 2020.
95 cf Pridemore, et al, (n 33) 1–2.
96 United Nations, 'Digital Financial Inclusion,' *International Telecommunication Union,
Issue Brief Series, Inter-agency Task Force on Financing for Development* (July 2016) http://
www.un.org/esa/ffd/wp-content/uploads/2016/01/Digital-FinancialInclusion_ITU_
IATF-Issue-Brief.pdf accessed 3 May 2020.
97 Ibid, 2.
98 cf Ozili (n 94) 16.
99 Ibid, 2.

generally available for borrowing, and increase the ease and rate of doing business.[100]

A connected discourse of financial inclusion is the emergence of financial technology (Fintech) companies that provide online and offline financial services to customers. The main attraction for Fintechs is rooted in generally faster provision of services of digital finance and sometimes the relatively lower charges they offer to customers compared to conventional banks.[101] Since Fintechs are relatively new compared to traditional brick-and-mortar banks, the former are usually advertised as offering improved services that save customers more time and money.[102]

Also, given that Fintechs do not usually handle deposits, the regulatory demands are typically lower compared to those imposed on traditional banks that hold customers' deposits and are required to strictly follow prudential guidelines when loaning money to customers.[103] So, given that regulation is relaxed in the operations of Fintechs and their interactions with the general public, sometimes they trick unsuspecting customers and charge them high fees, including a deliberate delay in the processing of complaints relating to failed transactions, because the customer's only way of communication is online as opposed to visiting a brick-and-mortar office.[104] Sometimes, the main interest of a Fintech company, which determines its legal jurisdiction in the event of a legal action, might be outside the environment where its financial services and products are patronized, thereby leaving dissatisfied customers extremely limited choices for resolving disputes.[105]

Even though there are a few criticisms against Fintechs and their business models which are allegedly exploitative, it cannot be denied that their financial services have improved the realization of financial inclusion, which is agreed to be an integral element of the solution to poverty.[106] They provide quicker financial services to customers; these services are often denied or delayed for several days or weeks in the traditional banking

100 Rui Han and Martin Melecky, 'Financial Inclusion for Financial Stability: Access to Bank Deposits and the Growth of Deposits in the Global Financial Crisis' (2013) World Bank Policy Research Working Paper 6577, 12. http://documents.worldbank.org/curated/en/850681468325448388/pdf/WPS6577.pdf accessed 12 May 2020.

101 cf Ozili (n 94) 8.

102 Consumer International, '10 Things Consumers Need to Know About Fintech' https://www.consumersinternational.org/news-resources/blog/posts/10-things-consumers-need-to-know-about-fintech/ accessed 1 May 2020.

103 cf Basel II Framework (n 46).

104 Victoria Pallien, 'The Modern-day Banking Experience: Brick & Mortar vs. Digital,' *Fintech News* (12 July 2019) https://www.fintechnews.org/the-modern-day-banking-experience-brick-mortar-vs-digital/ accessed 4 May 2020.

105 Rachel O'Grady, 'Fintech: A Bittersweet Inevitability?' *African Law & Business* (4 September 2018) https://iclg.com/alb/8502-fintech-a-bittersweet-inevitability accessed 12 May 2020.

106 cf GPFI (n 93) 2.

sector.[107] Also, since Fintechs are not highly regulated like traditional banks and often offer online services across jurisdictions, this gives them more space to be innovative and competitive and thus improve customers' experience and economic well-being.[108] Another recorded benefit is that Fintechs can provide small loans to financial consumers to solve their pressing problems.[109] Ordinarily, these consumers will not qualify for loans in the traditional banking sector and may not be in a position to provide collateral that will satisfy the various prudential guidelines that govern the banks in a particular system.[110]

Some underlying benefits of financial inclusion

Financial inclusion in developing countries typically results in women and poor people acquiring greater control over their finances, and this impacts on all other decisions that stem from household management including more children being enrolled in schools; more nutritious food being consumed to improve health; and more employment, gender equality, and general economic well-being in society.[111]

Toward realizing the World Bank's goal of universal financial access by 2020,[112] more than 1.2 billion people have been able to open bank accounts since 2011 and this is their entry point into the formal economy.[113] The only drawback here appears to be that a significant percentage of these accounts have never been used, perhaps due to the unaffordable fees for financial services or some other limiting factors such as old age, lack of education, and consumer protection mechanisms against the oppressive practices of the financial institutions or the activities of financial scammers.[114]

If the factors debilitating the aim of financial inclusion are addressed, it could lead to a profound improvement in the lives of people as envisaged by the World

---

107 cf Ozili (n 94) 8.
108 Ibid, 3.
109 Pratyush Chandramadhur, 'Instant Loans: How Consumers Can Finance Personal Needs from New Age Finance Companies,' *Financial Express* (17 March 2020) https://www.financialexpress.com/money/instant-loans-how-consumers-can-finance-personal-needs-from-new-age-finance-companies/1901067/ accessed 12 June 2020.
110 cf Ozili (n 94) 8.
111 Elizabeth Price, 'Financial Inclusion Is a Key Enabler to Reducing Poverty and Boosting Prosperity,' *The World Bank* (2 October 2018) https://www.worldbank.org/en/topic/financialinclusion/overview accessed 30 April 2020.
112 World Bank, 'UFA2020 Overview: Universal Financial Access by 2020' (1 October 2018) https://www.worldbank.org/en/topic/financialinclusion/brief/achieving-universal-financial-access-by-2020 accessed 10 May 2020.
113 World Bank, 'The Global Findex Database 2017' https://globalfindex.worldbank.org/node accessed 2 May 2020.
114 Tish Sanghera, 'Banking in India: Why Many People Still Don't Use Their Accounts,' *AJ Impact* (22 June 2019) https://www.aljazeera.com/ajimpact/banking-india-people-don-accounts-190621093947054.html accessed 9 May 2020.

Bank.[115] In many developing countries, mere ownership of accounts transforms people's lives by putting more money into their pockets in indirect ways. For example, in the Philippines, reports show that women who opened bank savings accounts became more empowered in their decision making which impacted positively on their households.[116] Similar progress was reported in Bangladesh whereby rural credits and digital finance have helped to improve the level of women's empowerment.[117]

In Nigeria and many other African countries, the rates at which criminals engaged in armed robbery and house burglary fell significantly following the banking reforms that saw the creation and operation of many digital bank accounts. People stopped carrying large amounts of cash in their pockets or travelling bags or keeping cash at home, and this reduced the incidents of robbery and enhanced the benefits associated with a low crime rate.[118] In Kenya, 88% of account owners use digital finance, and a study shows a link between this heightened use and improvement in personal and family well-being.[119]

Digital finance is also integral in reducing corruption and pilfering as was realized in Tanzania where payment of the entrance fee to a national conservation park was digitized and thus led to about a 40% reduction in leakages.[120] India's pensioners saw an improved income of about 47% when the country moved from cash to smart card payment of pension workers.[121] And in Uganda, the government's transition to digital bus tickets led to a 140% increase in its

115 cf Grandolini (n 91).

116 Nava Ashraf, et al, 'Household Decision Making and Savings Impacts: Further Evidence from a Commitment Savings Product in the Philippines' (2006) Center Discussion Paper No. 939, Yale University, 9. http://www.econ.yale.edu/growth_pdf/cdp939.pdf accessed 12 May 2020.

117 Syed Hashemi, et al, 'Rural Credit Programs and Women's Empowerment in Bangladesh' (1996) 24 World Development 4, 635–653.

118 Baba Iyodo, et al, 'Consequences of Bank Frauds on the Growth of Nigerian Economy' (2016) Global Journal of Management Perspective https://www.longdom.org/articles/consequences-of-bank-frauds-on-the-growth-of-nigerian-economy.pdf accessed 13 May 2020.

119 IFC, 'Digital Access: The Future of Financial Inclusion in Africa' (2018) World Bank Document, 33. http://documents.worldbank.org/curated/en/719111532533639732/pdf/128850-WP-AFR-Digital-Access-The-Future-of-Financial-Inclusion-in-Africa-PUBLIC.pdf accessed 10 May 2020. This World Bank Document also contains data in respect of other African countries.

120 United Nations, 'New United Nations Study: Digital Payments Could Boost Tax Revenue by Nearly US$500 Million Each Year and Drive Economic Modernization in Tanzania,' *Better Than Cash Alliance* (20 September 2016) https://www.betterthancash.org/news/media-releases/new-united-nations-study-digital-payments-could-boost-tax-revenue-by-nearly-us-500-million-each-year-and-drive-economic-modernization-in-tanzania accessed 2 May 2020.

121 Tihad Wald, 'Governments Can Fight Corruption by Joining the Digital Payment Revolution,' *World Economic Forum* (11 April 2018) https://www.weforum.org/agenda/2018/04/governments-join-digital-payment-revolution-fight-corruption/ accessed 11 May 2020.

revenue due to reduction in leakages.[122] The police in Afghanistan received full salaries comparable to a 30% raise for the first time when the government moved from cash to digital payment of salaries.[123]

The experiences above appear to be similar with what has happened around the globe since the advent of digital finance. The positive effects of digital finance are enormous and include financial inclusion, access to credit, reduction in poverty, lessened corruption of public officials, gender equality, ease of concluding financial transactions, and general progress of society.

Factors debilitating the full realization of financial inclusion

The positive effects of digital finance and how it improves financial inclusion rests on the presumption that the poor people seeking to be included have mobile phones, Internet connectivity, and enough education to operate and enjoy the financial services offered by Fintechs, whose operations are often not influenced or inhibited by geographical locations and unique realities of some consumers.[124] In any case, the effective use of digital finance has some correlations with high literacy level, knowledge, and banking experience.[125] In other words, it is easier on average, to achieve a higher financial inclusion among educated people who can easily appreciate the benefits of use and opportunity cost, such as payments of utility bills and money transfers to relatives and business partners without visiting a bank due to understanding of the opportunity costs.[126] In fact, those who use digital financial services and realize the underlying benefits might undertake the easier task of convincing their educated friends and family members to also use it. However, it is tougher to get people with little or no education to use digital finance, which debilitates the possibility of adequate financial inclusion.[127]

122 Sabahat Iqbal, 'A Public-Private Partnership to Digitize Bus Fares in Rwanda,' *CGAP* (27 December 2016) https://www.cgap.org/blog/public-private-partnership-digitize-bus-fares-rwanda accessed 9 May 2020.
123 Communications Team, 'Afghanistan: Moving Police Salary Payments to Mobile Accounts,' *Better Than Cash Alliance* (New York, 2 June 2016) https://www.betterthancash.org/news/blogs-stories/afghanistan-moving-police-salary-payments-to-mobile-accounts accessed 10 May 2020.
124 Leora Klapper, '5 Ways Digital Finance Can Help People Escape Poverty,' *World Economic Forum* (16 December 2016) https://www.weforum.org/agenda/2016/12/five-ways-to-help-more-people-benefit-from-digital-finance/ accessed 25 May 2020.
125 See the relevant case studies in Gyatri Murthy, et al, 'Fintechs and Financial Inclusion: Lessons Learned,' *CGAP Case Study* (May 2019) https://www.cgap.org/sites/default/files/publications/2019_05_Case_Study_Fintech_and_Financial_Inclusion.pdf accessed 11 May 2020.
126 Michale Rizzo, 'Digital Finance: Empowering the Poor via New Technologies,' *World Bank* (10 April 2014) https://www.worldbank.org/en/news/feature/2014/04/10/digital-finance-empowering-poor-new-technologies accessed 25 May 2020.
127 cf Ozili (n 94) 16.

Poor education or a total lack of it makes it difficult for a proper inclusion of this class of individuals into the financial system. First, given that digital finance is predicated on technology and most times requires a user to furnish personal data as a precondition for use, many uneducated or superstitious people suspect that a Fintech's demand for personal data as a prerequisite for using digital finance is part of a broader plan to lure them into acceptance of something evil and incongruous to their religious beliefs.[128] There are people, and this is more prevalent in developing countries, who superstitiously believe that microchips, computer software, 5 G network, etc., are specific diabolical means of achieving the evil plan against this superstitious demographic.[129] Some religious leaders assist in advancing this view, and their less critical congregations believe them, and as a result, detest the use of digital finance.[130]

Second, granted that digital financial services offer many benefits that could cure poverty, the costs of digital services and innovations are generally transferred to users, because absent any other source of funding, this is the major way Fintechs can make profits for their shareholders as well as invest more in research and development.[131] Yet, the service charges to users are often unaffordable to the unbanked demographic, whose patronage and continued use would have further reinforced the goal of financial inclusion.[132] In other words, those who can afford to pay for the services of digital finance seem to be those who already have bank accounts with traditional banks and enjoy the possibility and ease of linking their bank accounts with their Fintech-enabled accounts for transactions;[133] this group largely represents the educated banking demographic.

---

128 Ibid, 10.
129 Tim Adams, '5 G, Coronavirus and Contagious Superstition," *The Guardian* (26 April 2020) https://www.theguardian.com/world/2020/apr/26/5g-coronavirus-and-contagious-superstition accessed 6 May 2020.
130 Chris Oyakhilome, 'Implementation of 5 G,' *YouTube* (3 April 2020) https://www.youtube.com/watch?v=6ZQ2OgnajUs accessed 12 May 2020.
131 '[F]or unsecured consumer lending, for example, the weighted average cost of financing was 14 percent for lenders that did not have third-party backup servicers and 5.8 percent for those that had them. ...' Steve Fromhart and Chris Moller, 'Funding Takes Center Stage for Nonbank Online Lenders: Cost of Capital Survey Results,' Deloitte (9 July 2018) https://www2.deloitte.com/us/en/insights/industry/financial-services/cost-of-funding-survey-nonbank-online-lenders.html accessed 13 May 2020.
132 Asress Gikay, 'European Consumer Law and Blockchain Based Financial Services: A Functional Approach against the Rhetoric of Regulatory Uncertainty' (2019) 24(1) Tilburg Law Review, 27–48, 27. The author opines that 'the enthusiasts of the technology have claimed that cryptocurrencies will bank the unbanked, i.e., those who have no access to credit card or debit card and hence are excluded from the financial system. The claim proved to be false because (a) credit card or debit card is a perquisite for acquiring cryptocurrencies from exchange platforms in many cases and (b) cryptocurrencies are expensive, and transactions in them are risky that the unbanked is not inclined to engage in.'
133 However, note that some payment systems, for example, M-PESA, may not necessarily require users to own a bank account. See generally https://www.safaricom.co.ke/personal/m-pesa/getting-started/using-m-pesa accessed 27 May 2020.

Since most Fintechs deliver online financial services to customers across the globe and are not regulated by all the central banks where their customers are located, due to their distant jurisdictions and lack of a brick-and-mortar presence in most of the countries in which they operate, the fees and interests they charge for their products and services are not always regulated or capped, are not reflective of the economic situation of consumers in poor countries, and are typically being offered on a take-it-or-leave-it basis.[134] The fees are therefore generally unaffordable among the uneducated and poor people who are willing to patronize their financial services. Consequently, Fintechs tend to focus more on educated rich users who can easily understand their terms and conditions or are more able to afford professional guidance in understanding such contractual terms.[135] This situation whittles the World Bank's goal of universal financial access by 2020.[136]

Third, an inadequate level of financial and computer literacy is also a debilitating factor in the appreciation and use of digital finance. Without adequate knowledge in this respect, people are unable to effectively operate cell phones that support the use of digital finance and are generally unable to independently perform the same type of financial services, which they could perform with the assistance of their bankers if they were to visit brick-and-mortar offices.[137] Therefore, there is a correlation between education and financial inclusion – if the latter must be achieved, and if it is agreed to be a catalyst for economic empowerment, then education and financial inclusion must be viewed as the basic precondition for the eradication of poverty.[138]

Similarly, lack of the knowledge to use digital financial services owing to lack of education[139] could make the user more susceptible to scams by the tricks and manipulations of online fraudsters seeking to obtain the user's financial data for onward theft of their digital funds.[140] The unauthorized sale of financial data of

---

134 Peter Sandeen, "PayPal Steals from Its Customers with Hidden Fees' https://petersandeen.com/paypal-is-stealing/ accessed 19 May 2020.
135 cf Ozili (n 94) 10.
136 cf World Bank UFA 2020 (n 112).
137 cf Ozili (n 94) 17.
138 However, Stanescu argues that mere education of a consumer is not a panacea to vulnerability and some other factors must be addressed. Cătălin Gabriel Stănescu, 'The Responsible Consumer in the Digital Age: On the Conceptual Shift from "Average" to "Responsible" Consumer and the Inadequacy of the "Information Paradigm" in Consumer Financial Protection' (2019) 24(1) Tilburg Law Review, 49–67, 58. DOI: https://doi.org/10.5334/tilr.143 accessed 27 May 2020.
139 Peter J. Morgan, 'The Need to Promote Digital Financial Literacy for the Digital Age,' *T20 Japan* (15 March 2019) https://t20japan.org/wp-content/uploads/2019/03/t20-japan-tf7-3-need-promote-digital-financial-literacy.pdf accessed 27 May 2020.
140 Riju Dave, 'Don't Get Cheated by Online Fraudsters: Here's How to Protect Yourself," *The Economic Times Wealth* (1 August 2016) https://economictimes.indiatimes.com/wealth/plan/dont-get-cheated-by-online-fraudsters-heres-how-to-protect-yourself/articleshow/53462567.cms accessed 12 May 2020.

vulnerable consumers to unscrupulous buyers[141] and the eventual exploitation of data by fraudsters underline the extant inadequate security apparatuses and weak consumer protection regimes that frustrate the efforts toward financial inclusion via the Fintechs' digital financial services platforms.[142] The constantly accruing fear crystallizes the belief among victims of digital fraud,[143] especially the poor and uneducated, that it is simply a way to deprive them of their hard-earned money; in response, they keep their cash at home, which is also not immune to theft.[144]

Finally, it should be noted that while digital finance can lead to more financial inclusion that assists in eradicating poverty, it could also lead to the existence of digital financial data that could help governments to make effective plans on how to reach out to certain demographics especially in a crisis such as the Covid-19 pandemic, where many systems are thinking of ways to send palliatives to the most impacted population in society.[145] Also while the availability of digital financial data does not automatically lead to access to affordable credit, it is an integral part of it, since some form of data needs to be in existence before a Fintech or even a traditional bank is able to give favorable loans to financial consumers.

Revisiting the business models of Fintechs

It should be recalled that one of the major causes of the 2008 financial crisis was the unfair business practices against vulnerable consumers who were intentionally offered credits that they were incapable of repaying.[146] Yet, there is a growing similarity between the business model of banks in the pre-2008 era and that of Fintechs now[147] in that there is an increasing amount of reports against the latter for engaging in activities that deeply exploit the vulnerability of consumers.[148]

141 Michael Lynch, 'Fast Account Openings and Bots Increase Fraud Risk,' *Payments Source* (25 January 2019) https://www.paymentssource.com/opinion/fast-account-openings-and-bots-heighten-the-fraud-risk accessed 26 May 2020.
142 OECD, 'Digitalisation and Financial Literacy,' *G20/OECD INFE Policy Guidance* (2018) http://www.oecd.org/daf/fin/financial-education/G20-OECD-INFE-Policy-Guidance-Digitalisation-Financial-Literacy-2018.pdf accessed 27 May 2020.
143 cf Smith (n 23).
144 cf Ozili (n 94) 14.
145 Ibid, 11.
146 cf Giovanni, et al (n 10) 368.
147 Lauren Saunders, et al, 'Misaligned Incentives: Why High-Rate Installment Lenders Want Borrowers Who Will Default,' *National Consumer Law Center* (July 2016) https://www.nclc.org/issues/misaligned-incentives.html accessed 27 May 2020.
148 Christine Hines, 'Fintech Brings New Options and a Lingering Old Problem for Consumers,' *National Association of Consumer Advocates* (29 August 2018) https://www.consumeradvocates.org/blog/2018/fintech-brings-new-options-and-lingering-old-problem-forconsumers. See some useful cases: *FTC vs. Western Union Company* (March 2020), 'The $153 million distribution announced today brings some measure of justice for the elderly and other victims who were financially harmed by the fraudulent schemes in this

Thus, given that Fintechs have become alternative financial service providers but in many cases do not have any physical presence in some of the countries their customers come from, they tend to capitalize on the distant jurisdiction, the act of carrying out business transactions with customers solely via the Internet platform and not being regulated in such circumstances, to offer financial services on an unconscionable, take-it-or-leave-it basis.[149] Similarly, Fintechs involved in short-term lending, who in a discriminatory manner,[150] lent to vulnerable consumers at a high interest rate would most likely experience mass repayment defaults due to the Covid-19 pandemic.[151] It is possible in that case (especially for countries lacking a regulatory legal framework for a more civil, private debt collection mechanism like the U.S. Fair Debt Collection Practices Act)[152] for the Fintechs to engage in aggressive debt collection practices or to sell such debts to buyers at a discount, who in turn would engage in aggressive enforcement of the debts against vulnerable consumers that are already adversely impacted by the credit crisis.[153]

Another issue connected to this is that the services of banks are, in general, a little more unaffordable due to their being highly regulated to comply with numerous guidelines in order not to lose the deposits of customers to risky ventures. However, Fintechs do not face similar regulatory standards as conventional banks do since they do not collect and hold customers' deposits and oftentimes thrive by keeping a few brick-and-mortar offices compared to the traditional banks. Yet, even though they do not incur running expenses like the conventional banks do, there are still costs associated with their services, which enable them to keep their online platforms safe and constantly remain innovative

case,' said Assistant Attorney General Brian A. Benczkowski of the Justice Department's Criminal Division. https://www.ftc.gov/news-events/press-releases/2020/03/first-round-refunds-totaling-153-million-sent-consumers-result. For other similar cases wherein Fintechs exploited the vulnerability of consumers, see 'Cases Tagged with Fintechs' at https://www.ftc.gov/enforcement/cases-proceedings/terms/13309. Both websites accessed 26 May 2020.

149 An example is TransferWise. It renders financial services to over 7 million customers from 60 countries. But it is solely regulated by the UK Financial Conduct Authority. Except for customers residing in a few exempt countries, English law and courts entertain disputes of all other customers who have disputes with TransferWise. https://transferwise.com/terms-of-use-eea accessed 26 May 2020.

150 For a critique of this lending approach of Fintechs, see Robert Bartlett, et al, 'Consumer-Lending Discrimination in the Era of FinTech' (November 2018) https://faculty.haas.berkeley.edu/morse/research/papers/discrim.pdf accessed 25 May 2020.

151 Mugdar Variyar, et al, 'Alternative Lenders Power into Loans Overlooked by Banks,' *Economic Times* (7 October 2016) https://economictimes.indiatimes.com/small-biz/money/alternative-lenders-power-into-loans-overlooked-by-banks/articleshow/54728705.cms accessed 28 May 2020.

152 See generally, Cătălin Stanescu, *Self-Help, Private Debt Collection and the Concomitant Risks* (Springer 2015).

153 Gian Boeddu, et al, 'Protecting Financial Consumers during the COVID-19 Crisis,' *World Bank Blog* (8 May 2020) https://blogs.worldbank.org/psd/protecting-financial-consumers-during-covid-19-crisis accessed 27 May 2020.

so as to provide safe and reliable services.[154] However, the government of each country should recognize the duty to properly regulate the fees charged by Fintechs located in other jurisdictions, to their citizens so as to ensure the adequate protection of vulnerable consumers.

Part III: education and financial inclusion

The inseparability of education and financial inclusion

Some scholars have argued that a human right to credit or microcredit exists, because it could actually become the foundation on which other rights of people, especially the poor, would be achieved.[155] If poor people (a significant number of whom are vulnerable consumers)[156] acquire credit for onward investment, then they could in the long run get themselves out of poverty and be in a better position to enjoy other civil and political rights.[157] A corollary view that stems from the above line of thought and inquiry is whether there can be a right to financial inclusion, given that it has increasingly been accepted by national and international institutions like the United Nations and World Bank that owning and operating a bank account, saving and deposit facilities, and access to credit facilities on reasonable terms and conditions are the essential tools of eradicating poverty; in the same way, education, gender equality, freedom from discrimination, etc., can be recipes for human development because they unlock the dead capital in every reasonable person, especially the poor, toward improving their own lives.[158]

The argument undertaken in this chapter is not necessarily to advocate for a direct textual inclusion of the 'right to financial inclusion' into the various body of rights in the traditional instruments, but to adopt the 'functional approach'[159] to legal reasoning in inquiring whether the benefits accruing from financial inclusion are similar to those advocated for under the more traditional headings of rights, especially the right to education, which is regarded as a sure means by which an individual can empower themselves and become less susceptible to financial vulnerability. In essence, it argues that when the functional approach is applied, there is no fundamental difference in aim between the right to education

---

154 cf Ozili (n 94) 7.
155 See, generally, James Nickel, *Making Sense of Human Rights* (Oxford: Blackwell 2007).
156 Mauricio Garlado, 'Identifying Vulnerability to Poverty: A Critical Survey' (2018) 32(4) Journal of Economic Surveys, 1074–1105, 1077.
157 Richard Claude, 'The Right to Education and Human Rights Education' (2005) 2(2) Sur Rev. int. direitos human https://www.scielo.br/scielo.php?pid=S1806-64452005000100003&script=sci_arttext&tlng=en accessed 10 May 2020.
158 cf World Bank UFA 2020 (n 112).
159 See, generally, Bert van Roermund, 'Law and Functionalism: The Limited Function of Law' (2015) 4 Law and Method, 1 https://www.bjutijdschriften.nl/tijdschrift/lawandmethod/2015/04/lawandmethod-D-15-00001.pdf accessed 28 May 2020.

and the right to financial inclusion, because both rights seek to empower the individual; this should therefore underline the importance of the latter and make it an integral part of government policies.[160]

Thus, if the right to education has been well accepted as a human right, a case of functional equivalence could be made between it and financial inclusion, therefore, putting the latter on the same footing with the right to an education. The rest of the chapter shows how both rights are similar in functions, in that they assist vulnerable groups in society, such as women, minorities, and poor people to gain empowerment and possibly escape from poverty and financial vulnerability.

Basic education as human right

The right to a basic education has been widely recognized both at the national and international levels. The Universal Declaration of Human Rights, regarded as the most important and most subscribed rights instrument, states that:

(1) Everyone has the right to education. Education shall be free, at least in the elementary and fundamental stages. Elementary education shall be compulsory. Technical and professional education shall be made generally available and higher education shall be equally accessible to all on the basis of merit.
(2) Education shall be directed to the full development of the human personality and to the strengthening of respect for human rights and fundamental freedoms. It shall promote understanding, tolerance and friendship among all nations, racial or religious groups, and shall further the activities of the United Nations for the maintenance of peace.
(3) Parents have a prior right to choose the kind of education that shall be given to their children.[161]

Interestingly also, Article 13 of the International Covenant on Economic, Social, and Cultural Rights (ICESCR)[162] provides for a similar and enhanced set of rights vis-à-vis education by going beyond the basic primary education into the secondary and vocational types.[163] Hardly any modern constitution does not emphasize the importance of basic education, and each year, countries dedicate a

---

160 Gautam Kumar, 'Financial Inclusion as a Human Right, *India Fellow*,' 15 December 2018 https://www.indiafellow.org/blog/2018/12/financial-inclusion-and-human-rights/ accessed 12 May 2020.
161 Article 26 UDHR https://www.un.org/en/universal-declaration-human-rights/ accessed 12 May 2020.
162 ICESCR, available at https://www.ohchr.org/en/professionalinterest/pages/cescr.aspx accessed 12 May 2020.
163 See, generally, Fons Coomans, 'Justiciability of the Right to Education' (2009) 2 Erasmus L Rev 427.

significant portion of their resources for the education of their citizens, to among other things achieve the aim and objectives stated in the UDHR and other human rights instrument, such as the ICESCR which recommends secondary, vocational, and higher education, thus showing that the effort on education should transcend the teaching of pupils at the primary school level and progress to the education and empowerment of adults.[164]

Although ICESCR embodies rights that many developing countries still consider as nonjusticiable, the Supreme Court of India, for instance, has in at least two cases[165] upheld the right to education as a positive right. Similarly, Article 53 of the Kenyan Constitution guarantees every child the right to a free and compulsory basic education, and Section 39 of Kenya's Basic Education Act 2013 requires the government to 'ensure that children belonging to marginalized, vulnerable or disadvantaged groups are not discriminated against and prevented from pursuing and completing basic education.' It is proposed that developing countries in Asia and Africa should follow the Indian and Kenyan approaches, respectively, which treat education as a positive right.

The benefits of education and financial inclusion in the context of a credit crisis

First, education unlocks a person's hidden potentials which benefit them both in the short and long runs. In the short run, they are able to make informed and better choices from the array of options that are available to them. A careless choice due to inability to think for oneself could mar the progress of the decision maker at an early stage of life. This is especially true in the era of the Internet, which has given the freedom of self-publishing of information, some of which is fake, in order to achieve narrow interests that could damage the personal interest of an individual and their family. Thus, education helps an individual to carefully navigate through the myriad of information and become better able to make healthy choices that improve their well-being. In the long run, the aggregate of good decisions made as a result of the decision maker's education yields good results and puts them in the position of being competent participants on matters that affect them whether cultural, social, economic, and political issues; these abilities, enabled by education, make them better and productive citizens. With respect to financial inclusion in the era of the Internet, fake news, and scams,[166] a person's education helps them to protect their finances from being defrauded by

---

164 ICESCR, Article 13(2)(b) and (c).
165 See *Mohini Jain vs. State of Karnataka* [1992] 3 SCC 666; and later in *Unnikrishnan J.P. vs. State of Andhra Pradesh* [1993] 1 SCC 645.
166 NCLC, 'Consumer Concerns: Dreams Foreclosed: Saving Older Americans from Foreclosure Rescue Scams,' *Consumer Concerns* (January 2010) https://www.nclc.org/images/pdf/older_consumers/consumer_concerns/cc_dreams_foreclosed.pdf   accessed 26 May 2020.

scammers who are often posing as banks and charity organizations to obtain sensitive financial data.[167]

If use of digital finance is an integral element of financial inclusion, then it stands to reason that some education is needed for an individual to understand how to read and understand information on websites and on financial payment platforms so that they do not click on options that are detrimental to their financial interests. This is more so, considering that some Fintechs do occasionally introduce predatory practices that entrap some uneducated or absent-minded users, by presenting them with options to enter into a side agreement or perform a side transaction in the middle of a particular one, with the intention of causing them to incur unintended financial liabilities.[168] Yet, it is believed that due to little or no regulation of Fintechs, many of these predatory practices are likely to increase in the context of Covid-19, as more companies will become desperate about their cash flows and engage in more deceptive practices against financial consumers.[169] Education, whether the more basic, general type or bespoke consumer education, has become highly relevant these days as the sure way to protect consumers from the numerous deceptive practices seeking to make them poorer.[170]

Second, and stemming partially from the above point, education, especially in a democracy, tries to ensure that an individual exercising their rights to vote, presumably chooses the most competent candidate who can champion sustainable credit and consumer law reforms that will benefit consumers. This is particularly important given that the choice of bad leaders will mostly like lead to wrong national choices that eventually cause retrogression in society, if not globally. It is often said, for instance, that one of the major problems African countries suffer is bad leadership, and there is a compelling correlation between the general level of education and awareness in the African society and the types of leaders that are elected, who often do not appreciate the connection between adequate consumer protection and the general progress in society.[171]

167 Philip Seargeant and Caroline Tagg, 'Fake News: The Solution Is Education, Not Regulation,' *Times Higher Education* (29 December 2016) https://www.timeshighereducation.com/blog/fake-news-solution-education-not-regulation accessed 12 May 2020.
168 Ted Knutson, 'Small Businesses Harmed by Fintech Lenders, Entrepreneur Advocates Warn Congress,' *Forbes* (13 February 2019) https://www.forbes.com/sites/tedknutson/2019/02/13/small-businesses-harmed-by-online-lenders-entrepreneur-advocates-warn-congress/#57dfd2526dba accessed 12 May 2020.
169 cf Bartlett, et al, (n 150).
170 Vincent DiLorenzo, 'Fintech Lending: A Study of Expectations Versus Market Outcomes' (2018) https://ssrn.com/abstract=3247112; Fintech Lending Risks and Benefits, availabe at https://sites.duke.edu/thefinregblog/2018/11/14/fintech-lending-risks-and-benefits/ accessed 10 May 2020.
171 Sam Adeyemi, 'Africa Doesn't Need Charity, It Needs Good Leadership,' *World Economic Forum* (4 May 2017) https://www.weforum.org/agenda/2017/05/africa-doesn-t-need-charity-it-needs-good-leadership/ accessed 19 May 2020.

Third, education, depending largely on the level of it, improves the mind and equips the recipient with logical reasoning, practical skills, and the ability to make good judgments based on facts. Granted that a basic education may not be adequate to unlock all of a person's abilities, it is nonetheless better than no education at all. Thus, an educated person can easily recognize economic opportunities and know when they are being abused and financially excluded by government policies. In that case, they will know how or where to seek solutions and how to reach out to consumer protection bodies or legal aid groups, as opposed to rationalizing the harmful events on superstition and being totally unable to help themselves toward finding viable solutions to their problems. Even though it may not be said that lack of education directly causes poverty, there is an overwhelming correlation between being uneducated and financially vulnerable[172] and being an easy target of financial exploitation and exclusion without any meaningful counter-resistance.

Notwithstanding the important benefits education confers on a recipient and how it improves both the recipient and their society, it is still generally argued in some countries or by some scholars not to be made a positive right due to lack of affordability, in that a positive right, unlike a negative right, requires the government to invest resources toward the realization of that right – in this case, the basic education of a citizen. Many people contend that regardless of its unarguable benefits, the enormous amount of resources required is highly burdensome on taxpayers; depending on how economically stable a society is, this could be a herculean task to achieve. This appears to be the same type of argument against the proposal to regard financial inclusion as a positive right. However, an educated citizenry would constitute a high-quality labor force with more innovative ideas that can impact on society in many positive ways.

Part IV: conclusion

Credit has always been a crucial topic for market systems, and since the 2008 financial crisis, the global economy has been struggling to grapple with the best methods to increase access to it without causing untold hardships for consumers. The rules that govern credit use in large part are influenced by the interests of financial institutions that lobby lawmakers to pass laws that accentuate their interests. They are also equipped to find any loopholes in the law and possess enough resources to navigate safely away from legal restrictions that inure to the

172 Quacquarelli Symonds, 'What Effect Does Education Level Have on Wealth?' 'According to Eurostat data, the average salary for those with a high level of education (at least one year of tertiary education) in the EU was approximately 50% higher than those with a medium level of education (secondary/high-school), and a humongous 70% higher than those with only a low level of education (anything below secondary/high-school).' Studies on this topic conducted by the International Labor Organization in developing countries showed similar results. https://www.qs.com/what-effect-does-education-level-have-on-wealth/ accessed 27 May 2020. Also, cf Garlado (n 156) 1077.

benefits of consumers. The Covid-19 pandemic, which satisfies the features of a credit crisis, will cause banks to be reluctant in lending to consumers or will cause them to lend with unfavorable conditions. Each country will need to fathom to what extent interest rate capping on loans, especially consumer loans, will yield a balance of interests between financial institutions and vulnerable consumers.

It is interesting that many countries have already amended their insolvency legislation to disable or amend provisions on minimum debt value for statutory demand, grace period for repayment, and wrongful trading of directors. These amendments do not affect provisions of law that border on breach of fiduciary duties, such as fraudulent trading. This means that directors who embezzle corporate assets will still remain criminally liable. It is important that these amendments which tilt toward corporate rescue are undertaken so that courts will not be flooded with applications for insolvent liquidations of individuals and companies. In any case, informal debt restructuring mechanisms, for instance, the 'London Approach'[173] and other informal types, would likely be frequently utilized.

Finally, the use of digital finance is becoming mainstream and its popularity will increase as banks and financial institutions focus more on digital banking both as a partial solution to prevent wide spread of Covid-19 and to reduce operation costs by closing down some of their brick-and-mortar branches. Yet, many financial consumers, especially in developing countries, are not competent to use digital financial services and will become more susceptible to online fraud and data theft.[174] In the short term, this calls for consumer protection regulators to undertake an increased level of education for financial consumers tailored toward empowering them on how to safely use digital finance; for a long-term solution, the governments of countries must invest more in educating their citizens as a sustainable and preventive solution to being vulnerable to Internet fraud.

Also, if more people learn to safely use digital finance, it will lead to a more encompassing financial inclusion, which is noted to be an integral element in the cure of poverty. These aspirations cannot be possibly realized if a significant number of a country's citizens are unable to read and write. The chapter concludes with the idea that an increased level of formal education as envisaged by the UDHR and ICESCR treaties is the sustainable method of enhancing financial inclusion and curing poverty, given that an educated person is better able to safely use digital finance.

---

173 London Approach, https://www.bankofengland.co.uk/-/media/boe/files/quarterly-bulletin/ 1993/the-london-approach.pdf?la=en&hash=CDA5C88581160C72F37C5B6BC05FA303AA 400B58 accessed 30 May 2020.

174 cf Smith (n 23).

5 The payments revolution
Toward financial exclusion or inclusion?

Sabrina Rochemont[*]

Introduction

Payments used to be relatively straightforward: cash and cheques dominated daily transactions; bank accounts provided for more convenience through debit or credit cards and were a key access point to other financial services, such as savings and credit.[1]

In 2015, the World Economic Forum introduced the concept of a "fourth industrial revolution" toward a digital economy. Since then, the dynamics of the payments ecosystem have been confirming the trend, illustrating the pace of disruption for all stakeholders, in particular for consumers.

The digital revolution has already disrupted the status quo, with new players driving a "digital first" approach. Contactless payments have displaced cash for low-value transactions. Mobile network operators such as the MTN group[2] acquire bank licences; e-commerce platforms such as Alibaba[3] launch their own payment apps; and some businesses such as sports venues[4] prepare to accept cryptocurrencies.

This revolution benefits developing regions that have not yet established ubiquitous banking infrastructures and now embrace the powers of new technology to grant access to financial services. Simultaneously, developed countries

---

[*] Member of the Cashless Society Working Party, June 2020.

1 'Cards in the evolving European payments landscape,' Payments Europe, 2019, https://www.paymentseurope.eu/wp-content/uploads/2019/12/Payments-Europe-Report_Cards-in-the-evolving-European-payments-landscape.pdf accessed 15 April 2020.

2 Akwagyiram A., 'Nigeria's Central Bank Awards Financial Services Licence to MTN Subsidiary' *Reuters* (30 July 2019) https://af.reuters.com/article/investingNews/idAFKCN1UP0LR-OZABS accessed 15 April 2020.

3 'Alipay' https://intl.alipay.com/ accessed 15 April 2020.

4 'Watford Will Now Accept Bitcoin for Merchandise Purchases | Watford Observer' https://www.watfordobserver.co.uk/sport/17897688.watford-will-now-accept-bitcoin-merchandise-purchases/ accessed 15 April 2020.

have gradually evolved toward less-cash economies, with a diminishing role for cash in daily transactions.[5]

The Cashless Society Working Party,[6] hosted by the Institute and Faculty of Actuaries, has been researching a cashless society and de-cashing trends on a global basis since 2017,[7] with multiple findings being relevant to the topic of financial inclusion, or fair and non-discriminatory access to financial services. This chapter aims to communicate relevant findings from the Working Party: these resulted from monitoring social media and analysing international public data and some specialised reports on the topics of a cashless society and payment technologies. As payment themes and trends are global, this contribution draws from relevant international examples in both developing and developed regions.

This chapter will first remind readers about the functions of money; review the status of cash; and discuss new alternatives to cash that are on offer for consumers' convenience, such as digital wallets, mobile money, credits and local currencies, and cryptocurrencies. It also introduces the prospect of central bank digital currencies and the potential impacts on financial inclusion. It will then explore the reasons for the divisive nature of a cashless society amongst consumers. The chapter will finally draw some lessons for the fair and non-discriminatory access to financial services in developed countries.

Innovations in the payment ecosystem

The provision of money and means of payment used to be limited to cash, deposit, and checking accounts, the latter associated with cheques and payment (debit and credit) cards. However, players other than central and commercial banks have entered the established payments market with innovative instruments that have challenged the traditional definition of money, its functions, and intermediation: technology firms such as Google, Apple, Facebook, and Amazon now compete with commercial banks for the financial relationship with consumers.[8] Other innovators, such as bitcoin, also claim to be developing money, yet keep away from regulatory controls. Can cryptocurrencies qualify as money?

In order to protect consumers, legislators must comprehend the functions of money and the complexities of the emerging ecosystem.

5 Bank of England, 'Future of Finance: Review on the Outlook for the UK Financial System' 2019, pp 25–27 https://www.bankofengland.co.uk/-/media/boe/files/report/2019/future-of-finance-report.pdf?la=en&hash=59CEFAEF01C71AA551E7182262E933A699E952FC.
6 'A Cashless Society Working Party,' Institute and Faculty of Actuaries' 2017–2020 https://www.actuaries.org.uk/practice-areas/finance-and-investment/finance-and-investment-research-working-parties/cashless-society-working-party accessed 15 April 2020.
7 '*A Cashless Society: Benefits, Risks, and Issues - Abstract of the London Discussion* | British Actuarial Journal, Cambridge University Press, Volume 23 2018 e28 DOI:https://doi.org/10.1017/S1357321718000223.
8 Bank of England, 'Future of Finance: Review on the Outlook for the UK Financial System' 2019, p28 https://www.bankofengland.co.uk/-/media/boe/files/report/2019/future-of-finance-report.pdf?la=en&hash=59CEFAEF01C71AA551E7182262E933A699E952FC.

What is money?

Although most people use money on a day-to-day basis for the purchase of goods and services, the definition of money is abstract. Money is usually defined through its functions:[9]

- As a unit of account, money provides a common standard to measure the total volume of production, income, savings, wealth, etc.
- As a medium of exchange, money provides a common medium for the exchange of goods and services, which would otherwise have taken place with barter.
- As a store of value, money allows for wealth to be stored and for savings to occur.

As a result of these functionalities, a clear characteristic of whatever constitutes "money" requires it to be sufficiently acceptable and trusted.

Examples of money include notes and coins, fiat currency (i.e., legal tender whose value is backed by the government), and electronic money, which is the focus of payments innovation.

The Bank of England[10] has defined electronic money as cashless alternatives to physical notes and coins and calls out wrappers, mobile money, credits, and local currencies, as well as digital currencies. Each cashless means of payment has its own individual level of security, user protection, settlement time, ease of use, and associated costs and fees.

This section will explore changes in the use of cash, each cashless category, and implications for vulnerable consumers. In addition, it will introduce the potential for central bank digital currencies as a future innovation to influence the access of vulnerable consumers to financial services.

Cash, payment cards, and contactless payments

In developed countries, commercial bank accounts are the established means for consumers to store deposits, send and receive payments, and withdraw cash. Checking accounts function with cheque books and debit cards, now usually equipped with contactless technology.

Contactless card technology allows a consumer to present the card to a merchant terminal and pay without inserting the card or entering the PIN. The technology delivers major benefits in public transport systems, with numerous bus operators such as Lothian buses in Scotland[11] and

---

9 Tucker IB, *Survey of Economics* (9th edn, Cengage Learning 2015), pp399–400.

10 Bank of England, *'Quarterly Bulletin'* 2014 Q3 Volume 54 No 3 pp262–265. https://www.bankofengland.co.uk/-/media/boe/files/quarterly-bulletin/2014/quarterly-bulletin-2014-q3.pdf accessed 15 April 2020.

11 Rochemont S., 'A Cashless Society in 2019,' Institute and Faculty of Actuaries, 2020, p20 https://www.actuaries.org.uk/documents/cashless-society-2019.

Arriva buses[12] throughout the UK implementing contactless payments; some transporters become cashless through banning cash payments to save ticket-issuing time and therefore improve timetable reliability. However, cashless transport systems can be inconvenient to foreign visitors, who may not have access to a local bank account. Use of foreign contactless cards can result in disproportionate transaction and foreign-exchange fees,[13] as some banks charge minimum fees per foreign transaction.

Major public transport systems such as London's Oyster card enable consumers to top up with cash at underground stations. However, there is a risk that vulnerable groups would be unable to access other public transport systems if they ban cash, yet offer no local facilities at bus stops to top up or buy credits. Nevertheless, many vulnerable travellers would typically benefit from free transport passes or other concessions from the government or welfare organisations. These concessions may be limited in space, leading users to be confined to a territory.

The rise of contactless payments has led to major changes in the use of cash. Cash had been the traditional means of payment for low-value transactions. Contactless payments have challenged the market share of cash in countries such as France, the UK, and Sweden, due to their convenience: as these reduce friction in commercial transactions, both consumers and retailers save time. They can have unintended effects: the ease and speed of contactless transactions can cause issues with controlling household budgets and therefore can affect more vulnerable groups disproportionately, as the process removes the pain of consciously and physically parting with cash, a key self-control mechanism.[14]

The gradual shift away from cash to electronic payments implies an increasing reliance on private payment systems. Some high-impact technology incidents in 2018, such as those relating to the TSB bank in the UK and the VISA payments network in northern Europe, affected the availability of payment systems on a large scale and therefore impacted on consumers' ability to access their deposits.[15] These have focused the minds of regulators, while public inquiries were raised relating to the spate of incidents, in particular in the UK.

The situation presents economic challenges that adversely impact the cost of access to payments. Cash is inclusive, as its use is free to consumers at the point

12 mbH HI, 'Arriva to Launch Contactless Payments on Its Services in Derby' https://www.arrivabus.co.uk/midlands/latest/arriva-to-launch-contactless-payments-on-its-services-in-derby/ accessed 15 April 2020.
13 Jones R. and others, 'Holiday Money: How to Find the Best Cards and Currency Rates | Money | The Guardian' https://www.theguardian.com/money/2018/jun/23/holiday-money-best-cards-currency-rates-bank-charges-cash accessed 15 April 2020.
14 'Pain of Paying' Behavioraleconomics.com https://www.behavioraleconomics.com/resources/mini-encyclopedia-of-be/pain-of-paying/ accessed 15 April 2020.
15 Rochemont S., 'A Cashless Society in 2018,' Institute and Faculty of Actuaries, 2019, p18 https://www.actuaries.org.uk/documents/cashless-society-2018-cashless-world-motion-review.

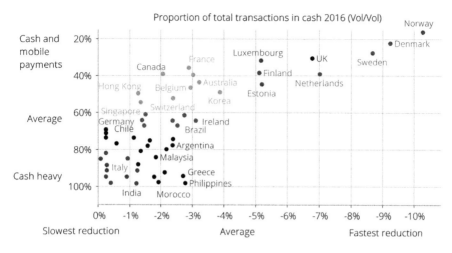

Figure 5.1 Proportion of total transactions in cash 2016, Future Of Finance © 2019 Bank of England.

of use and is financed as a public good, whereas private operators provide a commercial service for profit. Each transaction carries fees that are paid either directly by the consumer, or indirectly through business costs. An increase in noncash transactions means an erosion of the consumer's wallet if businesses are allowed to charge consumers transaction fees for using debit or credit cards. These fees have been a barrier to the growth of electronic transactions to such a degree that developing countries such as India[16,17] have lifted system fees, or subsidised them in order to achieve their strategic objectives: transaction fees disproportionally affect populations targeted by financial inclusion programmes. In Asia and Oceania, countries such as Australia have been investing in national payment platforms to empower competition and therefore decrease these costs.

The second economic impact from the reduction of the use of cash is the viability of cash machines, that directly impacts their availability to consumers. Wholesale distribution of cash involves a complex supply chain with high fixed costs and a transaction-based income.[18] The year-on-year reduction in withdrawals has been jeopardising the equilibrium of the ecosystem in developed countries. The situation is compounded by the loss of bank branches that have

16 Rochemont S., 'A Cashless Society in 2018,' Institute and Faculty of Actuaries, 2019, pp41–48 https://www.actuaries.org.uk/documents/cashless-society-2018-cashless-world-motion-review.
17 Rochemont S., 'A Cashless Society in 2019,' Institute and Faculty of Actuaries, 2020, p25 https://www.actuaries.org.uk/documents/cashless-society-2019.
18 'Access to Cash' (6 June 2019) https://www.psr.org.uk/psr-focus/access-to-cash accessed 15 April 2020.

also become unviable as banking has become digital. As a result, two phenomena have appeared in the UK: an increasing proportion of cash machines (ATMs) now charge consumers for each withdrawal. In addition, unviable ATMs and branches have been decommissioned.[19] Charging consumers every time they withdraw cash disproportionally impacts vulnerable groups, the very ones who are most likely to make frequent small withdrawals to manage their budget.

The issue of disappearing ATMs and bank branches has received increasing public attention and led to comprehensive reviews and surveys. In the UK, the Access to Cash Review[20] concluded that the most vulnerable groups of society use cash the most and therefore rely on the cash infrastructure. Cost of entry is a barrier to accessing digital services, which may also not be accessible to those with physical or mental health issues, and could be impractical or unsafe for people who rely on others to make their purchases.

The issue of availability of cash accelerated from 2018 to 2020, despite several central banks[21] reiterating that they are committed to issuing cash. The 2020 Covid-19 pandemic risks exacerbating the situation as retailers prefer the use of contactless payments, due to fears that coins and notes can transmit the virus. There is, however, limited evidence to support the claim that cards are safer,[22] amidst suspicion that businesses are leveraging the situation to discourage the use of cash for operational advantage.

In this section, we have explained how contactless card payments have eroded the role of cash for low-value transactions, with economic consequences for the viability of cash machines, as well as the cost of transactions directly impacting on the inclusiveness of payments.

The next sections will focus on cashless alternatives.

Cashless alternatives: wrappers

The Bank of England[23] describes the first category of cashless alternatives as 'wrapper' services that improve the user interface and accessibility of existing

19 Rochemont S., 'A Cashless Society in 2018,' Institute and Faculty of Actuaries, 2019, pp54–63 https://www.actuaries.org.uk/documents/cashless-society-2018-cashless-world-motion-review.

20 Access to Cash Review, 'Final report,' 2019, pp44–52 https://www.accesstocash.org.uk/ accessed 15 April 2020.

21 'Bank of England Welcomes Access to Cash Review | Bank of England' https://www.bankofengland.co.uk/news/2019/march/boe-welcomes-access-to-cash-review   accessed 15 April 2020.

22 Auer R. and others, 'Covid-19, cash, and the future of payments,' Bank for International Settlements Bulletin No 3, 03 April 2020 https://www.bis.org/publ/bisbull03.htm accessed 15 April 2020.

23 Bank of England, '*Quarterly Bulletin*' 2014 Q3 Volume 54 No 3 pp262–265 https://www.bankofengland.co.uk/-/media/boe/files/quarterly-bulletin/2014/quarterly-bulletin-2014-q3.pdf accessed 15 April 2020.

payment systems. Examples are digital wallets, such as Google Wallet or Apple Pay, which link consumers' bank and technology accounts, mobile phone numbers, and email addresses. In the Chinese AliPay and WeChat Pay solutions, consumers store a balance, which is linked to a bank account. These innovations therefore represent neither a new currency nor a new core payments system. Wrappers operate amidst complex layers of integration with nonfinancial businesses, such as social networks.[24]

Consumers make use of digital wallets through mobile applications and at points-of-sale with the Near Field Communication (NFC) technology, as well as online through Internet browsers. The use of these wrappers is commonly referred to as 'mobile payments,' which should not be confused with 'mobile money,' a different concept that is explored in the next section.

Convenience attracts consumers to such wrappers: the level of integration with social media, e-commerce, or technology platforms aims to remove the friction between the moment a consumer selects a product or service for sale, its purchase, and then its consumption. The ease of purchase can induce consumers into overspending through high volumes of low-value transactions and subscriptions to services that may not be deactivated once the consumer no longer needs them. Fast-tracked "one-click" systems, where consumers never log out of their wallets, may also be too fast and seamless for consumers with cognitive deficiencies to recognise that they have entered a commercial contract.

These digital wallets offer security elements to consumers, as sellers receive a token from the platform, instead of sharing users' bank account or payment card details. Buyers also have recourse against the seller through the wallet in the event of issues with the products, services, or delivery. Combined with ratings to measure each seller's reputation, these increasingly integrated e-commerce platforms appear to supply a consumer-focused environment.

However, some risks are associated with the type, size, and economic power of the platforms. An open market is in the interest of consumers, as healthy competition should lead to lower prices and better products and services. The commercial interest of the platforms that operate wallets is to increase market share away from the incumbents' more expensive services. Consumers should benefit from these dynamics,[25] unless anti-competitive practices arise: the power of retail and social media through their extensive consumer base may lead to the creation of closed-loop systems that exclude other payments from being accepted. There is a concern that consumers could become entirely tied to a

24 Bank of England, 'Future of Finance: Review on the Outlook for the UK Financial System' 2019, p28 https://www.bankofengland.co.uk/-/media/boe/files/report/2019/future-of-finance-report.pdf?la=en&hash=59CEFAEF01C71AA551E7182262E933A699E952FC.

25 Bank of England, 'Future of Finance: Review on the Outlook for the UK Financial System' 2019, p107 https://www.bankofengland.co.uk/-/media/boe/files/report/2019/future-of-finance-report.pdf?la=en&hash=59CEFAEF01C71AA551E7182262E933A699E952FC.

platform and may eventually lose choice of payment. This specific aspect led European regulators to open antitrust investigations against technology platforms in 2019,[26] in response to some practices and the prospect of a social media platform creating its own currency.[27]

Another risk derives from the vertical integration of consumers' experience: these platforms collate all browsing, consumption, and financial data, potentially leading to biases and unfairness if the same operator also seeks to upsell financial services such as credit or insurance to these consumers.

Some e-commerce platforms have developed payment systems ahead of financial services becoming available from other parts of the local ecosystem. An example is Indonesia, where ride-hailing firm Grab[28] had to create its own payment platform in order to boost its nonfinancial business. Such initiatives fast-track economic development. However, nonfinancial new entrants may not have the expertise to handle risks and operational issues associated with payments. As a result, consumer payment details and transaction data may be at increased risk of fraud or loss in the event of platform collapse. Indonesia's central bank suspended Grab's payment platform. Grab then invested in an established local digital payment platform.

In spite of the proposed benefits, the adoption of such wrappers has been slower to materialise than the market had predicted. Evidence from recent global surveys[29] points to levels of distrust toward social media and Internet companies, with wide regional variations: consumers in Western economies are generally hesitant when it comes to these businesses, with deteriorating levels of trust from 2017 to 2019. Other studies that have sought to analyse the underlying reasons in Finland[30] and Malaysia[31] identify security concerns as a primary inhibiting factor to adopting the technology. According to both studies, data privacy (i.e., the sharing of sensitive information with third

26 Rochemont S., 'A Cashless Society in 2019,' Institute and Faculty of Actuaries, 2020, p26 https://www.actuaries.org.uk/documents/cashless-society-2019.

27 Schroeder S., 'Facebook announces Libra cryptocurrency with a massive list of partners [WWW Document].' Mashable. 2019 https://mashable.com/article/facebook-libra/ accessed 15 April 2020.

28 'Grab Expands into Indonesia E-Payments, Taking Battle to Go-Jek - Nikkei Asian Review,' 2019 https://asia.nikkei.com/Business/Companies/Grab-expands-into-Indonesia-e-payments-taking-battle-to-Go-Jek accessed 15 April 2020.

29 '2019 CIGI-Ipsos Global Survey on Internet Security and Trust' (*Centre for International Governance Innovation*) 2019 https://www.cigionline.org/internet-survey-2019 accessed 15 April 2020.

30 Ates G., 'What are the reasons for not adopting mobile payments?' Master's Thesis, International Business Management with Fintech focus, Arcada, 2019, pp43–45 https://www.theseus.fi/handle/10024/261125.

31 Rahman M. and others, 'Is Malaysia ready to go cashless?' Kodisa International Conference ICBE 2019, pp141–148 http://www.supermanlee.com/kodisa2019/KODISA.ICBE2019_Proceedings.pdf.

	Ant Financial	Tencent	Google	Facebook	Amazon	Apple	PayPal
Type of firm	Online retail	Tech	Tech	Social media	Online retail	Tech	Electronic payments
Payment solutions	Alipay	WeChat Pay (previously Tenpay)	Google Pay (previously Google Checkout, Android Pay, Tez (India))	Facebook Messenger Payments and Whatsapp Pay (India)	Amazon Pay	Apple Pay	PayPal, Venmo, Braintree, Xoom
Launched	2004	2005	2011	2015	2007	2014	1999
Estimated number of users (data cannot directly be compared)	1 billion users[a]	1 billion users (of WeChat)[b]	25 million users[c]	2.4 billion active Facebook users[d] 210 million active Whatsapp India users[e]	33 million+ made a purchase via a "Pay with Amazon" button[f]	383 million users[g]	250 million users[h]
How it works	Balance stored in a digital wallet linked to a bank account or card. QR codes initiate payments	Balance stored in a digital wallet linked to a bank account or card	Payment cards linked to and authenticated by mobile phone; Credit transfers	Debit cards linked to Facebook Messenger	Embeds payment cards; credit transfers; direct debits; e-money online	Payment cards linked to and authenticated by mobile phone	E-money account can be funded through cards, credit transfers, and direct debits

a   See intl.alipay.com/.
b   See www.statista.com/statistics/255778/number-of-active-wechat-messenger-accounts/.
c   See economictimes.indiatimes.com/small-biz/startups/newsbuzz/google-pay-now-has-25m-monthly-active-users/articleshow/65865946.cms.
d   See www.statista.com/statistics/264810/number-of-monthly-active-facebook-users-worldwide/.
e   See www.ft.com/content/e045cdd2-0503-11e9-99df-6183d3002ee1.
f   See www.forbes.com/sites/greatspeculations/2017/02/14/heres-how-amazon-payments-can-drive-profitability-for-the-company/#63fc70a4d228.
g   See www.statista.com/statistics/911914/number-apple-pay-users/.
h   See www.paypal.com/uk/webapps/mpp/personal.

Figure 5.2 Overview of selected payment providers, Future of Finance © 2019 Bank of England.

parties) is related to trust and is another key barrier to shifting to this type of cashless payment.

Surveys on the topic of mobile payments typically exclude the perception and readiness of consumer groups that may not be the core commercial targets for these services: access to the Internet or a smartphone with a data package is a prerequisite to using digital wallets. Such access is also required to sign up to competitive offers from various providers. Vulnerable consumers who are unable to purchase, lease, or operate an Internet device are locked out from digital services that may be of benefit and improve their access to financial and non-financial services; they may instead suffer from a "poverty premium,"[32] a term that indicates that the poor pay more for essential goods and services than other groups in society. In this context, digital and financial exclusion may exacerbate the poverty premium.

An additional functionality within these digital wallets is the use of quick response (QR) codes for peer-to-peer payments. QR codes[33] have been used for over two decades in manufacturing industries and supply chains. Their use for payments is revolutionary, due to the lack of requirement for a business or retailer to invest in acquiring merchant networks with the associated purchase of point-of-sale equipment: consumers' smartphones are sufficient to enable a transaction on a peer-to-peer basis. As a result, these are beneficial to support financial inclusion of micro, mobile businesses, and for vulnerable individuals to receive money without bearing the security risks of cash. Trials in Scandinavia and the UK have equipped the homeless with a QR code on a printed card, linking the code to an individual bank account, so that anonymous donors can transfer money securely through their own digital wallet. However, beneficiaries might rely on accessing their account through intermediaries such as charities or partner banks. QR codes also assume access to a suitable smartphone and access to a telecom network to manage accounts and funds. If not available, this process risks impacting negatively on individual freedom and risks introducing financial abuse through intermediaries. QR codes also require a level of learning for usage, which may exclude the elder generation, or those with cognitive impairments, from donating safely while using the technology.

Central banks of countries with a low penetration of banking services have been embracing the potential for QR codes to equip consumers with a means of sending peer-to-peer payments, hence saving financial transaction fees that are one of the causes for poorer consumers to use cash instead of digital solutions in their countries. Such national QR code wrapper solutions have been implemented in a number of Southeast Asian countries,[34] eventually connecting with each other to enable more efficient cross-border payments. Recent evidence

---

32 Davies S. and others, 'The Poverty Premium' University of Bristol, http://www.bris.ac.uk/media-library/sites/geography/pfrc/pfrc1614-poverty-premium-key-findings.pdf, accessed 15 April 2020.

33 Chan J., 'The Rise and Rise of Quick Response Codes,' Institute and Faculty of Actuaries, 2019, pp9–16 https://www.actuaries.org.uk/documents/addendum-cashless-society-benefits-risks-and-issues.

34 Rochemont S., 'A Cashless Society in 2018,' Institute and Faculty of Actuaries, 2019, p17 https://www.actuaries.org.uk/documents/cashless-society-2018-cashless-world-motion-review.

indicates a rising trend of QR code deployment in African countries, such as Ghana[35] and Rwanda.[36]

However, QR codes present security risks[37] that are intrinsic to the nature of the code: a human eye cannot read the data within the code to validate its content; hence, it is possible the code contains instructions that do not match the user's intent or contains some additional code with fraudulent instructions. This vulnerability applies beyond payments, as a code within marketing or other material may also direct the consumer to unwanted content, or launch fraudulent programmes. Automated attacks have led a major Japanese retailer to cancel its QR code deployment in 2019,[38] due to programmes that defrauded funds from consumers' bank accounts.

This security issue is widely acknowledged as a rising concern that is related to the growing financial use of QR codes: the revision of the QR code ISO/IEC standard 18004:2015 to include financial application may be a way forward within the context of financial institutions aligning to the ISO 20022 universal financial industry message scheme.

In this section, we have introduced the concepts and applications of digital wallets and mobile payments. Despite their convenience, we have also indicated the risks that excessively powerful market players may lock consumers into their ecosystem with monopolistic behaviours; conversely, digital exclusion risks locking vulnerable consumers out of services that may benefit their welfare.

Cashless alternatives: mobile money

The previous section detailed mobile payments that assume consumers have access to a bank account, the prevailing scenario in developed countries.

Developing countries with high cash use tend to lack a banking infrastructure and to be associated with poverty and high levels of corruption. The banking infrastructure may only be partially developed or partially accessible. Branches may only be available in capital cities, and cash machines may be scarce as the

35 Entsie B., 'Ghana Adopts New Universal QR Code for Digital Payments, Here's How It Works [ARTICLE] - Pulse Ghana,' 11 March 2020 https://www.pulse.com.gh/bi/ strategy/ghana-adopts-new-universal-qr-code-for-digital-payments-heres-how-it-works/ zyz2w16 accessed 15 April 2020.

36 National Bank of Rwanda, 'Rwanda Payment System Strategy – towards a cashless Rwanda 2018-24,' 2018 https://www.bnr.rw/payment-systems/policies/?tx_bnrdocumentmanager_ frontend%5Bdocument%5D=209&tx_bnrdocumentmanager_frontend%5Baction%5D= download&tx_bnrdocumentmanager_frontend%5Bcontroller%5D=Document&cHash= 99f1bb2e46865242a30cbe8df8127020.

37 Chan J., 'The Rise and Rise of Quick Response Codes,' Institute and Faculty of Actuaries, 2019, p22 https://www.actuaries.org.uk/documents/addendum-cashless-society-benefits-risks-and- issues.

38 Liptak A., '7-Eleven Japan Shut down Its Mobile Payment App after Hackers Stole $500,000 from Users - The Verge' https://www.theverge.com/2019/7/6/20684386/7-eleven-japan- shut-mobile-payments-app-7pay-security-flaw-cybersecurity accessed 15 April 2020.

supply chain may not reach rural areas due to distance, security, and terrain. This weakness in the financial infrastructure has resulted in the demand for payment systems being unmet, a factor against economic development and individual welfare, as financial inclusion starts with payments.[39]

When banks are available, consumers face other barriers to opening bank accounts: Know Your Customer (KYC) and Anti-Money Laundering (AML) regulations require verification of identity, address, and the source of funds. In Africa, some countries do not have national identification schemes or other documentation to enable opening bank accounts. In addition, rural workers' earnings are seasonal and unreliable, making people hesitant to pay for financial services, and banks are reluctant to lend to risky consumers with no credit history. Furthermore, gender gaps[40] are associated with financial exclusion: the head of the family would control the household finances, thereby preventing access by family members, and depriving them from the prospect of building an independent financial record. Refugees also find themselves excluded from financial services in all regions[41] with consequences for the safety of their cash and their inability to receive support from friends and families.

In 2017, 1.7 billion people were unbanked, of which two-thirds had access to a mobile phone.[42]

Mobile money emerged as a solution in 2007 through the launch of M-Pesa in Kenya by mobile network operator (MNO) Safaricom: it is a new payment system, with money stored on a smart card or a system provider's books, but which continues to use national currencies. M-Pesa has since become a model for other countries that have derived initiatives from the success story of M-Pesa.[43]

The established network of Safaricom's airtime agents in the community has been the core resource to develop the relationship from the provision of telecommunications into financial services: consumers complete identification checks with a local agent, register a SIM card,[44] and receive a PIN number to complete the registration on their phone. This may be a 2G phone or a smartphone, as

39 Bank for International Settlements and others, 'Payment Aspects of Financial Inclusion in the Fintech Era,' p2 https://www.bis.org/cpmi/publ/d191.htm accessed 15 April 2020.
40 Osei-Tutu F. and Weill L., 'Sex, language and financial inclusion,' BOFIT Discussion Papers, Bank of Finland Institute for Economies in Transition, 2020 https://helda.helsinki.fi/bof/bitstream/handle/123456789/16993/dp0920.pdf;jsessionid=95C26671A5D0DE36D003AF3FE0491295?sequence=1.
41 Katholische Universität Eichstätt-Ingolstadt 'Internationale Studie Untersucht Integration von Flüchtlingen Im Finanzsystem,' IDW Online 28 May 2019 https://idw-online.de/en/news?print=1&id=716617 accessed 15 April 2020.
42 World Bank, 'Global Findex,' 2017 https://globalfindex.worldbank.org/ accessed 15 April 2020.
43 GSMA, 'What Makes a Successful Mobile Money Implementation? Learnings from M-PESA in Kenya and Tanzania | Mobile for Development,' 2009 https://www.gsma.com/mobilefordevelopment/resources/what-makes-a-successful-mobile-money-implementation-learnings-from-m-pesa-in-kenya-and-tanzania/ accessed 15 April 2020.
44 Safaricom, 'How to Register for M-PESA' https://www.safaricom.co.ke/personal/m-pesa/getting-started/register-for-m-pesa accessed 15 April 2020.

the service uses basic short message service (SMS) technology [other countries use the unstructured supplementary service data (USSD) standard] to send and receive money to phone numbers,[45] and other functionalities such as checking balances. The mobile (smartphone) application offers further services on smartphones such as bill management and overdraft facilities.

As a result, MNO consumers have been able to transact money between individuals and to pay for goods and services without requiring a bank account. The value of mobile commerce transactions in Kenya passed the KSh1 trillion ($10 billion) mark for the first time in the first quarter of 2018. The service now counts in excess of 30 million users in Kenya, has expanded to neighbouring countries, and has inspired new operators in Africa and Asia.[46,47] MNOs continue to acquire payment licences to meet the local regulatory requirements, with Ghana, Mauritius, and Nigeria being notable examples of countries in the process of modernising their regulatory frameworks to enable new business models.

In the case of M-Pesa, the funds received by Safaricom are deposited in several commercial banks, which are prudentially regulated in Kenya.[48] In addition, the funds are held by a trust and are therefore out of reach from Safaricom, which cannot access or use these, so this differentiates Safaricom from a bank. In the unfortunate event of Safaricom going bankrupt, the creditors of Safaricom would not have access to the M-Pesa funds. This is a requirement from the Central Bank of Kenya, which oversees M-Pesa. The funds remain at all times the property of M-Pesa users.

M-Pesa continues to develop its e-commerce ecosystem and has been celebrated internationally as a world-changing[49] innovation, with associated impacts on economic well-being and welfare: the Kenyan and Indian governments have been able to deliver welfare payments directly to recipients who previously had no bank account, such as spouses and vulnerable adults in precarious situations (e.g., retired farmers).

45 Hanouch M., 'What Is USSD & Why Does It Matter for Mobile Financial Services?' CGAP, 17 February 2015 https://www.cgap.org/blog/what-ussd-why-does-it-matter-mobile-financial-services accessed 15 April 2020.

46 Rochemont S., 'A Cashless Society in 2018,' Institute and Faculty of Actuaries, 2019, p17 https://www.actuaries.org.uk/documents/cashless-society-2018-cashless-world-motion-review.

47 Rochemont S., 'A Cashless Society in 2019,' Institute and Faculty of Actuaries, 2020, pp28–34, https://www.actuaries.org.uk/documents/cashless-society-2019.

48 Achord S. and others, 'A Cashless Society: Benefits, Risks and Issues (Interim Paper),' Institute and Faculty of Actuaries, 2017, pp40–42 https://www.actuaries.org.uk/documents/cashless-society-benefits-risks-and-issues.

49 'M-Pesa Puts Safaricom on Fortune's "Change the World" Firms Listing - Daily Nation' https://www.nation.co.ke/business/-Safaricom-on-Fortune-firms-listing/996–4723132-avoxxm/index.html accessed 15 April 2020.

However, M-Pesa's market dominance in Kenya has prompted calls for regulatory intervention against monopolistic behaviour,[50] as Safaricom controls the telecom's infrastructure that underpins the operation of M-Pesa, and competitors have not invested in alternative infrastructure. These competitors have argued for the infrastructure to be shared with other operators, and other stakeholders have called for mobile payments to be interoperable across systems. Despite regulatory intervention on interoperability, consumers continued to experience higher prices for transfers across networks, as well as delays and network errors through 2019.[51] Competitors have, however, gradually been able to dent M-Pesa's market dominance. Such concerns about market competition are shared in other countries where MNOs offer mobile money services, due to the similar control of the USSD infrastructure.

Mobile money users are particularly vulnerable to account fraud, such as SIM swap scams:[52] mobile phones, financial services, and other accounts are commonly secured through two-step verification. Fraudsters first obtain information about the target through social engineering or phishing techniques. Then they convince the telephone provider to transfer the victim's phone number to the fraudster's SIM. The latter then takes control of the victim's accounts, bypassing security features of accounts that rely on SMS on phone calls. Although these scams can affect other types of mobile wallets or wrappers, mobile money accounts are thought to be most targeted, with a resulting disproportionate impact on the poorest.

Mobile money has empowered individuals to finance micro businesses and therefore improve their own economic prospects, as other financial services such as loans and overdraft services have developed on M-Pesa. However, the delivery of free (welfare) money without sufficient levels of financial education is understood to have caused undesirable behaviour and contributed to a private debt situation in Kenya: gambling services and sports betting in particular grew in Kenya outside of regulatory controls. Consumers learnt to borrow to gamble and developed debt problems they could not tackle. The immaturity of local credit-checking processes compounded the issue, as consumers could keep borrowing unchecked, without the benefit of any early warning signals. Kenyan regulators therefore banned the use of M-Pesa for gambling in 2019.[53]

Mobile money has helped developing countries "leapfrog" over their weak banking infrastructure. Mobile network operators have become direct competitors to banks, fitting within new regulatory arrangements such as payment service provider licenses. This development has brought additional benefits such as

50 Rochemont S., 'A Cashless Society in 2018,' Institute and Faculty of Actuaries, 2019, pp28–32 https://www.actuaries.org.uk/documents/cashless-society-2018-cashless-world-motion-review.

51 Rochemont S., 'A Cashless Society in 2019,' Institute and Faculty of Actuaries, 2020, p24 https://www.actuaries.org.uk/documents/cashless-society-2019.

52 'SIM Swap Fraud Explained and How to Help Protect Yourself | Norton' https://us.norton.com/internetsecurity-mobile-sim-swap-fraud.html accessed 15 April 2020.

53 Rochemont S., 'A Cashless Society in 2019,' Institute and Faculty of Actuaries, 2020, p24 https://www.actuaries.org.uk/documents/cashless-society-2019.

traditional banks responding to competition by launching more inclusive services, leading to improved consumer choice.

While mobile money presents multiple challenges as explored in this section, its benefits are measurable on the African continent. The World Economic Forum has concluded: "Fixing global poverty is hard. But one solution might be as simple as using a mobile phone to access financial services."[54]

This chapter has examined mobile wallets and mobile money, both of which enable digital payments. These may be used to purchase credits and local currencies.

Credits and local currencies

Consumers can also buy credits in exchange for an alternative unit of account, which can be spent on a particular platform, such as online games. Local currencies are also credits, whereby people exchange national currencies for a local equivalent that can be spent in a defined geographic area to boost local sustainability. Credits and local currencies rely on users trusting a new currency as a unit of account and medium of exchange. Nevertheless, they generally make use of existing payment systems, including use of "wrapper"' services, to make transfers.

UK local currencies such as the Bristol Pound or Liverpool Pound are backed by and remain on a fixed exchange rate with sterling.[55] France counts nearly 40 local currencies, within a 2014 legal and regulatory framework[56] that fits within a social enterprise model. Rollon, launched in June 2018, is the first fully digital instance, exchanged at a 1:1 parity with the euro through a mobile application.[57] The converted euros are deposited with a partner regional commercial bank.

Festival organisers have also adopted credits, mostly as rechargeable bracelets or similar wearables, that are discarded at the end of the event or retained for the next iteration of the festival. These improve the consumer experience, as they save cumbersome cash handling in crowded venues. However, it can be difficult for festival goers to check their balances and track their spending. Consumers may also experience issues with accessing and claiming their balance at the end of festivals.

Other types of retailers use credits through mobile phone applications, whereby consumers transfer balances from their bank account to keep credits

54 Klapper L., 'How This One Change Can Help People Fight Poverty' (*World Economic Forum*), 2018 https://www.weforum.org/agenda/2018/08/reduce-poverty-give-poor-people-bank-accounts-leora-klapper/ accessed 15 April 2020.

55 Bank of England, '*Quarterly Bulletin*' 2014 Q3 Volume 54 No 3 pp262–265. https://www.bankofengland.co.uk/-/media/boe/files/quarterly-bulletin/2014/quarterly-bulletin-2014-q3.pdf accessed 15 April 2020.

56 'L'économie sociale et solidaire' (*Gouvernement.fr*) https://www.gouvernement.fr/action/l-economie-sociale-et-solidaire accessed 15 April 2020.

57 Berteau A., 'La Normandie Se Dote d'une Monnaie Locale et Numérique, Une Première En France', Le Figaro, Paris, 11 July 2018, Economie https://www.lefigaro.fr/conjoncture/2018/07/11/20002-20180711ARTFIG00121-la-normandie-se-dote-d-une-monnaie-locale-et-numerique-une-premiere-en-france.php accessed 15 April 2020.

with the retailer, to enable convenient services such as preordering drinks from chains of coffee shops.

As these credits cannot be used with other retailers or platforms, these are effectively closed-loop systems where consumers can no longer allocate funds for other uses and may be unable to transfer balances back to their account, hence committing to expenditure with the retailer. This raises concerns about the status of such credits and what recourse consumers have in the event of a scheme collapsing.

Digital currencies

Twelve years on from the great financial crisis in 2008, the lingering lack of trust in banks[58] is associated with the rising interest in payments outside the commercial banking system, with appeal for decentralised digital currencies. Bitcoin, the innovator, has been dubbed "the evil spawn of the financial crisis."[59]

The Bank of England defines a digital currency as "a scheme that incorporates both a new, decentralised payment system and a new currency. All the schemes exhibit a publicly-visible ledger which is shared across a computing network. A key defining feature of each digital currency scheme is the process by which its users come to agree on changes to its ledger (that is, [to agree] on which transactions to accept as valid). Most digital currencies are 'cryptocurrencies', in that they seek consensus through means of techniques from the field of cryptography. There are also a small number of digital currencies that seek consensus through non-cryptographic means."[60]

Since the launch of bitcoin, an array of digital companies has claimed to offer assets with the functionalities of a currency. However, few outside of the new industry agree that such assets qualify as money. Their volatility means they are a poor store of value. Their acceptance for transactions is not widespread, despite the industry's efforts to date, and their current technical limitations in terms of performance and capacity suggest they are not scalable enough for general use. As a result, most erudite financiers conclude that cryptocurrencies are speculative assets.[61]

Marketing messages for such assets appeal to vulnerable consumers, through elaborate schemes that offer a quick means to get rich, and as an anti-system,

---

58 Marcus G., 'The financial crisis and the crisis of trust in the banking sector of the advanced economies,' Bank for International Settlements, Rhodes University Business School strategic conversation series, Grahamstown, 10 October 2012 https://www.bis.org/review/r121011b.pdf.

59 Jones C., 'ECB Official Dubs Bitcoin "Evil Spawn of the Financial Crisis,"' Financial Times, London, 15 November 2018 https://www.ft.com/content/92c4737e-e8ed-11e8-885c-e64da4c0f981 accessed 15 April 2020.

60 Bank of England, '*Quarterly Bulletin*' 2014 Q3 Volume 54 No 3 pp262–265 https://www.bankofengland.co.uk/-/media/boe/files/quarterly-bulletin/2014/quarterly-bulletin-2014-q3.pdf accessed 15 April 2020.

61 Baur D. and others, *Journal of International Financial Markets, Institutions and Money*, Volume 54, May 2018, pp177–189 '*Bitcoin: Medium of exchange or speculative assets?*' https://doi.org/10.1016/j.intfin.2017.12.004.

libertarian solution,[62] an alternative to the global banking system that is believed to have excluded poorer members of society. Such messages echo the beliefs of gullible consumers: to sell a dream solution to improve their own welfare without barriers or controls from government or official organisations.

Such dreams of obtaining easy and independent money ignited further when social media platform Facebook announced in 2019 its project in partnership with other organisations to launch a cryptocurrency for use on its platform, aiming to resolve some of the known weaknesses of the banking system, such as inefficient cross-border transactions: their delays and costs negatively affect remittances, mostly used by expatriated workers to send money home to their families in need, usually in developing countries. The project also claimed its currency would improve financial inclusion,[63] granting accounts to the unbanked.

National regulators have taken diverse approaches toward these crypto-currencies: from China's bans to Singapore drafting an industry code of practice to the US Securities and Exchange Commission initiating lawsuits against businesses for selling unregulated securities.[64] However, they united with central banks and politicians against Facebook's project. One of the key concerns is the role of cryptocurrencies in facilitating crime. Celebrity-backed scams and Ponzi schemes, as well as the criminal laundering of money through crypto services that grant total anonymity, lead to the suspicion that cryptocurrencies are a scammer's paradise. Criminal activities using cryptocurrencies have also been directly impacting real life,[65] through the facilitation of ransomware attacks against public services in multiple countries, diverting local resources that could have been used toward productive purposes. Theft of crypto wallets through hacking attacks on cryptocurrency exchanges, as well as the SIM-swapping scams, disproportionally affect the more vulnerable, devastating their lives and savings.

The Onecoin scam[66] is an example that illustrates the vulnerability of naïve consumers to elaborate marketing ploys. In this instance, multilevel marketing was used to market a Ponzi scheme. The product consisted of educational packages delivered to mine a fake cryptocurrency that was believed to gain value as per the organisers' communications, although there was no platform for members to convert or sell them, or to buy goods or services. However, the organisation is

62 Stănescu C. G. and Gikay A. A., 'Technological Populism and Its Archetypes: Blockchain and Cryptocurrencies' [2019] Nordic Journal of Commercial Law 46 https://journals.aau. dk/index.php/NJCL/article/view/3442 accessed 13 June 2020.

63 'Zuckerberg: Libra As Financial Inclusion Tool' (*PYMNTS.com*, 23 October 2019) https://www.pymnts.com/facebook/2019/zuckerbergs-testimony-paints-libra-as-financial-inclusion-tool/ accessed 13 June 2020.

64 Rochemont S., 'A Cashless Society in 2019,' Institute and Faculty of Actuaries, 2020, p12 https://www.actuaries.org.uk/documents/cashless-society-2019.

65 Rochemont S., 'A Cashless Society in 2019,' Institute and Faculty of Actuaries, 2020, pp13–14 https://www.actuaries.org.uk/documents/cashless-society-2019.

66 'Cryptoqueen: How This Woman Scammed the World, Then Vanished - BBC News' https://www.bbc.com/news/stories-50435014 accessed 15 April 2020.

believed to have raised \$4bn through marketing the dream of a new free world where everyone could become rich, where everyone had access to money. The British Broadcasting Corporation podcast series[67] that investigated the scheme highlighted some devastating effects on local society when the organisation re-cruited members in Uganda through churches, depleting local resources, family life, and devastating local society.

Central bank digital currencies

Cash is a public good, yet its use has been declining in developed countries. The shift toward electronic payments means private, often foreign players may control a country's retail payment system, raising questions of sovereignty. In addition, the payments infrastructure in many jurisdictions is obsolete and requires up-grades. Some new technologies such as decentralised ledger technology or its blockchain instance have encouraged central banks to look into new models to facilitate national settlements' infrastructure and to consider the potential for issuing digital fiat money, under the concept of central bank digital currencies (CBDC). The prospect of a private digital currency gaining mainstream adoption has increased the urgency of such research.[68]

The concepts surrounding the possible issue of a CBDC are complex: they can include considerations for financial inclusion, although these may not be central to their design. Holding a retail (personal) account with a central bank may be a future solution for those unable to access commercial bank accounts, such as vulnerable groups.

At the time of writing this chapter, no clear model was available for such ac-counts, although the Bank of England has engaged in discussion[69] with stake-holders on the prospect and design of a future CBDC for the UK. Some smaller jurisdictions such as the Eastern Caribbean[70] have started implementing a CBDC with financial inclusion at its core, in order to address issues with access to and efficiency of payments across its number of islands. Some organisations suggest the use of mobile money[71] as a retail CBDC, to capture its benefits as well as addressing its risks, instead of creating new, more complex instruments.

67 'BBC Sounds - The Missing Cryptoqueen - Downloads' (*BBC*), 2019 https://www.bbc.co.uk/programmes/p07nkd84/episodes/downloads accessed 15 April 2020.

68 Ward O. and Rochemont S., 'Understanding Central Bank Digital Currencies (CBDC),' Institute and Faculty of Actuaries, 2019 https://www.actuaries.org.uk/documents/understanding-central-bank-digital-currencies-cbdc.

69 'Central Bank Digital Currency: Opportunities, Challenges and Design | Bank of England' https://www.bankofengland.co.uk/paper/2020/central-bank-digital-currency-opportunities-challenges-and-design-discussion-paper accessed 15 April 2020.

70 Eastern Caribbean Central Bank 'About the Project |' https://www.eccb-centralbank.org/p/about-the-project accessed 15 April 2020.

71 Cooper B. and others, 'The use cases for central bank digital currency for financial inclusion: A case for mobile money,' Cenfri, 2019 https://cenfri.org/wp-content/uploads/2019/06/CBDC-and-financial-inclusion_A-case-for-mobile-money.pdf.

One particular area of consideration for the design to benefit financial inclusion is: how would consumers access a CBDC? Countries such as China and the UK[72] are considering issuing them through existing financial institutions and payment providers. This intermediation model is likely, as a central bank would not willingly choose to be involved in retail banking, with its frequent account management activities. However, this mechanism of access may not address the known challenges of some consumers to access financial services through commercial operators, such as the cost of keeping an account.[73]

Another key question for the design of a retail CBDC in the context of financial inclusion and the interests of consumers is whether the account and transaction details should be kept at the commercial operator or be replicated in the central bank ledger. This would have implications for the portability of a CBDC account to other commercial operators, as well as the access to and use of transaction details.

An account that is held directly at a central bank would present some advantages as well as drawbacks for vulnerable consumers. Such access would enable demographic profiling and would facilitate the direct delivery of welfare[74] or helicopter money[75] to targeted recipients without relying on commercial operators to cascade monetary policy or various schemes. It would, however, potentially provide visibility of transaction details to representatives of government.

The advancement and implications of China's national reputation system highlight the known issue of trust in governments and the risks associated with a totalitarian state in the event that all payments become digital. A practical example of the consequences of such control is the purposeful use of Internet shutdowns to control dissident activity[76] in countries known to be led by authoritarian regimes.

One more implication to consider for the future access to a CBDC is a likely prerequisite for the implementation of a digital identity, in particular for countries lacking formal identity documentation. Such digital identity may help resolve the challenges of undocumented citizens, although they may present different challenges, related to the access and use of personal data. The deployment of India's biometric identification scheme, Adhaar, remains

72 Bank of England, 'Central Bank Digital Currency: Opportunities, Challenges and Design,' March 2020 http://www.bankofengland.co.uk/paper/2020/central-bank-digital-currency-opportunities-challenges-and-design-discussion-paper accessed 15 April 2020.

73 Institute and Faculty of Actuaries, 'IFOA response to the Discussion Paper on Central Bank Digital Currency,' June 2020 https://www.actuaries.org.uk/documents/ifoa-response-dp-central-bank-digital-currency.

74 'Are Central Banks Disconnected from Their Financial Inclusion Responsibilities? | Institute and Faculty of Actuaries' https://www.actuaries.org.uk/news-and-insights/news/are-central-banks-disconnected-their-financial-inclusion-responsibilities accessed 13 June 2020.

75 Helicopter money is a last resort type of monetary stimulus, which involves printing large sums of money and distributing it to the public to encourage people to spend more and thus boost the economy.

76 Rochemont S., 'A Cashless Society in 2019,' Institute and Faculty of Actuaries, 2020, pp26–27 https://www.actuaries.org.uk/documents/cashless-society-2019.

controversial,[77] despite its achievements in enabling access to bank accounts and delivering welfare programs.

In this section, we discussed the benefits and drawbacks of cashless alternatives. Although there is potential for technological innovation to improve the welfare of consumers that are so far locked out of digital services, careful consideration must be applied to manage their pitfalls.

Transition toward a less-cash society

Use of cash in developing countries can account for up to 90% of transactions and is associated with an informal economy, low levels of financial inclusion, and low tax receipts. This contrasts with developed countries that already have a mature payment ecosystem and are evolving toward a less-cash society.

The transition to a cashless economy would be a strategic choice and complex undertaking that requires a political will, as well as engagement of all stakeholders toward a shared goal. Conversely, the transition toward a "less-cash" society seems to be happening by stealth in developed countries, locking vulnerable groups out, and threatening wide-ranging societal disruption if not managed. The interests of the concerned stakeholders diverge, associated with tensions and distrust, that can lead to failed strategies if some stakeholders are neglected. For instance, in 2017 Nigeria attempted to impose a cashless society through bank payments.[78] However, the government did not engage with other stakeholders such as mobile network operators and nonfinancial business at that time, to ensure the infrastructure was in place. Chaos and popular backlash led to the policy being suspended within weeks, owing to insufficient preparation. The Nigerian government launched a new plan in 2018 that included the enablement of mobile money through the creation of new payment service banking licenses. The share of cashless transactions has been growing since.[79]

Consumer interests

Local development of infrastructure is an underpinning requirement for successful digitisation of an economy. It must include legal and consumer protection, electrical, network, security, and technology infrastructure. Other risks and issues are associated with the public's perception of a future without cash and should be taken into consideration when drafting public policy and legislation.

77 Bedi R. 'World's Largest Biometric ID System Approved by Indian Court as 1 Billion Enroll for Welfare and Tax' https://www.telegraph.co.uk/news/2018/09/26/worlds-largest-biometric-system-approved-indian-court-1-billion/ accessed 15 April 2020.
78 Rochemont S., 'A Cashless Society in 2018,' Institute and Faculty of Actuaries, 2019, p79 https://www.actuaries.org.uk/documents/cashless-society-2018-cashless-world-motion-review.
79 Rochemont S., 'A Cashless Society in 2019,' Institute and Faculty of Actuaries, 2020, p29 https://www.actuaries.org.uk/documents/cashless-society-2019.

A cashless society would affect each of the stakeholders differently, each with a complex set of tensions and interests that help explain the divisive nature of the concept. The potential benefits or otherwise of de-cashing depend on how individual players interpret it. In addition, governments and banks sometimes carry negative perceptions from consumers that affect trust in these institutions. A dominating perception is that the drive toward a cashless society is ultimately driven by the desire by certain bodies to exert maximum economic and social control and "coerce the untamed into the cogs of the financial system."[80]

Consumers' choice of payments and their convenience is an assertion of freedom, and possibly of political power. Innovators provide an alternative to banks, and the wider range of choice should lead to lower consumer costs. Electronic payments should protect consumers' interests though the reduction of fraud and theft, as well as a fair tax system though the reduction of cash payments. The public cost of producing and handling cash would disappear in a totally cashless society.

However, cash is a safety valve that empowers citizens against an omnipotent central bank and government. Consumers' views in developed countries show concern for a dystopian world, where all activities are electronically logged, and individual freedoms are lost through digital enslavement and opportunities for repression.[81] This issue draws strong views in countries where trust in government is low,[82] with suspicion of hidden agendas against some minority groups or toward totalitarian regimes: any dissident may become locked out of the economy and unable to survive if they are not compliant.

A cashless society is an ideal market-dominating position for banks: cash is their biggest competitor, yet it requires banks to resource its handling by maintaining cash machines and bank branches. The lack of trust in banks since the great financial crisis may be an explanation for the great cash paradox: despite the growth of digital payments, major central banks report a rise in the demand for cash since the crisis, with the unexplained ongoing growth of banknotes in circulation. The prospect of negative interest rates being imposed on personal accounts is another source of fear and another possible explanation for consumers keeping cash at home during years of low interest rates.

Beyond the convenience of digital payments, cash is free to use as a public good; electronic payments push the consumption of private services and draw fears of consumer protection if providers collapse, as well as the level of security that protects accounts, payments, and consumer data.

Consumers are attached to cash for its social value, for the intergenerational kindness of the tooth fairy, and for other customs that typically include a smile

80 Anonymous.
81 Achord S. and others, 'A Cashless Society: Benefits, Risks and Issues (Interim Paper),' Institute and Faculty of Actuaries, 2017, p55 https://www.actuaries.org.uk/documents/cashless-society-benefits-risks-and-issues.
82 '2019 CIGI-Ipsos Global Survey on Internet Security and Trust' (*Centre for International Governance Innovation*) https://www.cigionline.org/internet-survey-2019 accessed 15 April 2020.

with a discreet gift of a banknote or a coin. Debt support organisations and other financial experts also recommend using cash to manage expenditure[83] and to avoid overspending: a cash budget for a shopping trip or a social night out is an effective tool for self-control.

Digital natives may be more likely than older generations to adopt electronic budgeting tools, indicating this budgeting issue may be transitory. The transition toward digital payments can negatively affect the older generations, who may find new technologies financially, physically, or cognitively inaccessible. Digital exclusion would gradually lead to financial exclusion, as bank branches and cash machines became scarcer.

Cash is also a safeguard against the unavailability of the underpinning technical infrastructure: power fails; networks fail; point-of-sale machines fail; mobile phones can be stolen, lost, or broken; accounts and transactions can be hacked into; or access can be denied in error. Consumers have also become increasingly concerned about general environmental costs; payments have shifted from physical printing and distribution to electronic infrastructure,[84] with smart-phones, point-of-sale equipment, and data centres.

Financial exclusion is a particular risk: the dependency of noncash payments on the ability to access bank accounts, or smartphones with underlying reliable Internet infrastructure can gradually exclude the most vulnerable in society as they are unable to access goods and services.

Outlook for the fair and non-discriminatory access to financial services

Initiatives in developing countries point to a number of opportunities to improve fair and non-discriminatory access to financial services in developed regions that will impact on regulations.[85]

Mobile money (without a bank account) is still absent from the payments landscape of many developed countries, yet it has helped the unbanked in developing countries. The poor and unbanked are a minority market in the West, so the solution to include them may have to come from governments, instead of commercial organisations that might find such a project economically unviable. Even new banks rely on consumers' access to the Internet. Some established businesses such as mobile network operators could, however, contribute knowledge in the area.

83 Cauldwell M., 'How to Switch to Cash Only for Your Budget' https://www.thebalance.com/how-to-switch-to-cash-only-for-your-budget-2385691 accessed 15 April 2020.
84 Rochemont S., 'Issue 21- Environmental Sustainability of a Cashless Society,' Institute and Faculty of Actuaries, 2018   http://www.actuaries.org.uk/documents/environmental-sustainability-cashless-soociety.
85 Rochemont S., 'Coping in a Cashless Society,' Institute and Faculty of Actuaries, 23 October 2019 https://www.actuaries.org.uk/news-and-insights/news/coping-cashless-society accessed 15 April 2020.

Smartphones and Internet access are passports to financial inclusion, as they grant access to the best utility offers, financial management (including budgeting) and banking apps, job searches, social networks, knowledge sharing, and much more. Yet, poorer consumers may be unable to afford these. Governments may wish to evaluate mechanisms to equip financially excluded groups with smartphones and Internet access, comparing the costs and benefits of this with enabling payments through simple 2G mobile phones.

Proof of identity and address are required when opening bank accounts, to fulfil Know Your Customer and Anti-Money Laundering regulations. Governments could consider how those without any formal (paper) documentation such as identification or home address can create a digital identity, as this is a barrier to opening a bank account. As banks prepare to launch biometric payment cards (using fingerprints instead of PIN numbers for security), now may be an appropriate time to redefine documentation requirements and consider the benefits of National Digital Identification.[86]

Digital and financial literacy need developing amongst the vulnerable groups so they can access and use the tools effectively. Consumers who currently have no access to bank accounts or electronic means of payment may also find themselves vulnerable to aggressive commercial exploitation. Without digital and financial education, these new consumers are more likely to be abused by commercial organisations. Responsible provider behaviour needs nurturing in order to safely bring this new demographic into the formal economy. This will require a coordinated approach, with consumer protection at its core, between the private sector to uphold its duty of care and the public sector to develop and enhance financial literacy skills.

Conclusion

This chapter introduced a dynamic and increasingly complex payments ecosystem, developing as part of the digital revolution. New currencies, new payment systems, and nonfinancial players arise that have the power to financially include or exclude consumers.

Challenges and priorities depend on the level of local economic development. Some regions have leapfrogged over the need for the traditional banking infrastructure, using digital IDs and mobile money to equip the poor and formalise their economies. However, consumer protection tends to be a laggard in these regions.

In parallel, developed countries are experiencing a slow yet hardly managed transition toward a less-cash society, resulting in the loss of some infrastructure upon which people depend to access cash and financial services.

---

86 *World Bank*, 'Mission Billion: Transforming Countries and Empowering People through Digital Identity' (*World Bank Live*, 20 March 2019) https://live.worldbank.org/mission-billion accessed 15 April 2020.

The race for convenience and simultaneous trust crises highlight the tensions that now challenge legislators: while excess regulation can stifle innovation, new scenarios associated with transactional and personal data call for legislators to engineer their own "leapfrog" moment to accompany new ecosystem dynamics.

Bibliography

2019 'Cards in the evolving European payments landscape', Payments Europe, 2019, https://www.paymentseurope.eu/wp-content/uploads/2019/12/Payments-Europe-Report_Cards-in-the-evolving-European-payments-landscape.pdf accessed 15 April 2020.

'Nigeria's Central Bank Awards Financial Services Licence to MTN Subsidiary' *Reuters* (30 July 2019) https://af.reuters.com/article/investingNews/idAFKCN1UP0LR-OZABS accessed 15 April 2020.

'Alipay' https://intl.alipay.com/ accessed 15 April 2020.

'Watford Will Now Accept Bitcoin for Merchandise Purchases | Watford Observer' https://www.watfordobserver.co.uk/sport/17897688.watford-will-now-accept-bitcoin-merchandise-purchases/ accessed 15 April 2020.

Bank of England (n5; 8; 24; 25). 'Future of Finance: Review on the Outlook for the UK Financial System' 2019, https://www.bankofengland.co.uk/-/media/boe/files/report/2019/future-of-finance-report.pdf?la=en&hash=59CEFAEF01C71AA551E7182262E933A699E952FC.

'A Cashless Society Working Party', Institute and Faculty of Actuaries' 2017–2020, https://www.actuaries.org.uk/practice-areas/finance-and-investment/finance-and-investment-research-working-parties/cashless-society-working-party accessed 15 April 2020.

'A Cashless Society: Benefits, Risks, and Issues - Abstract of the London Discussion | British Actuarial Journal, Cambridge University Press, Volume 23 2018 e28 DOI: https://doi.org/10.1017/S1357321718000223.

Tucker I.B., *Survey of Economics* (9th edn, Cengage Learning 2015), pp 399–400

Bank of England (n10; 23; 55; 60), *"Quarterly Bulletin"* 2014 Q3 Volume 54 No 3 p 262–265. https://www.bankofengland.co.uk/-/media/boe/files/quarterly-bulletin/2014/quarterly-bulletin-2014-q3.pdf accessed 15 April 2020.

Rochemont S. (n11; 17; 26; 47; 51; 53; 62; 63; 71; 73; 74; 75), *'A Cashless Society in 2019'*, Institute and Faculty of Actuaries, 2020, https://www.actuaries.org.uk/documents/cashless-society-2019.

Rochemont S. (n15; 16; 19; 34; 46; 50), *'A Cashless Society in 2018'*, Institute and Faculty of Actuaries, 2019, https://www.actuaries.org.uk/documents/cashless-society-2018-cashless-world-motion-review.

mbH HI, 'Arriva to Launch Contactless Payments on Its Services in Derby' https://www.arrivabus.co.uk/midlands/latest/arriva-to-launch-contactless-payments-on-its-services-in-derby/ accessed 15 April 2020.

'Holiday Money: How to Find the Best Cards and Currency Rates | Money | The Guardian' https://www.theguardian.com/money/2018/jun/23/holiday-money-best-cards-currency-rates-bank-charges-cash accessed 15 April 2020.

'Pain of Paying' Behavioraleconomics.Com https://www.behavioraleconomics.com/resources/mini-encyclopedia-of-be/pain-of-paying/ accessed 15 April 2020

'Access to Cash' (6 June 2019) https://www.psr.org.uk/psr-focus/access-to-cash accessed 15 April 2020.

2019 Access to Cash Review (n20), *'Final report'*, 2019. https://www.accesstocash. org.uk/ accessed 15 April 2020.

Auer, R. and others, *'Covid-19, cash, and the future of payments'*, Bank for International Settlements Bulletin No 3, 03 April 2020, https://www.bis.org/ publ/bisbull03.htm accessed 15 April 2020.

'Facebook Launches Libra Cryptocurrency with a Massive List of Partners' https://mashable.com/article/facebook-libra/?europe=true accessed 15 April 2020.

'Grab Expands into Indonesia E-Payments, Taking Battle to Go-Jek - Nikkei Asian Review' https://asia.nikkei.com/Business/Companies/Grab-expands-into-Indonesia-e-payments-taking-battle-to-Go-Jek accessed 15 April 2020.

(n29; 77) '2019 CIGI-Ipsos Global Survey on Internet Security and Trust' (*Centre for International Governance Innovation*) https://www.cigionline.org/internet-survey-2019 accessed 15 April 2020.

Ates, G., *'What are the reasons for not adopting mobile payments?'* Master's Thesis, International Business Management with Fintech focus, Arcada, 2019 https:// www.theseus.fi/handle/10024/261125.

Rahman, M. and others, *'Is Malaysia ready to go cashless?'* Kodisa International Conference ICBE 2019, p 141–148 http://www.supermanlee.com/kodisa2019/ KODISA.ICBE2019_Proceedings.pdf.

Davies, S. and others, 'The Poverty Premium' University of Bristol, http://www. bris.ac.uk/media-library/sites/geography/pfrc/pfrc1614-poverty-premium-key-findings.pdf, accessed 15 April 2020.

Chan, J. (n33; 37), 'The rise and rise of Quick Response Codes', Institute and Faculty of Actuaries, 2019, https://www.actuaries.org.uk/documents/ addendum-cashless-society-benefits-risks-and-issues.

Entsie, B., 'Ghana Adopts New Universal QR Code for Digital Payments, Here's How It Works [ARTICLE] - Pulse Ghana', 11 March 2020 https://www.pulse. com.gh/bi/strategy/ghana-adopts-new-universal-qr-code-for-digital-payments-heres-how-it-works/zyz2w16 accessed 15 April 2020.

National Bank of Rwanda, 'Rwanda Payment System Strategy – towards a cashless Rwanda 2018-24', 2018 https://www.bnr.rw/payment-systems/policies/?tx_ bnrdocumentmanager_frontend%5Bdocument%5D=209&tx_bnrdocumentma-nager_frontend%5Baction%5D=download&tx_bnrdocumentmanager_frontend %5Bcontroller%5D=Document&cHash=99f1bb2e46865242a30cbe8df8127020.

Liptak A.,'7-Eleven Japan Shut down Its Mobile Payment App after Hackers Stole $500,000 from Users – The Verge' https://www.theverge.com/2019/7/6/ 20684386/7-eleven-japan-shut-mobile-payments-app-7pay-security-flaw-cybersecurity accessed 15 April 2020.

Bank for International Settlements and others, 'Payment Aspects of Financial Inclusion in the Fintech Era' https://www.bis.org/cpmi/publ/d191.htm accessed 15 April 2020.

Osei-Tutu, F., and Weill, L., 'Sex, language and financial inclusion', BOFIT Discussion Papers, Bank of Finland Institute for Economies in Transition, 2020, https://helda.helsinki.fi/bof/bitstream/handle/123456789/16993/dp0920. pdf;jsessionid=95C26671A5D0DE36D003AF3FE0491295?sequence=1.

Katholische Universität Eichstätt-Ingolstadt 'Internationale Studie Untersucht Integration von Flüchtlingen Im Finanzsystem', IDW Online 28 May 2019 https://idw-online.de/en/news?print=1&id=716617 accessed 15 April 2020

World Bank, 'Global Findex' https://globalfindex.worldbank.org/ 2017, accessed 15 April 2020.

GSMA, 'What Makes a Successful Mobile Money Implementation? Learnings from M-PESA in Kenya and Tanzania | Mobile for Development', 2009 https://www.gsma.com/mobilefordevelopment/resources/what-makes-a-successful-mobile-money-implementation-learnings-from-m-pesa-in-kenya-and-tanzania/ accessed 15 April 2020.

Safaricom, 'How to Register for M-PESA' https://www.safaricom.co.ke/personal/m-pesa/getting-started/register-for-m-pesa accessed 15 April 2020

Hanouch, M., 'What Is USSD & Why Does It Matter for Mobile Financial Services?' CGAP, 17 February 2015 https://www.cgap.org/blog/what-ussd-why-does-it-matter-mobile-financial-services accessed 15 April 2020.

Achord S. and others, (n48; 76) 'A Cashless Society: Benefits, Risks and Issues (Interim Paper)' Institute and Faculty of Actuaries, 2017, https://www.actuaries.org.uk/documents/cashless-society-benefits-risks-and-issues.

'M-Pesa Puts Safaricom on Fortune's "Change the World" Firms Listing - Daily Nation' https://www.nation.co.ke/business/-Safaricom-on-Fortune-firms-listing/996-4723132-avoxxm/index.html accessed 15 April 2020.

Klapper, L., 'How This One Change Can Help People Fight Poverty' (*World Economic Forum*), 2018 https://www.weforum.org/agenda/2018/08/reduce-poverty-give-poor-people-bank-accounts-leora-klapper/ accessed 15 April 2020

'L'économie sociale et solidaire' (*Gouvernement.fr*) https://www.gouvernement.fr/action/l-economie-sociale-et-solidaire accessed 15 April 2020.

Berteau, A., *'La Normandie Se Dote d'une Monnaie Locale et Numérique, Une Première En France'*, Le Figaro, Paris, 11 July 2018, Economie, https://www.lefigaro.fr/conjoncture/2018/07/11/20002-20180711ARTFIG00121-la-normandie-se-dote-d-une-monnaie-locale-et-numerique-une-premiere-en-france.php accessed 15 April 2020.

Marcus, G., *'The financial crisis and the crisis of trust in the banking sector of the advanced economies'*, Bank for International Settlements, Rhodes University Business School strategic conversation series, Grahamstown, 10 October 2012. https://www.bis.org/review/r121011b.pdf.

Jones, C., *'ECB Official Dubs Bitcoin "Evil Spawn of the Financial Crisis"* Financial Times, London, November 15, 2018 https://www.ft.com/content/92c4737e-e8ed-11e8-885c-e64da4c0f981 accessed 15 April 2020.

Baur D. and others, *Journal of International Financial Markets, Institutions and Money*, Volume 54, May 2018, pp 177–189 *'Bitcoin: Medium of exchange or speculative assets?'* https://doi.org/10.1016/j.intfin.2017.12.004.

Stănescu C-G. and Gikay A.A., 'Technological Populism and Its Archetypes: Blockchain and Cryptocurrencies' [2019] *Nordic Journal of Commercial Law 46* https://journals.aau.dk/index.php/NJCL/article/view/3442 accessed 13 June 2020.

'Zuckerberg: Libra As Financial Inclusion Tool' (*PYMNTS.com*, 23 October 2019) https://www.pymnts.com/facebook/2019/zuckerbergs-testimony-paints-libra-as-financial-inclusion-tool/ accessed 13 June 2020.

'Cryptoqueen: How This Woman Scammed the World, Then Vanished - BBC News' https://www.bbc.com/news/stories-50435014 accessed 15 April 2020

2019 'BBC Sounds – The Missing Cryptoqueen - Downloads' *(BBC)*, 2019 https://www.bbc.co.uk/programmes/p07nkd84/episodes/downloads accessed 15 April 2020.

Ward, O., Rochemont, S., *'Understanding Central Bank Digital Currencies (CBDC)'*, Institute and Faculty of Actuaries, 2019, https://www.actuaries.org.uk/documents/understanding-central-bank-digital-currencies-cbdc

'Central Bank Digital Currency: Opportunities, Challenges and Design | Bank of England' https://www.bankofengland.co.uk/paper/2020/central-bank-digital-currency-opportunities-challenges-and-design-discussion-paper accessed 13 June 2020.

Eastern Caribbean Central Bank 'About the Project |' https://www.eccb-centralbank.org/p/about-the-project accessed 15 April 2020

Cooper, B. and others, 'The use cases for central bank digital currency for financial inclusion: A case for mobile money', *Cenfri*, 2019, https://cenfri.org/wp-content/uploads/2019/06/CBDC-and-financial-inclusion_A-case-for-mobile-money.pdf.

Institute and Faculty of Actuaries, 'IFOA response to the Discussion Paper on Central Bank Digital Currency', June 2020, https://www.actuaries.org.uk/documents/ifoa-response-dp-central-bank-digital-currency.

Are Central Banks Disconnected from Their Financial Inclusion Responsibilities? | Institute and Faculty of Actuaries' https://www.actuaries.org.uk/news-and-insights/news/are-central-banks-disconnected-their-financial-inclusion-responsibilities accessed 13 June 2020.

Bedi, R. 'World's Largest Biometric ID System Approved by Indian Court as 1 Billion Enroll for Welfare and Tax' https://www.telegraph.co.uk/news/2018/09/26/worlds-largest-biometric-system-approved-indian-court-1-billion/ accessed 15 April 2020.

Cauldwell, M. 'How to Switch to Cash Only for Your Budget' https://www.thebalance.com/how-to-switch-to-cash-only-for-your-budget-2385691 accessed 15 April 2020.

Rochemont, S., 'Issue 21- Environmental Sustainability of a Cashless Society' Institute and Faculty of Actuaries, 2018, http://www.actuaries.org.uk/documents/environmental-sustainability-cashless-soociety.

Rochemont, S., 'Coping in a Cashless Society' Institute and Faculty of Actuaries, 23 October 2019 https://www.actuaries.org.uk/news-and-insights/news/coping-cashless-society accessed 15 April 2020.

World Bank 'Mission Billion: Transforming Countries and Empowering People through Digital Identity' (*World Bank Live*, 20 March 2019) https://live.worldbank.org/mission-billion accessed 15 April 2020.

Part II

6 Inside the black box

The impact of machine learning on the creditworthiness assessment

Joanne Atkinson[*]

Introduction

The Bank of England Prudential Regulation Authority's 2017 statement on consumer credit[1] indicated that while the market for consumer credit is continuing to expand, ensuring responsible lending remains a high priority. Responsible lending includes several factors, but a central element is the requirement to conduct a creditworthiness assessment[2] of the consumer in every case before deciding whether to extend credit, how much, and on what terms.

The means by which the creditworthiness assessment is conducted are evolving rapidly. In past years, creditworthiness might have been assessed via a face-to-face conversation or a review of the consumer's paper bank statements. Now it is much more likely to be conducted online via a complex assessment of thousands of readily available data points which make up the consumer's profile. The manner in which the creditworthiness assessment is conducted is not readily understood by consumers. Because it is often carried out using third-party software in the form of so-called black box products, it is frequently not fully understood by lenders either.

This chapter will outline the development of the creditworthiness assessment and explain the ways in which it has evolved. It will demonstrate that the assessment has developed much more quickly than the relevant statutory and other applicable regulation. It will analyse the conduct of the assessment, highlighting practices not contemplated in the current legal framework. Specifically, the legal and regulatory issues posed by the use of machine learning software to conduct the assessment will be examined. The chapter will begin by exploring the ways in which the creditworthiness assessment is currently regulated in the UK. As the UK approach is heavily informed by EU regulation, the relevant Directives and Articles will also be examined. Gaps in the effective protection of consumers will

---

[*] Principal Lecturer in Law, University of Portsmouth.
1 Bank of England, PRA Statement on Consumer Credit July 2017 https://www.bankofengland. co.uk/prudential-regulation/publication/2017/pra-statement-on-consumer-credit accessed 30 May 2019.
2 Financial Conduct Authority Policy Statement 18/19 Assessing Creditworthiness in Consumer Credit https://www.fca.org.uk/publication/policy/ps18–19.pdf accessed 30 May 2019.

be identified. In order to address the resulting questions about the effectiveness of current regulation, some comparative data from the United States will be analysed. The chapter will then examine the theoretical bases of regulation. The UK regime is predominantly based on the teachings of behavioural economics, and the merits of this approach will be evaluated. Alternative approaches to regulation in this area will also be considered. In particular, the emerging potential for a more fairness-based approach will be examined.

In conclusion, the view of the UK regulator that no further regulation is required in this area[3] will be challenged. Instead, it will be argued that a radical overhaul of regulation in this marketplace is needed to keep pace with developments on the ground.

The creditworthiness assessment

The Consumer Credit Directive (the Directive)[4] aims to facilitate a functioning market for credit across the EU. This means a market which provides sufficient protection for consumers while still allowing free and fair access to credit. One of the key aims of the Directive is to promote responsible lending. The role of irresponsible lending in generating the financial crisis of 2008 has been widely discussed,[5] and there is a clear imperative to avoid another credit crunch resulting from poor lending decisions, overextended borrowers, and widespread inability or failure to repay amounts loaned to consumers. The Directive seeks to address this by creating rules designed to ensure that lending to consumers is conducted in a responsible manner. Responsible lenders must (inter alia) consider the ability of the borrower to repay the loan amount before making a decision on whether to issue credit, the amount of credit, and any terms attached.[6] Credit should not be extended to consumers where it is clearly apparent from the outset that there are likely to be problems with repayment.[7] However, according to the Consumer Financial Services Action Plan, a functioning consumer financial market is also characterised by inclusivity and the availability of credit.[8] Therefore, both regulators and lenders must strike a delicate balance between encouraging participation in the market and ensuring that consumers are adequately protected from irresponsible and unscrupulous lending.

In order to prevent irresponsible lending, the Directive requires lenders to perform a creditworthiness assessment of every consumer before extending

---

3 ibid.
4 Directive 2008/48/EC of the European Parliament and the Council 23 April 2008.
5 See, e.g., M Konings, 'Rethinking Neoliberalism and the Subprime Crisis: Beyond the Re-regulation Agenda' (2009) Competition & Change Vol 13 No 2, 108–127.
6 Vanessa Mak, 'What is Responsible Lending? The EU Consumer Mortgage Credit Directive in the UK and the Netherlands' (2015) Journal of Consumer Policy 38, 411–430.
7 (n 2).
8 European Commission, *Consumer Financial Services Action Plan: Better Products, More Choice* COM2017/0139.

credit.[9] The Financial Conduct Authority guidelines indicate that creditworthiness comprises two factors.[10] First is the credit risk, which refers to the risk to the lender of the borrower defaulting or missing payments. The second component is affordability, which refers to the risk to the consumer resulting from difficulties repaying the debt. This might include a reduction in living standards because of sacrifices made in other areas to service the debt. Similar requirements on creditworthiness assessment have been transposed into the national laws of all member states, with some states going beyond the Directive's requirements and providing specific and detailed guidance on the application of the rule. In some states (e.g., Spain, Belgium), specific documents must be completed to evidence the assessment.[11] In the UK, the Financial Conduct Authority ("FCA") is the relevant regulator and has published rules and guidance which expand on the meaning of the Article 8 requirement and provide guidance on their application. The FCA guidance, which has recently been updated, places particular emphasis on the adequacy and proportionality of the assessment.[12] In other words, there is no single standard. The level of rigour of the assessment should reflect the amount, term, and other conditions of the product applied for. The majority of lenders now operate some form of risk-based pricing (a "rate for risk" model)[13] whereby the interest rate and terms of the consumer's contract are dictated by their profile as revealed by the creditworthiness assessment. The outcome of the assessment may therefore affect not only the decision of whether to extend credita but also the cost of any credit offered.

The term "creditworthiness" is a loaded one, carrying the implication that the worth of the prospective debtor is being assessed in a wider sense than simply their current financial status. Indeed, the assessment extends beyond the consumer's financial worth; it encompasses value judgements about reliability, integrity, honesty, and acceptability, among other things.[14] The consequences of passing or failing the assessment can be very significant. Consumers who are not deemed creditworthy by mainstream financial institutions are typically faced with a restricted choice of often more expensive and usually much less appealing alternatives such as seeking to access short-term high-cost credit products (including so-called payday loans), exploring peer-lending initiatives, or

---

9 Article 8, Directive 2008/48/EC.
10 FCA Handbook CONC 5.2 A.10. See also s.38(1) Financial Services & Markets Act 2000.
11 European Commission, *Mapping of national approaches in relation to creditworthiness under Directive 2008/48/EC on credit agreements for consumers* 9 October 2018 https://ec. europa.eu/info/files/mapping-national-approaches-relation-creditworthiness-assessment-under-directive-2008-48-ec-credit-agreements-consumers_en accessed 31 July 2019.
12 (n 2).
13 Risk Management Group of the Basel Committee for Banking Supervision, *Principles for the Management of Credit Risk* 2000 https://www.bis.org/publ/bcbs75.htm accessed 20 April 2020.
14 V Mak and J Braspenning, 'Errare humanum est: Financial Literacy in European Consumer Credit Law' J Consum Policy (2012) 33,307.

borrowing from friends and family. Ultimately, the only choice for this group may be to go without desired or needed items.[15] Consumers in this group may include sub-prime or near-prime consumers such as those on low incomes or those working in unstable employment or on zero hours contracts. They may also include those with thin credit files, meaning they have little or no documented financial history. Examples of thin-file consumers are those with a limited history of borrowing, those who have never had a bank account, or recent arrivals to the country in which the lender is situated.[16] All are at risk of financial exclusion,[17] although there is evidence to suggest that their current credit score does not necessarily provide an accurate reflection of the risk of their defaulting.[18] Given that one of the FCA's criteria for a functioning consumer financial market is inclusivity,[19] it is clear that making the correct assessment has much wider implications than the protection of the individual lender and borrower. Failure to frame the assessment correctly could affect the efficiency of the market by excluding potentially creditworthy and profitable borrowers. Making an incorrect assessment may mean denying credit to borrowers who could benefit, and who may in fact pose a low credit risk, thus causing unnecessary detriment. The question then arises as to who is best placed to make such a loaded assessment. The Directive places the responsibility on the lender, but as will be seen, the process used is not always transparent and may in fact be conducted remotely from the lender. Further, the criteria used in the assessment are not always easily discoverable and may well vary considerably from lender to lender.

Regulation in this area has generally encouraged a libertarian, subjective approach.[20] In the UK, the consumer credit regime has historically depended heavily on an *ex ante* form of regulation,[21] implementing a licensing system for credit intended to ensure that only ethical, financially sound, and reputable providers could enter the marketplace. Once licensed, those providers have been

---

15 Dr Lindsey Appleyard, Carl Packman, and Jordon Lazell, *Payday Denied: Exploring the lived experience of declined payday loan applicants* (2018) Coventry University Research Centre.

16 See, e.g., PWC *Banking the underbanked: the growing demand for near-prime credit* https://www.pwc.co.uk/industries/financial-services/insights/uk-consumer-credit-outlook/banking-the-underbanked-the-near-prime-segment.html accessed 1 May 2020.

17 M Konings, 'Rethinking Neoliberalism and the Subprime Crisis: Beyond the Re-regulation Agenda' (2009) Competition & Change Vol 13 No 2, 108–127.

18 N Newman, 'How Big Data Enables Economic Harm to Consumers, Especially to Low Income and Other Vulnerable Sectors of the Population' (2014) Journal of Internet Law, 11.

19 Financial Conduct Authority *Consumer Credit and Consumers in Vulnerable Circumstances* April 2014 http://debtfreeadvice.co.uk/images/Credit_In_Vulnerable_Circumstances.pdf accessed 4 December 2018.

20 See Milton Friedman, *Capitalism and Freedom* (University of Chicago Press 1962).

21 Ian Ramsey, *Consumer Law & Policy: Text and Materials on Regulating Consumer Markets* (3rd edn Hart Publishing 2012).

given a high degree of discretion in the way in which they select their custo-mers.[22] Indeed, the FCA prides itself on taking a principles-based stance which is flexible, forward-looking, and definitely not over-prescriptive. It states that "[i]n following our new rules and guidance, firms should use their judgement to de-cide what is appropriate in the circumstances".[23]

Credit scoring and credit reference agencies

Creditworthiness

Article 8 of the Directive states that Member States must ensure that,

> *"before the conclusion of the credit agreement, the creditor assesses the consumer's creditworthiness on the basis of sufficient information, where appropriate obtained from the consumer and, where necessary, on the basis of a consultation of the relevant database".*

As noted earlier, creditworthiness includes an assessment of both credit risk and affordability. Credit risk – the risk to the lender that the borrower will default – is relatively straightforward to assess, provided the consumer has a documented financial history. In the UK, the assessment is usually made online using the services of one of the three major credit reference agencies: Experian, Equifax, or TransUnion (previously CallCredit).[24] This assessment essentially uses evidence of past behaviour to forecast future conduct, specifically the likelihood of future default. There is no uniform way of assessing credit risk, and an assessment of the same consumer might produce a different risk rating depending on which agency is used. However, all credit reference agencies will typically use historical data on income, expenditures, and current and past borrowings together with informa-tion about previous defaults and recent credit applications. Some of these data are required to be disclosed by the consumer in the application for credit. The rest are drawn from publicly accessible sources such as the electoral roll and court records. Although this method of credit rating or credit scoring is generally accepted as the industry standard, it is flawed in several respects. First, it is by no means clear that information on past conduct is a reliable indicator of the ways in which a consumer might behave in the future.[25] A closer examination of other contextual information may be needed in order to generate more accurate pre-dictions. Further, the rules of scoring vary between lenders, are not always

---

22 ibid.
23 Financial Conduct Authority Policy Statement 18/19 Assessing Creditworthiness in Consumer Credit https://www.fca.org.uk/publication/policy/ps18–19.pdf at 1.17.
24 Joe Deville, 'Consumer credit default and collections: the shifting ontologies of market attachment' (2014) Consumption Markets & Culture, 17:5, 468–490.
25 P Kelly and M Barker, 'Why is changing health-related behaviour so difficult?' (2016) Public Health 136, 09–116.

disclosed, and can appear counterintuitive. For example, there is some evidence that a certain level of missed or late payments under past contracts may make a consumer a more appealing prospect to a lender, improving their credit score. This is because the penalties incurred will generate a greater profit than continuous timely payments, while not significantly reducing the probability of full repayment in due course.[26] It must be remembered that the assessment of credit risk is essentially a calculation of the risk to the lender, or viewed another way, the likelihood of the consumer generating a profit for the lender over the life of the contract.

A further shortcoming of the credit risk assessment is its reliance on the consumer's documented financial history. Assessing risk in this way via regression models discriminates against consumers lacking evidence of past dealings. This group includes younger consumers and recent arrivals to the jurisdiction as well as consumers who have never, or only recently, opened a bank account – consumers with thin credit files.[27] The somewhat circular nature of the assessment frequently means that consumers must take on debt before they can be allocated a credit score. Borrowers with no credit score – those already at the margins of society – are therefore penalised either by being excluded from credit or by having to access high cost credit on unfavourable terms to themselves. There is considerable evidence that such consumers are especially vulnerable to unexpected drops in income or items of expenditure, and without access to mainstream credit they can quickly accrue problem debt.[28]

This is an unhappy modern instance of Caplovitz's "poverty premium".[29] In a rate for risk marketplace, these consumers face exploitation by lenders charging higher than usual interest rates on any credit extended. It may be assumed that, simply by virtue of having a thin or nonexistent credit file, such consumers do pose a greater risk to lenders. However, in the absence of hard empirical data about the spending and repayment patterns of such consumers, this must remain an assumption.

Arguably, it may benefit credit risk calculations at the wider level to incorporate information from this group into the data pool used to generate the risk assessment. Because these consumers face exclusion from the mainstream

26 (n 2).
27 D Guegan and B Hassani, 'Regulatory learning: How to supervise machine learning models? An application to credit scoring' (2018) Journal of Finance and Data Science 4, 157–171.
28 Y Hartfree and S Collard, 'Locating credit and debt within an anti-poverty strategy for the UK' (2015) Journal of Poverty and Social Justice vol 23(3), 203–214.
29 David Caplovitz, *The Poor Pay More: Consumer Practices of Low Income Families* (New York Free Press of Glencoe 1963); See also S Davies, A Finney, and Y Hartfree, *Paying to be Poor: Uncovering the Scale and Nature of the Poverty Premium* University of Bristol Personal Finance Research Centre 2016.

credit market, their experiences are not factored into mainstream prediction models. However, it is well established that prediction models based on narrow data sets can be very inaccurate.[30]

Even where adequate credit data are available, there is evidence that using historical data to predict future behaviour is not always accurate or helpful,[31] particularly where the aim (or at least one aim) is to encourage more responsible behaviour in the future or to encourage consumers to adopt habits which will benefit themselves, such as financial planning and prudence. Research on the accuracy of such predictions in other contexts indicates that where consumers present a history of poor planning and decision making, the history could usefully be explored to find information about the root cause or causes of such behaviour, and then seek to address that cause in order to reduce the risk of more poor decisions in the future.[32] However, notwithstanding the flaws outlined above, the assessment of credit risk is at least linked to historical financial data, rather than seeking to generate predictions of future behaviour based on lifestyle factors.

Affordability

Affordability is a more complex measure. Whereas credit risk relates to the risk to the lender, affordability is concerned with the risk to the consumer. The affordability assessment seeks to quantify, inter alia, the risk of creating over-indebtedness.[33] It also aims to review the consumer's financial position in a more holistic manner, in order to assess the likelihood of the consumer suffering detriment in other areas in order to service the debt being applied for. This might entail cutting back on expenditure in other areas of the household budget to ensure repayments are met, or going without items or services to pay penalties if repayments are missed.[34] Consumers who experience a financial upheaval in the form of an unpredicted or unbudgeted event, such as job loss, will frequently fall back on credit cards and other forms of lending to maintain their lifestyle, incurring significant unexpected debt in the process.[35] Preventing unnecessary detriment is one of the main components of responsible lending.[36] However, the affordability assessment is necessarily a somewhat subjective one, because even

30 J Kruppa, A Schwarz, G Arminger, and Z Zielger, 'Consumer credit risk: Individual probability estimates using machine learning' (2013) Expert Systems with Applications 40, 5125–5131.
31 (n 27).
32 (n 25).
33 D Marron, 'Producing over-indebtedness' (2012) Journal of Cultural Economy 5:4 407–421.
34 (n 28).
35 Elizabeth Warren, 'Unsafe at any rate' (2007) Democracy Journal, Summer 8.
36 R Hodson, D Dwyer, and L Neilson, 'Credit Card Blues: The Middle Class and the Hidden Costs of Easy Credit' (2014) Sociological Quarterly 55, 315–340.

where common criteria are applied, the lending decision depends on an exercise of judgement by the individual lender. That judgement must incorporate a review of a wider set of information than simply documented income and existing debt. In order to assess affordability, the lender must seek to understand wider factors informing the consumer's lifestyle, expectations, and current habits, and then use that understanding to theorise about their prospective future financial behaviour. The assessment requires the lender to weigh these criteria before reaching an individual decision based on their own judgement of the applicant.

Historically, the affordability criterion might have been explored via a chat with the local bank manager. Such a person would most likely already have been acquainted with the borrower's circumstances and standing in the community. They may also have been able to assess whether the borrower was living within their means, or perhaps ascertain whether they had hidden sources of income or hidden financial responsibilities. More recently, a scripted telephone conversation may have been used to explore the consumer's lifestyle and existing commitments. These conversations can yield a very helpful rounded and in-depth understanding of individual consumers' circumstances, and a few smaller lenders still rely on a face-to-face affordability assessment. However, such conversations are necessarily time-consuming and intrusive. In a face-to-face assessment of an individual's worthiness, the risk of bias whether conscious or unconscious must remain. For most lenders, a face-to-face assessment is simply not commercially viable. Big data appears to offer a solution.[37] Indeed, there is a wealth of evidence that lenders are now routinely using data harvesting from the likes of Google and social media as part of the affordability assessment, and to cross-sell or upsell products to consumers.[38] However, unintended consequences flow from the substitution of a data-based assessment for a face-to-face discussion and these are explored below.

Machine learning and the creditworthiness assessment

In an age of big data and machine learning, automation of the creditworthiness assessment offers clear commercial benefits. There are obvious advantages in terms of the speed of response when credit is applied for, and lending decisions can now be taken almost instantaneously.[39] Indeed, there is anecdotal information

37 C K Livada, 'Assessment of consumers' creditworthiness' (2019) ERA Forum Vol 20 Issue 2, 225.
38 Guangming Guo, Feida Zhu, Enhong Chen, Qi Liu, Le Wu, and Chu Guan, 'From footprint to evidence: An exploratory study of mining social data for credit scoring' (2016) ACM Transactions on the Web. 10, (4), Research Collection School Of Information Systems; J Kruppa *et al.* (2013) 'Consumer credit risk: Individual probability estimates using machine learning', *Expert Systems With Applications* 40, 5125–5131.
39 QuickQuid (2020) www.quickquid.co.uk accessed 25 September 2019; Tendoloan (2020) www/tendoloan.co.uk accessed 25 September 2019; Satsuma Loans (2020) www.satsumaloans.co.uk accessed 25 September 2019.

about lenders actively slowing down their online responses – even adding a pause to the automated process during which consumers watch a timer running down – in order to reassure applicants that due care is being taken to review their data.[40] This aside, there are more serious implications resulting from the automation of the process, which are not contemplated under current UK regulation.[41] Increasingly, the creditworthiness test is being carried out using algorithm tools and machine learning not only to review historical conduct, but also to build a picture of their current status and habits in order to predict borrowers' likely future behaviour.

As noted earlier, the assessment of credit risk test has historically been ad-dressed by the use of historical data, and affordability by more current contextual data about the consumer's current financial status and outgoings. The use of machine learning however means that increasingly the lending decision is made on the basis of software-generated predictions about the future, rather than evidence of past conduct. Such predictions are based on an ever-increasing data set. Data on individuals can now be gathered from a huge array of thousands of data points which may reveal an individual's online as well as offline activities. Some obvious questions arise here about data protection, and these are begin-ning to be explored.[42] In most cases, the consumer's permission is sought for the lender to access a very wide variety of personal information, on the basis that this can help build a more accurate picture of their creditworthiness. However, lots of easily searchable data including individual profiles on social media sites for ex-ample are already in the public domain. This information can reveal many in-sights of interest to potential lenders. For example, an individual's online footprint may reveal where and how frequently they shop, their internet browsing habits, music playlists, and even personal emails and other commu-nication trails. This information in turn can feed into the creditworthiness as-sessment as it is revealing of the consumer's levels of impulsiveness, brand loyalty, the stability of their cash flow, spending habits, and so on.[43] Even the times of day when consumers are active online have a value in this data set as they can reveal information about working patterns, etc.

Harvesting of the aforementioned data from social media represents a key part of the process. Information about the age of consumers' social media accounts, the frequency of their use, and the number and profile of their connections can be used to extrapolate judgements about an individual's family and social

---

40 Westminster Business Forum Keynote Seminar: Priorities for consumer credit – the future for regulation, ensuring consumer protection and supporting inclusion, Transcript of pro-ceedings 6 December 2018.
41 See Financial Conduct Authority, FCA Handbook (TSO 2019).
42 See, e.g., Federico Ferretti, 'Consumer access to capital in the age of FinTech and big data: the limits of EU law' Maastricht Journal of European and Comparative Law (2018) Vol 25(4), 476.
43 T Alloway, 'Big Data: credit where credit's due', *Financial Times* (London 4 February 2015).

circumstances, the strength of their job security, their socioeconomic status, and possibly even their race.[44] All these data are then fed into the creditworthiness assessment. Although assessing creditworthiness is an inherently discriminatory process, there are clear risks here of discrimination for illegitimate and potentially unfair reasons creeping into the process. It is not clear whether or how lenders make use of information about a consumer's nationality, ethnic profile, religion, or age, although all of these are protected characteristics under the Equality Act 2010.[45] The lack of transparency in the assessment process means it is difficult to prevent biases from developing. There is no doubt that the use of so-called big data is revolutionising the way in which creditworthiness is assessed, along with all other aspects of financial underwriting and the financial services marketplace. As with all revolutions, the consequences are significant and wide-ranging, and many of them are unintended and not contemplated in the existing scheme of regulation.

The sophistication and complexity of the creditworthiness assessment means that lenders are no longer able to complete it in-house without specialist technological assistance. For many lenders, particularly smaller enterprises, this means purchasing a specialist software product which can be plugged in to their own existing systems and processes. Often, a product purchased off the shelf for this purpose will be supplied in a black box format. The term "black box" refers to a system where the input and output of the process are known, but how one is transformed into the other is not known.[46]

At the outset, the purchaser cannot see or access the workings of the product beyond setting the broad parameters of the assessment. Once the product begins to build up a data set and carry out assessments, it will typically use machine learning to refine and develop its calculations and predictions on an ongoing basis. Machine learning is a specific branch of artificial intelligence (AI). In rule-based AI, the same inputs will always generate the same outputs. However, machine learning is capable of evolving its algorithms as the available data set increases. In some cases, the developer may have conditioned the machine learning platform early in the process by ousting certain results which are undesired or obviously wrong. In many cases, however, the development simply occurs by acquiring a sufficient quantity of data, so that the number of false positive outputs is automatically lowered. Thus, the nature of the algorithms used in prediction are unknown even to their original developer. The use of machine learning may be argued to offer benefits to the consumer, as the further removed the product becomes from its human originators, the more conscious

44 (n 42).
45 Equality Act 2010, s.4.
46 Frank Pasquale (2015). *The Black Box Society: The Secret Algorithms That Control Money and Information*. Cambridge, Massachusetts; London, England: Harvard University Press.

and unconscious biases in the calculations are eliminated. Conversely, over time, machine learning may replace human biases with other forms of discrimination.[47]

However, it also raises a number of issues of regulatory concern. First, it is the lender who is responsible for conducting the assessment under FCA rules.[48] It is impossible for a lender to discharge this responsibility satisfactorily if the lender does not know or appreciate precisely how the assessment is carried out. The software provider is not responsible for the lending decision and does not have any contact with the end consumer borrower, so it is not helpful or appropriate to place any further responsibility on the supplier. There is thus a liability gap which persists inside the black box.

The General Data Protection Regulation (GDPR/Regulation) provides a partial solution to this problem.[49] Under the Regulation, solely automated decision making may not be used where the outcome has a legal or similarly significant effect, unless the consumer consents. Consumers may also request information about the logic employed in the decision-making process. Of course, where the process is very complex and obscure, it is questionable how much benefit an average consumer would gain from access to the algorithm even where a human explanation is provided. Many consumers rely on the credit-scoring reports referred to earlier even though these increasingly appear to be obsolete.[50]

Further, responsible lending is predicated on the requirement that lenders should treat borrowers fairly.[51] A key component of fairness is transparency.[52] It is difficult to see how the test can be transparent when lenders themselves may not be fully aware of what data are collected, how they are computed to compile a consumer's profile, or the metrics used to make an assessment.[53] The assessment is certainly not transparent to consumers, and misunderstandings abound among consumers about the way in which creditworthiness is assessed.[54] Even if the assessment were made transparent, it is doubtful whether this would offer any benefit to consumers; they would not be in a position to use the information provided to inform their own choices. First, the highly technical nature of the calculation is likely to be outside the grasp of the average consumer.[55] Further, as

---

47 Danielle Keats Citron and Frank Pasquale, 'The Scored Society: Due Process for Automated Predictions' (2014) Washington Law Review Vol 89 Issue 1, 1.
48 Rule 5, Financial Conduct Authority *Consumer Credit Sourcebook (CONC)* https://www. handbook.fca.org.uk/handbook/CONC/1/?view=chapter.
49 General Data Protection Regulation (EU) 2016/679.
50 Nikita Aggarwal, 'Big Data and the obsolescence of consumer credit reports' https://www.law. ox.ac.uk/business-law-blog/blog/2019/07/big-data-and-obsolescence-consumer-credit-reports accessed 28 April 2020.
51 Financial Conduct Authority, *Fair Treatment of Customers* https://www.fca.org.uk/firms/ fair-treatment-customers.
52 ibid.
53 (n 27).
54 See, e.g., https://www.which.co.uk/money/credit-cards-and-loans/credit-scores accessed 12 December 2019.
55 (n 18).

already explained, reputable lenders may not extend credit without conducting some form of creditworthiness assessment so consumers who exercise their right to opt-out of the test face alternatives of going without credit services or seeking credit from other sources, neither of which may be practical or desirable.

Finally, even if the conceptual issues around liability, fairness, and transparency can be resolved, it will be extremely difficult for the regulator to scrutinise the application of the test in these circumstances. Arguably, this will be the case whether the assessment is conducted via a black box product or not, because the sophistication of the calculations used means that a clear and binary regulatory judgement may not be possible or even appropriate.

An illustration: the Ford Motor Credit experience

Since 2017, Ford Motor Credit in the United States has been testing machine learning software to predict the likelihood of borrowers defaulting, with apparent success.[56] The test took a large set of anonymised loan application data and processed them via two separate prediction models. It then compared both sets of predictions with the actual incidence of default by consumers on their car loans. The first model used was a logistical regression model of the type traditionally used to assess creditworthiness. This model was used by Ford Credit's own loan underwriting team to make predictions about likely future loan performance and likelihood of default. The second model was a machine learning-based online software system provided by a third-party contractor, ZestFinance.[57] The system was a black box product[58] in the sense that its workings were not designed by or visible to the end user, Ford Credit's financial underwriters. What is known is that the software used contextual data which are not factored into traditional credit-scoring models to generate similar predictions. The product used machine learning to refine these predictions as it gathered data about more consumers. The contextual information examined by the software included facts disclosed in the application for credit but which are often discounted by traditional risk-scoring models; for example, whether a consumer used the same telephone number on successive applications (suggesting stability) or used a different number each time (suggesting lack of stability or fraud risk).[59] When the predictions were compared with the actual performance of the loans, the software was found to be more accurate than the traditional model (applying rule-based scoring to historical financial data) at predicting default. This is significant not because the software was faster or more efficient, but because it was using more holistic factors linked to current status to

---

56 Penny Crossman, 'Ford Credit puts AI to the test' *American Banker, Asset Securitisation Report* (October 2017) 22.
57 Zest Finance Inc (2020) www.zest.ai.
58 (n 46).
59 (n 56).

generate predictions about future behaviour, rather than documented historical data on past conduct. In other words, the assessment was based not on what consumers have done in the past, but what they are likely to do in the future.

Clearly, the initial results should be treated with a degree of caution, and it may be suggested that the underlying motivation for the experiment was to search for ways of lending more to a greater number of borrowers than ever. Nonetheless, the Ford Credit example is interesting because it represents a rare – possibly unique – direct comparison of the two main prediction models in analysing data about the same individuals.

Ford Credit viewed the early indications of the superiority of the machine learning platform as an unqualified success,[60] although it was quick to point out that further development work would be needed as the software continues to evolve, and also that although the software is a powerful tool, the lending decision would always be made by a human underwriter. The automated model does appear to offer several significant advantages. Assessing creditworthiness in this way offers a much better chance of being deemed creditworthy for un-banked or thin-file consumers, including younger consumers and consumers recently arrived from other countries. These customers might automatically be filtered out by an assessment based on historical data, even though they may well in fact be reliable and low-risk borrowers. In this way, the projection model appears to widen financial inclusion and simultaneously offer a potential boost to lenders.

However, from a regulatory perspective, the Ford Credit example offers a clear illustration of some serious potential risks. A lack of transparency in the assessment and decision-making process means that fairness cannot be guaranteed. It is by no means clear which factors form part of the decision-making process, so that while some of the historical bases for discrimination have been overcome, other new grounds may consciously or unconsciously be introduced. There is no indication in the reported information of how much influence nonfinancial considerations have in assessing creditworthiness. Similarly, it is difficult to ascertain how much weighting is applied to individual factors, and requiring disclosure of the process used does not guarantee disclosure of the weighting afforded to various factors. If the credit provider is able to cherry-pick the most profitable customers using sophisticated machine learning techniques, this may work directly against financial inclusion. There is a risk that lenders could circumvent current anti-discrimination laws via the use of proxies. Ultimately, it may operate to make the credit marketplace even less competitive for those on low incomes.[61]

---

60 (n 56).
61 Information such as postal codes or zip codes, for example, may be used as proxies for race or socioeconomic background; see, e.g., National Consumer Council (2004) *Paying More, Getting Less* (London, NCC).

Regulation: possible approaches

In beginning to formulate a possible regulatory approach to the developing creditworthiness assessment, it is necessary to balance a number of competing policy considerations. First is the imperative to avoid a repeat of the credit crunch of 2007–2008. The catastrophic consequences of irresponsible lending continue to have a ripple effect in the current financial marketplace so the prevention of market failure is a high priority for regulators. On the other hand, there is growing recognition that consumers who may previously have been classified as sub- or near-prime because of a lack of documented financial history may in fact present a lower credit risk than has previously been assumed.[62] There is also growing concern about the financial exclusion faced by certain sectors of the population[63] and a widespread desire to reinvigorate the retail financial services marketplace.[64] In order to reach an appropriate balance, a fresh and creative approach may be needed in order to improve inclusivity in the consumer credit sector.

Behavioural economics and information remedies

The modern paradigm for regulation of consumer markets is rooted in the behavioural economics movement.[65] Behavioural economics has been enormously influential in this context and its effectiveness and limits merit detailed evaluation. While there is no single definition of behavioural economics (or its later incarnations, variously known as "behavioural law and economics" and "the new law and economics"),[66] it clearly involves using theoretical tools from psychology to understand consumers' behaviour, choices, and decision making.[67] Classical economic theory is predicated on the assumption that consumers will shop around and actively exercise choice, rewarding traders who behave appropriately and ultimately driving those who do not out of business. The implicit assumptions about consumers' decision making in the classical model are just that: assumptions, not supported by empirical evidence. The idea that people do not always adhere to logic or rationality in their decision making was proposed by Adam Smith as long ago as 1776[68] and explored more recently by popular

62 (n 33).
63 C Walker, P Hanna, and L Cunningham, 'Parasitic Encounters in Debt: The UK Mainstream Credit Industry' (2015) Theory & Psychology Vol 25 Issue 2, 239–256.
64 (n 17).
65 (n 21).
66 F Rischkowsky and T Doring, 'Consumer Policy in a Market Economy: Consideration from the Perspective of the Economics of Information, the New Institutional Economics as well as Behavioural Economics' (2008) Journal of Consumer Policy 31, 285–313.
67 Daniel Ariely, *Predictably Irrational: The Hidden Forces that Shape our Decisions* (Harper Collins 2008).
68 Adam Smith, *An Inquiry into the Nature and Causes of the Wealth of Nations* (Strahan and Caddell 1776).

theorists such as Ariely.[69] The ways in which proven behavioural biases and other influencing factors can be used to help organisations and individuals make better choices were outlined to great acclaim in 2008 by Thaler and Sunstein.[70] They state that a nudge is "an aspect of choice architecture that alters people's behaviour in a predictable way".[71] The use of nudges as instruments of social policy was adopted by the UK Government in 2010 with the establishment of the so-called Behavioural Insight Team (a.k.a. the "Nudge Unit")[72] and by the White House which appointed Prof Sunstein as head of the Office of Information and Regulatory Affairs in 2011.[73] The concept of the nudge is based on a rejection of the classical economic assumption that consumers can be relied upon to drive competition by making rational, informed decisions.

Behavioural economists propose that while consumer behaviour may not always be rational, it is usually highly predictable.[74] For example, consumers are strongly influenced by factors such as the timing of decisions and the way in which choices are framed.[75] In general, consumers are poor at assessing probabilities; they care more about possible losses than potential gains, and they display a very strong inertia bias, or tendency to the status quo.[76] Notably, in the field of financial services, when presented with a choice (perhaps in the form of a selection from a list or a checkbox on an application form), consumers are disproportionately inclined to fall back on pre-selected default options even where these are suboptimal choices when assessed in terms of the interests of the consumer.[77] The predictability of outcomes resulting from an analysis of the factors affecting consumers' decisions can be capitalised upon by firms that may use this information to exploit consumers.[78] Clearly, the more data points captured by lenders, the greater the possibility of harm. Equally, however, argue its proponents, the very fact of this predictability can and should be used by regulators to assist or guide consumers to make better choices and to improve the effectiveness of regulation, and specifically of consumer remedies.

69 (n 67).
70 Richard Thaler and Cass Sunstein, *Nudge: Improving Decisions about Health, Wealth and Happiness* (Yale 2008).
71 ibid, 6.
72 P Ormerod, 'A Network is as Good as a Nudge for a Big Society' (2010) Financial Times London 15 September 2010.
73 J Weisman and J Bravin, 'Obama's Regulatory Czar Likely to Set a New Tone' (2009) Wall Street Journal 8 January 2009.
74 Mike Walker, Behavioural Economics: The Lessons for Regulators' (2017) European Competition Journal Vol 13 No 1, 1–27.
75 (n 67).
76 Richard Thaler and Cass Sunstein, 'Libertarian Paternalism is Not an Oxymoron' (2003) University of Chicago Public Law and Legal Theory Working Paper No 43.
77 (n 63).
78 (n 74).

Thaler and Sunstein characterise the nudge as a form of "libertarian paternalism",[79] and they acknowledge some potential objections to and shortcomings of the model.[80] However, other commentators have raised more fundamental ethical problems with their philosophy.[81] Nudges seek to bypass the consumer's conscious decision-making process, including all the unconscious biases which may influence that process, in order to nudge their choice in the preferred direction of the choice architect. It is difficult to reconcile this practice with the authors' claims to libertarianism and respect for individual autonomy.[82] Indeed, some commentators have gone so far as to suggest that nudges "express contempt and disrespect for individuals as rational beings",[83] and that their legitimacy as regulatory tools should therefore be questioned. Of course, this criticism assumes that individuals are rational beings whose choices are based on reason and evidence – an assumption which is energetically challenged by Thaler, Sunstein, and others.[84] Nonetheless, as mentioned above, the central tenets of behavioural economics have been enthusiastically embraced by regulators in the UK.

As a result of the insights offered by behavioural economics, the past decade has seen rapid development of demand-side remedies (also referred to as information remedies). These are regulatory interventions or nudges which are designed to improve consumers' decision making, and thus assist them to buy services or products which offer better value and are more suited to their needs, or to avoid buying those which are unsuitable for some reason. While making consumers better off as judged by themselves,[85] such measures were also thought to have the important secondary effect of improving competition in the marketplace, as ethical suppliers are rewarded with increased business while unethical or overly costly providers or those who are less effective at meeting consumers' needs must change or die out. Many demand-side remedies involve disclosure or information provision, aimed at rectifying the information asymmetry which often exists between consumers and suppliers. For example, prior to entering into a credit transaction, lenders must advise consumers of the cost of credit on an annual percentage rate (APR) basis, ensuring consistency and comparability of information.[86]

79 Richard Thaler and Cass Sunstein, *Nudge: Improving Decisions about Health, Wealth and Happiness* (Yale 2008), 5.
80 ibid, Ch 15.
81 See, e.g., D Hausman and B Welch, 'Debate: To Nudge or Not to Nudge' (2010) 18 Journal of Political Philosophy, 123.
82 L Bovens, 'The Ethics of Nudge' in T Grune-Yanooff and S Hansson (eds) *Preference Change: Approaches from Philosophy, Economics and Psychology* (Springer 2008).
83 Karen Yeung, 'Nudge as Fudge' (2012) 75(1) Modern Law Review 122–148, 137.
84 See, e.g, T Durkin, G Elliehausen, and T Zywicki, 'An Assessment of Behavioural Law and Economics Contentions and What We Know Empirically About Credit Card Use by Consumers' (2014) Supreme Court Economic Review Vol 22 No 1, 1–54.
85 (n 70).
86 Consumer Credit (Total Cost of Credit) Regulations 2010.

However, more recently, evidence has begun to emerge that these information remedies are not the panacea originally hoped for.[87] As more information is reviewed and generated in the credit transaction, there is a real risk of information overload for consumers, whereby important facts are obscured by the provision of swathes of technical detail.[88] Indeed, there is some evidence that disclosure of the APR, for example, can in fact be misleading for short-term borrowers.[89] In markets where competition is already low or where consumers are less engaged, it is also clear that demand-side remedies do not materially improve competition.[90] Therefore, if consumers are not inclined to be proactive and tend to stay loyal to one firm, other firms will not experience external pressure to perform better, and development may be stifled as it becomes very difficult for new and innovative providers to break into the market. Retail banking is a good example of this kind of marketplace, where customers have historically proved very resistant to moving their current accounts even where their experience of their current provider is poor. This remains the case even when banks take significant measures to improve transparency and cash incentives are offered by competitors.[91]

The effectiveness of demand-side remedies typically depends on an active margin of engaged consumers – those who are active in seeking information, using it to make choices, and calling suppliers to account when things go wrong – to protect the majority, who tend to be disengaged.[92] A central feature of demand-side remedies is the provision of information by traders. Yet there is evidence that this information is not readily received or understood by all consumers,[93] potentially placing those who may already be disadvantaged at an even greater disadvantage. In order for consumers to make informed choices about products and services, and to understand what redress they have if things go wrong, large amounts of sometimes complex information may need to be disclosed by traders. This information is often more easily accessed and understood by consumers who are educated, experienced, and in a position to make an active choice.[94] Those with few choices (e.g., sub- or near-prime borrowers seeking

87 A Fletcher, 'The Role of Demand-Side Remedies in Driving Competition: A Review for Which?' (2016) Centre for Competition Policy, University of East Anglia.
88 Geraint Howells, 'The Potential and Limits of Consumer Empowerment by Information' (2005) Journal of Law and Society Vol 32 No 3, 349–370.
89 S Agarwal, S Chomsisengphet, N Mahoney, and J Stroebel, 'Regulating Consumer Financial Products: Evidence From Credit Cards' (2015) Quarterly Journal of Economics 111–164.
90 Competition and Markets Authority, Financial Conduct Authority 'Helping People Get A Better Deal: Learning Lessons About Consumer Facing Remedies' (2018) UK Consumer Network.
91 Competition and Markets Authority 'Making Banks Work Harder for You: Retail Banking Market Investigation' 9 August 2016.
92 L Berg, 'Who Benefits from Behavioural Economics?' Economic Analysis and Policy 44 (2014), 221–232.
93 (n 74).
94 (n 66).

credit) may benefit far less from information disclosure, even though this group is arguably in greater need of protection from exploitation by unscrupulous traders.[95] There is some evidence that credit scoring in general is poorly understood by consumers and misconceptions abound.[96] In considering the complexity of the creditworthiness assessment, it is doubtful whether full disclosure of the information accessed by lenders or the algorithms used to process it would be of any great benefit to an average consumer. Furthermore, such disclosure may not even be possible given that, as has already been established, the nature and weighting of the information used and the content of the algorithm itself is frequently unknown to the lender. Consumers in this context are already overloaded with vast amounts of complex and sophisticated information.[97] Relying on the provision of further information is unlikely to assist consumers further and may even make the situation worse by obscuring key data which should inform decision making.[98]

In a marketplace where levels of engagement are varied, such as credit cards, overdrafts, motor vehicle finance, or other forms of short-term consumer lending, interventions designed to protect one group of consumers may well have a detrimental effect on other groups. For example, there are some indications that the cap on interest rates for short-term, high-cost credit has made credit more difficult to access for so-called sub- or near-prime borrowers, who are arguably those with the fewest choices of credit providers and the greatest need of credit facilities. The unintended consequence of this action has been to reduce inclusivity thereby making the market less efficient in its function. Thus, in terms of the design of demand-side remedies, one size does not fit all.

Engaged consumers, although often in the minority, may typically behave in more predictably sensible, prudent, and rational ways. They may be better able to access, understand, and use the information with which they are provided and thus be more effective in delivering the traditionally expected economic benefits of driving competition and transparency. It is therefore vital that they remain engaged. An overly paternalistic approach ("libertarian"[99] or otherwise) can be dangerous, resulting in active consumers becoming less active over time, as well as removing any intention of the disengaged majority to ever become engaged.[100] If regulators place too much emphasis on the demand side of the

---

95 See, e.g., S Davies, A Finney, and Y Hartfree, 'Paying to be Poor: Uncovering the Scale and Nature of the Poverty Premium' (2016) University of Bristol Personal Finance Research Centre.

96 See, e.g., M Lewis and A Roberts, 'Credit scores: bust myths and improve your score' *Money Saving Expert* 2019 https://www.moneysavingexpert.com/loans/credit-rating-credit-score/.

97 Geraint Howells, 'The Consumer Credit Litigation Explosion' (2010) Law Quarterly Review 126, 617.

98 (n 88).

99 (n 76).

100 (n 74).

relationship, the rewards of being engaged may diminish and they risk disincentivising consumers to join, or remain in, the active margin. This can lead to poorer outcomes for all.[101] Further, if enforcers play a reactive rather than proactive role, depending on consumers to initiate claims, there is a real risk that traders who breach the regulations will not be sanctioned and that consumers who suffer loss as a result will miss out on compensation.

Therefore, it is submitted that more radical regulatory action on the supply side is also needed to strike an appropriate balance and protect the interests of all consumer groups. There are some indications that a more robust approach to supply-side regulation is beginning to emerge. Supply-side measures are those which place rules around supplier behaviour, preventing harm from occurring, rather than putting choice in the hands of consumers and providing remedies after the fact when detriment occurs. Measures such as price regulation and stricter rules on competition are typically involved. Recent developments in the UK, such as the cap on payday loan charges[102] and the FCA's latest proposals on price regulation,[103] indicate that the tide may be turning on the behavioural approach. Regulators may now be developing an appetite for more robust and intrusive regulation on the supply side. While this is to be welcomed, the question remains of the form such regulation should take.

Alternative approaches to regulation

One frequently expressed criticism of the behavioural economics approach is that it is overly paternalistic and interferes with individual autonomy to an unacceptable extent.[104] Neoliberal models of regulation place a significant degree of responsibility on the consumer to become financially literate and to exercise informed choice.[105] However, this more rights-based approach, which purports to empower the demand side of the market, has been criticised for protecting least those whom it is intended to serve most: low-income or vulnerable consumers and those at the margins. Educated, middle-class consumers with a high degree of financial literacy draw the greatest benefit from an information-based scheme of regulation with informed choice at its heart.[106] Ironically, this group is least likely in fact to depend on compulsory disclosure of information, as they often have access to other sources of advice and information. Conversely, consumers who do not share these attributes may find the high volume of often technical information shared by lenders as part of compulsory disclosure (e.g.,

---

101 (n 87).
102 Financial Services (Banking Reform) Act 2013, s.131.
103 Financial Conduct Authority 'Fair Pricing in Financial Services' (October 2018) Discussion Paper 18/19 www.fca.org.uk/publication/discussion/dp18-09.pdf.
104 See, e.g., Karen Yeung, 'Nudge as Fudge' (2012) 75(1) MLR, 122–148.
105 (n 88).
106 (n 18).

statements of APRs) to be so inaccessible and opaque as to be completely un-helpful.[107] Therefore, an information-based regime could function to exacerbate existing inequalities.

One rationale frequently cited for extending regulation of consumer credit is the prevention of market failure.[108] The *ex ante* or administrative model of regulation manifested in the UK licensing regime is designed to make the marketplace safer and more competitive for consumers by preventing problems before they occur.[109] Conceived in the 1970s, it was intended to prevent loan sharks and other unscrupulous or unsuitable lenders from establishing a presence in the market.[110] The foundations of the regime are close supervision and en-forcement of compliance by the regulator (currently the FCA). While this pro-vides an example of supply-side action which is successful up to a point, it is administratively extremely costly and burdensome and the regime of the Consumer Credit Act 1974 has been heavily and repeatedly criticised for being overly detailed, complex, and technical, an issue only partly alleviated by the changes introduced in the Consumer Credit Act 2006. The *ex ante* model may prevent some problems from arising in the first place, but it does not offer many meaningful remedies for consumers when problems do occur. Much enforce-ment is carried out by the Financial Services Ombudsman, creating a further layer of administrative control without improving transparency.[111]

More recently, there are indications that an equity-based model of regulation of financial services is beginning to emerge.[112] The fair trade approach adopts the more successful elements of earlier regimes with the aim of ensuring an inclusive market and fair access to credit at reasonable prices. It has long been established that poor consumers are repeatedly penalised in the marketplace for being poor.[113] They are typically faced with fewer choices and, because they often have no savings, often pay a short-term premium for goods and services including financial services and credit. A fairness-based approach to regulation aims to avoid this double penalty or "poverty premium". It does so by emphasising the

---

107 (n 88).
108 Ian Ramsey, *Consumer Law & Policy: Text and Materials on Regulating Consumer Markets* (3rd edn Hart Publishing 2012), 43.
109 ibid, 388.
110 Crowther Committee, Consumer Credit: Report of Committee (Cmnd 4596).
111 Consumer Credit Act 2006, s.59.
112 M Kelly-Louw, J P Nehf, and R Rott (eds), *The Future of Consumer Credit Regulation: Creative Approaches to Emerging Problems* (Ashgate 2008).
113 David Caplovitz, *The Poor Pay More: Consumer Practices of Low Income Families* (New York Free Press of Glencoe 1963); S Davies, A Finney, and Y Hartfree, *Paying to be Poor: Uncovering the Scale and Nature of the Poverty Premium* (2016) University of Bristol Personal Finance Research Centre; Dr Lindsey Appleyard, Carl Packman, and Jordon Lazell, *Payday Denied: Exploring the lived experience of declined payday loan applicants* (2018) Coventry University Research Centre.

central importance of fairness in financial dealings. The FCA has repeatedly asserted that treating customers fairly is a central requirement for regulated firms.[114] Under reforms introduced by the Consumer Credit Act 2006,[115] the court has very wide powers to reopen credit agreements or cancel them altogether where it finds that the relationship between lender and borrower is unfair. The question of fairness is key to regulating the creditworthiness assessment, but in order to be effective, regulators must take a proactive rather than a reactive approach to this assessment.

The requirement of fairness

The idea of fairness underpins consumer credit regulation. However, a comprehensive and authoritative definition of fairness remains elusive. The unfair relationship test under s.140A-C of the Consumer Credit Act 1974 replaces the previous prohibition on extortionate credit bargains.[116] Under the old test, the court could make an order in connection with a credit agreement if it was held to be "extortionate". However, the statutory test of an extortionate bargain was strictly applied and difficult to satisfy; payments under such an agreement had to be "grossly exorbitant".[117] The unfair relationship test is much broader and more flexible. It covers the majority of credit agreements entered into by individual consumers.[118] The only agreements not subjected to the test are regulated mortgages (which are subject to separate and extensive regulation) and credit agreements where the borrower is a corporation.[119] The test gives the court extensive powers to revise the terms of a credit agreement or even to set it aside in its entirety where the relationship between lender and borrower is found to be unfair. It must be emphasised that the test extends further than an examination of the terms of the credit agreement. The whole of the relationship between lender and borrower fails to be scrutinised. This includes the terms of the credit agreement itself, the terms of any related agreement, the way in which the lender has exercised its rights under the agreement or a related agreement, and crucially, any other thing done or not done by or on behalf of the lender before or after the making of the agreement. Evidently, this covers the entire transactional history between the parties.[120] It also covers the actions of third

---

114 Financial Conduct Authority, *Fair Treatment of Customers* https://www.fca.org.uk/firms/fair-treatment-customers.
115 Consumer Credit Act 1974 s.140 A(1).
116 Consumer Credit Act 1974, ss.137–140 (repealed).
117 ibid.
118 Consumer Credit Act 1974, s.140A-C.
119 Consumer Credit Act 1974, s.189.
120 Sarah Brown, 'Consumer Credit Relationships – Protection, Self-interest/Reliance and Dilemmas in the Fight Against Unfairness: the Unfair Credit Relationship Test and the Underlying Rationale of Consumer Credit Law' (2016) Legal Studies Vol 36 No 2, 230–257.

parties. It is applied ex post facto so the relationship can be examined in a retrospective manner. In principle, the test would catch the creditworthiness assessment, rendering it liable to scrutiny to assess whether it has been conducted in such a way as to make the relationship between the parties unfair, to the detriment of the consumer.

The terms "fair" and "unfair" remain undefined in the legislation. The scheme of the Consumer Credit Act affords a very wide jurisdiction to the court. The question of fairness in the conduct of the creditworthiness assessment remains untested. It is clear that fairness comprises an element of transparency.[121] It is also undisputed that in order to demonstrate unfairness, a claimant does not necessarily have to show that there has been a breach of statutory or other duty.[122] The court can examine whether the lender has complied with expected standards of professional conduct, meaning that an unfair relationship may be found even if all elements of relevant statutory regulation have technically been complied with. Therefore, there are grounds to suggest that the conduct of the creditworthiness assessment should be subject to judicial scrutiny. In the case of *Plevin v Paragon Personal Finance Ltd*,[123] the Supreme Court handed down guidance on what will constitute an unfair relationship for these purposes. *Plevin* is best known in the context of payment protection insurance (PPI), and the decision paved the way for a wave of PPI-related claims by consumers in the UK in the years which followed. However, for these purposes, it also lays down some clear and helpful guidelines on the nature of unfair relationships.

The claimant Mrs Plevin took a personal loan from Paragon through an intermediary company. The intermediary recommended Mrs Plevin take out a policy of payment protection insurance on the loan, on which it took an undisclosed commission. One of the issues for the court was whether the intermediary was acting "on behalf of" the lender. In the *Plevin* case, the court decided that it was not. Lord Sumption opined that the words "on behalf of" denoted agency; in order to render a relationship unfair, the act or omission complained of must engage the responsibility of the lender as if the lender had done or not done the act itself. Although there was no such relationship of agency in *Plevin*, the creditworthiness assessment clearly does engage the lender's responsibility to the borrower. Therefore, even if the software used to conduct the creditworthiness assessment is provided by a third party and the lender does not have knowledge of the mechanics of the black box assessment, it is something done "by or on behalf of" the lender and thus is caught by the test.

Once a consumer complains that the credit relationship is unfair, the burden of proof is on the lender to demonstrate that it is fair. The difficulty for lenders is that because the creditworthiness assessment is often not transparent even to the

121 *Harrison v Black Horse Ltd* [2011] EWCA Civ 1128.
122 *Patel v Patel* [2009] CTLC 249.
123 *Plevin v Paragon Personal Finance Ltd* [2014] UKSC 61.

lender, it is virtually impossible to show whether or not it is fair. If the lender cannot show that a practice is fair, then the court must conclude for the claimant consumer and make whatever order it considers necessary. Arguably, a creditworthiness assessment which militates against financial inclusion cannot be fair. In a competitive marketplace, the right of the lender to choose their customer may be viewed as being important as the right of the consumer to make an informed choice of lender.[124] However, it is suggested that lenders are using the assessment to "cherry-pick" only the most profitable customers and offering preferential rates to some groups of customers based on criteria which are quite possibly discriminatory and certainly not clear and transparent.[125] There is a dearth of evidential data in this area, and it is suggested that further research is needed to inform any review of regulation. Nonetheless, questions are raised about the nature of responsible lending and financial inclusion.[126] In any event, it is suggested that practices such as these may well be unfair within the broad test prescribed by the CCA.

Where a credit relationship is found to be unfair, the court has a wide discretion with regard to remedies. One route available is to set aside the credit agreement. Rendering a credit agreement unenforceable is a recurring sanction under the CCA regime. However, it has been argued that, particularly where the sanction is triggered by minor errors, trivial fault-free breaches, or software problems, it is a disproportionate response.[127] Moreover, it is difficult to see how unenforceability provisions can be constructive if the ultimate goal of the regulatory regime is financial inclusion. The aim of improving inclusivity may be better served, for example, by making the agreement enforceable only with leave of the court, and subject to certain conditions.[128] Therefore, if the question of fairness is to be reviewed in the context of the creditworthiness assessment, the range of available sanctions must also be considered.

Conclusion

The requirement to conduct a creditworthiness assessment of the consumer before deciding whether to extend credit is a central component of responsible lending.[129] The process by which the assessment is conducted has undergone a very rapid evolution. Whereas once it may have been carried out in person and face to face, it is now more likely to be undertaken remotely and via an AI-based

---

124 (n 17).
125 (n 21).
126 P Skinner, 'Caveat Creditor: Difficulties in Unfair Relationship Claims' (2015) Butterworths Journal of International Banking and Financial Law, 555–557.
127 Richard Mawrey, 'NOSIA than thou? Unenforceabiity provisions in consumer credit regulations' (2019) Butterworths Journal of International Banking and Financial Law.
128 Sarah Brown, 'The Unfair Relationship Test, Consumer Credit Transactions and the Long Arm of the Law' (2009) LMCLQ, 90–112.
129 Directive 2008/48/EC of the European Parliament and the Council 23 April 2008.

software application rather than an individual. Assessing creditworthiness via machine learning in this way appears to offer a route to access mainstream credit for consumers who have no credit history, are in unstable employment, have thin credit files, or might be otherwise classified as sub- or near-prime. The experience of Ford Motor Credit is an example of how an automated assessment could help to encourage fairer access to credit and invigorate the marketplace, while also offering a more complete and accurate means of assessing consumers' creditworthiness. However, it also raises some serious regulatory issues.

The way in which the assessment is conducted is not transparent. Because many lenders simply use so-called black box software products, there is no way for consumers or regulators to scrutinise the way in which the assessment is carried out. This therefore means that the fairness of the assessment cannot be effectively regulated, checked, or guaranteed. The current scheme of regulation, which is rooted in the philosophy of behavioural economics, is inadequate to regulate this form of assessment. Information disclosure and information remedies are the main tools of a behavioural economics-based model of regulation. However, where the information used is not known to the lender and may be so complex, technical, and voluminous as to be overwhelming to the consumer, the remedies offered are not helpful or meaningful to consumers.[130] If the assessment is to be adequately regulated, other models of regulation such as rights- or fairness-based models must be examined.

Currently, online or automated conduct of the assessment is not explicitly contemplated in the Financial Conduct Authority's sourcebook.[131] This means that there is no guidance for lenders on its responsible or ethical use. The GDPR offers a partial solution, but this is of limited use where the process of assessment is very complex or the relative weighting of assessment criteria is not known or disclosed. The CCA 1974 does contemplate a need for lenders to act fairly in their dealings with consumers. This is encapsulated in the unfair relationship test in s.140A-C of the CCA 1974. The broadly drafted test is sufficiently wide to catch both the content and conduct of the creditworthiness assessment. However, the question of what fairness requires in this context has not yet been tested by the court. What is quite clear is that a lender subject to a complaint of unfairness by a consumer will face considerable difficulty in seeking to defeat such a complaint. One must therefore conclude that the current regulatory regime is not equipped to deal with the issues arising from an automated creditworthiness assessment.

There are some indications of change on the horizon. In 2016, the FCA set up a regulatory sandbox,[132] which is a test environment within which businesses can test new or innovative business propositions in a controlled environment, with

130 (n 88).
131 Financial Conduct Authority, FCA Handbook (TSO 2019).
132 https://www.fca.org.uk/firms/regulatory-sandbox accessed 20 September 2019.

access to real consumers and subject to regulatory supervision. This indicates a willingness on the part of the regulator to engage with new and potentially disruptive ways of doing business which is encouraging. As currently set up, the sandbox test is initiated by businesses approaching the FCA, and subjects are selected by the regulator from the proposals it receives. To date, no testing has been completed of creditworthiness software. It is submitted that regulatory testing of a black box creditworthiness assessment is urgently needed for all the reasons set out above. This will require the regulator to seize the initiative and set a new agenda in this area. A fresh and creative approach to regulating the assessment could bring about a welcome improvement in fair access to credit for all consumers.

7 Consumer peer-to-peer lending and the promise of enhancing access to credit

Lessons from the Netherlands

*Martha Elisabeth Buit**

Introduction

Credit is indispensable for the modern consumer. Access to credit allows consumers to meet their basic needs and to enhance their social welfare, also enabling markets to function and stimulating economic growth.[1] However, access to credit is not as self-evident as it seems. Vulnerable consumers (such as low-income people, the unemployed, minorities or migrants, persons with disabilities, young people, and oftentimes women) are at risk of having only limited to no access, often being left with unsustainable options, such as payday lending with its exorbitant interest rates.[2] Furthermore, since the 2008 financial crisis, the opportunities for consumers to gain access to credit have become further limited, as traditional incumbent lenders, such as banks, tend to refuse credit to high-risk consumer groups despite their increased needs to obtain it.[3]

---

* PhD candidate at the Groningen Centre for European Financial Services Law, University of Groningen, the Netherlands. E-mail: m.e.buit@rug.nl. The author would like to express her sincere thanks and gratitude to Prof. O. O. Cherednychenko, Prof. M. H. Wissink, Dr. M. Duchateau, A. R. Voorwinden, B. Tadema, E. Bambrough, and M. Windsma for their valuable suggestions and comments on the previous versions of this chapter.
1 O. O. Cherednychenko, 'The EU Charter of Fundamental Rights and Consumer Credit: Towards Responsible Lending?' in H. Collins (ed.), *European Contract Law and the Charter of Fundamental Rights* (Intersentia 2017), 139.
2 E. Macchiavello, *Microfinance and Financial Inclusion. The Challenge of Regulating Alternative Forms of Finance* (Routledge 2018), 7–9. See also Financial Conduct Authority, *Consumer Vulnerability* (Occasional Paper No. 8 2015).
3 Ibid., 17; C. R. Everett, 'Origins and Development of Credit-Based Crowdfunding' (2014), SSRN Electronic Journal http://doi.org/10.2139/ssrn.2442897 accessed 30 June 2020, 1, 12; I. J. Galloway, 'Peer-to-Peer Lending and Community Development' (2009), 39 *Community Investments Center Working Contribution Federal Reserve Bank of San Francisco*, 1, 1; C. Corr, 'Alternative Financial Credit Providers' (2007) https://www.semanticscholar.org/paper/Alternative-Financial-Credit-Providers-in-Europe-Corr/fd5c8a3125c5357895 4655199fc8e4e5fac84bab#citing-papers accessed 30 June 2020; A. Schwienbacher and B. Larralde, 'Crowdfunding of Small Entrepreneurial Ventures', in D. Cumming (ed.), *Oxford Handbook of Entrepreneurial Finance* [Oxford University Press (forthcoming) 2010], 1, 20; I. Akkizidis and M. Stagars, *Marketplace Lending, Financial Analysis, and the Future of Credit. Integration, Profitability and Risk Management* (Wiley 2016), 30; Commission,

In response to this credit crunch, consumer-peer-to-peer lending (consumer P2PL) has become one of the biggest alternative financing methods in the EU consumer credit market. As the first platform, the British Zopa, started to operate in 2005, the post-crisis period has witnessed a significant growth of P2PL, which has been characterized as a sustainable and trustworthy alternative to bank finance.[4] In particular, it is often observed by academics and the industry that consumer P2PL enhances access to credit for consumers who are not able to obtain it from a bank.[5]

This chapter focuses on the question of whether consumer P2PL has the potential to enhance access to credit. Based on the empirical research on the Dutch consumer P2PL platforms' business models and a legal analysis of the European and Dutch regulatory framework, this chapter will show that access to credit through P2PL is not as self-evident as it may seem at first sight. It is argued that, in order for consumer P2PL platforms to be able to meet the needs of consumers who cannot obtain credit from traditional lenders, the applicable regulatory framework should enable such platforms to do so.

The chapter is divided into three sections. Section 2 discusses the background of P2PL as well as the business models of the Dutch consumer P2PL platforms which provide unsecured consumer lending. Building on this empirical evidence, Section 3 examines whether the platforms are regulated as "credit providers" under the Consumer Credit Directive[6] (CCD) and Dutch financial supervision law. It investigates whether the platforms are obliged to perform the

Proposal for a Regulation of the European Parliament and of the Council on European Crowdfunding Service Providers (ECSP) for Business ['COM(2018)113 final'] https://ec. europa.eu/info/law/betterregulation/initiatives/com-2018-113_en accessed 30 June 2020, 1.

4 R. Lenz, 'Peer-to-Peer Lending: Opportunities and Risks' (2016) 7 European Journal of Risk and Regulation https://papers.ssrn.com/sol3/papers.cfm?abstract_id=2912164 accessed 30 June 2020, 1, 3–4; B. Zhang a.o., *Sustaining Momentum: The 2nd European Alternative Finance Industry Report* (2016), Cambridge Centre for Alternative Finance https://www. jbs.cam.ac.uk/faculty-research/centres/alternative-finance/publications/sustaining-momentum/#.Xvw8zudcLb0 accessed 30 June 2020, 14.

5 Macchiavello (n 2), 219; O. O. Cherednychenko and J. M. Meindertsma, 'Irresponsible Consumer Credit Lending in the Post-Crisis Era: Is the Consumer Credit Directive Fit for its Purpose?' (2019) 42 Journal of Consumer Policy, 483, 498; H. Kim and L. De Moor, 'The Case of Crowdfunding in Financial Inclusion: A Survey' (2017), 26 *Strategic Change*, 193, 194; A. Bachmann a.o., 'Online Peer-to-Peer Lending – A Literature Review' (2016), 16 *Journal of Internet Banking and Commerce*, 1, 3. See also Commission, *Unleashing the Potential of Crowdfunding in the European Union, Communication from the Commission to the European Parliament, the Council, the European Economic and Social Committee and the Committee of the Regions* COM(2014)172 https://ec.europa.eu/info/publications/communication-crowdfunding_en accessed 30 June 2020, 2, where the Commission envisages the great potential of crowdfunding in general to complement traditional sources of finance.

6 Directive 2008/48/EC of the European Parliament and the Council of 23 April 2008 on credit agreements for consumers and repealing Council Directive 87/102/EEC (Consumer Credit Directive).

creditworthiness assessment, which in turn may obstruct consumers' access to credit. Particular attention is given to the regulatory style of the Dutch Authority for the Financial Markets (*Autoriteit Financiële Markten;* AFM) and its influence on the platforms' substantive obligations towards consumers. In addition, the legal framework is analyzed, in particular in light of the empirical evidence concerning how the platforms deal with credit risk and consumer access to credit. Section 4 provides some final remarks on the potential of consumer P2PL to enhance financial inclusion.

Before we can proceed with the analysis, however, some remarks as to the methodology are in order. First, it goes beyond the scope of this chapter to investigate who exactly the vulnerable consumers in the field of financial services are, specifically the ones who cannot gain access to bank credit. The chapter assumes such consumers exist and need credit, focusing on the issue of whether the CCD or Dutch financial supervision legislation enables them to engage in P2PL.[7] Second, the empirical analysis involved the examination of the business models of the existing Dutch consumer P2PL platforms that provide unsecured consumer installment credit. In the Netherlands, up until April 2019, three platforms provided such credit, namely Lender&Spender, Lendex, and Geldvoorelkaar.nl. As of April 2019, Geldvoorelkaar.nl only allows small- and medium-sized enterprises to make use of their platform. Nonetheless, this platform has been included in this study because it uses a P2PL business model which is also common in other European countries. Further, some empirical evidence concerning consumer access to the investigated P2PL platforms is discussed, focusing on the publicly available evidence on their websites concerning the creditworthiness assessments as well as an interview conducted with Lender&Spender. In order to identify the business models of the three platforms, public information on their websites, general terms and conditions, and loan agreements were examined. In particular, the questions of which entity/ entities (the lenders and/or the platform) fund(s) the loan amount and who the contractual counterparty of the consumer-borrower is have been considered. The analysis has identified two main business models: Model A (new; used by Lender&Spender and Lendex) and Model B (the client segregated account model; previously used by Geldvoorelkaar.nl). These business models – and thus not individual P2PL platforms – will be used for the legal analysis to answer the

---

7 See, e.g., IPSOS, *Consumer vulnerability across key markets in the European Union – Final Report* (European Commission 2016) https://op.europa.eu/en/publication-detail/-/ publication/d1af2b47-9a83-11e6–9bca-01aa75ed71a1/language-en accessed 30 June 2020, 335 ff; Financial Conduct Authority, *Consumer credit and consumers in vulnerable circumstances* (2014) https://www.fca.org.uk/publications/research/consumer-credit-and-consumers-vulnerable-circumstances accessed 30 June 2020; CIVIC Consulting, *The Overindebtedness of European Households: Updated Mapping of the Situation, Nature and Causes, Effects and Initiatives for Alleviating its Impact* (European Commission 2013) https://ec.europa.eu/info/business-economy-euro/banking-and-finance/consumer-finance-and-payments/retail-financial-services/credit/consumer-credit_en accessed 30 June 2020.

question of whether the platforms using a particular business model can and should be seen as "credit providers."

Consumer P2PL

Background

The post-crisis regulatory environment in the EU forced banks to reduce their credit risk.[8] This, in combination with transaction costs incurred for processing small loans to low-income individuals, made it unappealing for banks to provide credit to such consumers.[9] This meant that consumers with little to no credit history, low or fluctuating income, and sometimes even the middle-income consumer found it increasingly difficult to receive finance. Additionally, many households and other parties withdrew from the traditional financial markets, with the banks' conventional role as credit providers being criticized and put in the spotlight of public opinion.[10] Combined with a low-interest rate environment, both capital holders and capital seekers turned to alternative market infrastructures that enable consumers and businesses to enter into direct, disintermediated relationships with lenders without the need for a single point of control.[11] In turn, this led to the growing popularity of P2PL. In 2017, European consumer P2PL provided around €1,392 million worth of consumer loans, accounting for the largest share of European alternative finance (namely, 41% of the total volume).[12] These data do not include the United Kingdom which has the largest P2PL market in Europe, adding up to a total of £1.4 billion.[13] At the same time, the Dutch consumer P2PL market remains significantly underdeveloped, with an estimation of around €6.1 million.[14]

---

8 Credit risk refers to the possibility of a loss resulting from a borrower's failure to repay a loan or meet the contractual obligations. See T. van Gestel and B. Baesens, *Credit Risk Management. Basic Concepts: Financial Risk Components, Rating Analysis, Models, Economic and Regulatory Capital* (Oxford University Press 2009), xi.

9 S. Johnson, A. Ashta, and D. Assadi, 'Online or Offline? The Rise of Peer-to-Peer Lending in Microfinance' (2010) 8 *Journal of Electronic Commerce in Organizations*, 26.

10 L. Pelizzon, M. Riedel, and P. Tasca, 'Classification of Crowdfunding in the Financial System,' in P. Tasca, T. Aste, L. Pelizzon, and N. Perony (eds.), *Banking Beyond Banks and Money. A Guide to Banking Services in the Twenty-First Century* (Springer 2016), 6.

11 European Banking Authority, *Discussion Paper on the EBA's Approach to Financial Technology (FinTech)* (2/2017) https://www.eba.europa.eu/-/eba-publishes-a-discussion-paper-on-its-approach-to-fintech accessed 30 June 2020, 6.

12 Ziegler a.o., *Shifting Paradigms. The 4th European Alternative Finance Benchmarking Report* (2019), Cambridge Centre for Alternative Finance https://www.jbs.cam.ac.uk/faculty-research/centres/alternative-finance/publications/shifting-paradigms/#.Xvw8IedcLb0 accessed 30 June 2020, 16, 31.

13 B. Zhang a.o., *The 5th UK Alternative Finance Industry Report* (2018), Cambridge Centre for Alternative Finance https://www.jbs.cam.ac.uk/faculty-research/centres/alternative-finance/publications/5th-uk-alternative-finance-industry-report/#.Xvw8hedcLb0 accessed 30 June 2020, 35.

14 Ziegler a.o. (n 12), 85.

Banks are still the world's largest supplier of credit.[15] In comparison with the overall market volume of unsecured bank loans, the market share percentage of P2PL in 2015 has been estimated to be around 1% in Europe and 2–3% in the United Kingdom.[16] However, P2PL shows extreme annual growth rates of 80% to 100% on average indicating that P2PL will become even more significant in the near future.[17] The aforementioned is underwritten by the European Commission (EC) which, even though the P2PL market is still developing, has recognized P2PL as an important source of nonbank finance and made its continued growth part of the deeper and safer development of a European Single Market for consumer credit.[18] On a systemic level, P2PL increases competition in the financing market and is a stimulus for further financial innovation. In consumer credit markets, P2PL may not only expand financing opportunities but also provide consumers with easier and faster access to credit on better terms and conditions than those of an incumbent institution.[19]

However, there are also risks involved in P2PL.[20] With respect to access to credit, the most immediate negative consequence is over-inclusion of consumers, which can result in overindebtedness. Not only does the expansion of lending mean that riskier loans are granted, but also that new, riskier borrowers from low economic groups enter the market.[21] Furthermore, P2PL platforms can have perverse incentives to over-include borrowers as these platforms use a fee structure that aims to maximize the number of established loans between lenders

15 Akkizidis and Stagars (n 3), 30; Galloway (n 3), 1.
16 Lenz (n 4) 3–4.
17 Ziegler a.o. (n 12), 16; Zhang a.o. (n 4), 14.
18 Commission, *Consumer Financial Services Action Plan: Better Products, More Choice, Communication from the Commission to the European Parliament, the Council, the European Central Bank, the European Economic and Social Committee and the Committee of the Regions* (COM(2017)139) https://ec.europa.eu/info/publications/consumer-financial-services-action-plan_en accessed 30 June 2020, 8–9; Commission, *Crowdfunding in the EU Capital Markets Union, Commission Staff Working Document* SWD(2016)154 https://ec.europa.eu/info/publications/crowdfunding-eu-capital-markets-union_en accessed 30 June 2020, 30–31; COM(2014)172 (n 5), 11–12.
19 COM(2014)172 (n 5), 4–5, 9.
20 See, for an overview, E. Macchiavello, 'Financial-Return Crowdfunding and Regulatory Approaches in the Shadow Banking, FinTech and Collaborative Finance Era' (2017) 14 European Company and Financial Law Review, 662, 669–671; Lenz (n 4); SWD(2016)154 (n 18), 16; COM(2014)172 (n 5), 5–8.
21 G. Comparato, 'The Rationales of Financial Inclusion' (2015) 11 *ERCL*, 22, 33; Cherednychenko and Meindertsma (n 5), 484; I. Domurath, 'A Map of Responsible Lending and Responsible Borrowing in the EU and Suggestions for a Stronger Legal Framework to Prevent Over-indebtedness of European Consumers' in H. W. Micklitz and I. Domurath (eds.), *Consumer Debt and Social Exclusion in Europe* (Taylor & Francis Ltd 2015), 155, 159–160; A. Rona-Tas, 'The Role of Credit Bureaus in Globalised Economies: Why They Matter Less Than We Think and How They Can Matter More' in H. W. Micklitz and I. Domurath (eds.), *Consumer Debt and Social Exclusion in Europe* (Taylor & Francis Ltd 2015).

and borrowers. In other words, the more loan agreements are concluded on a platform, the more fees the platform will collect.[22]

At the same time, P2PL platforms depend on their reputation for further growth and the continuation of their activities.[23] As relative newcomers in the industry who are highly dependent on attracting new borrowers and lenders, these platforms need to make sure that their borrowers and lenders have trust in them and the P2PL industry in general. Hence, platforms need to be financially and operationally resilient, maintain their reputation, and build customer trust. All this is linked with the way they manage and lower their credit risk.[24] In general, the more financially vulnerable a consumer is, the higher the default risk. Developing an effective credit assessment plays an important role in preventing over-inclusion in the credit market.[25] The regulatory approach to P2PL with respect to the consumer's creditworthiness assessment is discussed below. But first the two identified business models, Model A and Model B, are described.

The empirical analysis of Dutch consumer lending platforms' business models

As mentioned earlier, three unsecured consumer lending platforms have been analyzed with respect to their business model features (specifically the money lending streams and contractual relationships), with the two models being identified. First, the characteristics of Model A platforms will be discussed, after which follows a similar analysis regarding Model B platforms.

The P2PL process at Model A platforms commences when a consumer submits an online loan application on the platform's website. During this phase, the borrower indicates the required amount and maturity of the loan and submits all required documents for the credit risk analysis. If the application is successfully submitted, the platform processes it and conducts its own assessment of the underlying credit risk. In case of approval, the platform finances the loan from its own funds and transfers the requested amount directly to the borrower. The platform then transfers the claims that arise from the loan agreement to the lenders through acts of assignment.[26] These lenders – who are mostly consumers – have gained

---

22 E. A. Omarini, 'Peer-to-Peer Lending: Business Model Analysis and the Platform Dilemma' (2018) 2 International Journal of Finance, Economics and Trade, 31, 40.

23 Ibid, 38–39.

24 Ibid, 40.

25 Ibid, 40; see also A. Mehrotra, 'Financial Inclusion Through FinTech – A Case of Lost Focus' [2019] *International Conference on Automation, Computational and Technology Management*, 103, 105.

26 In the Netherlands, acts of assignment are defined as a way to transfer a registered claim to a third party. In case of P2PL, acts of assignment ex art. 3:84/94 Dutch Civil Code entail that the loan agreement between the borrower and platform remains. The only difference is that – after the acts of assignment – the lenders become the creditors of the claims that arise out of the loan agreement. The acts are undisclosed when the original creditor does not mention to the borrower that the lenders become the creditors of the claim. The consequences of this

access to the platform by signing a user agreement. Although lenders may determine the amount they want to invest through the platform (which varies from hundreds to thousands of euros), they are not able to choose to finance a particular loan as the transfer of the claims is executed on a pro rata basis, depending on the amount each lender lends out. The money flows through a third-party account (*Stichting Derdengelden;* TPA) set up by the platform, except for the pre-financing from the platform to the borrower.[27] Therefore, the lenders fund the loan even though the loan origination stems from the platform. This construction has consequences for the contractual relationships. As the platform is the entity that advances the loan amount to the borrower, the contractual relationship concerning the loan agreement is between the platform and the borrower. This contractual relationship continues to exist, even when the platform enters into separate agreements with the lenders.

Contrary to Model A, Model B has already been described in the academic literature and is called the "client segregated account model," which is used by UK-based platforms such as Zopa.[28] When a borrower's loan request is approved, the request is placed on a website where individual lenders can choose the loans they want to invest in. After a request is fully funded, the lenders pay the amount they want to lend to a TPA, which transfers the loan amount directly to the borrower. Consequently, Model B platforms neither prefinance nor fund the loan in any way. Moreover, borrowers and lenders face each other as contractual counterparties in the loan agreement.

form are not further discussed here. However, it is important to differentiate acts of assignment from "transfer of contract" ex art. 6:159 Dutch Civil Code (*contractsovername*) where the entire contractual position is transferred to another party. Under this article, the lenders would become the new contractual counterparty of the consumer-borrower (which would make the situation – after the transfer of contract – identical to that of Model B).

27 In general, a TPA is an independent foundation with its own board and bank account that exists to keep all the cash flows of third parties separated from that of the platform. When a platform goes bankrupt, the money stored at the TPA is not affected by the bankruptcy. In practice, the TPA can be seen as an extension of the platform, see Lenz (n. 4), 17; O. Havrylchyk and M. Verdier, 'The Financial Intermediation Role of the P2P Lending Platforms' (2018) 60 *Comparative Economic Studies*, 115, 119. Therefore, this chapter regards the TPA solely as an executive body that is used by the platform to transfer money from and to the lenders and borrowers. As the platform is fully responsible for the actions of the TPA under Dutch law, the legal status of the TPA is not discussed separately.

28 Lenz (n 4), 8. See for more information on other business models: E. Kirby and S. Worner, *Crowd-funding: An Infant Industry Growing Fast* (2014) International Organization of Securities Commissions Research Department Staff Working Paper 3/2014 http://www.memofin.fr/uploads/library/pdf/Crowd-funding-An-Infant-Industry-Growing-Fast[1].pdf accessed 30 June 2020; 16 ff.; F. Brunetti, 'Web 2.0 as Platform for the Development of Crowdfunding,' in R. Bottiglia and F. Pichler (eds.), *Crowdfunding for SMEs. A European Perspective* (Macmillan Publishers Ltd. 2016), 64 ff.; S. Sharma and N. Lertnuwat, 'The Financial Crowdfunding with Diverse Business Models' (2016) 2 *Journal of Asian and African Social Science and Humanities*, 74, 82 ff.

As Section 3 will show, it matters when a platform uses a business model comparable or equal to Model A or Model B as platforms only have an obligation to assess a consumer's creditworthiness when they can be legally qualified as a "credit provider" in accordance with the CCD and Dutch financial supervision legislation.

Regulating access to credit in consumer P2PL: lessons from the Netherlands

In 2016, the EC declared that there was no strong case for EU level policy intervention as consumer P2PL is still a fast-developing market, operating on a predominantly local scale.[29] In 2017, an impact assessment led to the proposal of a regulation that introduces a European license for business P2PL and equity-based crowdfunding platforms to offer cross-border services in Europe.[30] However, (cross-border) lending services in relation to consumers are excluded from the scope of the proposal.[31] Therefore, the CCD and Member States' legal frameworks regulate consumer P2PL. In both the CCD and Dutch financial supervision law, "credit providers" have an obligation to perform a creditworthiness assessment. Therefore, the legal definition of a credit provider will be discussed, followed by an assessment of whether Model A and Model B platforms fit into this definition (Section 3.1). Subsequently, the legal requirements of the creditworthiness assessment will be explained to examine the strictness of the assessment (Section 3.2). Finally, the credit risk standards used by the platforms are analyzed in light of the findings from the empirical analysis of their business models (Section 3.3).

Platforms as "credit providers" under the CCD and Dutch law

In order for the platforms to fall within the framework of the CCD, the models have to be regarded as "credit providers."[32] In short, the CCD applies to credit agreements in which a creditor (i.e., a natural or legal person in the course of its trade, business, or profession) grants or promises credit to a consumer.[33] Evidently, the drafters of the CCD designed the legislation concerning the creditworthiness assessment with the conventional borrowing model in mind.[34] The standard P2PL business model (Model B) does not fit into this legal framework, insofar as these platforms do not act as lenders. Generally, they are not

29 SWD(2016)154 (n 18), 31.
30 COM(2018)113 final (n 3).
31 Ibid, 2, 13.
32 Article 3 CCD.
33 Article 3(b) CCD.
34 Cherednychenko and Meindertsma (n 5), 506.

the counterparty of the borrower nor do they finance the loan, implying that they do not grant credit, nor promise it. The latter is a significant difference in comparison to traditional credit providers, as the loans do not enter the platforms' balance sheet. As a result, these platforms fall outside the CCD's scope of application when it comes to certain credit provision articles, such as the creditworthiness assessment.[35] On the other hand, Model A platforms do grant credit, even though they only prefinance the loan. This means that such platforms will most likely fall under the scope of the credit provision measures of the Directive.

As for the applicability of the Dutch standard of a "credit provider," the models can be qualified comparably to the standard of the CCD. Most rules on credit provision, including those on the consumer's creditworthiness assessment, are laid down in the Dutch Financial Supervision Act (*Wet op het financieel toezicht*, Wft). According to the Wft, there has to be a "professional credit provider" who, in short, either makes a direct or indirect sufficiently determined proposal to enter into a credit agreement as the *counterparty* of a consumer, or takes over the claims under the credit agreement from the original credit provider.[36] Platforms with a business model structure as the one in Model A will qualify as professional credit providers. However, platforms under Model B do not, as they are neither the counterparty of the consumer nor the financier of the loan. Nevertheless, in practice, the AFM qualifies them as credit providers as well, preventing the provision of credit from being an unregulated activity and, potentially regulating the platforms stricter than required by law.[37]

The regulatory approach of the AFM towards consumer P2PL

For consumer P2PL platforms, the AFM applies a uniform standard of consumer protection and access as – irrespective of the actual business model of a platform – the regulator regards all consumer P2PL platforms as the counterparty of the consumer-borrower. The AFM has not explicitly indicated the reasons for this (potential) expansion. In my view, Silverentand rightly points out that the AFM wanted to avoid the possibility that the provision of consumer credit would be an unregulated activity in the case of P2PL, and perceived P2PL platforms as the designated parties to burden with the requirements for licensed credit providers.[38] Otherwise, this obligation would fall on the lenders – a highly diverse

---

35 See also Cherednychenko and Meindertsma (n 5), 506–507. However, as these platforms can be qualified as credit intermediaries under article 3(f) of the CCD, they would have to comply with certain obligations concerning, for example, the provision of information that are similar to those of credit providers.

36 Article 1:1 under "offering" sub a jo. 1:1 under "offeror" jo. 2:60 Wft.

37 This information was obtained through an interview the author conducted with the AFM. See also L. J. Silverentand a.o., *Hoofdlijnen Wft (Recht en Praktijk nr. FR6)*, (Kluwer 2018), 415–416.

38 Ibid, 415–416.

group that can consist of tens to hundreds of retail and/or institutional entities.[39] Requiring each of them to obtain a license to provide credit would make P2PL impracticable. From the perspectives of ensuring a high level of consumer protection, legal certainty and uniformity of the law, it is a highly justifiable regulatory style. However, it is arguably one that conflicts with the rationale of maximum harmonization of the CCD as imposing stricter legal requirements other than those falling on credit intermediaries would be inconsistent thereto. Also, such regulation could hinder platforms in further innovating their business models and/or services let alone, as will be discussed below, influence the accessibility of them.[40]

Regardless, in the Netherlands, both Model A and Model B P2PL platforms are subject to licensing requirements connected with the provision of credit and must comply with the substantive obligations resulting therefrom.[41] The current regulation requires all platforms to comply with general reporting requirements towards the AFM, as well as far-reaching prudential and conduct of business rules, which could be perceived as burdensome by small and new credit providers. In terms of prudential rules, one can think of suitability, professional competence, and reliability requirements for directors or other personnel, as well as requirements concerning the business operations and control structure.[42] Concerning rules of conduct, platforms have to introduce a method of complaint handling and comply with credit registration requirements, (pre-)contractual information and advertising requirements, a general duty of care, certain commission rules, as well as perform a creditworthiness assessment.[43] The latter will be discussed below in more detail.

The criteria of the creditworthiness assessment according to the CCD and Dutch law

The creditworthiness assessment aims to protect consumers against overindebtedness and insolvency. More specifically, consumers must be protected against the irresponsible granting of credit agreements which are beyond their financial capacities.[44] Against this objective, it is surprising that article 8 of the CCD only imposes a general obligation on the lender. Before the conclusion of a

---

39 G. J. Brugman, 'Wijzigingen in de regeling inzake crowdfunding', [2016] *Beleggingsbelangen*, 31, 33.
40 However, other than briefly stating these problematic aspects, the chapter does not lend itself for an elaborate discussion. For more information, see M.E. Buit, 'Consumenten-peer-to-peer lending-platformen als kredietaanbieders. Een heroverweging noodzakelijk?' (2020), 6 *Tijdschrift Financieel Recht in de Praktijk*, 53-60.
41 Article 2:60 Wft.
42 Article 2:63 Wft.
43 Article 4:32–4:37a Wft.
44 Case C-565/12 *LCL Le Crédit Lyonnais SA vs. Fesih Kalhan*, para. 42–43; see also Domurath (n 21), 162.

credit agreement or subsequent credit increase, the lender has to assess the consumer's creditworthiness "(…) on the basis of sufficient information, where appropriate obtained from the consumer and, where necessary, on the basis of a consultation of the relevant database."[45] The Directive does not specify what has to be understood under the term *sufficient information* and when a consumer is *creditworthy*. In addition, how a consumer's creditworthiness can be determined is undefined, and the question of what the lender must do in case of a negative creditworthiness assessment is not addressed by the Directive. As far as the latter is concerned, the CCD contains no provision that obliges the lender to warn the consumer in case of the negative outcome of the assessment or to deny credit altogether. Accordingly, the Directive leaves Member States with a wide margin of appreciation to fill in these open-ended norms.[46]

The Court of Justice of the European Union (CJEU) affirms that this margin of appreciation exists.[47] More specifically, the CJEU states that for the assessment of creditworthiness, credit providers have a margin of discretion to determine whether the information at their disposal is sufficient to assess the consumer's creditworthiness or whether it must check that information against other evidence.[48] The sufficiency of the information is to be determined on a case-by-case basis. Different factors can be considered, such as the circumstances in which the credit agreement is concluded, the loan amount, and the personal circumstances of the consumer.[49] The credit provider may carry out the assessment solely based on the information supplied by the consumer (provided that the information is sufficient). Yet, mere unsupported declarations by the consumer may not in themselves be sufficient. They must be accompanied by supporting evidence.[50] Therefore, while the credit provider does not have a structural obligation to verify all the information provided, it is obligated to perform further checks in the case of unsupported information.[51]

In the Netherlands, the creditworthiness assessment of article 8 of the CCD was transposed into financial supervision law, particularly the Wft and the Decree on the Conduct of Business Supervision of Financial Undertakings under the Wft (*Besluit Gedragstoezicht financiële ondernemingen Wft*; Bgfo). Based on this

---

45 Article 8(1) CCD; see also Cherednychenko and Meindertsma (n 5), 500.
46 Therefore, one may question to what extent the CCD actually achieves its goal of full harmonization. For more information, see Cherednychenko and Meindertsma (n 5), 507, specifically footnote 75; O. O. Cherednychenko and J. M. Meindertsma, 'Verantwoorde kredietverstrekking aan consumenten in een multilevel governancesysteem' (2014) 13 *Tijdschrift voor Consumentenrecht & Handelspraktijken*, 181, 183.
47 Case 449/13 *CA Consumer Finance SA/Bakkaus en Bonato* [2014] ECLI:EU:C: 2014:2464, para. 36.
48 Ibid, para. 36.
49 Ibid, para. 37.
50 Ibid, para. 39.
51 Ibid, para. 39.

legislation, a professional credit provider must perform a creditworthiness assessment of the consumer-borrower prior to the conclusion of a loan agreement (or an increase in the credit amount) in order to prevent overindebtedness (*overkrediterinng*).[52]

The process involves three steps. First, the provider has to obtain information concerning the borrower's financial position.[53] Second, the provider needs to assess whether the granting of (more) credit is responsible (*verantwoord*).[54] Third, the lender has to decide on the consumer's credit application. If the provision of (more) credit is irresponsible (*onverantwoord*), the provider is not allowed to enter into a credit agreement with the consumer-borrower (respectively grant more credit). This means that the credit provider must refuse to provide the credit (*weigeringsplicht*), which is one of the most far-reaching duties in Dutch law.[55] In the event a credit provider does not comply with these requirements, the AFM, depending on the severity of the act, may issue a warning, give instructions, impose a penalty payment (*last onder dwangsom*) or an administrative fine (*bestuurlijke boete*), revoke a license, or even report a criminal offence to the Public Prosecution Service (*Openbaar Ministerie*).[56]

Whether or not the provision of credit is responsible remains an open standard that has to be applied by the credit provider. Yet, neither the Wft nor the Bgfo contain detailed legal rules as to how this should be done.[57] Concerning the first step of the assessment, the parliamentary history of the implementation of the CCD in Dutch law mentions that a proper assessment of the financial position of the consumer involves the following: The provider must gather information concerning the income of the consumer (such as the source and level of the income); certain fixed expenses (i.e., rent, mortgage, alimony, and health insurance); and the consumer's ability to repay the loan. Here, a weak or insecure position of the consumer (e.g. a young person with low income) increases the chance that the provision of credit would be irresponsible.[58]

In the second step, the lender is required to formulate, document, and apply the criteria under which it assesses the consumer's creditworthiness.[59] However,

---

52 Article 4:34(1) Wft.

53 Article 4:34(1) Wft; see also Cherednychenko and Meindertsma (n 46), 184. In addition, the Dutch meaning of the term "responsible" in relation to the creditworthiness assessment should not be confused with the *obligation of responsible lending* of which the creditworthiness assessment forms an important part. For more information concerning this obligation, see Domurath (n 21).

54 Article 4:34(1) Wft; See also Ibid, 184.

55 Article 4:34(2) Wft; See also Silverentand a.o. (n 37), 382.

56 S. H. L. Niessen and B. J. M. van de Wetering, 'De bijzondere bancaire zorgplicht bij overkrediteering. N.a.v. HR 16 juni 2017, ECLI:NL:HR:2017:1107' [2017] *Nederlands Tijdschrift voor Handelsrecht*, 228, 234.

57 Cherednychenko and Meindertsma (n 46), 184.

58 See the Dutch parliamentary history referred to as *Kamerstukken II* 2009/10, 32 339, nr. 3, 36 (*MvT*).

59 See articles 113–115 Bgfo. Under article 113 Bgfo, a credit provider cannot enter into a

again, legislation does not further elaborate on the question of how the lender has to do this. The AFM has indicated that it considers the codes of conduct of branch organizations as the minimum requirements for a proper creditworthiness assessment.[60] This implies that credit providers have the option (not the obligation) to implement higher restrictions to the access to credit, but cannot lower the standards. The codes of conduct of the Dutch Banking Association (*Nederlandse Vereniging van Banken;* NVB) and the Dutch Association of Finance Companies (*Vereniging van Financieringsondernemingen in Nederland;* VFN) are applicable to P2PL.[61] Both codes are a form of self-regulation to promote what the Dutch banking industry and other credit providers consider responsible lending practices regarding consumer credit, containing (among others) an elaboration of the creditworthiness requirements.[62]

For the assessment of whether the granting of credit is responsible for a consumer, the basic principle of both codes of conduct is that the consumer always has sufficient resources to meet his or her basic needs and to pay his or her fixed costs. Both codes of conduct distinguish between four types of households: single, single with children, cohabiting/married, and cohabiting/married with children. As a general rule, at least 15% of the net income (after deduction of the

credit agreement (of €1000 or higher) when he has not obtained adequate written information concerning the financial position of the consumer in order to assess the creditworthiness of the consumer-borrower. Article 114 Bgfo states that a credit provider of a loan which exceeds €25,000 must consult the data registered at the National Credit Register. Therefore, the formulation of these articles is very open and does not contain specific instructions. See J. M. Van Poelgeest, 'Comments on art. 4:34 Wft', in H. M. Vletter-van Dort a.o. (eds.), *SDU Commentaar Wet op het financieel toezicht* (2015) https://www.legalintelligence.com/documents/24577042?srcfrm=basic+search& docindex=0&stext=J.M.Van Poelgeest%2C 4%3A34 Wft&rid=18eb96a6-efd6-49ba-b4b4-8d8bd5da44ee accessed 30 June 2020.
60 J. M. Meindertsma, 'De kredietwaardigheidstoets in het privaatrecht' [2017] *Tijdschrift voor Consumentenrecht en handelspraktijken*, 115, 117; Silverentand a.o. (n 37), 382.
61 Meindertsma (n 60), 117; J. M. van Poelgeest, *Kredietverstrekking aan consumenten* (Kluwer 2015), 64–65; Cherednychenko and Meindertsma (n 46), 184–185. In short, the NVB consists of the heads of banks operating in the Netherlands and functions as the link between the banking sector, the government, and the public to achieve a strong, healthy, and internationally competitive banking system for the Dutch and foreign banks and credit institutions operating in the Netherlands. See NVB, *Dutch Banking Association (Nederlandse Vereniging van Banken)* (30 June 2020) www.nvb.nl/english/dutch-banking-association-nederlandse-vereniging-van-banken/ accessed 30 June 2020. The VFN is an overarching organization consisting of all sorts of credit providers. It looks after the common interest of their members and promotes a healthy development of the Dutch financial market in general. See VFN, *Wie we zijn* (30 June 2020) www.vfn.nl accessed 30 June 2020.
62 VFN, Normen en gedragscodes (30 June 2020) www.vfn.nl/gedragscodes/; NVB, Gedragscode consumptief krediet (30 June 2020) https://www.nvb.nl/publicaties/gedragscodes/gedragscode-consumptief-krediet/.

standard housing costs and basic income standard) must be available for repayments.[63] When assessing repayment capacity, both codes of conduct maintain a monthly repayment capacity of at least 2% of the amount of credit in the case of installment credit.[64] Lastly, to determine the maximum amount of credit, the net income of the consumer is seen as the starting point from which the costs of living, rent, and other fixed costs have to be deducted.[65]

Overall, the creditworthiness assessment under Dutch law takes a borrower-focused approach.[66] This approach not only focuses on the question of *whether* the consumer can repay the loan (lender-focused), but also *how* the consumer can repay. This assessment requires the credit provider to stand in the shoes of the borrower and assess to what extent these obligations (could) harm the consumer's financial position.[67] For example, the credit provider is required to assess whether the consumer has the long-term ability to repay the loan in a sustainable way (e.g., not having to sell one's house or car, drastically change their household, or frequently default on paying fixed expenses).[68]

In sum, it is not always easy for credit providers to implement the standards correctly, given the fact that they are applied in the circumstances of a specific case. However, the codes of conduct give credit providers further guidance as to the criteria to be used when assessing the consumers' creditworthiness. These are also the requirements that the platforms have to implement in their credit risk analyses. Through these requirements, an attempt is made to strike a balance between the prevention of overindebtedness and the inclusion of consumers in the Dutch credit market. Although credit providers have some leeway in determining the level of credit risk analysis, this leeway is limited. For example, the platforms can choose to enhance the monthly repayment capacity from 2 to 4% or demand that a higher percentage of net income is available for repayments. As such, in practice, room for differentiation seems to result in narrower access to the platforms for consumers rather than the broader one.[69]

---

63 The net income is the net monthly income, without health care, holiday, school, and travel allowances; child benefits; and any tax refunds for medical expenses. At least the following sources of income may be taken into account when calculating the net income: income from permanent employment, a fixed 13th month, a partner's tax credit, and/or government benefits for young disabled persons, persons suffering from a long-term illness, or other similar schemes. Other allowances with a permanent nature may also be considered.
64 Article 6 Code of Conduct VFN and article 7 Code of Conduct NVB.
65 Cherednychenko and Meindertsma (n 46), 185.
66 Cherednychenko and Meindertsma (n 5), 488; Meindertsma (n 60), 117.
67 Ibid, 118.
68 Ibid, 117; see also Van Poelgeest (n 61), 72–73;Cherednychenko and Meindertsma (n 5), 6.
69 This information was obtained through an interview the author conducted with Lender&Spender.

The application of the creditworthiness assessment by the Dutch P2PL platforms

How the leeway available to P2PL platforms within the regulatory framework for the creditworthiness assessment has been used can be exemplified by the Model B platform when it still provided consumer credit. The latter operated risk categories, allowing the lenders to choose a higher rate of return combined with a higher default risk. The interest rate assigned to the borrowers depended on the risk category they were placed in [with 1 being the safest category and 6 being the one with the highest chance of default (corresponding with a start-up)]. These risk classifications represent the payment capacity of the borrower – that is, the maximum financial leeway a borrower has to repay the debt with interest. Almost all consumers were classified in categories 1–3 (the low-risk categories), although no statements can be made based on public information relating to the level of differentiation between these categories.

However, now only Model A platforms are available for consumers in the Netherlands. Such platforms apply a set interest rate which is derived from the chosen ratio between the amount and maturity of the loan and also operate an automated system that is used to select the "creditworthy" consumers at the gate. The platforms have determined a maximum of credit risk and will not allow borrowers to acquire a loan above this threshold. Concerning the strictness of the assessment, Lender&Spender indicated that it exclusively allows consumers who can obtain a bank loan, implying that only creditworthy consumers, as determined by the Dutch financial supervision law and self-regulation, can access the platform.[70] To be more precise, the platform estimates that 80% of the Dutch consumers are eligible to obtain credit from a bank, out of which Lender&Spender focuses on the top 20% only allowing access for consumers with a permanent employment contract or retired employees under the condition that they have never experienced repayment difficulties in the past.[71] In doing so, the platform operates a stricter creditworthiness assessment than banks. According to the platform, the reason behind the exclusion of consumers who cannot turn to banks for credit is that the practice is too risky, for both lenders and borrowers.[72] The maximum interest rate of 14%[73] on consumer loans in the

---

70 This information was obtained through an interview the author conducted with Lender&Spender.
71 J. van Weerdt, *Vormen consumentenleningen een aantrekkelijke belegging?* (29 April 2019) https://www.participaties.nl/Feature/477834/crowdfunding/Vormen-consumentenleningen-een-aantrekkelijke-belegging.aspx accessed 30 June 2020.
72 Ibid.
73 Due to the COVID-19 pandemic, the maximum interest rate on consumer loans is temporarily lowered to 10% as of August 2020. The measure will apply until 1 March 2021 and can be extended for a maximum of 6 months. See Rijksoverheid (17 september 2020) https://www.rijksoverheid.nl/onderwerpen/bescherming-van-consumenten/vraag-en-antwoord/wat-is-kredietvergoeding-en-wat-is-het-maximale-kredietvergoedingspercentage accessed 17 september 2020.

Netherlands in relation to the credit risk makes the practice unsustainable. In addition, the platform also wants to prevent consumers from ending up in financial difficulties due to the loan. Due to the strict legislation concerning the provision of credit, combined with the focus on the upper segment of the market, the platform expects an annual default rate of 0.5% (compared to a general default rate in the Dutch consumer credit market that lies between 0.5 and 2.5%).[74]

Consequently, the platform limits access further than legally required. As explained above, such a practice is allowed under European and Dutch law. Although the desire to protect the consumer underlies the aforementioned choices of the platform, the fact that only a specific group of consumers is allowed (which happens to be the one that poses the least risk of default) seems to be also driven by business-oriented motives, such as reducing the overall credit risk of the company and enhancing the trustworthiness of the platform. This raises concerns about consumer access to the P2PL market. If P2PL is indeed designed to serve the needs of less well-off consumers who cannot easily obtain credit from a bank, financial regulators should rather encourage their access to P2PL rather than restrict it.

Final remarks

That consumer P2PL expands financial access for consumers who cannot obtain bank financing is not as self-evident as it appears at first sight. Overall, consumers who cannot afford a loan from a bank will have difficulties obtaining one from the Dutch P2PL platforms. On the positive side, this may protect consumers against overindebtedness. After all, a credit request must not be granted if it is clear upfront that the consumer is not able to meet his or her repayment obligations. However, this does not mean that all consumers – except for the least risky ones – need to be shunned. Nevertheless, this is the current practice at one of the platforms investigated in this chapter. Even though default rates as low as 0.5% may inspire confidence in the market and enhance the reputation of the platform and the industry, the current approach does not contribute to financial inclusion. Instead of increasing the range of consumers who can obtain credit, it makes it a market for the most well-off consumers only, increasing competition for that specific group.

The way in which P2PL is regulated can obstruct or facilitate financial inclusion. If the platforms are regulated in the same way as traditional lenders, as under Dutch law, they will use the creditworthiness assessment criteria which are equal or even stricter than those used by traditional credit institutions and may even adopt other aspects of their business model.

Whether the current (or even a higher) level of inclusion is desired depends on the role the EU and Member States wish consumer P2PL to play in their credit market(s). However, the EU could provide guidance to Member States regarding the role of consumer P2PL and recommend an appropriate legal

---

74 Ibid.

response. In particular, it could shed light on the extent to which consumer P2PL platforms must have room to experiment with the level of inclusion so as to realize their full potential as a sustainable and trustworthy source of finance for less well-off consumers.

Bibliography

Akkizidis I. & Stagars M., *Marketplace Lending, Financial Analysis, and the Future of Credit. Integration, Profitability and Risk Management* (Wiley 2016).

Brugman G.J., 'Wijzigingen in de regeling inzake crowdfunding' (2016) 6 *Vakblad Financiële Planning* 31–33.

Brunetti F., 'Web 2.0 as Platform for the Development of Crowdfunding', in R. Bottiglia & F. Pichler (eds.), *Crowdfunding for SMEs. A European Perspective* (Macmillan Publishers Ltd. 2016).

Buit M.E., 'Consumenten-peer-to-peer lending-platformen als kredietaanbieders. Een heroverweging noodzakelijk?' (2020), 6 *Tijdschrift voor Financieel Recht in de Praktijk*, 53–60.

Cherednychenko O.O., 'The EU Charter of Fundamental Rights and Consumer Credit: Towards Responsible Lending?' in H. Collins (ed.), *European Contract Law and the Charter of Fundamental Rights* (Intersentia 2017).

Cherednychenko O.O. and Meindertsma J.M., 'Verantwoorde kredietverstrekking aan consumenten in een multilevel governancesysteem' (2014) 13 *Tijdschrift voor Consumentenrecht & Handelspraktijken*, 181–191.

Cherednychenko O.O. and Meindertsma J.M., 'Irresponsible Consumer Credit Lending in the Post-Crisis Era: Is the Consumer Credit Directive Fit for its Purpose?' (2019) 42 *Journal of Consumer Policy*, 483–519.

CIVIC Consulting, 'The Over-indebtedness of European Households: Updated Mapping of the Situation, Nature and Causes, Effects and Initiatives for Alleviating its Impact' (European Commission 2013) https://ec.europa.eu/info/business-economy-euro/banking-and-finance/consumer-finance-and-payments/retail-financial-services/credit/consumer-credit_en accessed 30 June 2020.

Commission, *Proposal for a Regulation of the European Parliament and of the Council on European Crowdfunding Service Providers (ECSP) for Business* ('COM(2018) 113 final') https://ec.europa.eu/info/law/betterregulation/initiatives/com-2018-113_en accessed 30 June 2020.

Commission, *Consumer Financial Services Action Plan: Better Products, More Choice, Communication from the Commission to the European Parliament, the Council, the European Central Bank, the European Economic and Social Committee and the Committee of the Regions* (COM(2017)139) https://ec.europa.eu/info/publications/consumer-financial-services-action-plan_en accessed 30 June 2020.

Commission, *Crowdfunding in the EU Capital Markets Union, Commission Staff Working Document* (SWD(2016)154) https://ec.europa.eu/info/publications/crowdfunding-eu-capital-markets-union_en accessed 30 June 2020.

Commission, *Unleashing the Potential of Crowdfunding in the European Union, Communication from the Commission to the European Parliament, the Council, the European Economic and Social Committee and the Committee of the Regions* (COM (2014)172) https://ec.europa.eu/info/publications/communication-crowdfunding_en accessed 30 June 2020.

Comparato G., 'The Rationales of Financial Inclusion' (2015) *11 ERCL*, 22–45.

Domurath I., 'A Map of Responsible Lending and Responsible Borrowing in the EU and Suggestions for a Stronger Legal Framework to Prevent Over-indebtedness of European Consumers' in H.W. Micklitz and I. Domurath (eds.), *Consumer Debt and Social Exclusion in Europe* (Taylor & Francis Ltd 2015).

European Banking Authority, *Discussion Paper on the EBA's Approach to Financial Technology (FinTech)* (2/2017), https://www.eba.europa.eu/-/eba-publishes-a-discussion-paper-on-its-approach-to-fintech accessed 30 June 2020.

Everett C.R., 'Origins and Development of Credit-Based Crowdfunding' (2014), *SSRN Electronic Journal* http://doi.org/10.2139/ssrn.2442897 accessed 30 June 2020, 1–32.

Financial Conduct Authority, *Consumer Vulnerability* (Occasional Paper No. 8 2015).

Financial Conduct Authority, *Consumer credit and consumers in vulnerable circumstances* (2014), https://www.fca.org.uk/publications/research/consumer-credit-and-consumers-vulnerable-circumstances accessed 30 June 2020.

Galloway I.J., 'Peer-to-Peer Lending and Community Development', (2009) *39 Community Investments Center Working Contribution Federal Reserve Bank of San Francisco*, 1–15.

Havrylchyk O. and Verdier M., 'The Financial Intermediation Role of the P2P Lending Platforms' (2018) *60 Comparative Economic Studies*, 115–130.

IPSOS, *Consumer Vulnerability Across Key Markets in the European Union – Final Report* (European Commission 2016) https://op.europa.eu/en/publication-detail/-/publication/d1af2b47-9a83-11e6-9bca-01aa75ed71a1/language-en accessed 30 June 2020.

Johnson S., Ashta A. and Assadi D., 'Online or Offline? The Rise of Peer-to-Peer Lending in Microfinance' (2010), *8 Journal of Electronic Commerce in Organizations*, 26–37.

Kim H., and De Moor L., 'The Case of Crowdfunding in Financial Inclusion: A Survey' (2017), *26 Strategic Change*, 193–212.

Kirby E. and Worner S., *Crowd-Funding: An Infant Industry Growing Fast* (International Organization of Securities Commissions Research Department, Staff Working Paper 3/2014, 2014) http://www.memofin.fr/uploads/library/pdf/Crowd-funding-An-Infant-Industry-Growing-Fast[1].pdf accessed 30 June 2020.

Lenz R., 'Peer-to-Peer Lending: Opportunities and Risks' (2016), *7 European Journal of Risk and Regulation*, https://papers.ssrn.com/sol3/papers.cfm?abstract_id=2912164&download=yes1 accessed 30 June 2020, 688-700.

Macchiavello E., *Microfinance and Financial Inclusion. The Challenge of Regulating Alternative Forms of Finance* (Routledge 2018).

Macchiavello, E., 'Financial-Return Crowdfunding and Regulatory Approaches in the Shadow Banking, FinTech and Collaborative Finance Era' (2017) *14 European Company and Financial Law Review*, 662–722.

Mehrotra A., 'Financial Inclusion Through FinTech – A Case of Lost Focus' [2019] *International Conference on Automation, Computational and Technology Management*, 103–107.

Meindertsma J.M., 'De kredietwaardigheidstoets in het privaatrecht' (2017) *Tijdschrift voor Consumentenrecht en handelspraktijken*, 115–122.

Niessen S.H.L., and Van de Wetering B.J.M., 'De bijzondere bancaire zorgplicht bij overkreditering. N.a.v. HR 16 juni 2017, ECLI:NL:HR:2017:1107' (2017) *5 Nederlands Tijdschrift voor Handelsrecht*, 228–238.

Omarini E.A., 'Peer-to-Peer Lending: Business Model Analysis and the Platform Dilemma' (2018) *2 International Journal of Finance, Economics and Trade*, 31–41.

Pelizzon L., Riedel M. & Tasca P., 'Classification of Crowdfunding in the Financial System', in P. Tasca, T. Aste, L. Pelizzon, N. Perony (eds.), *Banking Beyond Banks and Money. A Guide to Banking Services in the Twenty-First Century* (Springer 2016).

Rona-Tas A., 'The Role of Credit Bureaus in Globalised Economies: Why They Matter Less Than We Think and How They Can Matter More' in H.W. Micklitz and I. Domurath (eds.), *Consumer Debt and Social Exclusion in Europe* (Taylor & Francis Ltd 2015).

Schwienbacher A. and Larralde B., 'Crowdfunding of Small Entrepreneurial Ventures', in D. Cumming (ed.), *Oxford Handbook of Entrepreneurial Finance* (Oxford University Press (forthcoming) 2010).

Sharma S. & Lertnuwat N., 'The Financial Crowdfunding with Diverse Business Models' (2016) *2 Journal of Asian and African Social Science and Humanities*, 74–89.

Silverentand L.J., *Hoofdlijnen Wft (Recht en Praktijk nr. FR6)* (Kluwer 2018).

Van Gestel T. and Baesens B., *Credit Risk Management: Basic Concepts: Financial Risk Components, Rating Analysis, Models, Economic and Regulatory Capital* (Oxford University Press 2009).

Van Poelgeest J.M., *Kredietverstrekking aan consumenten* (Kluwer 2015).

Van Poelgeest J.M., 'Comments on art. 4:34 Wft', in H.M. Vletter-van Dort (and others) (eds.), *SDU Commentaar Wet op het financieel toezicht* (2015), <https://www.legalintelligence.com/documents/24577042?srcfrm=basic+search&docindex=0&stext=J.M.Van Poelgeest%2C 4%3A34 Wft&rid=18eb96a6-efd6–49bab4b4–8d8bd5da44ee accessed 30 June 2020.

Zhang B., Wardrop R., Ziegler T., Lui A., Burton J., James A. and Garvey K., *Sustaining Momentum: The 2nd European Alternative Finance Industry Report* (Cambridge Centre for Alternative Finance, 2016) <https://www.jbs.cam.ac.uk/faculty-research/centres/alternative-finance/publications/sustaining-momentum/#.Xvw8zudcLb0 accessed 30 June 2020.

Zhang B., Ziegler T., Mammadova L., Johanson D., Gray M. and Yerolemou N., *The 5th UK Alternative Finance Industry Report* (Cambridge Centre for Alternative Finance, 2018) <https://www.jbs.cam.ac.uk/faculty-research/centres/alternative-finance/publications/5th-uk-alternative-finance-industry-report/#.Xvw8hedcLb0 accessed 30 June 2020.

Ziegler T., Shneor R., Wenzlaff K., Odorović A., Johanson D., Hao R., Ryll L., *Shifting Paradigms. The 4th European Alternative Finance Benchmarking Report* (Cambridge Centre for Alternative Finance, 2019) <https://www.jbs.cam.ac.uk/faculty-research/centres/alternative-finance/publications/shifting-paradigms/#.Xvw8IedcLb0 accessed 30 June 2020.

8 Digital debt collection
Opportunities, abuses and concerns

Cătălin-Gabriel Stănescu

Introduction

Since its inception, debt collection has been one of the most dynamic industries. Throughout its millenary existence, debt collection has evolved together with law and technology, proving to be as adaptable as it was lucrative. This process is most evident in the 20th and 21st centuries, when legislation has imposed more and more limits on the debt-collector's range of methods that could be used to extract payment. The techniques employed by the industry have moved from face-to-face discussions and house visits, to written communications (*via* letters, telegrams), the use of telephone, and other means of distance communication, culminating with emails, text messages (SMS), social media, phone apps, and blockchain-based systems.[1]

The debt collection industry has been at the forefront of innovation, being among the first to employ automatization in its activity. Debt collectors have also been one of the main collectors and interpreters of big data in order to extract information that will help them maximize their recovery rates.[2] Moreover, the industry has constantly turned to using other disciplines (psychology and econometrics) and to experimenting (consumer-debtor behaviorism)[3] in the development of its collection methods *via* data gathering and interpretation, standardization, algorithmic scoring, and profiling of debtors. The purpose was twofold: (a) to take advantage of scientific discovery and innovation in order to maximize returns and[4] (b) to stay ahead of the law.[5]

---

1 See, for instance, Jonathan M. C. (Chadds Ford Rosenoer, PA, US), MANAGEMENT OF CONSUMER DEBT COLLECTION USING A BLOCKCHAIN AND MACHINE LEARNING (International Business Machines Corporation (Armonk, NY, US), United States 2018 http://www.freepatentsonline.com/y2018/0285971.html accessed 28 April 2020.

2 Joe Deville, *Lived Economies of Default: Consumer Credit, Debt Collection and the Capture of Affect* (Taylor and Francis, 2015), 105.

3 Id. at 97–99.

4 Id. at 85–89.

5 Colin Hector, 'Debt Collection in the Information Age: New Technologies and the Fair Debt Collection Practices Act', (2011) 99 California Law Review 1601, 1614.

The use of technological innovation has brought significant gains. Computerization has made the debt collection market global and uniform. Debt collectors can now handle more accounts, generating higher returns with the use of less resources.[6] On their end, consumers benefit from better calculations of their debts, better management of their accounts, and less recovery fees.

All the above came at a cost. An activity that was mainly about personal inter-relations is increasingly alienated and impersonal, as it shifts from direct individual contact, toward mass communication, via standardized and automated messages addressed to pools of debtors with similar features. Debt collectors have learned to circumvent old and static legal protections and to exploit the legal gaps generated by technological innovation.[7] Consumer-debtors find themselves victims of targeting and abusive practices, which are not yet covered by the law. In the end, many of the technological developments employed in debt collection maintain the industry at the fringes of legality and ethics.

A brief literature review

The disruptive effects of new technology employed by debt collection agencies have caught the attention of both academics and consumer advocates, mainly on the American shore of the Atlantic.

In 2006, Lauren Goldberg listed a plethora of issues affecting the FDCPA.[8] Among them, she mentioned the use of new technology to target vulnerable groups of consumers (women, the elderly, low-income individuals, or migrants) for collection.[9] She cited media reports of what she called "unfair discrimination" and proposed three solutions: (a) to incorporate a code of ethics in the FDCPA, (b) to ban any form of discrimination based on inherent characteristics (such as age or sex) in collection practices, either within the FDCPA or by enacting separate legislation, and (c) to increase transparency by public disclosure of relevant statistical information about contacted debtors, which would reveal potential discriminatory patterns.[10]

In 2009, the Fair Trade Commission (FTC) issued a Report – The Challenges of Change – in which it concluded that the FDCPA must be modernized to take account of changes in technology, especially those in communication technology. While the FTC clearly stated that debt collectors should be able to use all communication technologies, it opined that the law should be crafted to avoid the unfair usage of such technologies to deceive or abuse consumers.[11]

---

6 Deville, 2015, p. 88.
7 Hector, California Law Review (2011) 1616–1617.
8 Lauren Goldberg, 'Dealing in Debt: The High-Stakes World of Debt Collection after FDCPA,' (2006) 79 Southern California Law Review 711.
9 Id. at 736–738.
10 Goldberg, Southern California Law Review (2006) 740–741.
11 FTC, 'Collecting Consumer Debts: the Challenges of Change' (Federal Trade Commission, 2009), p. vi.

In 2011, Collin Hector drew attention to the fact that although new technologies provide conveniences for collectors and consumers alike, they also create the potential for new forms of deception and raise novel privacy concerns.[12] His paper on debt collection in the information age refers to several US cases where debt collectors have resorted to deceptive uses of social media and other new communication mediums (emails and SMS) in their collection strategies. In his opinion, the main problem was the failure of the legislator to update the existing legislation.[13] He observed that despite what he called a dramatic transformation of the industry, which was moving forward, the regulatory landscape remained largely backward looking. Conclusively, he called for both a comprehensive reform of the national legislation (mainly the FDCPA) and a proactive stance of the supervisory agency.[14]

The issues raised by the debt collectors' use of social media in their relationship with the debtors were also addressed by Eliberty Lopez in 2013.[15] She listed several ways in which debt collectors use social media to track consumers' common names, unlisted phone numbers, and address changes in order to find out whether, despite unpaid debt, consumers still made purchases. The listed cases suggest that this sort of information is used frequently to harass or shame consumers into paying their debts.[16] As solutions to prevent violations of FDCPA on social media platforms, she suggested four different types of action: (a) self-regulation of said platforms (by which they should actively deter FDCPA violations); (b) state criminal actions to prevent impersonation on social media; (c) federal action and calls for the Consumer Financial Protection Bureau (CFPB) to examine and rate the compliance of debt collectors with the FDCPA; and (d) an amendment of the FDCPA on a similar line with that suggested by Hector.[17]

Issues with the use of new technology in debt collection are also reported in Europe, although the academic discussion is almost absent. Note that the intricacies of employing new technology in debt collection are addressed from the perspective of creditors and debt collection companies.

In 2008, Mark Opperman[18] cited several internal reports of the debt collection industry concerning the failures of the new technologies (such as predictive dialers) that were supposed to aid debt collectors in improving their productivity and maximizing operations efficiency. At the time, the technology was not always intelligent enough to distinguish between real debtors and answering machines, which not only wasted resources and time, but also could generate breaches of

---

12 Hector, California Law Review (2011).
13 Id. at 1621.
14 Id. at 1633.
15 E. Lopez, 'Debt Collectors Disguised As Facebook "Friends": Solutions to Prevent Violations of the Fair Debt Collection Practices Act on Social Media Platforms' (2013) 65 Rutgers Law Review.
16 Id. at 925–926.
17 Id. at 948–949.
18 Mark Oppermann, Debt collection difficulties? (2008) CREDIT MANAGEMENT.

the communication laws.[19] His article suggested another type of solution: using a newer and better messaging technology.[20]

In 2016, Heather Greig-Smith reported on the industry's attempt to catch up with technology and millennials' habits, while still acting within the boundaries of the law.[21] She ventured that messaging apps like WhatsApp will take off for the debt collection industry in the future. She listed several reasons, the most important being that SMS and emails are used less, the messages are encrypted and offer better security, and messaging apps show when and if the message has been received and/or read.[22] However, the use of social media platforms, such as Facebook, in collection was presented as being of low priority for collection efforts,[23] the main focus being on multichannel integrated approaches and mobile and bot communication with the debtor, leading toward an increased digitization of the sector.[24]

Chapter's aim, methodology, and structure

The above (summarized literature and its findings) reflect not only on the phenomenon and its challenges, but also the differences in approach between the two sides of the Atlantic (reflected by the juxtaposition of US and UK examples).

As will be shown in the next section (The Federal Debt Collection Practices Act (FDCPA) – policies and aims), the US has been on the forefront of both debt collection innovation and regulation of abusive debt collection practices, with the FDCPA being adopted back in 1977. However, its legislation has remained largely outdated, and the issues posed by the new technologies have been mostly resolved by case law and broad judicial interpretation of the old act. Thus, the focus of articles and reports has been mostly on identifying issues and suggesting solutions. It should be mentioned here as well, that the main problems are not those of using technology or collecting data, but the manner and purposes for which they are used and how to protect vulnerable groups of consumers from abuse.

One may also notice that the articles mentioned have revealed some challenges raised by the use of newer technologies in debt collection, which the FDCPA has not envisioned. Given the significant transformation and expansion of digitalization at all levels of society in the past decade, one needs to ask what technology introduces that the law is ill equipped to deal with. Would amendments and clarifications offer adequate solutions (as was suggested by the authors mentioned in the previous section), or will digitalization of debt collection be a game

---

19 Id. at 20.
20 Id. at 21.
21 Heather Greig-Smith, What's App With Digital Debt Collection? see id. at (2016).
22 Id. at 17.
23 Id. at 18.
24 Id. at 19.

changer that will require a complete redesign of fair debt collection practices laws? This chapter seeks to fill in the literature gap by providing an answer to these questions.

For this purpose, the chapter uses the FDCPA as a benchmark since it is one of the oldest and most influential fair debt collection practices acts. The focus is on its foundational policies, aims, and solutions as an archetype of legislation struggling with the challenges posed by increased usage of technology and digitalization. In addition, the chapter refers to several patent applications filed in the US that would change, to a greater or lesser extent, the debt collection industry. Their analysis is useful to reveal some of the opportunities and risks that technological innovation might bring for consumers, businesses, and policy makers.

The chapter has three main parts. The first one provides a background to the topic, by introducing the concepts of debt collection and the key policies behind the adoption of the FDCPA. The second addresses the phenomenon of digital debt collection, exemplified by four patent applications of inventions that would ultimately turn debt recovery into a fully automated process. The third part addresses the potential benefits and risks of digital debt collection, as they stem from the detailed analysis of the most recent patent applications discussed. The chapter concludes with the summary findings.

The Federal Debt Collection Practices Act (FDCPA) – policies and aims

In 1977, the US Congress enacted the FDCPA with the aim of prohibiting abusive, harassing, and deceptive debt collection practices and protecting interstate commerce. Two main policy goals lay at its foundation: (a) protecting consumers from egregious debt collection practices and (b) protecting ethical debtors from competitive disadvantages caused by those businesses engaging in unfair practices.[25]

When the FDCPA was implemented, Congress found "abundant evidence of the use of abusive, deceptive, and unfair collection practices, by many debt collectors." In its opinion, these contributed to the high number of "personal bankruptcies, marital instability, loss of jobs and *invasions of individual privacy*" (emphasis added),[26] despite the availability of ethical and lawful means for the effective collection of debts.[27]

Most of the practices banned by the FDCPA dealt with aspects of communications with consumers or third parties (time, location, ancillary requests,

---

25 § 802 FDCPA (15 USC 1692a) – Congressional findings and declarations of purpose https://www.ftc.gov/enforcement/rules/rulemaking-regulatory-reform-proceedings/fair-debt-collection-practices-act-text#802 accessed 21 September 2019.
26 § 802 FDCPA (USC 1692a) (a) – Abusive practices.
27 Id. at (c) – Available nonabusive collection methods.

message, language, and disclosure),[28] harassment or abuse,[29] false or misleading representations including usage of deceptive forms,[30] and other unfair practices.[31] These were supported by a wide range of private[32] and administrative[33] remedies that consumers could assert against abusive debt collectors as well as by certain positive obligations imposed on debt collectors (notice and validation of debt, suspension of collection).[34]

As mentioned, the protections offered by the FDCPA were also meant to remove the legal void[35] and the economic incentives for debt collectors to engage in unfair practices.[36] In the view of Congress, the business model of the collection industry encouraged collection by any means.[37] The American legislator sought to ensure that those businesses that did not engage in unlawful or unethical behavior were not competitively disadvantaged or adversely affected by unscrupulous undertakings.[38]

Nevertheless, at the time when the FDCPA was implemented, the world was a vastly different place. The first commercial automated cellular network was only launched in 1979, in Japan, followed by the Nordic Mobile Telephone system in Denmark, Finland, Norway, and Sweden.[39] The first commercially available mobile phone was launched in 1983, but the industry did not take off until the early 1990s [when the digital cellular technology (GSM)[40] and the short messaging services (SMS) were launched in Finland] and reached its peak at the beginning of the new millennium, when the third generation (3G) was launched in Japan.[41] At the end of the first decade of the 21st century, 3G networks were

---

28 § 804 FDCPA (USC 1692c) – Acquisition of location information; § 805 FDCPA (USC 1692d) – Communication in connection with debt collection, and § 808 FDCPA (USC 1692g) (7)– (8) – Unfair practices.
29 § 806 FDCPA (USC 1692e) – Harassment or abuse.
30 § 807 FDCPA (USC 1692f) – False or misleading representations, § 812 FDCPA (USC 1692k) – Furnishing certain deceptive forms.
31 § 808 FDCPA (USC 1692g) (1)–(6) – Unfair practices.
32 § 813 FDCPA (USC 1692l) – Civil liability.
33 § 814 FDCPA (USC 1692m) – Administrative enforcement.
34 § 809 FDCPA (USC 1692h) – Validation of debts.
35 Id. at (b) – Inadequacy of laws. In the words of the US Congress "existing laws and procedures for redressing these injuries are inadequate to protect consumers."
36 Id. at (e) – Purposes.
37 § 802 FDCPA (15 USC 1692d) – Interstate Commerce.
38 Id. at (e) – Purposes.
39 https://web.archive.org/web/20081022043906/http://www.tekniskamuseet.se/mobilen/engelska/1980_90.shtml accessed 21 September 2019.
40 http://www.umtsworld.com/umts/history.htm accessed 21 September 2019.
41 Id.

overwhelmed by the expansion of streaming media, which led to the emergence of broadband technologies labeled as 4G and LTE.[42] At the end of 2017, the number of mobile broadband subscriptions globally reached 4.3 billion,[43] while in 2018 they become predominant and more affordable than fixed broadband.[44]

Of significant importance for the rapid development and radical changes in connectivity and communication via the Internet was the rise of the smartphone, a mobile device combining the functions of phones, cameras, and computers. While at their outset smartphones were designed for business purposes, the unveiling of the first iPhone in 2007[45] turned smartphones into an immensely popular, globally distributed device, without which our lives would be unimaginable today. By 2013, 1 billion smartphones were in use worldwide.[46] The wide presence and usage of mobile devices capable of connecting to the Internet has changed not just the life or people, but also businesses. A study concluded that, by 2012, four out of five people used mobile devices in the US to shop online.[47] Mobile apps are omnipresent in areas such as communication, social relations and networking, fitness, and education.

The financial industry quickly adapted to the trend of digitalization and now offers mobile banking services, including contactless payment, and so do the debt and data collection industries. It is safe to say that none of these were envisioned when the FDCPA was adopted and it should not come as a surprise that currently the legislation appears ill-suited to deal with the challenges posed by the new realities, as exemplified by the literature review.[48]

However, until amendments are implemented, any legal threats posed by the widespread usage of new technologies must be assessed under the two-pronged test established under the FDCPA. Thus, where debt collectors resort to a new technology in their collection process, its legality must be determined depending on whether the outcome (a) is an unfair or abusive practice on the consumer and

42 https://www.itu.int/en/ITU-D/Statistics/Pages/stat/default.aspx accessed 21 September 2019.
43 International Telecommunication Union (ITU)'s ICT Facts and Figures 2017, 4 https://www.itu.int/en/ITU-D/Statistics/Documents/facts/ICTFactsFigures2017.pdf accessed 21 September 2019.
44 Id. at 5. See also the ITU's Measuring the Information Society Report. Executive Summary 2018, 2 https://www.itu.int/en/ITU-D/Statistics/Documents/publications/misr2018/MISR2018-ES-PDF-E.pdf accessed 21 September 2019.
45 Luke Dormehl, Steve Jobs gave the iPhone its grand unveiling 8 years ago today, (9 January 2015) https://www.cultofmac.com/308585/steve-jobs-gave-iphone-grand-unveiling-8-years-ago-today/ accessed 21 September 2019.
46 ITU estimates that at the end of 2018, 51.2% of the global population, meaning 3.9 billion people, were using the Internet. For country-based statistics, see https://www.itu.int/en/ITU-D/Statistics/Pages/stat/default.aspx accessed 21 September 2019.
47 <https://www.comscore.com/Insights/Press-Releases/2012/9/Retailers-Carving-Out-Space-in-the-M-Commerce-Market?cs_edgescape_cc=DK accessed 28 April 2020.
48 *Supra* A Brief Literature Review.

(b) generates unfair competition for other debt collectors. Nevertheless, before analyzing the intricacies of digital debt collection, the chapter first investigates the relationship between debt collection and technological innovation.

Debt collection and technological innovation

As I have mentioned, debt recovery moved from face-to-face encounters and house visits toward written letters and phone calls, before moving towards digitalization and full automation. It required many resources and kept returns at a certain minimum due to the limited number of accounts that each debt collector could handle on his own. Debt collectors have increasingly turned to science (e.g., psychology, sociology, experimentation, econometrics[49]) and to emerging technologies to enhance productivity and maximize recovery rates,[50] although not everything that followed has been positive.

The disruptive and adverse effects of technology were felt both by consumer-debtors and by the industry. Regarding the former, the use of new technologies allowed debt collectors to circumvent the existing laws and to exploit legal gaps, thus exposing consumers to new types of abuse. With regard to the latter, those who embraced technological innovation have gained a significant competitive advantage, for they quickly became able to handle more clients and make more recoveries, while employing less people and spending less resources, in comparison to agencies that still relied on traditional methods and were ultimately absorbed or pushed out of business.

This for has been the case in the US, where debt collection agencies started using sophisticated automated processes in early 1960s both to assist in their back offices and in their communications with debtors. A decade later, by using IBM punch card machines, one US company claimed that automation helped with the automatic preparation of collection notices, with managing follow-ups, and with preparation of forwarding notices to other collection agencies to enlist their help in the collection process.[51] The result was not just a significant improvement in the company's activity, but it also increased the number of consumer-debtors subjected to collection practices within a short span of time and caused a disruption of the collection market for the new breed of collection agencies relying on technology became a major threat to smaller companies.[52]

The last 30 years have taken the collection industry even further. The appearance and wide spread of mobile communication, increased usage of ubiquitous computing and technologies of statistical modeling, algorithmic (credit) scoring and expansion of coding and software, data collection, and trading have

49 Deville, 2015, 95–103.
50 Hector, California Law Review (2011), 1603.
51 Deville, 2015, 88.
52 Id. at 88.

brought with them a plethora of benefits for business and new threats for consumers, especially with regard to new deceptive practices and violations of privacy.[53] Given that the regulatory response is slow in keeping up with innovation, the new threats are not easily resolved under the existing legal frameworks (assuming they exist in the first place).

The legal void or gray areas are dangerous also due to their potential to encourage collection agencies to engage in a "race to the bottom," where unscrupulous debt collectors will take advantage of the technologies and the legal uncertainties they create in a manner which will endanger the welfare of consumers and competitiveness of the market. It is why the past decade has seen so many calls in the US to update the legislation and ensure that the policies lying at the foundation of the FDCPA are not rendered useless by new technology.

The calls are to a great extent limited and can be grouped into two main categories: (a) communication and (b) violation/invasion of privacy. In the first category, one may find the use of voicemails, contacts via Facebook, and other social media sites. Scholars that addressed the topic seem to be of the opinion that since the existing legal framework is technologically neutral, only minor amendments are needed, in the sense that the legal definition of communication should place more emphasis on content and practical consequence of communication, than on form.[54]

In the second category, one may find the use of devices that help hide or alter the caller's ID, data gathering under false pretenses, the use of social media to publicly post information that shames consumers into paying their debts, outsourcing consumer-debtor databases, and ultimately, targeting debtors who are more likely to pay.

Several considerations derive from the above. First, the mentioned issues do not stem from technology, but from the way it is used. There is a legitimate right of debt collectors to employ and use all available technologies during their business. This is recognized by scholars and supervisory authorities, alike. However, the latter also agree that the law must be crafted to prevent collectors' use of technologies in an unfair, deceptive, or abusive manner toward consumers.[55] Second, while all those mentioned were (and still are) legitimate concerns, they no longer reflect the realities of today. Digitization has expanded to an extent that would have been hard to imagine even a decade ago, when most of the mentioned papers were published. Due to its high degree of adaptability and responsiveness to innovation, the debt collection industry has been no exception.

Thus, in the following section, the chapter examines two major aspects influencing digital debt collection with the benefits and concomitant risks they

---

53 Hector, California Law Review, (2011), 1605.
54 Id. at 1626–1628.
55 Consumer Federation of America, Collecting Consumer Debts: The Challenges of Change (2007), vi.

generate: (a) full automatization of collection and (b) data collection and algorithmic decision making.

Digital debt collection: on the path for further disruption

The previous section introduced the manner in which the debt collection industry has evolved and adapted to change – whether societal, legal, or technological – never abating from its ultimate goal: maximizing recovery rates and profits. What house visits, phone calls, and even letters had in common was human involvement and personal interrelations. However, humanity is more connected and network dependent; platform economy is at its peak; algorithms play an omnipresent role in our lives (be it credit scoring, personalized advertisement, or music suggestions); and bots control news flows, commentary sections, and chatrooms. It was only a matter of time until the debt collection industry tried to cash in on the new reality, via fully automated debt recovery.

In the US, several patent applications have been filed in the attempt to create an automated debt collection system, either in full or in part. Their common background is the debt collection industry's need to minimize costs and resources in the recovery process while maximizing return. A short overview helps explain the kind of systems that could transform the industry as well as the type of procedures and the risks that consumers might face in the upcoming years.

Enhancing debt collection using statistical models

One of the patent applications proposes an automated system designed to evaluate individual debt holder accounts and to predict the amount that will be collected on each account, based on learned relationships among known variables.[56] The predictive model is generated using historical data of delinquent debt, the collection methods used, and the success of the collection methods.[57]

What the algorithm sets out to do is constantly monitor and update consumer-debtors' behavior scoring and cross-reference it to other data such as credit scoring, historical information, etc. On this basis, the algorithm generates a payment projection score, used to estimate the likelihood that the debtor will eventually pay. The projection is then used to prioritize the collection cases that will be worked.

US inventors are aware that such payment projection models are already used by debt collectors, typically employing the information readily available –

56 Mia Shao, Scott Zoldi, Gordon Cameron, Ron Martin, Radu Drossu, Jenny Zhang, and Daniel Shoham, 'Enhancing Delinquent Debt Collection Using Statistical Models of Debt Historical Information and Account Events' (2000) https://patentimages.storage.googleapis.com/26/f3/c6/1f03eb0354396e/US7191150.pdf accessed 21 September 2019.
57 Id.

account holder's name, address, social security number, and monthly balances. However, they claim that the variables are not updated throughout the collection process and the payment projection model does not take advantage of information obtained during the collection itself. The answer is an improved method for analyzing delinquent debt accounts that uses not only available information, but the collector's notes as well and evaluates the effectiveness of various collection methods.

The model is solely designed to improve collection rates by prioritizing debts and targeting consumers whose behavior indicates they are most likely to pay. While the system might generate results that may amount to targeting certain vulnerable categories of consumers, it is not much different from how the industry has operated until now.[58] The creditors enjoy total freedom in choosing whom they can pursue, they can even forgive part or the entirety of the debt, and thus, they will argue there is nothing illegal or discriminatory about it. However, as evidenced by the literature review, things are not always as clear cut, especially in cases where there is an overlap between those deemed more likely to pay and vulnerable consumer-debtors targeted for their vulnerability (age, gender, disability). Whether a mere perverse effect of the inherent nature of the industry or a deliberate practice, a solution to targeting vulnerable consumers should be found.

Method and system for prioritizing debt collections

Another US patent application also envisions a system configured to generate priorities in debt collection.[59] In the inventors' view, debt collection management requires setting priorities on the order and vigor with which the debt collector pursues debtors, for the purpose of maximizing returns.

This is something that the industry has been attempting since its inception – especially since the mid-20th century – only this time, algorithms and artificial intelligence (AI) replace psychology and professional know-how. As the inventors put it, their invention provides a systematic, objective, and consistent way of assigning priorities to debt collection efforts, which makes it easy to use by any debt collector, regardless of experience.[60] Information is, as always, the key ingredient. In this case, the system receives debt-related information from the collectors and compares it with prestored information, after which it queues the delinquent accounts as per the priority value generated from the prestored information. Among the factors are the number of days past due for the debt, the

---

58 Deville, 2015, 133–134.
59 Burl Shannon Hinkle and Jeffrey L. Grubb, Method and System for Prioritizing Debt Collection (2007) https://patentimages.storage.googleapis.com/1d/de/ca/b4a28d229fcc4e/US7254558.pdf accessed 21 September 2019.
60 Id.

debt's value, the consumer's credit score, the consumer's internal payment history score, etc.

This proposed system does not collect debts in an automated way. It only pools and prioritizes them for the debt collector, to maximize efficiency. As a tool aiding the activity of debt collectors, this invention should pose little ethical-legal issues. The problematic aspect is that AI decides not only the order but also recommends the "vigor" with which the process should be followed. Too much vigor might amount for an unfair practice – be it harassment, psychological abuse, or invasion of privacy – however, these could be handled by applying *in extenso* the existing rules, on a case-by-case basis.

The automated first party debt collection system

The third US patent application concerning debt collection envisions a web-based system that a company could use in its debt recovery.[61] Various systems are advertised as being able to automatically commence a campaign to collect the debt, using several strategies that rely on: (a) the type, amount, or importance of the debt; (b) the likelihood of it being collected; and (c) any other relevant factors.

This kind of system would rely on information received from a client computing system. The information would include the name of the debtor, contact information, and the amount. An algorithm would decide the proper classification for the debt and a strategy for recovering it and ultimately will process the payment received, either in partial or in full satisfaction of the debt.[62]

The disruptive effect of this invention is clearly visible. Having access to such a system would enable creditors to attempt recovery of their debts without resorting to or paying for the services of a specialized debt collector. In addition, the system would be virtually able to employ and retrieve any kind of information concerning the debtor that is available on the Internet. The debtor's physical address, phone number, email address, social media identifier, and instant messaging ID could be submitted and stored by the debt collection system for later use, thus placing the consumer's privacy at significant risk.

The algorithm would also enable the system to generate a collection score and to categorize how to approach the debtor in recovery. It will take into account a series of factors such as the age of the debt, the debtor's age, available communication means, the amount to be recovered, type of service or product from which the debt arose, historical data concerning the debtor's activity, and any other combination of criteria in factors deemed important by the creditor. In this manner, the debt collection system can select, on its own, the best approach for recovery of the debt.[63]

61 Volker Neuwirth, Automated First Party Debt Collection System (2014).
62 Id.
63 Id.

AI would be able to replace completely human interaction in debt collection. The application mentions several examples of approaches, which could be used by the system and its recovery attempts: standard and custom emails, voice calls or messages, SMS texts, social media communications, instant messages, or a combination of all the above.[64] This plethora of options available for AI reveals the wide range of consumer-debtor's vulnerability in the digital age.

The implementation of such system opens the door for potential abusive practices that might elude the provisions of the FDCPA. Since the system is advertised for original creditors, in case the AI's strategy results in violations of the federal act, they would face no liability because the FDCPA does not apply to their category.[65] Moreover, even if consumer-debtors chose to resort to an action in tort, since there is no human involvement of the user in decision making and in the collection process,[66] it would be difficult to identify the liable party: is it the beneficiary, the coder, the developer, or AI itself?[67]

Additional issues concern communication with the debtor. As the inventor puts it, "virtually any type of contact information can be employed by the debt collection system […] As new social media platforms or other contact methods are developed and popularized, such platforms or other contact methods could also be used."[68] The message conveyed is that there is no escape for the debtor on the Internet. As emphasized by the literature review, it is still debatable if the usage of voice calls, instant messages, SMS, or social media communications falls under the coverage of the FDCPA, and US courts have been divided on the topic. The current expansion of digitization increases uncertainty – for both consumers and businesses – about what is now deemed reasonable and how the law should be applied to it.

System and method for debt collection

The latest US patent application addressed by this chapter envisions a web system and a method for debt collection that would help creditors and be compliant with the FDCPA.[69] This ambitious project relies on debtors' concern for their online reputation, which would motivate them to search online and initiate their own communication with a debt collector.

Like the previous project, the system would use computer databases, hardware and software to store the data, automatic web page generators, and landline and

---

64 Id.
65 § 803 (3) and (6) (15 USC 1692b) – Definitions.
66 Neuwirth, 2014, 12. "[T]he debt collection system, rather than the end user, can select the best approach for recovering a debt, thereby relieving the user from much of the burden of collecting a debt."
67 The situation is different in fair debt collection practices acts adopted at the state level.
68 Neuwirth (2014), 10.
69 Zhengping Zhang, System and Method for Debt Collection (2016).

wireless connections to the Internet.[70] For each debtor whose data is input in the system, the web page generator will automatically create a consumer profile in the form of a web page. The creditors who share the same debtor would be able to share data and consolidate the debtors' information.[71]

Debtors would be informed by the system on their outstanding debt and be allowed to dispute it on a forum made available by the system. All registered users would be able to see the information exchanged by the parties in the dispute and would cast a vote, on which position is more trustful.[72]

The envisioned system would generate enormous pools of data creating a significant privacy issue for the consumer-debtors involved. In addition, the system relies heavily on predetermined standardized templates and AI decision making to ensure compliance with the existing laws.[73] A more detailed discussion on the ethical-legal risks raised by this proposal takes place in the next section.

What is apparent from the proposed inventions is that at the beginning, a wide range of tools such as mathematical representations and predictive models, algorithmic scoring, and decision making were used solely to enhance and maximize the productivity of debt collectors, by prioritizing debts and identifying consumers most likely to pay. The legal and ethical questions raised by these proposals are (a) whether these tools end up targeting vulnerable consumers and generate a form of quasi-discrimination and (b) whether the collection, processing, and usage of collected data violate the consumers' expectation of privacy.

However, the more recent proposals aim, on the one hand, to remove humans from the debt collection process by relying entirely on AI decision making and, on the other hand, to remove debt collectors from the business of debt collection, while still conducting the recovery process, in a manner consistent with existing laws. None of the solutions proposed is fully transparent about the content of their algorithms and how the variables are being used; however, the disruptive effects – for both consumers and industry members – are clearly visible.

The questions raised by the latter proposals, assuming these inventions (and others like them) will materialize are (a) how can we ensure adequate protection and compliance with the legal standards and policies of the regulatory framework in place and (b) would normative amendments and changes of the current regulatory frameworks suffice or is there a need for a complete redesign of fair debt collection practices laws?

The benefits and risks posed by a potential materialization of full digital debt collection as well as proposed answers to the questions are provided in the following section.

70 Id. at 2.
71 Id. at 3.
72 Id. at 3, 5–6.
73 Id. at 4–5.

Digital debt collection meets the law

Not all countries have implemented fair debt collection practices laws.[74] Engaging in digital debt collection in one of these countries would mean operating in an almost complete legal void. Therefore, in such a case, the question is how to design a fair debt collection practices law in the first place, keeping in mind the technological advancement and the increased use of AI in debt collection. This situation will not be addressed here.

As the last patent application states, the greatest challenge of full automatization and reliance on AI is to build a "fair, open, and accessible collection system overcoming the obstacles posed by debtors seeking to avoid repayment, while *complying with all the laws* (emphasis added)."[75] The starting point in overcoming this challenge lies not with mathematics, statistics, or the law, but with shame and psychology, the first scientific tool employed by the industry: the debtors' concern for their [online] reputation.[76]

The question is what kind of information that would affect the debtors' reputation would encourage them to search online and contact creditors on their own accord, given that the FDCPA clearly forbids public shaming and disclosing information about the debt or the debtor's status as a debtor to third parties.[77] There is an obvious contradiction between what the invention seeks to achieve – a reverse in the need to open communication channels, by shifting it from the debt collector to the debtor – and what it might actually have to do in order to make it happen ("enables the debt information to be fully accessible and searchable except the debtors' identities [...], enables the names of the debtors to be publicly searchable without indications of their debts"). If such data remain anonymous, there is no risk for the debtors' privacy, and they would have no incentive or reason to contact the debt collector. Nevertheless, a first potential incongruence between the invention and the existing law is apparent.

The matter of contacting third parties for accessing information is also problematic. The web-based system envisions contacts with relatives, neighbors, friends, and legal representatives of the debtor, but also with other third parties, such as employers, authorized entities, or prospective landlords. By law, these

74 For instance, out of the 28 EU Member States (including the UK), the only ones that have a sector-specific fair debt collection practices law are Belgium, Denmark, Finland, Germany, Greece, Latvia, the Netherlands, Romania, Sweden, and the UK. It should also be mentioned that these laws vary significantly in coverage and scope.
75 Zhang, 2016, 1. He further adds: "it is desirable to build a FDCPA-compliant, web-based system that enables creditors to store the information about debtors and debts, enables the debt information to be fully accessible and searchable except the debtor's identities, enables debt purchasers, service providers, or debtors to contact creditors, enables the names of the debtors to be publicly searchable without indications of their debts, enables creditors to exchange information about the debtors with authorized entities and enables debtors to dispute or negotiate with creditors" (2).
76 Id. at 2.
77 § 805 FDCPA (15 USC 1692c) (b) - Communication with third parties.

categories should be contacted only once (with exceptions) and only in connection to the debtors' location. Would a constant monitoring of their online searches and communications be covered by the law? It is difficult to assess.

The three big novelties that would be brought to life by the system and method for debt collection, however, have to do with massive data collection and sharing, online validation of the debt, and fully automated debt collection.

Data collection and sharing

The web-based system envisioned by Mr. Zhang's patent application is mainly a massive tool for data collection and storage, creating databases of debtors and making them available for interested parties.[78] It "allows creditors to input and store debtors' account information and enables all users – creditors, collection service providers, debt purchasers, legal service professionals, information querists, and debtors – to communicate with each other for collecting debts, negotiating settlements, resolving disputes, trading debts, exchanging information and providing legal or financial services."[79] In addition, creditors who have one common debtor will "automatically form a closer relationship as 'friends' to exchange or consolidate the debtor's information."[80]

Practically, what the system does is generate a web page (profile) for each debtor, although it claims not to reveal any information, other than his or her name and location. All these pages would be "searchable at least by the unique queries – the names [...] on the internet or the home page of the system's website. Creditors can be contacted through hyperlinks in the webpage."[81] In other words, they would be widely accessible.

The purpose of the web page is to stir the curiosity of consumer-debtors surfing the Internet and to encourage them to contact the creditors on their own will, either to find out why their name is listed, or to ask for their data to be removed. Since they will first have to verify their identity, the system forces debtors or third parties to provide personal information (such as the last four digits of their personal security number), which can be then verified and stored in the database.[82]

Other querists can also be a relative, a friend, a neighbor, a coworker, or an authorized person, conducting a background check for the purpose of housing, employment, or loan. All these categories will be asked to classify themselves before engaging in communication with the creditor and to submit the supporting document required. Authorized querists, such as landlords, will have secured a written consent from the debtor; therefore, they will be entitled to a full disclosure from the creditor's side, without violating the existing law. In the

---

78 Zhang, 2016.
79 Id. at 2.
80 Id. at 3.
81 Id. at 3.
82 Id. at 5.

absence of consent from the debtor, the unauthorized querist would be treated as "a neighbor" or "friend" of the debtor and be allowed to provide certain information about the debtor, but not to acquire any information.

Several issues emerge. First, the system would collect data not only about the targeted consumer-debtor, but also about all querists and third parties from the debtor's closer or wider circle, as they will need to verify their identity via attachments that remain in the system. Moreover, most of these parties would not fall into the protected categories covered by the FDCPA in connection to communication,[83] because the federal act limits protection to the consumer's spouse, parent (if the consumer is a minor), guardian, executor, or administrator.

Second, the debt collector communicating with any person other than the consumer for the purpose of acquiring location information about the consumer should identify himself and not use any language or any symbol that would indicate the debt collector is in the debt collection business.[84] The language of the act, however, seems to suggest that the situation described concerns communications initiated by the debt collector for the purpose of acquiring a location of the debtor, and not those initiated by the third party, in which case, the FDCPA might not actually apply. This apparent legal uncertainty allows the system to collect as much data as possible about the debtor, although the intention of the legislator appears to have been to limit it to location only.

More uncertainty is caused by the following section of the FDCPA, which states that except for the purpose of acquiring a location of the debtor or where reasonably necessary to effectuate a post-judgment judicial remedy, the debt collector is not allowed to communicate, in connection with the collection of any debt, with any person other than the consumer (unless expressed prior consent of the consumer has been given directly to the debt collector).[85] Since the boundary between obtaining information on the debtor's location and communication about collection of the debt might not be easy to establish and the information is provided at the initiative of the third party, it may be very difficult to establish a violation of the FDCPA.

Third, the creation and publication online of a debtor's data that did not originate from the debtor – like in the case of social media information, which is published voluntarily by the debtor – would create significant individual privacy issues and have an unnerving effect on debtors. Since the web system would simply publish the name and location of the debtor, without disclosing more information on the reasons for doing so, it is hard to ascertain how debtors would be affected. The inventor relies on a psychological effect that would motivate the debtor to contact the creditor on its own initiative, which would enable the creditor to (a) update the consumer's data in the database and (b)

---

83 § 805 (d) of FDCPA (15 USC 1692d) – Communication in connection with debt collection.
84 § 804 (1) and (5) of FDCPA (15 USC 1692c) – Acquisition of location information.
85 § 805 (b) of FDCPA – Communication in connection with debt collection.

avoid liability under the FDCPA. Nevertheless, the debtor could assert that the publication of his name and location data on the Internet amounts to a harassing, oppressing, or abusive practice in connection to the debt.[86]

Similar claims regarding misleading representations could be made in regard to asking the debtor to validate his information on the web system, before he can contact the creditor or the system administrator.[87] While the law seems to be well-suited to deal with this matter, the legal issues stem once more from the reversed pattern of communication. Thus, if the debtor acquiesces to the terms and conditions of the site and voluntarily initiates a conversation by submitting a document to verify his identity, the web system might claim legitimacy as defense against FDCPA violations.

Online validation of debt

The web system also envisions a type of online-dispute resolution mechanism, which will take place on a forum thread page. This mechanism is in fact a form of debt validation, where debtors can challenge the claims of their creditors and submit evidence against them. In addition, since the "thread" is initiated by the debtor, the system (which would most likely have terms and conditions attached to it) is authorized to allow the creditor to disclose detailed debt information on the forum. What makes this system unique is the fact that the thread is open to all registered users of the system (collection and legal service professionals), who will be able to comment and vote on which side of the dispute is more trustful. Thus, the ultimate decision on debt validation is removed from the hands of the creditor/debt collector and turned to a wider public, which will act as a sort of jury.

Debt validation is one of the most important safeguards granted to consumers by the FDCPA.[88] The law enables the consumer to notify the debt collector in writing that the debt, or any portion of it, is disputed, in which case the debt collector must obtain verification of the debt from the original creditor or provide a copy of the judgment thereof. No other information or guideline is mentioned in the FDCPA on how the debt collector should verify the debt.

This raises several legal-ethical concerns. While subjecting the verification of the debt to a panel of online users consisting of debt collectors, creditors, and debt purchasers is most likely not what the legislators had in mind, the FDCPA does not ban it either. One cannot help but wonder what the outcome would be if the result of the voting is rigged using bots or incentivized users. What is the overall legitimacy of a debt (in)validation provided by an extrajudicial body of users that is not sanctioned by law, but by consent to the web system's terms and conditions? Since the users vote but do not issue a "reasoned" opinion, would the consumer be able to challenge the validation of the debt and on which grounds?

---

86 § 806 of FDCPA (15 USC 1692e) – Harassment or abuse.
87 § 807 of FDCPA (15 USC 1692f) – False or misleading representations.
88 § 809 of FDCPA (15 USC 1692h).

Automated debt collection

The debt collection process is automated in its entirety (although human involvement still occurs for the administration and maintenance of the system). Once the system receives debt data, it automatically creates a web page and posts them on the Internet via a web server. Compliance with the FDCPA is, allegedly, ensured by using different predetermined templates, adapted to the situation, and the person is subjected to collection efforts. Therefore, the web pages will differ, depending on whether the debtor is a natural or a legal person.

If the debtor is a person (consumer), the web page will disclose the full name and last known location, or where the debt incurred, with no indication of the debt. Each web page will have a hyperlink HTML form, and attachments will be sent to the creditor by email. The hypertext will indicate that someone holds information about a named person or that someone is seeking communication with him or her. On the form, there will be check boxes where users will indicate who they are and their quality, after which they will be required to "validate" the completed form by uploading documents to support their claim. The system will then "advise" the creditor how to respond to remain compliant with the FDCPA, in a manner which could be described as "bot-compliance."

According to the patent application, this system would enable more means of communication than email, such as phone calling, texting, or instant messages, would support mobile display for smartphone users, and would have an integrated payment service.

This brings us back to the issue of liability. Assuming the web system provides wrong advice or adopts what is later considered an unfair practice, who will bear responsibility for the damages caused? I identified two situations. The first concerns the relationship between the creditors, debt collectors, or other users of the system. The matter will likely be settled contractually according to the terms and conditions of the web system. The second concerns the relationship between the aggrieved debtors and debt collectors. Will those behind the web system be assimilated with or considered an agent of the debt collector, or will the debt collector continue to bear liability regarding the consumer, retaining a recourse against the system? Analyzing all the legal implications would exceed the purposes of this chapter so they will not be detailed here.

This section showed that implementing inventions such as those discussed above is not always as clear cut and compliant as advertised. On the contrary, their design brings to light an entire array of issues and challenges that may fall either within the gray area or outside the boundaries of the law. Many of these issues could probably be addressed via an extensive or functional judicial interpretation of the law, to ensure adequate consumer protection. Others, however, might fall within the ambit of data privacy laws, agency laws, or tort laws, which would mean the FDCPA is not well suited to deal with all matters concerning digital debt collection.

Conclusion

This chapter started by emphasizing that debt collection was, is, and will most likely remain one of the most innovative and adaptive industries in the world. Its success depends on these two features. Several patent applications (most of them successful) serve as evidence that the industry is looking for ways to improve its efficiency while minimizing the resources involved. The wave of digitalization, the use of algorithmic decision making, and the transition toward AI-controlled software is contributing further to both the development and the transformation of the sector. A full digital debt collection process in the near future is not an unreasonable prediction.

While the industry changes and evolves with technology, consumers face new debt collection practices that may be abusive or unfair. At the same time, the law remains static and appears to be ill equipped to deal with the digital era. Given that the FDCPA was designed at a time when digitalization was a sci-fi topic, it is in great need of an update.

Nevertheless, this chapter revealed that most of the issues could be tackled by a functional, extensive interpretation of the FDCPA, or by amending its wording to expand its scope or increase its clarity. Although disruptive in effect, digitalization – at least to the extent portrayed by the patent applications reviewed – does not appear to be a game changer that requires a complete redesign of the entire system. The FDCPA needs an improvement, not a legislative revolution. Not yet.

Bibliography

Consumer Federation of America. *'Collecting Consumer Debts: The Challenges of Change. Comments to the Federal Trade Commission Regarding the Fair Debt Collection Practices Act'* (2007).

Deville, J. *'Lived Economies of Default: Consumer Credit, Debt Collection and the Capture of Affect'* (Taylor and Francis, 2015).

Federal Trade Commission, *'Collecting Consumer Debts: The Challenges of Change. A Workshop Report'* (February, 2009).

Goldberg, L. *'Dealing in Debt: The High-Stakes World of Debt Collection after FDCPA'*, *Southern California Law Review*, 2006.

Greig-Smith, H. *'What's App With Digital Debt Collection?'* (Credit Management, Stamford, 2016).

Hector, C. *'Debt Collection in the Information Age: New Technologies and the Fair Debt Collection Practices Act'* (2011) *California Law Review*.

Hinkle, Burl Shannon and Grubb, Jeffrey L., 'Method and System for Prioritizing Debt Collection' (2007), available at: https://patentimages.storage.googleapis.com/1d/de/ca/b4a28d229fcc4e/US7254558.pdf.

International Telecommunication Union Measuring the Information Society Report, available at https://www.itu.int/en/ITU-D/Statistics/Documents/publications/misr2018/MISR2018-ES-PDF-E.pdf.

International Telecommunication Union, ICT Facts and Figures (2017), available at: https://www.itu.int/en/ITU-D/Statistics/Documents/facts/ICTFactsFigures2017.pdf.

Lopez, E. *'Debt Collectors Disguised as Facebook "Friends": Solutions to Prevent Violations of the Fair Debt Collection Practices Act on Social Media Platforms'* (2013) *Rutgers Law Review.*

Neuwirth, V. 'AUtomated First Party Debt Collection System' (2014), available at: https://patentimages.storage.googleapis.com/b9/17/38/aaadc869f8751c/US20140188716A1.pdf.

Oppermann, M. *'Debt collection difficulties?'* (Credit Management, Stamford, 2008).

Rosenoer, J.M.C. (Chadds Ford, PA, US). *'Management of Consumer Debt Collection Using a Blockchain and Machine Learning'*, (United States, International Business Machines Corporation [Armonk, NY, US], 2018), available at: http://www.freepatentsonline.com/y2018/0285971.html.

Shao, Mia, Zoldi, Scott, Cameron, Gordon, Martin, Ron, Drossu, Radu, Zhang, Jenny and Shoham, Daniel. 'Enhancing Delinquent Debt Collection Using Statistical Models of Debt Historical Information and Account Events' (2000), available at: https://patentimages.storage.googleapis.com/26/f3/c6/1f03eb0354396e/US7191150.pdf.

Zhang, Z. 'System and Method for Debt Collection' (2016), available at: https://patentimages.storage.googleapis.com/88/c3/be/f87776c5571d24/US20160232605A1.pdf.

9 Financial conduct in the UK's banking sector

Regulating to protect vulnerable consumers

Holly Powley and Keith Stanton

Introduction[1]

In a modern society, all adults need access to the financial system in order to conduct their lives. They need to buy food and pay for housing and other utility services. Those without full access to the financial system may well pay a 'poverty premium.' For example, fuel costs will be higher for those who are unable to pay suppliers by direct debit or who are supplied by means of prepaid metres. A significant proportion of the UK's population are regarded, for various reasons, as 'potentially vulnerable.' Many are financially vulnerable:[2] they lack the means to cope easily with illness, unemployment, or unexpected expenditure. Other consumers might find that their age makes them vulnerable. Consumer vulnerabilities may well create other problems: there is evidence that persons with mental health problems have a higher rate of financial problems than the general population. The vulnerable may be also be less able to shop the market for the most advantageous deals. It is in neither the bank's nor the consumer's interest for an individual's financial problems to increase to the extent that they become unmanageable or for consumers to purchase a financial product without fully appreciating its features.

---

1 Note on sources. A considerable amount of the UK legislation on this issue is to be found in the FCA's Handbook https://www.handbook.fca.org.uk/. The Handbook, which is effectively delegated legislation supplemented by guidance, is split into a number of sourcebooks which regulate particular issues and sectors of the industry. For present purposes, the most important sourcebooks are: the Principles for Businesses (abbreviated as PRIN); the Banking: Conduct of Business Sourcebook (BCOBS), the Mortgages and Home Finance: Conduct of Business Sourcebook (MCOB), the Consumer Credit sourcebook (CONC), and the Dispute Resolution: Complaints part (DISP). For the sake of simplicity, all references in this chapter to sections of the Handbook will use the abbreviations. It should be noted that the UK has used the Handbook as the vehicle by which EU legislation is introduced into domestic law. Thus, the core rules in MCOB 11.6 which deal with responsible lending are derived from Article 18 of the Mortgage Credit Directive (Directive 2014/17/EU). The consumer credit creditworthiness assessment provisions now found in CONC 5.2A implement (in considerably expanded form) the UK's obligations under Article 8 of the Consumer Credit Directive (Directive 2008/48/EC).

2 FCA, *Guidance for Firms on the Fair Treatment of Vulnerable Customers GC19/3* (2019) 7.

Bank treatment of vulnerable consumers is a high profile issue in the UK. The Financial Conduct Authority (FCA), the UK's conduct regulator, is currently consulting on improved guidance for the financial services industry on the subject.[3] The FCA continues to expressly state that its work on vulnerability is a major priority, even at a time when it is faced with the immense challenges of Brexit and coronavirus.[4] The fact that the FCA sees the protection of vulnerable customers as a priority area of work reflects the fact that one of its statutory objectives is consumer protection.[5] This work on vulnerability is part of a wider process being conducted across the economy, by bodies such as the UK Regulators Network,[6] the Competition and Markets Authority,[7] and the House of Commons Treasury Committee.[8] The impact of coronavirus on the economy has actually emphasised that resources need to be devoted to the protection of the vulnerable.

This paper will survey these developments and place them in the context of the discussions of banking practices and culture which have taken place in the aftermath of the 2008 crash. It will be argued that the attention placed on the treatment of vulnerable consumers is an example of the fact that the role of retail banks as public utilities is increasingly recognised. The current picture shows that English law and regulation give considerable and increasing protection to vulnerable consumers in certain areas, such as lending. However, the wide range of vulnerabilities which can face banks and the impact of technological developments mean that more needs to be done to achieve a comprehensive result. Problems remain in relation to staff being able to identify and respond appropriately to different forms of vulnerability, the design of products, and communications with customers and standards of service. The existing measures which protect the vulnerable in their dealing with banks in certain contexts need to be embedded in a wider culture in which all those working in banks, the Board, those developing products and employees dealing with consumers, are alert to the need to identify consumers with vulnerabilities and treat them appropriately.

After a description of the UK's system of regulation of banks, this paper will discuss the nature of vulnerability: emphasising how the breadth of the concept creates problems for those charged with designing and providing protection for the vulnerable. We will then consider the wide range of measures which are currently in place, demonstrating that they tend to deal with particular issues rather than being parts of a comprehensive approach. The paper will then analyse the implications of the FCA's proposals for reform and assess the FCA's response to the coronavirus crisis. It will be argued that it is expected that vulnerability will continue to

---

3 *Ibid*; the most recent document. See also Nisha Arora, 'Our approach to ensuring firms treat vulnerable customers fairly' (5 March 2020) https://www.fca.org.uk/news/speeches/our-approach-ensuring-firms-treat-vulnerable-customers-fairly accessed 19 May 2020.

4 FCA, *Business Plan 2020/21* (April 2020) 4.

5 Financial Services and Markets Act 2000, ss 1B(3)(a) and 1C.

6 UK Regulators Network, *UKRN Annual Report 2020/21 and Work Plan* (April 2020), 16.

7 See the material at: 'Vulnerable customers' https://www.gov.uk/government/publications/vulnerable-consumers accessed 19 May 2020.

8 Treasury Committee, *Consumers' Access to Financial Services* (HC 1642, 13 May 2019).

feature prominently on the regulatory agenda: recent developments highlight the increasing social role that banks play. The regulator now expects banks to show that they give consideration to the fair treatment of consumers and if banks cannot demonstrate this, they are at risk of enforcement action. The profits of the bank and the interests of shareholders are no longer the sole concern from a conduct perspective: the culture of the institution is.

The UK's regulatory system

The UK's regulatory system is complex, with responsibilities split between two authorities: the Bank of England and the FCA. It is the FCA's Handbook that is at the centre of the conduct regulatory system which applies to banks. The Handbook contains high-level Principles which are to be applied by authorised businesses along with Rules to be complied with and Guidance for institutions on how the rules should be applied.[9] The work currently being conducted by the Authority on vulnerability is intended to provide firms with additional guidance on what they need to do to comply with the Principles.

FCA rules and guidance are supplemented by industry work on improving the treatment of vulnerable consumers. Industry initiatives range from additional high-level standards setting out good practice for the treatment of vulnerable consumers through to dedicated codes of practice for dealing with issues that have been identified as a cause of vulnerability. For example, the trade body UK Finance, in conjunction with the Money Advice Trust charity, has developed nine high-level principles for firms dealing with vulnerable consumers, emphasising the importance of information and support. The Banking Standards Board, an independent body evaluating the culture of banking institutions, has developed a Consumer Framework[10] setting out five key principles of good practice for banks to follow when engaging with consumers, utilising an outcomes-focused approach and making specific reference to vulnerable consumers: firms should be thinking about what vulnerable consumers need in their interactions with them. This is consistent with the holistic, consumer-focused approach encouraged by the FCA. Other nonprofit organisations have issued good practice guidelines covering topics that can impact vulnerability.[11]

All of the Rules in the FCA's Handbook concerning the treatment of vulnerable customers are legally enforceable: a private person damaged by breach of such a rule can seek compensation in the courts.[12] However, this remedy is rarely used as

---

9 The provisions can be identified in the Handbook by reference to the letter after the number of the provision – R denotes the provision is a Rule and G denotes guidance. The Principles are contained in a separate section of the Handbook – entitled PRIN – and can be located at PRIN 2.1.

10 Banking Standards Board, *Consumer Framework* (2019).

11 For example, the Money Advice Liaison Group, *Good Practice Awareness Guidelines on Debt and Mental Health* (2015) http://malg.org.uk/wp-content/uploads/2017/03/MALG-Debt-and-Mental-Health-Guidelines-2015.pdf accessed 22 May 2020.

12 Financial Services and Markets Act 2000 s 138D.

the governing legislation establishes a free to use dispute resolution system in the form of the Financial Ombudsman Service (FOS).[13] The FOS resolves disputes between consumers and banks according to what it determines as having been fair and reasonable in all circumstances of the case.[14] It is important to appreciate that, when making such a determination, the FOS is required to take into account a variety of factors. These include the law, the FCA's rules and issued guidance, industry codes of practice, and what is considered to be good industry practice.[15] It follows that a voluntary code of practice drawn up by an industry body such as the Lending Standards Board or UK Finance to govern the conduct of its members toward vulnerable consumers can have legal relevance in determining the outcome of a claim brought to the FOS.[16] Similarly, the FCA's generally stated Principles for Businesses (discussed in more detail below), which do not ground a cause of action in court proceedings, can be used before the Ombudsman.

In addition to these possibilities of remedies in favour of consumers, the FCA can, as part of its supervisory role, take enforcement action against an authorised firm for breach of the Principles and rules contained in its Handbook.[17] Such proceedings can result in the firm being fined and may lead to compensation being paid to damaged customers.

The FCA has been clear: firms need to demonstrate that they are taking consumer vulnerability into account if they are to comply with the Principles for Businesses,[18] the overarching conduct obligations. If they cannot show this, the FCA can take enforcement action for breach. Penalties for noncompliance are unlimited and can be significant. A firm which fails to take proper account of the interests of vulnerable customers could have broken a number of Principles. They are:

2   A firm must conduct its business with due skill, care and diligence.
3   A firm must take reasonable care to organise and control its affairs responsibly and effectively, with adequate risk management systems.
6   A firm must pay due regard to the interests of its customers and treat them fairly.
7   A firm must pay due regard to the information needs of its clients, and communicate information to them in a way which is clear, fair and not misleading.
9   A firm must take reasonable care to ensure the suitability of its advice and discretionary decisions for any customer who is entitled to rely upon its judgment.

---

13 Financial Services and Markets Act 2000 Part XVI.
14 Financial Services and Markets Act 2000 s 228(2).
15 DISP 3.6.4R.
16 See, for example: FOS DRN9194958.
17 See the FCA's *Enforcement Guide* published as the EG section of its Handbook at https://www.handbook.fca.org.uk/handbook/EG/2/?view=chapter accessed 22 May 2020. For example, the FCA has recently fined banks in the Lloyds Bank group £64,046,800 for breaches of Principles 3 and 6 in relation to their dealing with vulnerable and other customers in arrears on their mortgages. FCA, *Final Notice: Lloyds Bank PLC, Bank of Scotland plc, and The Mortgage Business Plc* (11 June 2020).
18 Nisha Arora (n 3).

Approached from this perspective, duties owed to vulnerable consumers are a component part of the general duties which banks owe to their consumers: this entails a flexible and tailored response. Firms need to organise their businesses in a manner which enables them to deal proactively, responsibly, and fairly with vulnerable consumers. The FCA has emphasised that the modern 'outcomes-based' approach to regulation which it uses means moving away from a box-ticking approach and toward a culture within institutions where banks and their staff consider whether they are doing the 'right thing' for the consumer.[19] There is no doubt that this is seen as part of the emphasis on developing cultures in banks which move away from the focus on profits that contributed to the 2008 crash. Banks are being asked to give the interests of their consumers priority over their own commercial interests. In short, banks are expected to spend money in order to ensure that vulnerable consumers have proper access to the financial system and are treated empathetically when they encounter problems. It is unlikely that declining to provide banking services to a consumer because they are deemed to be vulnerable, for example, fits comfortably with this expectation.

Defining and understanding vulnerability

A central issue is the need to identify vulnerability. This is difficult because of the great variety of factors which can render a consumer vulnerable. The FCA has developed its approach to vulnerability over the past few years, following the publication of its occasional paper on the topic[20] and is currently consulting on guidance to assist firms in developing their internal regimes to aid vulnerable consumers. The FCA has acknowledged that there are major challenges: 'defining vulnerability can be difficult and a prescriptive regulatory approach will be ineffective.'[21] This reflects reality: vulnerable groups are not homogenous and to define them as such risks pursuing a one-size-fits-all approach that does not acknowledge or address the consumer detriment that could arise. The FCA considers that there is a need for greater clarity to assist those confronting vulnerability issues in banks. It aims to give firms a better appreciation of the practicalities so that their culture and practices provide better protection for the needs of the vulnerable. Reflecting that approach, vulnerability is defined in general terms in the consultation:

> A vulnerable consumer is someone who, due to their personal circumstances, is especially susceptible to detriment, particularly when a firm is not acting with appropriate levels of care.[22]

19 FCA, *Business Plan 2020/21* (n 4) 12.
20 FCA, *Occasional Paper No 8: Consumer Vulnerability* (February 2015).
21 FCA, *Business Plan 2019/20 (2019)* 24.
22 FCA, *Guidance for firms* (n 2) 6.

It has identified four factors which act as drivers to create vulnerability:

> *Health* – health conditions or illnesses that affect the ability to carry out day-to-day tasks.
> *Life events* – major life events such as bereavement or relationship breakdown.
> *Resilience* – low ability to withstand financial or emotional shocks.
> *Capability* – low knowledge of financial matters or low confidence in managing money.[23]

The FCA has emphasised that every customer is potentially vulnerable.[24] Vulnerability can be permanent, sporadic, or temporary and is focused on individual context.[25] Set against the discussions surrounding culture within banks, an approach that requires a move away from clear categories and toward understanding individual consumers and their circumstances holistically makes sense. However, it requires a significant amount of understanding on the part of bank management and their staff.

Many factors can affect whether a consumer should be considered vulnerable such as to require bank staff to take action to mitigate that vulnerability. There is no exhaustive list of factors to consider. Vulnerability can be triggered by illness (including stress), hearing and sight problems, unemployment, homelessness, bereavement, age, criminal convictions, family problems, financial difficulties, financial capability, language and literacy issues, domestic abuse, substance abuse, gambling, and unfamiliarity with information technology. It is important to state that vulnerability might not be obvious or visible to those dealing with the consumer, and the consumer might not disclose it. Vulnerability is also not a fixed state: unexpected life events, such as illness, can lead to a consumer being vulnerable, if only for a very short time. The actions of firms dealing with consumers can also operate to induce or accentuate the vulnerability of consumers. For example, access to banking services has been central to the recent discussion on bank activities, with issues such as availability of accounts, cash and payment services, branch closures, telephone, and online banking and information provision. Issues relating to the cost of loans and overdrafts, financial resilience, managing bank accounts when a customer is ill, communication needs, and the treatment of consumers who are in default continue to feature prominently in the discourse surrounding consumer treatment and banks.[26]

Consumers can experience more than one vulnerability, and experiencing harm in one area can trigger vulnerability in another: vulnerabilities can

---

23 *Ibid* 6.
24 *Ibid* 6.
25 FCA, *Business Plan 2019/20* (n 4) 24.
26 For discussion, see Financial Services Consumer Panel, *Annual Report 2018/19* (2019).

intertwine, and vulnerability is rarely self-contained. Vulnerability can arise as a result of factors personal to the consumer, it can be caused as a result of things that happen to the consumer and can arise as a result of a bank's actions. These categories are not exclusive. Statistics highlight the impact of the breadth of vulnerability: 74% of consumers who experienced a problem with retail banking in 2017 were identified as showing 'characteristics of potential vulnerability'[27] and over half of adults (25.6 million) in the UK have at least one characteristic which renders them 'potentially vulnerable.'[28]

In order to understand what can drive vulnerability, the well-known challenges in the banker-customer relationship provide a good starting point: there is an information asymmetry. The manner in which information is communicated can make it difficult for consumers to understand bank products. A bank will be more familiar with its business than consumers. The consumer might not be able to identify potentially unfair terms in a contract or they could be at risk of exploitation. Accessing, and understanding, unfamiliar financial products may, therefore, induce vulnerability: approximately 24 million people do not feel confident making decisions about financial products.[29] Consumers can struggle to identify products or services that are appropriate for their needs. Bank actions can exacerbate this: terms and conditions used by banks can be lengthy,[30] complicated, and intimidating for consumers to understand.

Vulnerability can increase with age, due to health issues. Similarly, young adults who are unfamiliar with banking products and services may be vulnerable when dealing with banks. Illness introduces other challenges: consumers, or their representatives, need to continue running their financial lives if they are to avoid difficulties: a friend or family member might need to obtain a power of attorney or use some other method to operate a consumer's bank accounts. Financial problems, such as enduring or increasing levels of debt or a poor credit record, may well lead to a person being vulnerable.[31] Mental health problems are experienced by 46% of consumers with problem debt.[32] Over 30%[33] of the UK's population lack financial resilience; they have very limited savings to fall back on when faced by a financial emergency. In 2017, 13% of UK adults were found to have no cash savings, and a further 32% only had savings of between

27 FCA, *FCA Mission: Our Future Approach to Consumers* (November 2017) 24.
28 FCA, *The Financial Lives of Consumers Across the UK, Key findings from the FCA's Financial Lives Survey 2017* (June 2018) 77.
29 Money and Pensions Service, *Transforming customer wellbeing: What can retail banking do to build financial capacity?* (June 2019) 3.
30 For example, the terms and conditions used by one bank were the same length as Dickens' 'A Christmas Carol': Treasury Committee, *Consumers' Access to Financial Services* (n 8) 48.
31 This area is commonly dealt with in language which does not expressly refer to 'vulnerability.' The Consumer Credit Sourcebook chapter of the FCA's Handbook deals with customers 'in financial difficulties (CONC 1.3.1G).' Not all customers who are in financial difficulties are vulnerable, but many will be.
32 Money and Pensions Service, Financial capability report, p. 9.
33 FCA, *The financial lives of consumers* (n 28) 81.

£1 and £1,999.[34] These people are likely to resort to high cost borrowing to meet unexpected expenditure or everyday living costs. Access can impact resilience: in 2017, there were 1.23 million adults in the UK without a bank account,[35] yet it is estimated that this costs each of them on average an extra £485 annually through loss of discounts on energy, phone, and broadband available to those who pay by direct debit. They are also likely to face difficulties in obtaining loans due to the lack of a credit rating. These statistics highlight the numerous forms of vulnerability that can impact consumers in their interactions with their banks and in their wider lives.

Internet access is an important factor in access to bank facilities in the modern technological environment, yet in 2017, 5 million adults in the UK had never accessed the Internet.[36] Internet usage declines after the age of 50,[37] and it is used less by those on lower incomes.[38] The move toward online service provision can therefore exclude certain groups of consumers and thus exacerbate vulnerability, for example, living in a rural area can exclude access to online services if there is no, or poor, Internet coverage. Mobile banking applications require consumers to have a device that can support such activities, and updates to security requirements can mean that older devices do not support banking apps at all. The rapid growth of online and mobile banking has the potential to leave many consumers struggling to manage their finances and contact their bank. Nevertheless, online banking services can pose alternative challenges. Consumers, especially those with low IT literacy, risk being alienated by the technology needed to access these services. It can be intimidating for consumers who do not fully understand how to use the system provided by their bank. The increasing use of social media channels to engage with customers can be exclusionary and the role that 'chat-bots' often play in the online help setting can frustrate consumers who are struggling to explain the issue they are confronted with. It might be that the consumer terminates an attempt to contact the bank when faced by difficulties or does not contact the bank at all. It should not need to be said that the bank's online system needs to be resilient: IT collapses have highlighted the challenges that consumers can face when systems stop working.[39]

Branch and ATM closures have exacerbated the difficulties consumers can experience and can thus induce vulnerability. Over two-thirds of bank branches in the UK have closed in the last 30 years,[40] and while decisions on branch

---

34 *Ibid* 76.
35 University of Birmingham, *Financial Inclusion Annual Monitoring Briefing Paper* (2018) 1.
36 National Audit Office, *Vulnerable Customers in Regulated Industries* (March 2017) 6.
37 Oxford Internet Institute, *Perceived Threats to Privacy Online: the Internet in Britain* (September 2019) 5.
38 *Ibid* 6.
39 Treasury Committee, *IT Failures in the Financial Services Sector* (HC 224, 28 October 2019).
40 Chiara Cavaglieri, '*Can the Post Office Really Plug the Gap as Bank Branches Are Shut Down?*' *Which.co.uk* (London, 16 November 2018) https://www.which.co.uk/news/2018/11/can-the-post-office-really-plug-the-gap-as-bank-branches-are-shut-down/accessed 29 May 2020.

closure are commercial decisions for banks to make, they can have a significant impact on consumers, particularly the vulnerable. Increased distances to travel to a branch can hinder those who have reduced mobility or who live in rural areas: one-fifth of consumers now have to travel over three kilometres to get to the nearest bank branch.[41] This can limit the products and services available to different customers and can operate to exclude certain customer groups. Research in Bristol, for example, indicates that those living in deprived areas face greater difficulties accessing the cash infrastructure.[42] It also reduces the options available to consumers in terms of how they engage with their bank account. The number of free to use ATMs is decreasing, and not all ATMs offer the necessary accessibility features that blind or deaf customers might require to be able to use that machine.[43] Use of the Post Office as an alternative to branch banking is often stated as a counterpoint to the problems posed by closure:[44] it provides consumers with an alternative mechanism to access cash and can lessen the impact of branch closures, but Post Office branches are also in decline and do not have the capabilities to handle the variety of issues that can be dealt with in a bank branch. Barclays' plans (now reversed) to withdraw from the Post Office scheme highlight the shortcomings of relying on this infrastructure to facilitate access to the banking system.[45] The needs of consumers who might be deemed vulnerable are unlikely to be addressed through this mechanism.

Alternatives to branch banking can exacerbate consumer vulnerability. The increased distance between the bank and the consumer reduces the opportunity for the parties to develop a relationship and minimises the bank's ability to identify when a consumer needs support. This is a recognised problem in relation to banks' handling of powers of attorney and other cases of persons representing bank customers.[46] It also raises questions about how a bank engages with consumers when it needs to provide information and warnings about developments that could induce vulnerability, such as new forms of scams. Vulnerable consumers are likely to use the fewest channels of communication with their bank, and it could be that the branch has been their most reliable means of accessing information.[47] This also has implications for financial education initiatives, such as those designed

---

41 *Ibid.*
42 D Tischer, J Evans, and S Davies, '*Mapping the Availability of Cash: A Case Study of Bristol's Cash Infrastructure*' (May 2019).
43 Treasury Committee, *Consumers' Access to Financial Services* (n 8) 41.
44 Treasury Committee, *Consumers' Access to Financial Services: Government Response to the Committee's Twenty-Ninth Report* (HC 1642, 8 May 2019).
45 The decision was reversed following criticism from public and industry bodies: Barclays, 'Barclays and the Post Office Banking Framework' (24 October 2019) https://home.barclays/news/press-releases/2019/10/barclays-and-the-post-office-banking-framework/ accessed 1 June 2020.
46 FCA, *Occasional Paper* (n 20) 41-2.
47 See, for example, discussions above regarding Internet usage and drivers of vulnerability.

to reduce susceptibility to fraud: banks need to consider how they contact their consumers.

Banks systems (online and otherwise) can also be unintentionally designed in ways which create or increase stress and thus vulnerability. Systems need to be flexible to ensure that those who are less technologically able can use the system for their purposes. A bank also needs to provide mechanisms to allow consumers to cope with unexpected changes. Take the instance of a consumer who has unexpectedly fallen ill: there could be challenges for a carer in finding out about that consumer's essential finances if they only receive online bank statements. It is expected that banks will balance the need for access and communication against the risks of fraud.[48] Ultimately, the consumer will experience greater harm if they cannot run their financial life.

The current picture

There are a significant number of provisions in place in the UK that provide degrees of protection for consumers in vulnerable situations and thus require banks to adjust product and service provision in certain circumstances: this section will provide a summary of these measures. As discussed at the start of this chapter, the means of enforcement in the event of noncompliance depends on the type of provision; however, all will be relevant to the FOS if a complaint is submitted to it. Currently, this protection is provided by a variety of sources, ranging from the general law through to bank-specific regulation and industry good practice. Law, regulation, and practice in this field has developed in a piecemeal manner. This is a complex area which banks need to incorporate into their procedures if they are to achieve good practice.

Access to banking

Problems surrounding access to banking can exacerbate vulnerabilities of all kinds, with difficulties ranging from not being able to open a bank account to challenges accessing and operating an existing account. A number of provisions exist to ensure that banking is an inclusive industry.

The Payment Account Regulations 2015[49] aim to ensure that everyone has access to the banking system. By requiring designated banks[50] to make 'basic' bank accounts available,[51] they create a right for consumers to open and use a bank account. A 'basic' bank account is fee free and provides the consumer with access to payment services but not to loans. As a result, the bank does

---

48 FCA, *Guidance for Firms* (n 2) 54.
49 Implementing the EU's Payment Accounts Directive (Directive 2014/92/EU) 2014.
50 Nine UK banks are designated. 'Basic Bank Accounts' (December 2019) https://www.gov. uk/government/collections/basic-bank-accounts accessed 17 June 2020.
51 Regulations 19-27.

not have to be concerned with the consumer's credit rating. In 2019, there were 7.4 million 'basic' accounts open at the designated banks in the UK.[52] However, 1.23 million adults still do not hold a bank account in the UK,[53] and evidence indicates that a majority of these people do not know of the availability of 'basic' accounts.[54] There is a view that some banks are reluctant to publicise the availability of such accounts because the lack of overdraft facilities means that it is not profitable to offer them.[55] Other barriers, such as the documents needed to prove identity and address, have also been identified as making it difficult for some of the most vulnerable members of society, such as the homeless, those living in refuges, asylum seekers, and those leaving prison, to open such accounts.[56] The UK government wants the industry to be flexible in relation to the documents it is prepared to accept as proof of identity from customers who cannot meet standard verification requirements.[57]

In some instances, individual banks have developed their own voluntary initiatives to attempt to overcome the challenges presented by consumers who do not have identification documents. For example, HSBC has developed procedures to overcome these problems both for victims of human trafficking and modern slavery[58] and also for the homeless.[59] Lloyds Bank, as part of its 'Helping Britain Prosper Plan,' has introduced a similar scheme for the homeless, in partnership with charities in certain UK cities.[60] Nevertheless, protections here are not consistent or widespread: certain schemes are only available at certain branches.[61]

However, a line is drawn between the needs of the customer and the interests of the bank. This is particularly apparent in situations where banks make decisions about the services provided to customers. For example, the Payment Services Regulations 2017[62] permit a bank to close a consumer's

---

52 HM Treasury, *Basic bank accounts: July 2018 to June 2019* (December 2019) 5.

53 University of Birmingham, *Financial Inclusion Annual Monitoring Briefing Paper 2018*, (n 35) 1.

54 FCA, *FCA Mission: Our Future Approach* (n 27) 24.

55 Treasury Committee, *Consumers' access to financial services* (n 8) 10.

56 *Ibid* 12.

57 Treasury Committee, *Consumers' access: Government response* (n 44) 2–3.

58 HSBC, 'HSBC UK Provides Support for Survivors of Human Trafficking' (28 June 2019) https://www.about.hsbc.co.uk/news-and-media/hsbc-uk-provides-support-for-survivors-of-human-trafficking accessed 21 May 2020.

59 HSBC, 'Together we thrive' < https://www.hsbc.co.uk/togetherwethrive/ accessed 21 May 2020.

60 Lloyds Bank, 'Banking for Homeless People' https://www.lloydsbankinggroup.com/our-purpose/helping-people/making-banking-easier-for-homeless-people/ accessed 21 May 2020.

61 George Steer, 'Flaw highlighted in HSBC Bank Scheme for Homeless' *Financial Times* (London, 12 December 2019). https://www.ft.com/content/1cc6405b-69ec-4f19-9913-4d3af8ebc000 accessed 21 May 2020.

62 Reg 51(4).

account by giving two months' notice. UK Finances' Principles for Exiting a Customer[63] state that 'financial inclusion considerations and sensitivities of the customer, for example, customer vulnerability,' should be taken into account when doing this, but do not indicate that banks should continue to provide banking services to consumers where they do not wish to do so, even when the consumer is vulnerable. The Access to Banking Standard[64] has been developed (by industry, overseen by the Lending Standards Board) to respond to concerns regarding the number of bank branch closures. However, the Standard does not require banks to keep branches open: it sets out the procedure banks should apply before finalising the closure. Banks agree to identify affected consumers (consumers whose accounts are held by that branch), communicate the closure plans to those consumers, and provide information on how they can continue to access the service. Where a consumer has been identified as vulnerable, banks agree to contact them and find out if they require any further assistance:[65] they are not required to refrain from closing the branch.

Operation of accounts

At a general level, the Equality Act 2010 contains provisions that make unlawful discrimination on the basis of disability. It requires all businesses (including banks) to make reasonable adjustments to enable customers to access services.[66] This may require making available auxiliary aids such as a portable induction loop for people with hearing aids; British Sign Language interpreters; providing information in alternative formats, such as Braille or audio CDs; and extra staff assistance. Banks are now making considerable efforts to make their services accessible. Special debit cards are being issued to consumers with visual impairments, and ATM machines are being fitted with braille and audio facilities. Consumers are also being advised by their banks on how to use the accessibility features on their mobile phones to assist banking transactions. This area of law, which requires banks to devote resources to adapt their provision to meet the needs of vulnerable consumers, is enforced by the Equality and Human Rights Commission rather than the FCA. A consumer who claims to have been disadvantaged by a breach of the Act can claim compensation in the County Court.[67]

There have also been industry-wide developments concerning the operation of accounts. The Financial Abuse Code of Practice, introduced by UK Finance, provides guidance to banks on how to treat consumers who have been subject to financial abuse.[68] Such abuse, which is regarded as a species of domestic violence, covers a variety of situations such as where a person has been left penniless

---

63 UK Finance, *Principles for Exiting a Customer* (June 2019) https://www.ukfinance.org.uk/system/files/Principles-for-Exiting-a-Customer.pdf accessed 21 May 2020.
64 Lending Standards Board, *Access to Banking Standard* https://www.lendingstandardsboard.org.uk/wp-content/uploads/2017/07/Access_to_Banking_Standard.pdf accessed 21 May 2020.
65 *Ibid* 2.
66 Equality Act 2010, s 20.
67 Equality Act 2010, ss 113 and 119.

by the acts of an estranged partner emptying a joint bank account or has discovered that all means of identifying themselves to the bank have been removed so that they can no longer operate a joint account.[69] Notably, the Code indicates that staff should be empowered to override standard procedures in order to respond to the needs of the consumer. The Code lays down six principles designed to cover situations in which a person is suffering financial abuse at the hands of another. Central to the operation of the Code is Principle 5, which contains provisions designed to ensure that the consumer can regain control of their finances and indicates that firms can waive normal rules where appropriate, such as by accepting communications through third parties, accepting refuges and safe houses as consumers' addresses, and acceptance of nonstandard proof of identity. In the context of physical abuse, banks must not reveal the address of the place of safety at which the consumer is living.[70] Banks are setting up dedicated domestic and financial abuse procedures to provide support for consumers facing such problems.[71]

Recognising that family members of vulnerable consumers can also experience difficulties when dealing with banks has led to the development of codes of practice to address common situations. The Bereavement Principles,[72] for example, aim to ensure that those reporting a death to a firm only have to do so once (and that they are treated with compassion when they do), although the LSB noted in its Vulnerability Principles review that this has not been fully implemented by the firms involved in the review.[73] The Principles to Improve Customer Access[74] handle situations where a third party might need to access a vulnerable consumer's account, for example, during illness. They emphasise the importance of providing clear information to the third party on what they can/cannot do when accessing the account.

68 UK Finance, *Financial Abuse Code of Practice* (2018) https://www.ukfinance.org.uk/system/files/Financial-Abuse-Code-of-Practice.pdf accessed 1 June 2020.
69 Katy Austin, 'The Bank Sent My Safe House Address to My Abusive ex' *BBC News* (London, 26 August 2019) https://www.bbc.co.uk/news/business-49281219 accessed 21 May 2020.
70 Ombudsman News, Issue 127, August 2015, 11.
71 Lloyds Bank, 'Supporting Victims of Domestic and Financial Abuse' https://www.lloydsbankinggroup.com/our-purpose/helping-people/supporting-victims-of-domestic-and-financial-abuse/ accessed 21 May 2020.
72 British Bankers Association (BBA), *Bereavement Principles* (February 2016) https://www.bba.org.uk/wp-content/uploads/2016/03/BBA01-458427-v1-Bereavement_Principles.pdf accessed 21 May 2020.
73 LSB, *Financial Services Vulnerability Taskforce: Principles and recommendations* (October 2018) 10.
74 BBA, *Principles for Third Party Access* (June 2017) https://www.bba.org.uk/wp-content/uploads/2017/06/BBA01-477720-v1-BBA_Third_party_access_Principles.pdf accessed 21 May 2020.

Lending and financial vulnerability

Lending is an area in which substantial controls which can protect vulnerable consumers exist. They aim to ensure that individuals do not take on unsustainable levels of borrowing (responsible lending) and to provide assistance for those who default in repaying loans. UK law,[75] and the EU law on which some of it is based, impose different controls on consumer credit [76] and mortgage borrowing.[77] However, the underlying policies are the same in both areas.

As we have seen,[78] a significant proportion of the UK population is financially vulnerable because they have no or only limited cash savings to fall back on if their income is reduced (e.g., by illness or unemployment) or if they face unexpected expenditure (such as a repair bill). For such people, borrowing may be a necessity, but can lead to a spiral of increasing, and ultimately unmanageable, debt. There is a balance to be struck here between allowing people to borrow to meet urgent needs and ensuring that those in difficult circumstances are not exploited or left trapped with an impossible burden of increasing debt. Lending is, of course, a major source of income for retail banks, credit card companies, and other more specialised financial services firms. In recent years, the UK has taken a number of measures designed to protect people who need to borrow money. All of these measures show banks being compelled to adopt practices designed to avoid consumers becoming burdened by unmanageable debt and to assist those who are so burdened to overcome their problems.

First, payday lending (high-cost short-term credit) is an area in which financially vulnerable consumers have been exploited by lenders imposing very high interest rates on short-term unsecured borrowing. In 2015, the FCA placed constraints on such lending.[79] These controls have capped the charges and interest which can be levied on such loans.[80] Firms are also banned from rolling over such a loan into a new one on more than two occasions.[81] Promotions concerning such lending must carry a warning that serious money difficulties can result from late repayments.[82] These measures, combined with a stringent application by the FOS of the requirement that such firms conduct a proper creditworthiness assessment prior to making a loan, have had a drastic impact.

---

75 The UK law and guidance on its application is contained in the FCA's CONC and MCOB sourcebooks. The LSB's Standards of Lending Practice is an industry code of practice which expands on the CONC requirements.
76 Consumer Credit Directive (Directive 2008/48/EC).
77 Mortgage Credit Directive (Directive 2014/17/EU).
78 Above, section 3.
79 In 2017, the FCA calculated that 3.1 million adults in the UK had used high-cost borrowing in the previous 12 months. FCA, *The Financial Lives of Consumers (n 33)* 62.
80 CONC 5A.2.2R and 3R.
81 CONC 6.7.23R. Procedural requirements (including warnings) also apply to refinancing of a high-cost short-term loan.
82 CONC 3.4.1. R.

What was a growing and widely publicised market has gone into decline with firms which specialised in such lending going out of business. Following the changes, it was reported[83] that Wonga had reduced the annual percentage rate (APR) on its lending from 5,853 to 1,509%.[84] Wonga collapsed in 2018 following heavy financial losses resulting from the new regulatory rules and many compensation claims alleging mis-selling of loans. In the last year, QuickQuid, then the largest payday lender, PiggyBank Loans, and Peachy have also collapsed. The extent of these firms' potential liability for conducting inadequate creditworthiness assessments on consumers[85] appears to be the cause of these failures.

Second, the overdrafts market, used by many consumers who are in financial difficulty, has been reformed to meet the criticism that banks have been levying unreasonable charges on consumers who overdraw their current accounts. Banks are now required to send a warning to consumers whose current accounts are close to being overdrawn.[86] Research has concluded that such alerts reduce the charges being paid to banks by consumers in relation to unarranged overdrafts by 25%.[87] The charges have also become regulated. Since April 2020, banks must apply a single, published, interest rate to all overdrafts on a consumer's account (whether preauthorised or not).[88] Transaction charges for being overdrawn can no longer be made in addition to interest charges.[89] The aim is to make overdraft charges easier to understand and to use competition to keep them down. The FCA has estimated that 70% of those bank consumers who use overdrafts will pay less or see no change under the new system and that the cost of borrowing £100 through an unarranged overdraft is expected to drop from a typical £5 per day to under 10p per day.[90] Firms are now also required to monitor overdraft usage over time,[91] determine whether usage indicates a consumer is in financial difficulty, and communicate with consumers where there is repeat usage of the overdraft facility.[92] This is important in giving assistance to those financially vulnerable consumers

---

83 Rupert Jones, 'Wonga cuts cost of borrowing, but interest rate still 1,509%' *The Guardian* (London, 16 December 2014) https://www.theguardian.com/business/2014/dec/16/wonga-cuts-cost-borrowing-interest-rate accessed 29 May 2020.

84 It can, of course, be misleading to consider the annual cost of a loan which is only intended to be owed for a short period of time (Wonga's average loan term was 17 days).

85 See discussion on page 221–222.

86 Retail Banking Market Investigation Order 2017, Article 23.

87 Competition and Markets Authority, *Sending out an SMS: The Impact of Automatically Enrolling Consumers Into Overdraft Alerts* (2018) 4.

88 CONC 5C.2.1R.

89 CONC 5C.2.1R.

90 FCA, 'New Overdraft Rules Mean 7 Out of 10 People Will Be Better Off or See No Change' https://www.fca.org.uk/news/press-releases/new-overdraft-rules-mean accessed 15 May 2020.

91 CONC 5D.2.1R Firms are expected to identify whether a customer who repeatedly uses an overdraft facility is a customer that shows signs of potential financial difficulties or whether they are a consumer that does not. There is no definition of repeat use – it is for firms to determine.

92 CONC 5D.3.1R.

who are at particular risk of incurring regular charges for overdraft borrowing.[93] New rules requiring the cost of overdraft borrowing to be presented in a consistent format by all banks are designed to remove the information hurdles that customers experience and remove hidden costs associated with overdraft usage.[94] All of these measures reduce the possibility of unmanageable debt arising.

Third, measures have been taken to control lending on credit cards. In 2016, FCA research concluded that 5.6 million credit card customers in the UK had potentially problematic borrowing on their account.[95] Problematic borrowing was defined as a consumer being in default, having had a balance of over 90% of the credit limit for more than a year or only making the minimum repayments on the account. The FCA accepts that consumers who stay indebted to credit card companies over a long period of time are profitable for banks, but regards this situation as damaging to consumers because borrowing on a credit card is expensive and such borrowing may signify serious financial problems.[96] The measures introduced in the light of this research show that the Authority is prepared to sacrifice the banks' interests in favour of vulnerable consumers. In relation to financial vulnerability, the most important change has been to put credit card companies under an obligation to seek to identify customers in financial difficulty[97] earlier and to take appropriate steps at set points to assist those customers to repay the debt. In addition, as a way of reducing the overall debt on an account, a bank must set the minimum required monthly repayment on a credit card account at an amount equal to at least that amount which repays the interest, fees, and charges that have been applied to the consumer's account, plus 1 percentage of the amount outstanding.[98] The FCA estimates that these measures will decrease bank revenue by between £310 million and £1.3 billion per year.[99] Some banks[100] are now offering repayment plans for larger purchases made on credit cards. If a consumer accepts this, the borrowing on those items is steadily reduced by a fixed monthly sum and the risk of the borrowing turning into long-term debt is removed.

These specific changes are in addition to long-standing bodies of regulation which by controlling lending protect vulnerable consumers. A satisfactory creditworthiness assessment is a required precondition to a bank making a

---

93 FCA, '*High-Cost Credit Review: Overdrafts Consultation Paper and Policy Statement*' CP18/42, 2018.
94 BCOBS 7.6A.1R and 8.2.3.R.
95 FCA *Credit Card Market Study Final Findings Report* 2016 para 1.30.
96 FCA *Credit card market study: Persistent debt and earlier intervention – feedback to CP17/43 and final rules* PS 18/04 2018 para 1.8.
97 CONC 6.7.3AR.
98 CONC 6.7.5R.
99 FCA, '*High-Cost Credit Review*' (n 99) para 1.13.
100 EG Barclays, 'Installment Plan' https://www.barclaycard.co.uk/personal/customer/instalment-plan; NatWest, 'Existing Credit Card Customers: Instalment Plans' https://personal.natwest.com/personal/credit-cards/existing-customers/instalment-lending.html accessed 16 June 2020.

consumer loan[101] or lending on a mortgage.[102] The purpose of these provisions is the protective one of ensuring that consumers do not enter into unsustainable borrowing: it is not to ensure that the bank's lending is secured.[103] The consumer credit provisions are currently generating a large number of claims made to the FOS against payday loan companies on the basis that consumers were allowed to take out loans which they were unlikely to be able to repay without difficulty. In one case,[104] the consumer had taken out and repaid a number of small loans over a short period of time before more substantial sums were borrowed by further loans. The ombudsman considered that the pattern of borrowing should have put the lender on notice that the consumer was in financial difficulties (he was in fact gambling heavily) and that it had failed to undertake an adequate creditworthiness assessment at the time that the further loans were sought. The fees, charges, and interest on those loans were to be repaid to the consumer.

During the course of a loan, banks are expected to monitor the borrowing in order to identify signs of the consumer encountering financial difficulties.[105] They should ensure that consumer-facing employees are trained to do this.[106] Where necessary, they should also consider how they communicate with vulnerable consumers regarding debt issues. For example, a bank should produce a tailored response to a consumer who informs it that mental health difficulties mean he finds it difficult to discuss his affairs by telephone and does not have a fixed address.[107]

Consumers who are in default on their loans are commonly vulnerable as a result of financial problems. Banks are required to have policies and procedures for dealing with those whose accounts fall into arrears[108] and, specifically, to ensure fair and appropriate treatment of consumers who the firm understands or reasonably suspects to be particularly vulnerable.[109] As in relation to the coronavirus crisis, a bank might need to grant a consumer a 'payment holiday' to enable the consumer to manage their affairs if they are unable to work. The fair treatment principle[110] requires that consumers who are in default are treated empathetically and that efforts are made to resolve the problem by agreement: for example, by rescheduling payments in a way that is affordable.[111] Banks should

101 CONC 5.2A.4R.
102 MCOB 11.6.2R.
103 FOS, DRN1953728.
104 *Ibid.*
105 CONC 6.7.2(1) R and 6.7.3AR.
106 LSB, *Standards of Lending Practice: Personal Customers* (2016) 8.
107 FOS, DRN0228524.
108 CONC 7.2.1(1) R, MCOB 13.3.1R. FCA: *Final Notice, Lloyds Bank PLC, Bank of Scotland plc, and The Mortgage Business Plc* (11 June 2020).
109 CONC 7.2.1(2) R, MCOB 13.3.1CR.
110 PRIN 6, CONC 7.3.2G.
111 CONC 7.3.4R, MCOB 13.2.2AR.

advise such a consumer to seek the assistance of a debt advice body.[112] If a bank is aware that a consumer may lack the mental capacity to make decisions about their debts, it must suspend any debt collection process.[113] This provision can be very important if a consumer is unable to engage with the bank because of serious illness.

Fraud

Measures also exist which provide vulnerable persons with protection against Authorised Push Payment scams: those in which a customer is deceived into transferring money through the banking system to a fraudster. The LSB administers a voluntary code, the Contingent Reimbursement Model Code, which came into force in 2019.[114] All of the major retail banks have signed up to it. The Code states the procedure to be followed to determine whether a consumer should be reimbursed in the event of such a misdirected payment. The Code expressly refers to vulnerability and requires banks to take additional measures to identify and protect such customers.[115] A finding that a consumer is vulnerable will have a significant impact on the outcome: a consumer deemed vulnerable will receive full reimbursement from the bank irrespective of whether they ignored warnings that the transaction might be fraudulent.[116]

Gambling

A number of UK banks offer gambling blocks to consumers in order to protect those who consider their gambling to be problematic. These are voluntary developments; not all banks offer the facility, and there are considerable variations in what is offered.[117] In some cases, it is also possible for a consumer to block other forms of expenditure.[118] There are also variations of approach if a consumer subsequently seeks to remove a block from an account. While some banks place no restriction on removing a block,[119] others impose a 48 -hour cooling-

---

112 CONC 7.3.7AG, see also MCOB ch13.4.
113 CONC 7.10.1R.
114 LSB, *Contingent Reimbursement Model Code for Authorised Push Payment Scams* (2019) https://www.lendingstandardsboard.org.uk/wp-content/uploads/2019/05/CRM-code.pdf accessed 26 May 2020.
115 *Ibid*, SF1(4).
116 *Ibid*, R2(3).
117 The NatWest block only applies to Mastercard credit cards. See 'Struggling Financially: Gambling Block' https://personal.natwest.com/personal/life-moments/Struggling-financially/managing-your-gambling.html#how-it-works accessed 27 May 2020.
118 Barclays permits a customer to block payments to various categories of businesses. See 'How do I block merchants to a certain type of merchant in my Barclays app?' https://www.barclays.co.uk/help/mobile-banking/spending/merchant-control/accessed 17 June 2020.
119 EG NatWest (n 117).

224 Powley and Stanton

off period or require the consumer to discuss the issue with a member of staff before the block is removed to meet the risk of a consumer making an impulsive decision to start gambling again.[120]

Reforms and challenges

The regime covering bank interactions with vulnerable consumers is a complex and fragmented one. Banks should treat customers fairly, but it can be difficult for staff to understand what is expected of them when dealing with consumers in vulnerable situations. Rules and guidance cover bank behaviour in certain situations, but detailed rules cannot capture every type of vulnerability given the dynamic nature of consumer characteristics. FCA rules might require banks to take steps to comply with one regime, but industry guidance could suggest overriding standard procedures when certain vulnerabilities are present as, for example, in the case of nonstandard identification. It can also be hard for consumers to know what to expect from their bank: not all banks are signatories to voluntary codes, and banks have different internal processes.

Failure to identify vulnerability can have a significant impact upon the well-being of the consumer. However, the reality is that some consumers conduct their affairs at a considerable remove from their bank and banks are handling millions of transactions daily: vulnerabilities may be difficult to identify. Even where some vulnerabilities are obvious, it might still require effort to determine the impact of the vulnerability on the individual. Banks need to have systems in place to try to identify these consumers and take steps to mitigate harm they could face. The challenge for banks and their staff, therefore, is identifying vulnerable consumers and understanding the impact of the vulnerability on the consumer's needs. The challenge for regulators is ensuring that there is an appropriate framework in place to provide this protection.

The FCA is of the view that whilst some firms are making progress in their treatment of vulnerable consumers, the position remains far from perfect.[121] The proposed guidance on the topic[122] (the final publication has been delayed due to the coronavirus) is intended to assist firms with understanding what is expected of them when dealing with vulnerable consumers in order to comply with the Principles for Businesses. The guidance will be designated 'non-Handbook guidance' (adding greater complexity to an already confusing collection of regulation, industry guidance, and good practice) and will not be prescriptive: firms will be given a range of options rather than a checklist as to what must be done.

---

120 Monzo, 'How to block gambling spending from your Monzo account' (June 2018) https://monzo.com/blog/2018/06/19/gambling-block-self-exclusion accessed 30 May 2020.
121 Nisha Arora (n 3).
122 FCA, *Guidance for firms* (n 2) 3.

This is intended to permit flexibility in firms' implementation to respond to the needs of the markets they operate in.

The FCA's overall aim is that 'doing the right thing for vulnerable consumers (is) deeply embedded in the culture of firms' and 'that the outcomes experienced by vulnerable consumers are at least as good as those of other consumers.'[123] The guidance will inform the FCA's supervision of firms and could be relevant in enforcement proceedings and in compensation claims taken by individuals to the FOS. The themes in the proposed guidance draw on the FCA's earlier work on the topic: staff should deal with consumers as individuals and should understand the sector they operate within so that characteristics that could induce or accentuate vulnerability are identified. Staff should be able to provide appropriate support to the consumer and an understanding of the needs of vulnerable consumers should be incorporated into the management of the business.[124] Firms should take a proactive approach to understanding the nature and extent of vulnerability in the market they serve and to identifying vulnerable consumers.[125] Training, internal systems and innovation, and the culture of the firm are central to the firm's success.

Training

Staff dealing with vulnerable consumers should aim for a 'good outcome' that meets the needs of the individual consumer.[126] This positions bank staff at the centre of the vulnerability regime: appropriate training should be in place to support staff with understanding what vulnerability means and gaining the confidence to handle the vast array of situations consumers might experience.[127]

Staff need to be trained on the breadth of vulnerability, recording information regarding vulnerability, and tailoring service provision to meet consumer needs. Practically, this requires staff to be granted flexibility to guide conversations and training on how to enact this within the scope of their role. This is particularly important for frontline staff who are the initial point of contact for a vulnerable consumer and who might need to respond to a consumer's needs by diverging from normal processes. Staff need to be trained to deal empathetically and appropriately in such situations, ensuring that they are aware of the options available to them to meet the needs of the consumer. Systems offering staff the ability to diverge from normal processes in appropriate circumstances need to be in place.

Training poses challenges for banks: staff engage with thousands of consumers every day. Prescriptive rules increase the risk that banks pursue a 'tick

---

123 *Ibid* 15.
124 *Ibid*, Proposed Guidance para 16.
125 *Ibid* para 28.
126 *Ibid* para 27.
127 *Ibid* para 21.

box' approach and thus the desire to avoid them is understandable, but the lack of specific rules covering these situations can make it difficult for firms to develop internal approaches to handle vulnerability processes at a sufficiently detailed level to ensure that staff do consider vulnerability. Consistent treatment will continue to be an issue and ongoing monitoring has a large part to play in a firm's procedures.

Training also poses challenges for bank staff: staff need to identify signs of vulnerability and determine how to respond appropriately to individual consumers.[128] They need to know how to record the information correctly, for recordkeeping and to avoid the consumer repeating the information later. A number of tools exist to support staff in this process, designed to help staff access and record information about different types of vulnerability from consumers. For example, the 'TEXAS'[129] tool is widely used across the sector to handle disclosures with regard to mental health,[130] yet the scope of vulnerability issues means that this technique is not appropriate for all situations. The 'IDEA technique'[131] is an alternative that can be used to structure conversations with consumers presenting other vulnerabilities. A number of other tools can provide staff with direction as to questions to ask consumers, yet there is a risk that staff are overwhelmed by different procedures for different scenarios and fail to listen to information provided by the consumer, thus failing to respond to their needs. It is also important that staff are able to 'signpost' the consumer to other services, such as charities, that can provide specialised support for individuals: the expectation is not that banks will know everything, but staff need to be trained on where the consumer can access help if necessary.

Firms have worked with charities and consumer associations to develop training for staff (e.g., measures to support consumers with cancer). However, specific training on particular types of vulnerability can produce alternative difficulties, including confirmation bias where staff only identify those vulnerabilities that fall within the scope of their training and miss others.[132] This is not to argue against training, but highlights the pitfalls: designing training with suitable coverage to empower staff to respond flexibly and appropriately to the wide range of vulnerabilities that could lead to consumer harm can be difficult.

---

128 FCA, *Final Notice* (n 17).
129 TEXAS: Thank the customer for the information, Explain how the information will be used, eXplicit consent, Ask three key questions, Signpost to additional help.
130 University of Bristol Personal Finance Research Centre, *Vulnerability: A Guide for Debt Collection, 21 Questions, 21 Steps* (March 2017) 24.
131 IDEA: Impact; Duration; Experiences; Assistance.
132 UK Finance and Money Advice Trust, *The UK Finance Vulnerability Academy: Improving Outcomes for Customers in Vulnerable Circumstances*, Webinar (February 2019).

Systems and innovation

The draft guidance states that firms should consider the characteristics and needs of vulnerable consumers when designing products and communications in order to anticipate and proactively address difficulties that vulnerable consumers might have during a product's life.[133] For example, problems can arise when products (such as short-term loans) are likely to be sought by persons in financial difficulty and when there are a number of similar, but complex, competing products on offer in the market (as applies in the context of motor vehicle finance). Good design is also relevant to communication systems which should be designed in order to ensure that vulnerable consumers do not have difficulties in communicating with a firm[134] or in understanding the nature of products.[135] Systems need to make it easy for consumers to divulge information about their vulnerabilities,[136] and digital channels of communication should be configured in a way that alerts human advisers that a customer is displaying behaviour which suggests vulnerability.[137]

There have been significant developments with technology offered by firms, potentially improving how consumers engage with their bank and address areas of vulnerability. Enhanced analytics offered by online banking apps can help consumers to manage their finances and track their spending, providing them with greater control over their financial life,[138] and enable banks to identify consumers who might be experiencing financial difficulties. Technology can reduce the cost of service provision and allow banks to pass these savings on to consumers. Open banking can help a bank develop a better understanding of the consumer's profile and of potential drivers of vulnerability. The UK Regulators Network is considering whether wider data sharing on consumer vulnerabilities between firms in core sectors could reduce the need for consumers to repeat information about vulnerability regularly.[139]

However, consumers need to have access to both the Internet and a banking app to utilise these benefits: IT solutions are only solutions if they can be used by those who need them. Trust is required in open banking technology if consumers are to consent to their personal information being shared: currently consumers are concerned about data storage and privacy.[140] Open banking guidance

---

133 FCA, *Guidance for firms* (n 2), Proposed Guidance para 58.
134 *Ibid* para 76.
135 *Ibid* para 97 and 98.
136 *Ibid* para 35.
137 *Ibid* para 38.
138 Open Banking, *Open Banking and Vulnerable Consumers* https://www.openbanking.org.uk/insight/vulnerable-customers/ accessed 29 May 2020.
139 UK Regulators Network, *UKRN Publishes Follow-up Report on Water and Energy Company Data Sharing to Support Vulnerable Customers* (1 November 2018).
140 Open Banking, *Consumer Priorities for Open Banking* (June 2019) 31. https://www.openbanking.org.uk/wp-content/uploads/Consumer-Priorities-for-Open-Banking-report-June-2019.pdf accessed 30 May 2020.

emphasises the need for firms to engage with vulnerable consumers throughout the process to ensure that they are aware how their data will be used,[141] but it remains to be seen how open banking will evolve.

Product design teams should be aware of the needs of vulnerable consumers and incorporate features to support those needs. Diversity within product design teams is important to ensure different experiences are considered throughout the process. Training design teams on vulnerability is also necessary. The development of procedures by some banks that required consumers to have mobile phones to authenticate payments, to implement the Strong Customer Authentication rules,[142] highlights the challenges that can be faced by some consumers when their needs are not considered in the design process.[143] It is likely that errors of this kind will disproportionately impact the vulnerable, including older members of society and those on lower incomes.

Wider concerns about technological developments need to be considered in this context. In-built bias in algorithms could fail to acknowledge vulnerability or exaggerate it. The example of the Apple Card algorithm potentially introducing gender bias to credit limit decisions highlights one challenge.[144] While some drivers of vulnerability are easily identifiable (e.g., age), it is much harder to identify health issues. Overreliance on machine learning could lead to consumers being sold inappropriate products, data could tell a narrative that does not reflect the consumer's reality, and overuse of technology to engage with consumers can discourage some from using the service. Relying on technology to identify vulnerability should be avoided.

Bank culture

Complying with the FCA's approach requires the development of a corporate culture that values individuals and focuses the retail bank's operations toward the fair treatment of vulnerable consumers:[145] the internal culture of a bank impacts how consumers are treated. The move to grant staff greater flexibility when dealing with vulnerable consumers is a positive development, allowing staff to tailor an approach that provides a solution to challenges the consumer

---

141 Open Banking Implementation Entity, 'Customer Experience Guidelines' (2018) 13. https://www.openbanking.org.uk/wp-content/uploads/Customer-Experience-Guidelines-V1.3.0.pdf#page=13 accessed 1 June 2020.

142 Regulation 100, Payment Services Regulations 2017.

143 Treasury Committee, *Oral evidence: The work of the Financial Conduct Authority* (HC 475, 2019) Q560 per Catherine McKinnell MP.

144 Reuters 'Apple Card Issuer Investigated After Claims of Sexist Credit Checks' *The Guardian* (London, 10 November 2019) https://www.theguardian.com/technology/2019/nov/10/apple-card-issuer-investigated-after-claims-of-sexist-credit-checks?CMP=share_btn_tw accessed 1 June 2020.

145 FCA, *Guidance for firms* (n 2), Proposed Guidance para 19.

faces. However, moving staff away from a sales-driven, target-based approach will continue to be a challenge. As the FCA has highlighted, while there is evidence of changes to culture in terms of the 'tone from the top', effecting culture change at the mid-level of firms is much harder, given the incentives which have driven much of their career.[146] The culture of each institution needs to be a positive one if the necessary flexibility is to result in good outcomes. Consistency of treatment remains a concern given the silos that can exist in different business areas, in different regions, individual branches, and call centres. As UK Finance highlight, staff knowledge and understanding is one aspect of ensuring a cohesive approach to vulnerability, but this needs to be accompanied by improvements to the 'environment' within which staff are working.[147]

Regulation

Unintended consequences of regulatory change are important: rules designed to reduce vulnerability for some can induce vulnerability in others. For example, it is unclear where consumers who relied on payday lenders are accessing lending services now, with the collapse of many payday loan providers. There are concerns that the setting of interest rates at 39.9% APR by many overdraft providers indicates anti-competitive practices[148] following the introduction of the FCA's new rules on overdraft charges and worries over consumers who might be worse off as a result of the introduction of the rules.[149]

Changes in the style of regulation can also cause problems for consumers. For example, the increasing use of guidance by the regulator could lead to consumers having reduced options to challenge a firm's misconduct, as guidance is not enforceable in the courts (it is, of course, relevant to regulatory enforcement activity and complaints to the FOS). Outcomes-focused regulation will achieve little if an outcome such as 'consumers must be treated fairly' is supplemented by detailed guidance, thus returning to a position of box-ticking, yet encouraging all firms to pursue their own approaches makes it harder for supervisors to identify what is happening within individual banks.

---

146 FCA, *Senior Managers and Certification Regime Stocktake Report* (August 2019). https://www.fca.org.uk/publications/multi-firm-reviews/senior-managers-and-certification-regime-banking-stocktake-report accessed 1 June 2020.

147 UK Finance, *Improving Outcomes for Vulnerable Customers* (August 2018) https://www.ukfinance.org.uk/blogs/improving-outcomes-vulnerable-customers accessed 29 May 2020.

148 FCA, 'New Overdraft and Pricing Measures Letter' (28 January 2020) https://www.fca.org.uk/publication/correspondence/overdraft-pricing-letter-firms.pdf accessed 16 May 2020.

149 Julia Kollewe, 'UK Banks Told to Explain 40% Overdraft Rates', *The Guardian* (London, 28 January 2020) https://www.theguardian.com/business/2020/jan/28/uk-banks-overdraft-rates-fca accessed 29 May 2020.

Coronavirus and vulnerability

The coronavirus pandemic has given rise to widespread vulnerability: individuals have been faced with a number of drivers of vulnerability, including illness, bereavement, the loss of work, and/or a reduced income.[150] Changes to business operation and the move toward contactless payment to limit the spread of the virus have exacerbated difficulties for those who rely on cash for payments rather than cards.[151] Branch hours have been reduced as banks struggle with staffing demands, illness, and uncertainty. New measures had to be introduced quickly to provide consumers some element of control over their financial affairs. The government announced that mortgage holders would be eligible to apply for a payment holiday;[152] the FCA extended this support to other forms of consumer finance, including credit cards[153] and personal loans,[154] and has indicated that banks should assess the cost of overdraft borrowing for affected consumers.[155] Consumers who have high-cost, short-term credit products are eligible for a one-month payment freeze, and no interest should be accrued during this period – in light of the short-term, but expensive, nature of the product.[156] The credit rating of consumers who use these facilities should not be affected.[157] There are a number of options banks can employ when providing support to affected consumers, depending on the finance needs of the consumer, but banks are not expected to engage in investigations as to the consumer's circumstances.

These facilities have predominantly been introduced through temporary guidance, setting out the FCA's expectations for banks dealing with consumers during this period,[158] with changes to rules where necessary to permit banks to operate in

---

150 Developments after 3 June 2020 are not covered. Further guidance is expected.

151 The contactless payment limit increased to £45 (from £30) at the start of the coronavirus crisis. This development was expedited in response to the coronavirus. See https://www. ukfinance.org.uk/press/press-releases/contactless-limit-uk-increases-%C2%A345-today accessed 3 June 2020.

152 FCA, *Mortgages and Coronavirus: Our Guide for Firms* (March 2020) https://www.fca. org.uk/firms/mortgages-coronavirus-guidance-firms accessed 30 May 2020.

153 FCA, 'Credit Cards and Coronavirus: Temporary Guidance for Firms' (April 2020) https://www.fca.org.uk/publications/finalised-guidance/credit-cards-retail-revolving-credit-coronavirus-temporary-guidance-firms accessed 30 May 2020.

154 FCA, 'Personal Loans and Coronavirus: Temporary Guidance for Firms' (April 2020) https://www.fca.org.uk/publications/finalised-guidance/personal-loans-coronavirus-temporary-guidance-firms accessed 30 May 2020.

155 FCA, 'Overdrafts and Coronavirus: Temporary Guidance for Firms' (April 2020) https:// www.fca.org.uk/publications/finalised-guidance/overdrafts-coronavirus-temporary-guidance-firms accessed 30 May 2020.

156 FCA, 'High-cost Short-term Credit and Coronavirus: Temporary Guidance for Firms' (April 2020) https://www.fca.org.uk/publications/finalised-guidance/high-cost-short-term-credit-and-coronavirus-temporary-guidance-firms accessed 30 May 2020.

157 FCA, *FS20/3: Temporary Financial Relief for Consumers Impacted by Coronavirus: Feedback and Draft Guidance and Rules* (April 2020) 7.

158 FCA, 'Coronavirus (Covid-19): Information for Firms' (March 2020) https://www.fca. org.uk/firms/information-firms-coronavirus-covid-19-response accessed 30 May 2020.

accordance with the guidance.[159] The FCA has been clear: banks need to treat consumers fairly. If they don't, they are at risk of enforcement action:[160] this forms part of the Principle 6 obligation for banks to treat customers fairly.[161] If a consumer is facing financial difficulties as a result of the coronavirus, banks should be prepared to offer the temporary measures covered in the guidance to relieve pressures on the consumer.[162] If a consumer mentions information to their bank that indicates that they could be experiencing financial difficulties, the bank should ask whether the consumer would like the bank to consider giving support.[163] When determining whether to provide support in the form of a mortgage payment holiday, the bank must consider what is in the best interests of the consumer – it is expressly stated that banks should not consider their own commercial interests when making this decision.[164] This support has been comprehensive: as of 29 May 2020, 3.3 million payment holidays had been granted to consumers.[165] These measures will be expensive for banks. As loan periods and payment plans are extended to support consumers in financial difficulty, banks will not receive repayment as expected (although consumers will eventually repay the full debt as the length of payment plans are extended). Reductions in interest charged will be a direct hit to banks given the extent to which these charges contribute to bank profit.

The FCA's guidance indicates that the options for responding to consumer difficulty during the coronavirus period set the minimum expectations – if firms believe they need to provide further support to treat consumers fairly, they should. The FOS has emphasised that bank treatment of consumers at this time goes to the 'heart of what it means to act fairly and reasonably,'[166] stating that it will assess firms' standards against the guidance in place at the time.[167] Banks have been proactive in responding to the crisis: a number of banks have developed bespoke systems to provide support to those who need it. The dramatic increase in the number of consumers attempting to contact bank call centres led to a number of banks introducing dedicated telephone

---

159 For example, CONC 6.7.18R on refinancing agreements has been disapplied in the context of consumers who have been impacted by the coronavirus.
160 FCA, *Business Plan 2020/21* (n 4) 10.
161 See (n 152–n 156).
162 FCA, 'Overdrafts and coronavirus' (n 154).
163 See (n 152–n 156).
164 The guidance is reviewed on a regular basis.
165 UK Finance, 'Lenders Approve Almost 1.5 Million Payment Holidays on Credit Cards and Personal Loans' (29 May 2020) https://www.ukfinance.org.uk/press/press-releases/lenders-approve-almost-1.5%20million-payment-holidays; 'Lenders are Committed to Providing Support to those Borrowers that are Impacted by Covid-19' (22 May 2020) https://www.ukfinance.org.uk/press/press-releases/lenders-are-committed-to-providing-ongoing-support-to-those-borrowers-that-are-impacted-by-Covid-19 accessed 30 May 2020.
166 FOS, *Plans and Budget 2020/21* (2020) 5 https://www.financial-ombudsman.org.uk/files/271092/strategic-plans-budget-2020-21.pdf accessed 24 May 2020.
167 FOS, Correspondence with the FCA (16 April 2020) https://www.financial-ombudsman.org.uk/files/273748/FOS-Letter-to-FCA-on-circumstances-from-Covid-19-16042020.pdf accessed 24 May 2020.

lines for elderly consumers and National Health Service staff.[168] Access to cash has been problematic, and the identification of certain consumers as more vulnerable to the coronavirus has led to some banks (and the Post Office[169]) developing a cash delivery service: if a consumer has to self-isolate at home, their bank might deliver cash to them when requested.[170] NatWest has introduced a system where a consumer can grant a third party access to cash withdrawals from their account for up to three hours after contacting the bank to request the service.[171] They also offer a 'companion card' that can be topped up with funds from a consumer's account to give to a third party to make purchases on their behalf.[172] Many banks have increased the level of digital support available to consumers to help them improve their confidence with online banking and have actively sought to identify and contact affected consumers. To support those who might be unfamiliar, or uncomfortable, with accessing online banking, some banks offer virtual digital banking lessons.[173] Banks also now permit flexibility for consumers seeking to access funds in fixed term savings account, permitting withdrawals without financial penalties on the value of the savings.[174] However, the challenges surrounding technology and vulnerability remain: it is likely that the most vulnerable will be least able to access these services. Additionally, there is inconsistency in both the support and information provided to consumers by different institutions, with some banks utilising a number of tools and others providing little.

While the financial measures cannot be expected to continue indefinitely, it would not be surprising if banks continued to utilise some of these new support tools after the crisis. Banks have responded quickly to a rapidly evolving situation, and this has required innovation in unexpected aspects of the banking service – to ensure that those who might experience challenges in overseeing their financial lives are supported. Given the FCA's emphasis on the fair treatment of vulnerable consumers before the coronavirus crisis, it is unlikely that the significant advancements in support will be wound back fully – particularly with regard to the flexible provision of services for those who are deemed vulnerable.

168 Sam Meadows, 'What Each Bank is Doing to Help Older Vulnerable People and NHS Workers' *The Telegraph* (London, 8 April 2020) https://www.telegraph.co.uk/personal-banking/current-accounts/bank-help-older-vulnerable-people-nhs-workers/ accessed 24 May 2020.

169 BBC News, 'Coronavirus: Post Office to Deliver Cash to the Vulnerable' (22 April 2020) https://www.bbc.co.uk/news/business-52384053 accessed 24 May 2020.

170 Kim Kaveh, 'Banking During Lockdown: Cash Deliveries, Dedicated Telephone Numbers and More' Which.co.uk (12 May 2020) https://www.which.co.uk/news/2020/05/how-banks-are-helping-vulnerable-customers-during-the-coronavirus-crisis/ accessed 24 May 2020.

171 NatWest, 'Personal Banking' https://personal.natwest.com/personal/banking-with-natwest/banking-for-everyone.html#everyone accessed 24 May 2020.

172 *Ibid.*

173 It is worth noting that Barclays ran its 'Digital Eagles' scheme prior to the coronavirus crisis. See https://www.barclays.co.uk/digital-confidence/eagles/ accessed 3 June 2020.

174 Which?, 'Coronavirus: What It Means for Mortgages, Credit Cards, Loans and Savings' (22 May 2020) https://www.which.co.uk/news/2020/05/coronavirus-what-it-means-for-mortgages-savings-borrowing-and-benefits/#Savings accessed 4 June 2020.

There is a longer-term concern with some of these developments, however: reductions in the acceptance of cash and the faster push toward digital banking has meant that the provision of these services is more at risk than previously. Cash has rapidly become stigmatised as businesses associate it with heightened risks of spreading the virus.[175] The episode has also highlighted the challenges that banks can face when reconciling vulnerability concerns with other processes. For example, Virgin Money was heavily criticised for closing credit card accounts at the height of the crisis in the UK,[176] although it is possible that these measures were planned as part of Virgin's compliance with the FCA's initiative to identify consumers with problematic levels of credit card debt. Virgin ultimately suspended the closures due to the impact of the virus. Several banks have struggled to balance account requirements, such as requiring a consumer to conduct certain account functions in branch only, with the fact that the consumer is elderly, and therefore should be self-isolating at home in line with the governmental advice.[177] Compliance with the guidance has also emphasised the risk of unintended consequences arising from quick implementation of regulatory reform: some consumers who have agreed payment holidays with their banks have received letters from their banks warning them that they have missed payments. Banks are required to send these letters to comply with the Consumer Credit Act 1974; however, not all banks have warned consumers of their obligations under this Act, thus exacerbating stress at what is already a difficult time for many.[178] Questions also arise regarding the impact of payment holiday measures on credit ratings: despite FCA guidance that consumer credit ratings should not have an adverse mark if a consumer takes a payment holiday, some banks have failed to follow this guidance. It has also been acknowledged that lenders will be able to identify which consumers have had payment holidays.[179]

175 Hilary Osborne, 'UK Government Urged to Protect Access to Cash for Most Vulnerable' *The Guardian* (London, 2 June 2020) https://www.theguardian.com/money/2020/jun/02/government-urged-to-protect-access-to-cash-for-most-vulnerable? accessed 4 June 2020.
176 Miles Brignall, 'Virgin Money Suspends Thousands of Credit Cards with no Warning' *The Guardian* (London, 6 May 2020) https://www.theguardian.com/money/2020/may/06/virgin-money-suspends-thousands-of-credit-cards-with-no-warning accessed 24 May 2020.
177 Harry Brennan, 'Banks Shamed in to Retraining Staff After Asking Vulnerable to Break Self-isolation Rules' *The Telegraph* (London, 9 May 2020) https://www.telegraph.co.uk/personal-banking/current-accounts/banks-shamed-retraining-staff-asking-vulnerable-break-self-isolation/ accessed 24 May 2020.
178 Patrick Collinson, 'Borrowers on Payment Holidays to Receive 'Thuggish' Debt Letters' *The Guardian* (London, 3 June 2020) https://www.theguardian.com/money/2020/jun/03/borrowers-on-payment-holidays-to-receive-thuggish-debt-letters accessed 4 June 2020.
179 Leah Milner, 'Payment Holidays may Hit Credit Ratings' *Mortgage Strategy* (London, 5 June 2020) https://www.mortgagestrategy.co.uk/analysis/payment-holidays-may-hit-credit-ratings/ accessed 17 June 2020.

Overall, the impact of the FCA's approach during this period is that consumer financial well-being has taken priority over the profit of banking institutions. This reflects the flexibility the FCA seeks to engender within banks when it comes to consumers: they must consider the needs of vulnerable consumers and act appropriately. The status of these temporary provisions as guidance does not mean that banks can avoid providing consumers with support in favour of their own profit: the FCA has expressly stated that it considers these measures to form part of the Principle 6 obligation to treat customers fairly.[180] Poor practice will not be tolerated[181] and the content of the guidance will be relevant if enforcement action is required. The coronavirus guidance reflects the moves seen elsewhere in the banking consumer protection landscape in the UK: retail banks conduct an essential social function, and they should not exploit consumers who need access to these services.

Conclusion

The requirement placed on retail banks to protect their customers during the coronavirus crisis has emphasised both the social role that the FCA expects them to play and the fact that a great proportion of society can be rendered vulnerable by unexpected changes. These banks have been expected to bear significant costs in order to minimise the impact of the crisis. This is the latest and most important example of the move to emphasise the social protective role of banks, part of which has been the move to provide increased and more comprehensive protection for vulnerable members of society.

The current treatment of vulnerable customers reveals its ad hoc development. Considerable attention is currently being paid to the subject in an attempt to provide more comprehensive protection. But, the issue is not easy to resolve. The variety of circumstances which can be classified as vulnerability, and the fact that customers may be vulnerable in more than one way, make it very difficult to give comprehensive guidance. Detailed rules may provide easy solutions for problems which occur regularly, but they risk the possibility that other scenarios will go unprotected. On the other hand, reliance upon general principles or a move to outcomes-focused regulation may ensure that unforeseen problems are covered, but they may lack the precision needed to give adequate guidance to the staff who are dealing with customers in all areas in which the issue may arise.

The push toward increased reliance on IT solutions in the industry carries considerable risk of creating vulnerabilities as some consumers fail to engage with the technology and are increasingly distant from their banks. Systems must be properly designed to meet the needs of different vulnerabilities. Challenger banks, particularly those which only operate online, need to be aware both of the

---

180 See (n 152 – n 156).
181 FCA Business Plan 2020/21 (n 4) 10.

need to engage with consumers in a way which will identify vulnerabilities and of their obligation to make their services accessible.

The various forms of vulnerability and the fact that a large percentage of the population have characteristics which make them potentially vulnerable mean that the issue needs to be considered in relation to many transactions. There is a need for banks to engrain a culture in staff at all levels of the bank that consumers need to be treated as individuals and that products and decisions about products need to reflect the needs of each consumer, including those who are vulnerable. The fact that the FCA regards working with firms in order to transform the culture in the industry as one of its current priorities is a very positive sign. The introduction of the Senior Managers and Certification Regime is a move in the right direction. However, the practical difficulty of changing the culture in the devolved retail banking industry should not be underestimated.

Placing emphasis on the particular needs of individual consumers and their vulnerabilities creates problems for institutions which aim to issue standard guidelines to staff as a way of controlling the conduct risks which are created by a devolved workforce. Firms face a considerable problem in ensuring that policies on vulnerability operate successfully at the customer-facing level. There is a significant training need, and the training needs to be designed to handle the variety of vulnerabilities which may present. Training also needs to avoid confirmation bias causing staff to miss some vulnerabilities.

There are tensions inherent in this area. The achievement of an inclusive financial system which treats vulnerable consumers well does not remove some of the fundamental challenges: a financially distressed consumer does not become a good credit risk and eligible for a loan simply because their problems are identified. Banks remain public companies for whom the risks of subprime lending are well recognised. Established retail banks are under pressure to stay competitive. Enhanced consumer protection costs banks money at a time when established banks are running a large and underutilised branch network in competition with wholly online rivals. This is resulting in increased levels of automation and the closure of branches, both of which can dilute the relationship with customers (and can exacerbate some forms of vulnerability).

It is generally agreed that banks need to produce an inclusive offering and that steps need to be taken to ensure that this is achieved. It cannot be acceptable for banks to exploit the vulnerabilities of consumers. As the FCA has said, 'Vulnerable consumers may be more likely to experience harm' (than others) and if it does occur 'the impact on vulnerable consumers is likely to be greater than for other consumers.'[182] It is clear that important protections exist and that further progress is being made. However, there is a need for a more comprehensive framework of controls. It is hoped that the FCA's current work on the topic will result in one.

---

182 FCA, *Guidance for firms* (n 2) 9.

10 Are some classes of consumer-investors of collapsed pyramid and Ponzi schemes vulnerable?

A multi-jurisdictional perspective

Tibor   Tajti   (Thaythy)[1]

List of abbreviations and acronyms

bus.	–	Business
Bankr.	–	Bankruptcy
CEE	–	Central and Eastern Europe
CGAP	–	Consultative Group to Assist the Poor
EU	–	European Union
FTC	–	Federal Trade Commission (United States)
HUF	–	Hungarian Forints (national currency)
MLM	–	Multi-level Marketing Scheme
NB	–	National Bank
OXFAM	–	Oxford Committee for Famine Relief (UK)
SEC	–	Securities and Exchange Commission (United States)
SFO	–	Serious Fraud Office (United Kingdom)
UCPD	–	Directive 2005/29/EC (11 May 2005) concerning unfair business-to-consumer commercial practices in the internal market [European Union]
UDIS	–	Unlicensed Digital Investment Schemes
UK	–	United Kingdom
US	–	United States

1 Professor of law and Chair of the International Business Law Program at the Department of Legal Studies of Central European University(CEU), Budapest–New York– Vienna [https://www.ceu.edu]. Contact email: tajtit@ceu.edu. This paper served as the basis for the presentation of the author at the international conference 'Fair and non-discriminatory access to financial services' organized by the Faculty of Law of the University of Copenhagen on 26–27 September 2019. The author would like to express his gratitude for the exchanges related to this study to Professors Catalin Gabriel Stanescu (University of Copenhagen), Asress Adimi Gikay (Brunel University, London, UK), Károly Bárd (CEU), Csongor Nagy (Law School Szeged, Hungary), Su Su Mon (Yangon University, Myanmar), Ni Ni Win and Nan Kham Mai (both from Mandalay University, Myanmar), and Akshaya Kamalnath (Auckland University of Technology, New Zealand), to Matthew deCloedt (CEU SJD candidate), my former master's students Ma. Ricca Pearl Sulit from the Philippines (now attorney at the Department of Finance of the Philippines) and John Jay Laylo (now attorney-at-law in Manila), as well as to Maria Bertel (University of Innsbruck, Austria) and Juha Tuovinen (Finland), researchers at CEU in 2019/2020.

Introduction

The Prime Policy question: the legitimacy and repercussions of the "greedy and gullible" assumption[2]

Notwithstanding the growing scholarship on both pyramid and Ponzi schemes as specific types of financial fraud and vulnerable consumers, very few publications are devoted to the theoretical and practical implications of how collapses of pyramid and Ponzi schemes affect consumer-investors, especially those pushed to the peripheries of the socioeconomic system: the vulnerable classes. This is to a great extent attributable to the assumption that the consumers who dare to invest in these particular types of scams are inherently "**greedy** and **gullible**," who therefore are fully aware of how extremely speculative and risky such investments are and that the schemes are doomed to collapse.[3] Consequently, they cannot qualify as vulnerable deserving extra-regulatory protections.

The assumption survives irrespective that precise empirical and quantitative data on the various classes of impacted consumer-investors often are lacking and thus neither the existence, nor the want of vulnerable classes of consumer-investors could conclusively be proven. Often, the negative stance is based on a single, or a few eclectically selected high-profile cases, typically originating from one (or few) jurisdictions, hardly epitomizing the full spectrum of known types of schemes.

The answer to the initial question of whether *all* consumer-investors of these scams *per se* and unconditionally are to be treated as "greedy and gullible" is crucial because if the verdict is in the affirmative that would make any inquiry into the question of whether the existence of vulnerable classes of consumer-investors is to be recognized academic and superfluous. What this chapter desires to show is that the issue is much more nuanced, context-dependent, and variegated and what inevitably doubts the sweeping nihilism hidden in the greedy and gullible line of argumentation. This normative position, however, is limited to and qualified by the admittance that not all consumer-investors of pyramid and Ponzi schemes

---

2 This idea is expressed in different wordings yet normally it is greed and gullibility – or "*unbound and unreasonable trust*" – mentioned as main reasons why investors into pyramid and Ponzi schemes are condemned by the public and part of the academia. As Mervyn K. Lewis put it: "*A common view is that the victims of Ponzi schemes have only themselves to blame. After all, they handed over the money for investment, in which case they are either greedy or gullible.*" [Emphasis added] Mervyn K. Lewis, *Understanding Ponzi Schemes – Can better Financial Regulation Prevent Investors from being Defrauded?* (Edward Elgar, 2015), at 119. [Hereafter: Mervyn 2015].

3 For a list of publications representing the "*highly judgmental [cultural accounts] blaming consumer irresponsibility and even dishonesty*" see Jean Braucher, 'Theories of Overindebtedness: Interaction of Structure and Culture' Theoretical Inquiries in Law 7.2 (2006), at 324. [Hereafter: Braucher – Overindebtedness 2006]. For the publications representing the other, for consumers more benevolent ending of the spectrum of over-indebtedness theories, see Id. note 3 at 324.

deserve heightened regulatory protections. The task of law is, indeed, to replace the sweeping greedy and gullible assumption with a balanced formula that does not a priori and unconditionally reject the idea that pyramid and Ponzi schemes and vulnerable consumer-investors are completely incompatible categories.

Averting right at the beginning the accusation of not seeing the forest for the trees, a brief reminder that the greedy and gullible narrative might unduly narrow the ensuing elaboration's focus is due. Namely, the overarching concern that permeates the ensuing discussion relates to one of the chief moral values embraced by contemporary legal systems: elimination and punishment of fraud. Pyramid and Ponzi schemes are nothing else but scams, "artworks" of swindlers and con artists, peculiar and dangerous forms of financial fraud. Hence, it is the moral duty of all legal systems to eradicate them, though optimally their emergence should be prevented. As empirical evidences have amply proved, unfortunately that is hardly possible: the number of cases in which they have escaped detection even by experts numbers in the hundreds if not thousands. In other words, if it would have been possible to prevent their formation, there would be no need for the supplementary greedy and gullible narrative, nor for this writing. How and whether these moral considerations on the tasks of legal systems impact the question of whether the consumer and especially the vulnerable consumer-investor deserves the auxiliary regulatory protections of the legal system, however, are to be left to a future study.

The ancillary cognitive problem: how easily detectable the true nature of schemes is?

When pondering on whether and what kinds of policies would be justified in this context, it ought to be borne in mind that the schemes generate as well cognitive problems as understanding their true nature and consequently their detection, may amount to a major challenge especially for financially illiterate consumers additionally being devoid of financial means to obtain expert advice. This is so because they tend to appear in such "legitimate" guises that prevent easy recognition of their fraudulent nature for what it is apposite to bestow them, especially Ponzi schemes, with the characterization of "chameleons of finance."

Ample empirical evidence is available from all over the world proving that often even the expert staff of various governmental bodies, from company registries, to consumer protection – and financial supervisory agencies have failed to realize what in reality was ongoing behind the façade. The more case studies from more niches of the globe are taken a look at, the more conspicuous and pervasive this realization becomes. From a policy point of view, the lesson boils down to the following. As experts have often failed on this front, obviously it is neither equitable nor legitimate to expect consumer-investors to outperform professionals.

Modern systems tend to take notice of this hurdle and regulatory agencies routinely resort to the technique of red flagging, displaying the key features based on which average consumers should be in the position to unmask the schemes.[4] As red flags have proved to be impotent tools in quite a number of cases, obviously they cannot be reckoned with but as limited-utility supplements. This is another ancillary argument in favor of cutting back the reach of the greedy and gullible assumption.

A further point on the online risks increasingly lurking on consumer-investors needs to be made. Namely, the possibility of replicating off-line patterns by creating digital Ponzi schemes further exacerbates the task of capturing the true nature of schemes thanks to the spreading of such new technologies as blockchain and cryptocurrencies, or inventing novel methods of exploiting the expanding mobile telecommunication networks. Now the promoters of the schemes cannot only more easily and cheaply reach an ever greater number of vulnerable investors, but the geographic horizons of their activities have radically been expanded, too. Recovering anything from crashed online schemes, existing somewhere in the "ether," the imaginary world having no fixed location, additionally is multiple times harder compared to their off-line kin.

Proving the existence of and justifying the need for heightened regulatory protections of vulnerable consumer-investors as victims of collapsed pyramid and Ponzi schemes

To corroborate and illustrate these assertions with concrete case studies and empirical evidences, as well as to ameliorate the pertaining parochial scholarship, an analysis based on the following three main prongs is offered.

After these introductory notes, definitions, and terminology caveats, first, an overview of the most important empirical studies and data on the micro- and macroeconomic impacts of collapses follows. These have a ternary purpose. On one hand, they sketch how collapses of pyramid and Ponzi schemes affect consumer-investors *directly*, from the financial to the less palpable psychological consequences. The chief point is that collapsed schemes may generate, as many historic examples suggest, tens if not hundreds of thousands of consumer-investors losing their life savings, becoming unbanked, and not capable of making the required deposits necessary for extension of credits. On the other hand, reference is made to the broader socioeconomic effects of foundered scams and how these may *indirectly* affect vulnerable consumer-investors. On top of these comes a caveat on the reasons why regulatory or other steps are taken upon collapse of a scheme. Namely, often the consumer-protection concerns are overshadowed by macroeconomic ones. Simply fear from systemic risk to the problems mass withdrawals of deposits from banks may cause to the financial

---

4 The US SEC lists as red flags – warning signs – of Ponzi schemes seven items (e.g., high investment returns with little or no risk, unregistered investments, secretive and/or complex strategies, and difficulty receiving payments). See https://www.sec.gov/fast-answers/answersponzihtm.html accessed 16 May 2020.

system and the economy are the ones that induce fast and far-reaching steps and less the worries for the fate of consumer-investors, even if of a vulnerable sort.

Second, a seminal typology of schemes is offered from the perspective of consumer-investors. Especially those types of scams are identified and commented upon in case of which one could presume – based on the unique historic or socioeconomic circumstances, or empirical evidences are already available – that they tend to involve larger numbers of vulnerable consumer-investors. The typology serves also the purpose of showing that certain peculiar types of scams are especially susceptible to involving consumer-investors, best exemplified by affinity and schemes camouflaged as MLMs.

Third, to remedy the parochialism of scholarship and better corroborate the above, it is pivotal to embrace a multi-jurisdictional perspective involving not only developing but also emerging markets as well as transitory systems. Bringing a larger number of empirical evidences from significantly varying economies and differently developed legal systems is the token not only of a more balanced spectrum of collapsed schemes but also of a more nuanced and better supported answer to the central question of whether vulnerable consumer-investors exist, and which of their classes deserve heightened regulatory protections.

The expanding regulatory reactions as proofs of the gravity of the problem

In support of the normative position propounded, it ought to be added as well that the very existence and nature of regulatory responses, or the legal tools regulators in various jurisdictions employ to tackle the schemes, are indirect proofs both of the very existence of the problem as well as the gravity of our subject matter. The motivations may differ, and the fear from systemic risk and other major financial-cum-economic threats admittedly may be the main driving force behind the growth. Still, not all regulatory reactions address only these and there is growing sensitivity also vis-à-vis the dire position of vulnerable consumer-investors. This is a complex topic to be discussed in another work. Here, only the following needs to be sketched.

Regulatory reactions understandably differ though some rapprochement in-between some of the observed systems could be noted (especially the EU and the US). The US model (federal laws combined with the laws of the various states) is one of the most tested and developed patterns with most developed express and articulated policies, but it is also unique in the sense that besides employing consumer protection laws it also engages securities regulations. This is best visible in case of pyramid schemes camouflaged as MLMs, which have come within the purview of both the Federal Trade Commission (FTC) and the Securities and Exchange Commission (SEC) as well. The US is also the country that has been leading the global rankings as far as the Ponzi scheme-detection success rates is concerned during the last few decades.

The incomplete law of the EU, as supplemented by the laws of the Member States, is, as opposed to the US, such a Janus-faced model to the regulators of

which only pyramids, and pyramid schemes camouflaged as MLMs, and the pertaining consumer-protection aspects are only of high priority for the time being. Ponzi schemes are given considerably less attention to (if any), in clear contrast to the US.

Many African, Asian, and Latin-American countries often are rather featured by regulations of ambulatory nature reacting to impinging collapses. One of the most recent examples is Myanmar, where,[5] for example, pyramid schemes camouflaged as MLMs prompted passage of radical laws. India has also struggled with similar maladies yet in 2019 it managed to pass a comprehensive piece of legislation that strives to eliminate all forms of unregulated deposits from the market; a category extending also to Ponzi and pyramid schemes camouflaged as MLMs.

Last, one should not forget about the thousands of vulnerable consumers of countries that have had no sector-specific regulations whatsoever, the number of which is not negligible either. Unless a genuine welfare system exists in them (which often is not the case), the thoughts raised in this chapter apply to them with heightened force, too.

Equipped with this succinct synopsis of a paper dealing with a topic normally figuring only on the fringes (if at all) of contemporary mainstream legal scholarship, it is time to proceed to the particularities.

Definitions, terminology caveats

The comprehension of the ensuing discussion requires a clarification of the meaning of the legal categories playing a central role herein: vulnerable consumers and the "schemes." In case of schemes, the connotation of various local language equivalents may be different from the English ones used herein and may cause misunderstandings. As hardly could one speak of a consensus on which classes of consumers qualify as vulnerable consumers either, and as consumers are within the purview of more legal disciplines, in particular consumer protection and securities laws, a brief explicatory comment should be welcome as well.

Consumers, investor-consumers, and vulnerable consumers

The class of 'vulnerable consumers' is the focal point of this book, and thus this chapter as well. Who qualifies as such, however, not only differs in various legal systems, but is also hotly debated. In the EU, for example, the 2005 Unfair Commercial Practices Directive (UCPD)[6] is typically invoked to shed light on this issue though this piece of legislation fails to provide a definition.

---

5 Nan Kham Mai, 'Analytical Study on the Legality of Multi-Level Marketing' (2019) XVII(8) Journal Myanmar Academy of Arts and Science 191–204.
6 Directive 2005/29/EC (11 May 2005) concerning unfair business-to-consumer commercial practices in the internal market. [Hereafter: UCPD].

Who are deemed to be "vulnerable consumers" in Europe consequently is to be extrapolated from the definition of "average consumer" as the benchmark of the Directive, who is "reasonably well-informed and reasonably observant and circumspect, taking into account social, cultural and linguistic factors, as interpreted by the Court of Justice [...]."[7] Yet that the drafters of the UCPD realized that special protections are needed by some specific classes of consumers, more exposed to unfair practices, could indirectly be concluded from the list of blacklisted practices, and from a single section[8] that links vulnerability to "identifiable groups of consumers who are particularly vulnerable [...] because of their mental or physical infirmity, age or credulity [...]."[9]

The European Commission's 2016 gigantic project devoted to the same topic, resulting in a 834 -pages-long Final Report,[10] just confirmed that no commonly subscribed to definition of vulnerability could be found in Europe, partly because the concept is not static. The available sources, instead of attempting to define it, are rather "ex ante assessments of the likelihood of a potential negative outcome in terms of consumer well-being."[11] The Report did note, however, that the class of vulnerable consumers ought to be divided into more dimensions, perceived "as a spectrum rather than a binary state" and observed with different lenses in various sectors of the economy. This indirectly proves the legitimacy of the holistic approach applied herein, putting into the center vulnerable consumers not only from the perspective of consumer protection but also of securities laws.

Notwithstanding the context-specificity of this Europe-centered definition yet reckoning with its indeterminacy, one could easily realize how unfit it is for non-European contexts. It is an exacerbating factor that often actually there is no statutory, or at least commonly subscribed to, definition of vulnerable consumers in other countries as well as a result of what it is hard to point at a firm formulation, be it in positive law, or in scholarly works. The one enshrined into the South African Consumer Protection Act from 2008 might, however, help illuminate how drastically the prevailing local conditions may impact who is regarded as vulnerable. Namely, in South Africa besides minors and elderly, those with low literacy or limited fluency in the language used, low-income persons as well as people who live in remote, isolated, or low-density population

---

7 UCPD Recital 18.
8 For a critical analysis, see Jules Stuyck, Evelyne Terryn, and Tom van Dyck, Confidence through Fairness? The New Directive on Unfair Business-to-Consumer Commercial Practice in the Internal Market, (2006) 43, Common Market Law Review 107–152, at 121 et seq.
9 UCPD Article 5(3).
10 European Commission, *Consumer Vulnerability across Key Markets in the European Union – A Final Report* (January 2016), available at https://ec.europa.eu/info/sites/info/files/consumers-approved-report_en.pdf accessed 17 May 2020.
11 Id. at 9.

areas or communities would qualify as well.[12] In other words, some groups of consumers that would qualify as vulnerable in Europe would not necessarily qualify as such in South Africa. In the US, to make the picture even more complicated, vulnerability is further nuanced depending on whether consumer or rather securities law considerations are applied to determine who deserves extra protections.

There is, however, a common denominator for Europe and South Africa (and beyond): systems increasingly recognize that some classes of consumers are vulnerable and deserve more protections than the consumers posited as benchmarks. The legitimacy of the very existence of the class is not questioned. What is disputed is which groups of consumers deserve special treatment, why, and in which circumstances? Such national variations make opting for any specific national model as a benchmark for the category of vulnerable consumers for a multi-jurisdictional study like this problematic. For our purposes, rather it suffices to depart from such a general perception of the category of "vulnerable consumer" that reckons with the existence of more subclasses of needy consumers that deserve heightened protections of the regulatory system, whether unbanked or not.

A comment ought to be added also on the expression "consumer-investor." Namely, contrary to Europe, in the US, pyramid and Ponzi schemes are within the purview of not only the Federal Trade Commission (FTC) which is in charge of enforcement of antitrust and consumer laws, but also of the Securities and Exchange Commission (SEC) – presumably one of the most efficient agencies mandated to enforce securities laws since its creation in 1934. As one should expect, these use the terminology of their respective fields of law, the FTC speaking of "consumers" and the SEC "investors" or "consumer-investors." Yet, behind these labels, the very same "individuals" may be hidden. The leading MLM-related securities case from 1974, *SEC v. Koscot Interplanetary Inc.,*[13] involved "**individuals**" attracted to join the scheme as "beauty advisors" with the prospect of later, if successful, becoming "supervisors" or retail "managers" or "distributors" being at the top position of the scheme. These individuals, once they have invested their moneys, are then spoken of as "investors." As the holding concluded: "[…] the manner in which Koscot purveyed its enterprise to potential investors contravened the anti-fraud provisions of the [1934 Securities Exchange] Act." [Emphasis added]

Perhaps even more direct language could be found in the document of the US Senate's Special Committee on Aging titled "Old Scams-New Victims: Breaking the Cycle of Victimization" from 2005. Commenting on the reasons leading to the formation of the Corporate Fraud Task Force triggered by the Enron fiasco, noted

---

12 See Jacolien Barnard, 'Where does the Vulnerable Consumer Fit in? – A Comparative Analysis' (Fall, 2014) 18 Journal of Consumer & Commercial Law 2 . The definition derives from the purpose of the CPA that is to "*promote and advance the social and economic welfare of consumers in South Africa by reducing and ameliorating any disadvantages expressed in accessing any supply or goods or services by consumers.*" Id. at 5.

13 *Securities and Exchange Commission v. Koscot Interplanetary, Inc.* United States Court of Appeals, Fifth Circuit, 1974, 497F.2d 473.

that: "Although the term 'corporate fraud' implies a business fraud, the victims are the consumer investors who trusted the integrity of the firm." [Emphasis added][14]

In light of the above, the phrases consumer and investor, "vulnerable consumer," or "consumer-investors" will be interchangeably used in this chapter, following the dominant vocabulary used in the jurisdiction or context concretely spoken of. The reader is advised to bear these caveats in mind when reading the ensuing text.

It should be added that this chapter's primary aim is not to add another page to the European mainstream discourse, which is already abundantly rich and multi-faceted. It is rather a multi-jurisdictionally focused paper that is limited to a relative simple and straightforward task: shedding light on the existence and myriad questions corollary to the dire position of vulnerable consumers of collapsed pyramid and Ponzi schemes (including MLMs).

The repercussions of the differing connotation of the terms "pyramid" and "Ponzi" schemes

The variations in the local language nomenclatures as far as pyramid and Ponzi schemes are concerned, in case of a comparative piece like this, may considerably blur the picture and cause misunderstandings. A brief on terminology is therefore necessary.

The starting point relates to etymology. Namely, often the connotations of the domesticated local language terms could be linked to the features of that particular type of scam that left a more lasting imprint on the financial history of the observed country. For example, while in India, Myanmar, or Sri Lanka, pyramid schemes disguised as multi-level marketing (MLM) businesses have recently triggered regulatory reactions, the Albanian pyramid schemes of the mid-1990s were forms of shadow banks, or "informal lending companies" as characterized by Jarvis.[15] For scholars from these countries, therefore, it is the "pyramid scheme" expression that rings the bell, and the expression "Ponzi scheme" may not necessarily be even known. In Hungary, for example, this presumably is so because it has a specific crime the designation of which contains exactly the phrase "pyramid game" but not the term "Ponzi." Consequently, the reader

---

14 Special Committee on Aging, US Senate, Old Scams-New Victims: Breaking the Cycle of Victimization, 109th Congress, 1st Sess. (27 July 2005).

15 Chris Jarvis, 'The Rise and Fall of Pyramid Schemes in Albania' (IMF Working Paper 99/98, 2000) at 6, available at https://www.imf.org/en/Publications/WP/Issues/2016/12/30/The-Rise-and-Fall-of-the-Pyramid-Schemes-in-Albania-3161 accessed 17 May 2020. [Hereafter: Jarvis Paper 2000]. The Albanian 'shadow banks' appeared as companies and cooperatives, more precisely, nine named as 'Renting Associations' and two as 'Foundations'. As Abrahams described: *"Technically all the 'companies' were illegal because they did not have banking licenses. But the authorities allowed them to function because they said they were not officially banks. Both the government and the international financial institutions tolerated their activity to support the struggling state banks."* See Fred C. Abrahams, *From Dictatorship to Democracy in Europe* (New York University Press, 2015), at 174.

should be prepared that the used nomenclature here may not fully fit with the ones used by local languages and that often different terms are used for the same phenomenon by different authors. For instance, while the renowned political commentator and author Thomas L. Friedman[16] spoke of the Albanian schemes as "Ponzis," for the senior IMF economist Chris Jarvis, they were "pyramid schemes."[17] To economists, both are frequently simply bubbles.[18]

Although often no clear differentiation is made between pyramid and Ponzi schemes, and the usage is inconsistent, still they could quite clearly be differentiated. The key distinguishing factor is that while pyramids are focused on and thrive from recruitment (participative factor), Ponzis do the same through continuous raising of "new" money from "new" investors. The latter are often characterized by not having a "revenue-producing activity other than the continual raising of the new funds."[19] That is why Investopedia speaks of Ponzis as "fraudulent investment management services" and the promoters as "portfolio managers"[20] – who formally could appear in the guise of a CEO of a cooperative, company, or charity organization. Although it is common to them that above-the-average, if not excessive purported returns are promised, the income in case of the first depends on whether new members could be recruited; the other lives if new investments could be ensured from ever newer generations of investors. Both collapse once no new members or new investors can be found.

It makes sense to differentiate two types of pyramid schemes. Namely, the detection of so-called naked pyramids is easy because these live exclusively from new recruits. Where pyramids are regulated, they are typically illegal. The situation is a bit more complicated when recruitment is combined with sale of certain products. In the EU and US, in case of such recruitment-cum-product schemes, the key factor that distinguishes legal schemes from illegal ones is linked to the source of income: if income from recruitment dominates, regardless of whether there is income from some economic activity as well,[21] the scheme is deemed illegal. This combined features is also the reason why such pyramid

16 Thomas L. Friedman, *The Lexus and the Olive Tree* (Anchor Books, 2000), at 156.
17 *See* Jarvis Paper 2000 the title of which is "The Rise and Fall of the Pyramid Schemes in Albania." [Emphasis added] See supra note 17.
18 As Porras put it "*[t]he term bubble is used to refer to asset prices that are not justified by the assets' fundamentals or what can be understood by their 'intrinsic value.' [...].*" Eva Porras, *Bubbles and Contagion in Financial Markets*, vol. 2: Models and Mathematics (1st ed., Palgrave Macmillan, 2017), at 131.
19 Bryan A. Garner (editor-in-chief), *Black's Law Dictionary* (DeLuxe 7th ed., West, 1999).
20 Investopedia at https://www.investopedia.com/ask/answers/09/ponzi-vs-pyramid.asp accessed 5 May 2020.
21 As the SEC put it on its website, "*In the classic 'pyramid' scheme, participants attempt to make money solely by recruiting new participants.*" See SEC, Pyramid Schemes at https://www.investor.gov/protect-your-investments/fraud/types-fraud/pyramid-schemes accessed 17 May 2020. As Black's puts it: "*[A pyramid scheme is a] property-distribution scheme in which a participant pays for the chance to receive compensation for introducing new persons to the scheme, as well as for when those new persons themselves introduce participants.*"

schemes are harder to detect. This may happen in case of MLMs, which – as forms of direct, person-to-person sales – closely resemble pyramids. Pyramids disguised as MLMs present exactly for this reason, the existence of a thin blue line that separates them, a sui generis problem for regulators, as will be seen below. The nomenclature is further complicated by the fact that in the various US states a handful of expressions are used to refer to pyramid schemes, from "pyramid sales schemes," to "pyramid promotional" or "chain distribution schemes," through "pyramid distribution plans," or even "chain letter plans" or "pyramid clubs."[22]

Such problem of differentiation does not exist in case of Ponzi schemes, at least if the above definition is subscribed to: all Ponzi schemes are deemed to be illegal. The problem is that seeing what is really happening behind the "corporate veil" is often hard as the outward image does not reveal anything about the true nature of the venture. As many of the chronicled cases below will show, often even the regulators are incapable of detecting Ponzis in due time. Instead of a simple formula, they rather advise consumer-investors to pay attention to red flags as signs that behind a legitimate-looking entity a Ponzi scheme is hidden. The US SEC, for example, lists the following red flags on its website: high investment returns with no or little risk, unregistered investments and unlicensed sellers, secretive and/or complex strategies, and difficulties with paperwork or getting payments as well as "overly consistent returns" that do not fall notwithstanding the changed market conditions.[23]

Illegal schemes are criminalized though the approaches differ: some countries combat them through the general crime of fraud and yet a few have specific nominated crimes like Austria[24] and Hungary using specifically the expression "pyramid scheme" or "pyramid game."[25] In other words, in these countries (together with a few others), the law subsumes Ponzi schemes under the designation of "pyramid schemes."[26] In jurisdictions where that is the case, research for materials on "Ponzi schemes" in local languages would normally not yield results notwithstanding that in fact such schemes did come into existence, as it would be in Hungary. Simply, in this country the law has failed to develop to the

---

22 See, e.g., Jon M. Taylor, *The Case (for and) against Multi-Level Marketing* (Consumer Awareness Institution 2012), Appendix 2E.

23 SEC, Fast Answers – Ponzi Schemes https://www.sec.gov/fast-answers/answersponzihtm.html accessed 17 May 2020.

24 See § 168a of the Austrian Penal Code 1974 (as amended in 2019) (*"Strafgesetzbuch"*) – *"Ketten oder Pyramidenspiele."*

25 See § 412 of the Hungarian Criminal Code (*"Büntetőtörvénykönyv"*) [Law No. 100 of year 2012 on the Criminal Code].

26 See, e.g., Interpellation No. 2315/J XXV.GP filed on 27 August 2014 related to Lyoness International AG (joint-stock company) at https://www.parlament.gv.at/PAKT/VHG/XXV/J/J_02315/fname_362303.pdf accessed on 17 May 2020, in which the following German terms were used: *"Pyramidenspiel,"* as well as *"Pyramiden, bzw. Schneeballsystem."* These in English, metaphrased, ought to be translated as "pyramid game" and "pyramids, to wit, avalanche systems." The phrase Ponzi scheme is not appearing in the four-page document.

point where sharp differentiation of the two kin categories would trigger the interest of lawmakers as of yet.

Another factor obscuring the picture is that pyramid and Ponzi schemes are generic terms that cover a large variety of real-life schemes, most with a façade having, or closely resembling legitimate business forms or transactions. This will be visible from our typology of schemes below.

It may cause misunderstandings as well that some languages use terms the meaning of which do not even come close to the English "pyramid" or "Ponzi scheme" expressions, like the German snowball (avalanche) system – "*Schneeball System.*" Some Central European languages refer to them as "games." For example, the two Hungarian dominant expressions metaphrased, "pilot-game" ("*pilótajáték*") and "pyramid-game" ("*piramisjáték*"), stress the "game-nature" of the schemes notwithstanding that pyramid and Ponzi schemes are everything but games save for the simplest gifting schemes: wiring of small amounts of money to the previous generations of investors. Although the Austrian Penal Code uses the term "game" as well, the designation "chain" ("*Kette*") is also in circulation. Romanian language likewise has such a tandem: besides the "*joc piramidal*" (pyramid game) the "*schema piramidala*" (pyramid scheme). A 2009 Kenyan report mentioned even the expression of "merry-go-round schemes."[27]

The US-originated expression "Ponzi scheme" is, however, gradually being adapted by other languages as well, at least, in Europe.[28] As known, the designation was born out of the early 20th century fallen scheme orchestrated by an Italian immigrant, Charles Ponzi, a swindler and con artist, operating in the US.[29] Although it was not him who invented this particular type of fraudulent investment scheme, for some unknown reason, it became named after him, at least, in the English-speaking world and increasingly elsewhere, too.

Considering the above, whenever the spoken-of-jurisdiction makes a clear differentiation between the two categories and the two terms (as is the case in the

---

27 Kenyan Ministry for Cooperative Development and Marketing, *Report of the Task Force on Pyramid Schemes* (2009), at 16. The Report can be downloaded at https://pdfslide.net/technology/report-of-the-taskforce-on-pyramid-schemes.html accessed 17 May March. [Hereafter: 2009 Kenyan Taskforce Report].

28 For example, the French "*système de Ponzi,*" the Italian "*schema Ponzi,*" the Dutch "*Ponzifraude,*" or the Spanish "*esquema Ponzi.*" Some more recent German sources began to use also the "*Ponzi-Masche*" or the "*Ponzi-scheme*" expressions. For the latter, see Robert Kilian, 'Zur Strafbarkeit von Ponzi-schemes – Der Fall Madoff nach deutschem Wettbewerbs- und Kapitalmarktstrafrecht,' HRRS 10, No. 7/2009, at 285–290, available at http://www.hrr-strafrecht.de accessed 17 May 2020. The process of adaptation of the expression in Central and Eastern European countries (CEE) is well on its way, too. In Slovak language, besides the "*Ponziho schéma*" and the "*pyramidova schema,*" the game version is also known as "*Ponziho hra.*" Further, while the Croatian expressions are "*Ponzijeva i piramidalna shema,*" the Serbian is "*piramidalna i Poncijeva prevara;*" the latter already containing the word "fraud."

29 For a synoptically chronicled saga of Charles Ponzi, see, e.g., Mervyn 2015, note 4 supra, at 32–40.

US), the established usage pattern will be followed with respect to that particular jurisdiction in this paper as well. Elsewhere, the local variant will be used as well save when a distinction is to be made. In practical terms, this may mean that the Hungarian, Romanian, or Serbian language metaphrased expression of "pyramid scheme" could encompass also what in the US would be referred to as "Ponzi schemes." These European indeterminacies notwithstanding, the EU's above-mentioned Unfair Commercial Practices Directive category of "pyramid schemes"[30] most presumably does not extend to Ponzi schemes, or it is highly contentious whether it does.

Why study the socioeconomic effects of collapsed pyramid and Ponzi schemes on vulnerable consumers?

The magnitude of the problem

The sheer number of vulnerable consumers – often reaching tens or hundreds of thousands – harmed by fallen schemes is *per se* such a grave reason that does not allow for neglect of the topic. If we take only the US, which is the country presumably with the richest pool of pertinent quantitative and qualitative data, regulatory responses as well as publications on the topic[31] indicate that "about two million individuals fall victim to pyramid schemes and related fraudulent business opportunities each year."[32] The numbers inherently are more prohibitive in emerging financial systems, even if normally only rough estimates could be found.

Yet even in the US it is hard to forge a more or less precise account on the number of consumers impacted by these forms of financial pathology because the "victims of pyramid schemes are the least likely to report they have been defrauded."[33] An exacerbating factor is that often the marginalized and vulnerable communities are reached through their affinity, being part of a

---

30 See para 14 of UCPA Annex I entitled "Commercial Practices which are in all Circumstances Considered Unfair" which lists "Establishing, operating or promoting a pyramid promotional scheme where a consumer gives consideration for the opportunity to receive compensation that is derived primarily from the introduction of other consumers into the scheme rather than from the sale or consumption of products."

31 See, e.g., Tamar Frankel, *The Ponzi Scheme Puzzle: A History and Analysis of Con Artists and Victims* (OUP 2012); Kathy Bazoian Phelps and Hon. Steven Rhodes, *The Ponzi Book: A Legal Resource for Unraveling Ponzi Schemes* (LexisNexis, 2012) or David E.Y. Sarna, *History of Greed* (Wiley, 2010). [Hereafter: Sarna History of Greed 2010].

32 Anderson, K.B., *Federal Trade Commission. Consumer Fraud in the United States, 2011: The Third FTC Survey.* Available at https://www.ftc.gov/sites/default/files/documents/reports/consumer-fraud-united-states-2011-third-ftc-survey/130419fraudsurvey_0.pdf accessed 17 May 2020. Cited by Stacie A. Bosley, Marc F. Bellemare, Linda Umwali, and Joshua York, 'Decision-making and Vulnerability in a Pyramid Scheme Fraud' (2019) 80 Journal of Behavioral and Experimental Economics 1–13, at 1. [Hereafter: Bosley et al. 2019].

33 Bosley et al. 2019, at 2.

community which they trust. Hence, the collapse in such cases is not merely an individual tragedy but something more: an event that may denigrate the entire community within which it could escalate to a "stigma of reporting"[34] preventing the community members from airing their mistreatment. No wonder that "the literature on Ponzi schemes remains, to a large extent, anecdotal."[35]

Where, however, the economic and other negative consequences of collapsed schemes have been taken note of, normally because of the magnitude of the scheme and the systemic risk it embodies, targeted responses did ensue in various forms; proving the very existence and gravity of our subject matter. Mention should be made, for example, of the US SEC Pyramid Scheme Task Force in 2014[36] that dealt with the multipronged regulatory background, court precedents, as well as "376 Ponzi schemes prosecuted by the SEC [...] between 1988 and 2012 in the US" or the establishment of the UK Serious Fraud Office[37] that targets, among others, pyramid and Ponzi schemes as forms of "serious or complex fraud." Elsewhere, the regulatory responses are typically limited, more of ad hoc nature, if there is any until the threshold, or shadow of, systemic risk is reached; as the recent developments, for example, from Myanmar illustrate.

The number of vulnerable consumers affected: estimates and some quantitative data

As already stressed, not all fallen schemes involve vulnerable consumers, nor are there often precise, statistical, or other quality quantitative data on the proportion of harmed vulnerable consumers in these fiascos. The evidences often are anecdotal, but this should not lead to the conclusion that they are *a priori* unsuitable for analysis. It has not been contested by anybody, for example, that the overwhelming part of the more-than-ten-thousand victims of the collapsed Hungarian real property investment cooperatives were pensioners (many presumably qualifying as vulnerable).[38] Or, that the Colombian DMG and

---

34 Bosley et al. 2019, at 12.
35 Marc Hofstetter, Daniel Majía, José Nicolás Rosas, and Miguel Urrutia, 'Ponzi Schemes and the Financial Sector: DMG and DRFE in Colombia' (2018) 96 Journal of Banking and Finance 18–33, at 18. [Hereafter: Hofstetter et al. 2018].
36 See, e.g., the opening remarks of Andrew Ceresney, Director of the Division of Enforcement given at the *UIC-SEC Joint Symposium to Raise Public Awareness: Combating Pyramid Schemes and Affinity Frauds*, 2 March 2 2016. Available at https://www.sec.gov/news/speech/ceresney-remarks-joint-symposium-raise-public-awareness-03022016.html accessed 17 May 2020.
37 See the website of the agency at https://www.sfo.gov.uk/?s=ponzi&lang=en accessed 17 May 2020.
38 Hungary was a communist country before the fall of the Berlin Wall (9 November 1989). Notwithstanding that it was called the "happiest barrack in the Communist camp," with one of the highest living standards in the Eastern Block. Irrespective that Hungary was part of the same state with Austria until the end of WWI, it was not in the position to decrease the economic gap that persist between the two countries up until present day. See about those

DRFE[39] schemes included eventually all income groups, even "high-profile businesspersons and politicians (DRFE even offered special rates to government employees)"[40] who admittedly could not be classified as vulnerable deserving regulatory protections. Though as the Consultative Group to Assist the Poor (CGAP) noted: "[...] from the perspective of poor customers of financial services, both pyramid schemes (also known as Ponzi schemes) and identity fraud loom large [...]."[41]

Still, parallel with the development of consumer laws and the increased sensitivity to peculiar problems of the neediest and most risk-exposed classes of consumers, quantitative data are increasingly becoming available. A 2018 research based on 376 Ponzi schemes in which the US SEC took enforcement actions between January 1988 and August 2012, for example, involved about 17% elderly, 10% family members or friends, and 10% members of affinity groups linked by religion as victims.[42] Here, especially the elderly should be taken as a vulnerable class of consumers though the opinion of experts differ on whether elderly are more vulnerable to victimization than other categories of consumers. A similar dilemma is whether educated consumers are less exposed than

---

early transitory years in the article by Celestine Bohlen, Hungarians are Thriving, Gloomily, The New York Times (24 June 1991). Hence, to understand why large numbers of Hungarian pensioners have joined the real property investment cooperatives, one should bear in mind also the data on pensioners' living standard – conspicuously and significantly being lower compared to the country's western neighbors. For example, the average monthly pension in December 2004 was 56,244 HUF, or roughly 230 Euros. In December 2005, that increased to 62,879 HUF, or approximately 248 Euros. For exchange rates of Hungarian Forints per year, see https://arfolyam.iridium.hu/en-GB/EUR/2005-12#table accessed 3 May 2020. For English language statistical data on average monthly pensions, see the related web page of the Hungarian Statistical Office (KSH) at https://www.ksh.hu/docs/eng/xstadat/xstadat_annual/i_fsp001.html accessed 3 May 2020.

39 DRFE stands for "*Dinero Rapido Facil y en Efectivo*," or "Quick and Easy Money in Cash."

40 Hofstetter et al. 2018, note 37 supra, at 20.

41 CGAP, *A Guide to Regulation and Supervision of Microfinance* (CGAP/World Bank 2012), at 66 file:///E:/5%20Law%20Growth%20the%20Micro%20Perspective%20HUNG/32%20Microfinance/Microfi-nance-in-Myanmar-Unleashing-the-potential2017The-Business-of-Transition-Law-Reform-Development-and-Economics-in-Myanmar(1).pdf accessed 17 May 2020. [Hereafter: CGAP Microfinance Study 2012].

42 Stephen Deason, Shivaram Rajgopal, Gregory Waymire, and Roger White, *Accounting Lies and Fraud: A Case Where the Two are Separable* (12 March 2018), unpublished manuscript. The first version of the paper under the title *Who Gets Swindled in Ponzi Schemes?* is available at https://www0.gsb.columbia.edu/mygsb/faculty/research/pubfiles/12962/ponzi%20draft%20may%2013%202015.pdf accessed 17 May 2020. [Hereafter: Accounting Lies 2018]. The study focused on the role of accounting in the context of Ponzi schemes and found that provision of fraudulent financial statements and false auditor claims increases the duration of Ponzi schemes; false accounting statements may be exploited by fraudsters to increase their payouts and avoid due-time detection; and false accounting (lies) generates trust in the offered scam and may legitimize them. The study found also that the accounting profession's roles have neither been given proper attention to so far in the US, nor have the participating accountants been properly penalized. It is also interesting that the mean (median) Ponzi scheme had a duration of between three and four years. Id at 3.

the others,[43] and consequently therefore whether the uneducated should be a priori looked upon as a special class of vulnerable consumers. A study from 1995 found, for example, that "contrary to what one might expect, demographic variables such as education, income, or age do not significantly influence an individual's likelihood of succumbing to a fraud attempt."[44] This finding, less sympathetic to the cause of vulnerable consumers, is equally indeterminate as the concrete numbers hidden behind the "non-significant influence" presumption yet which should also count, just as the alterations in the numbers caused by the shifted contexts. The same study presumed, and the collected data partially confirmed, however, that most of the citizen-victims lived in nonurban locations, or that the somewhat higher number of Ponzi schemes in Florida could be attributed to the higher number of elderly (pensioners) living there. In other words, correlations do exist between the vulnerability of some identifiable classes of consumers and victims of fallen schemes.

These data from the US corroborate the fact that even if developed regulations are in place, that does not make the risks lurking on vulnerable consumers disappear, as a recent study on "social capital"[45] from the US suggests. Social capital is perceived as social norms of "neighborhood networks" that "encourage the participation and cooperation among members of a group,"[46] among others, in

---

43 For an overview of US studies dealing with the profiles of Ponzi organizers and their victims as well as the accompanying US scholarship, see, in particular, Chapter 4, "A Profile of the Con Artists and their Victims" in: Tamar Frankel, *The Ponzi Scheme Puzzle: A History and Analysis of Con Artists and Victims* (Oxford Scholarship Online, April 2015). In this book, Frankel, one of the most renowned US experts of the field, spoke of the role of education in risk tolerance as unclear (see the title of sub-section E on page 143). As she noted, although "*people with higher education can evaluate risks better than people who are less educated, [...] [higher education] does not shield investors, especially those who have a taste for experimenting. For example, education does not seem to undermine or erase popular beliefs completely.*" In other words, at least, as US studies suggest, although some firm correlations can, indeed, be drawn yet none of them is 100% correct as behavior, perceptions and the individual background of consumer-investors differ radically on more fronts. Frankel relied in her book on NASD (now FINRA) *Investor Fraud Study* (12 May 2006), as a crucial yet limited-utility source for empirical and behavioral data specifically on financial fraud. Limited in the sense that no single factor impacting the behavior of consumer-investors could explain all the cases. As Drew and Cross put it on the role of financial literacy drawing on the NASD 2006 study: "*[while the Study provides] useful insights into why financial literacy may be correlated with higher levels of victimization, [these findings may primarily be exploited for us to better understand] how the financial literacy curriculum could be redesigned in order to more effectively tackle financial fraud.*" Quoted from Jacqueline M. Drew and Cassandra Cross, Fraud and its PREY: Conceptualizing Social Engineering Tactics and Its Impact on Financial Literacy Outcomes, in: Tina Harrison (ed.). *Financial Literacy and the Limits of Financial Decision-Making* (Palgrave Macmillan, 2016), at 329.

44 Richard M. Titus, Fred Heinzelmann, and John M. Boyle, 'Victimization of Persons by Fraud' (January 1995) 41(1) Crime & Delinquency 54–72, at 60.

45 John (Jianqiu) Bai, Chenguang Shang, Chi Wan, and Yijia (Eddie) Zhao, 'Social Capital and Individual Behavior: Evidence from Financial Advisers' (January 2020), available at SSRN.

disciplining the financial advisory community. As they suggest, in communities where the intensity of social capital is stronger,[47] that attenuates the likelihood of financial adviser misconduct. In such communities, it is observable that misbehaving advisors leave and move to less cohesive neighborhoods. As the US financial advisory industry plays a crucial role in helping households make investment decisions and in total manages over $30 trillion in investable assets,"[48] misconduct has serious consequences, especially for the elderly. This is because "Americans age 50 and above [are] those most in need of quality financial advice [as they are] the least likely to pursue it, making them more susceptible to predatory pitches."[49]

The presumption that large number of vulnerable consumers fell victims of collapsed pyramid and Ponzi schemes could be easily illustrated both by historic and some more recent examples from around the world. Thus, in case of the gigantic Russian MMM scheme or the collapsed Albanian shadow banks, one could hardly find even estimates on the number of harmed vulnerable consumers. What is known is that a large portion of the citizenry were involved in these schemes, not just a limited number of privileged high-income investors as it was in the case of Madoff. Yet if one knows that thanks to the devastating economic policies of the preceding communist regimes in those days the overwhelming part of the population were genuinely poor people, financially uneducated, and surviving in a corrupt system full of regulatory gaps (or without any financial regulation protecting investors), it should not be doubted that many of the affected individual investors were vulnerable consumers in all senses of this notion.[50]

46 The authors of the study refer to Jacobs, J., the Death and Life of Great American Cities (Vintage, New York, 1962), Putnam, R.D., Bowling Alone: America's Declining Social Capital, in: Culture and Politics (pp. 223–234) (Palgrave Macmillan, New York, 2000), and Fukuyama, F., Social Capital and the Modern Capitalist Economy: Creating a High Trust Workplace, 4 Stern Business Magazine (1997), 1–16 in defining social capital. See US Social Capital Study 2020, note 43 supra, at 8.

47 As Bartalos summarized, reflecting on the study, while "[t]he states ranking highest in social capital are Utah, Wyoming, Colorado, North Dakota, South Dakota, Nebraska, Iowa, Minnesota, Wisconsin, Maine, New Hampshire, and Vermont," the lowest ranking states are in the southwest and include, among others, Georgia, Florida, and the lowest-ranking Louisiana. See Greg Bartalos, 'Where Crooked Advisers Thrive' (26 November 2019) RIA INTEL (electronic journal of the financial advisory industry), available at https://www.riaintel.com/article/b1j68ywn9d31h9/where-crooked-advisors-thrive accessed 17 May 2020. [Hereafter: Bartalos – Crooked Advisors].

48 Id. Introduction at 3.

49 See Bartalos – Crooked Advisors, note 47 supra.

50 Jarvis' description of the socioeconomic and political conditions prevailing in Albania before the arrival of capitalism should explain why could pyramid schemes emerge at all. As he put it: "*Albania started the transition process from central planning as the most isolated, undeveloped, and poor country in Europe. Albania had for centuries been largely unknown and inaccessible, and from 1945 to 1985 its isolation was compounded by the rigid dictatorship of Enver Hoxha. Communism in Albania was founded on complete reliance on central planning, the elimination of almost all forms of private property, and the idealization of national self-reliance as a guiding tenant of economic policy. In practice, this led to a virtual cutting off of the country from outside influences and*

The same could be presumed as to contemporary emerging financial systems today. For example, Myanmar had been until very recently (2011) an isolated military system,[51] which as such prevented its citizens from being exposed to and learning about the risks corollary to the world of capital markets and generally finance. Similarly instructive are the empirical evidences from India, where the number of unbanked people living in deep poverty and yet having been involved in MLM (direct) selling,[52] some being pyramid schemes disguised as MLM businesses, has been comparably extremely high. On top of that, most of these schemes operated within legitimate business forms, unhindered by governmental bodies in charge for quite some time, suggesting to consumers trusting the system that their activities were legal.

In brief, it is safe to work with the assumption that the collapse of many of the known past schemes have, indeed, involved a significant number of vulnerable consumers, notwithstanding the lack of precise quantitative data and the predicament generated by the unusual importance of anecdotal evidences. Technological advancements may help improve the situation. Yet as vulnerable consumers presumably will remain as reserved to talk about their precarious position caused by collapsed schemes in the future as in the past, one should not reckon with fast fundamental improvements on the front of easier access to increasingly more precise data on vulnerable consumers either.

Trust shock

Several other forceful reasons justify discussing the effects of collapsed pyramid and Ponzi schemes on vulnerable consumers. No financial expertise is needed to realize that, for example, the fall of the Albanian pyramid schemes collapsing the government and leading to riots with more than 2,000 people being killed, inevitably undermined confidence in the financial and entire legal system, which had lasting effects for generations.[53] Large-scale schemes inevitably have such consequences even if the percentage of a country's population affected by the

---

information. The result was that when transition eventually began, in 1991, the country had been reduced to desperate poverty and the vast bulk of the population was completely unfamiliar with market institutions or practices." [Emphasis added] Jarvis Paper 2000, note 15 supra, at 2.

51 See in general on Myanmar, Melissa Crouch and Tim Lindsey (eds.), *Law, Society and Transition in Myanmar* (Bloomsbury, 2014). [Hereafter: Crouch and Lindsey Myanmar 2014].

52 According to the estimates, about 4 million people were involved in direct selling already in 2010–2011, a number that has further increased in the meantime. See Bibek Debroy, *Report on Direct Selling Industry in India – Appropriate Regulation is the Key (FICCI and Indicus Analytics*, April 2013), at 11. Available at http://ficci.in/spdocument/20237/report-mark.pdf accessed 17 May 2020.

53 See Arnisa Gorezi and Evgjeni Bashari, 'Enforcement of Contracts in Albania – Overcoming Dilemmas in an Emerging Market' in Stefan Messmann and Tibor Tajti (eds.), *The Case Law of Central and Eastern Europe – Enforcement of Contracts,* vol. I (European University Press, Bochum-Germany 2009), section 1.3. at 52–57.

collapses is not as high as in Albania or Russia. Consider the example of the less spoken of Colombian schemes of DMG and DRFE, which were closed by the Colombian government in November 2018 yet which at that time "had over half a million customers[54] and [investments reaching] 1.2% of Colombia's annual GDP."[55]

In systems with a low level of the rule of law, the shock is further exacerbated by the dysfunctional insolvency law system because normally nothing can be recovered in the insolvency proceedings opened upon the fall of the scheme simply because the insolvency framework does not work. In the US, the contrary may be the case as best illustrated by the aired recoveries-related data from the aftermath of the collapse of the Madoff scheme. The still functioning web page of the "Madoff Recovery Initiative" heralds historically rarely heard of high rates of recoveries and distributions to victims.[56] This could hardly be even calculated with in emerging legal systems in which bankruptcy law is the stepchild not only of the legal system but also for the overwhelming part of the society, businessmen, and citizens alike.

Financial exclusion

The collapse may cause financial exclusion as well because the consumer-investors having lost their savings would not be in the position to make the required down payments or pay the fees that would allow them to qualify for loans or other financial products. This line of reasoning applies *a fortiori* to vulnerable classes of consumers. If the collapse results additionally in loss of, all or a significant part, of the regular income of a family's single breadwinner – as it may be when a scheme camouflaged as an MLM collapses – that might further deepen poverty.

A related development is, as some recent empirical evidences reveal, that

---

54 Colombia's population in 2019 was around 49 million.

55 Hofstetter *et al.* 2018, note 35 supra, at 18.

56 The Madoff Recovery Initiative website with data is at https://www.madofftrustee.com/ accessed 17 May 2020. See Tunku Varadarajan, 'The Amazing Madoff Clawback - How two lawyers, Irving Picard and David Sheehan, have recovered 75 cents on the dollar of the stolen money—many times the usual rate in such cases' (30 November 2018) Wall Street Journal, available at http://webreprints.djreprints.com/4482040774476.html. Both websites accessed 30 October 2019, when the distributions from the customer fund reached $11.758 bn. This success from ten years of groundbreaking work by Irving Picard (trustee), David Sheehan, and Stephen Harbeck is to be partially ascribed to FBI investigations and to the use of the 1970s Securities Investor Protection Act that made oversight by the Securities Investor Protection Corporation (SIPC – a nonprofit created by the act of Congress to protect clients of bankrupt brokerage firms) and distributions possible. Brokerage customers get based on the act of a limited insurance (maximum of $500,000 for securities and cash, and maximum of $250,000 for cash held with the bankrupt broker). Website is at https://www.sipc.org/ accessed 17 May 2020.

pyramid schemes often are looked upon by the neediest in emerging systems as more promising alternatives for escaping poverty even to microfinance arrangements.[58] Although the short history of microfinance as a way to help those at the bottom start doing business is far from being unscathed, unbanked people in emerging economies often end up investing their family savings in pyramid schemes, some disguised as MLMs or cooperatives, doomed to collapse *ab initio* instead of opting for microfinance. As is noted in a 2012 CGAP study:

> "Pyramid schemes are especially relevant to microfinance when they target victims who are less educated about and experienced with financial services. The schemes sometimes assume, or mimic, a regulatory form that is also used by legitimate microfinance providers—e.g., pyramid schemes have often been structured as financial cooperatives. In the short term, this hurts legitimate institutions that lose customers to high- yielding pyramid schemes."[57]

Whether the shifted orientation of vulnerable consumers – for the benefit of whom otherwise microfinance programs have been, indeed, conceived in the first place – is due to the job-like features of MLMs, the negative reputation microfinance gained in some parts of the world, the combination of the two, or rather the lure of high profits driven by sheer greed could hardly be sufficiently precisely determined. Although one could hardly speak of a trend either, the records mention more than a few cases. Yet the practice itself should concern us for two key reasons. On the one hand, it is worrisome given that pyramids inevitably collapse and may drag into the abyss of poverty hundreds if not thousands of the neediest. On the other hand, it is a living yet indirect proof of how the neediest consumer classes in emerging economies, rural regions, and other identifiable communities living in the least developed geographic regions of the world may perceive MLMs, some of which if unmasked would be pyramids.

Impact on the banking and economic system

Carvajal et al.[59] identified further negative consequences of unregulated investment schemes – including pyramid and Ponzi schemes – based on data from the Caribbean, which is another region of the world that has a significant number of vulnerable consumers. These considerations may serve as invaluable lessons especially to other similarly situated countries around the globe. Let us briefly list them here, leaving their in-depth study to economists.

First, they divert deposits from banks, so less will be available for lending and

---

58 CGAP Microfinance Study 2012, note 2 supra, at 69.
57 CGAP Microfinance Study 2012, Id. at 69.
59 Carvajal, A., Monroe, H.K., Wynter, B., and Pattillo, C.A., 'Ponzi Schemes in the Caribbean' (IMF Working Paper 09–95, 2009).

boosting entrepreneurship for the creation of jobs. Or, "savings [are diverted] from productive to unproductive uses and, in some cases, from the domestic economy to foreign destinations."[60] Second, loss of the money in the schemes may result in more nonperforming bank loans and increased loan delinquencies. Third, they generate artificially high levels of consumption based on the promised abnormal profits ("paper profits") or early withdrawals of the investments (if possible, at all). Fourth, if bailout of banks or other important financial institutions is inevitable and resorted to, fiscal costs are imposed.[61]

Systemic risk

The collapse of pyramid and Ponzi schemes, best illustrated by the fallen Albanian shadow banks in 1996–1997,[62] may lead to the collapse of the entire financial, economic, and even governmental system. This was possible in Albania because it was the poorest post-socialist country of Europe on the eve of the fall of the Berlin Wall, with a population that had been completely isolated from the West during the previous regime. Consequently, capitalism dawned virtually overnight on the Albanian society made only of peasants and military men and after decades of living surrounded by 173,371 concrete bunkers. Not only were experts in banking and finance lacking, but the new classes of politicians knew very little about these areas of economy. Moreover, top-level politicians themselves participated and benefited from the schemes.

Contrary to Albanians in the 1990s, current experts and politicians of Myanmar, Sri Lanka, or India better understood, or so it seems, what threats are inherent to some MLM schemes involving hundreds, if not thousands, of vulnerable consumer-investors as they imposed significant restrictions, or simply banned all MLM schemes. It seems that the experiences of other countries with MLMs were heeded by the regulators of these countries, and they recognized that the fall of such major schemes may endanger the financial system's stability as well. The systemic risk inherent not only to MLMs but also other types of pyramid and Ponzi schemes, however, is not something to be left only to the pages of financial history books. The lesson that should be heeded by emerging (and other) financial systems is that it may reappear elsewhere any time in similar or different forms from the above.

Security and sociopsychological risks

The collapse of schemes and the corollary losses (often of all personal or family savings) of consumers generate psychological shocks leading to depression, suicides, various illnesses, and breaking up of marital or other social ties. The true dimensions of these tragic consequences can hardly be quantified yet undoubtedly are losses not only for the affected individuals but also for the economy and society.

The rage and feeling of helplessness may find expression in milder or more

---

60 Hofstetter et al. 2018, note 35 supra, at 18.
61 Id.
62 Jarvis Paper 2000, note 15 supra.

violent forms of individual, group, or mass actions. The collapse of the Hungarian real property investment cooperatives during the first decade of the 21st century, for example, resulted in peaceful public demonstrations only.[63] However, some people took justice into their own hands, as in the defenestration of the directors of one of the Kenyan collapsed schemes.[64] Yet things may also escalate drastically as was the case in Albania, where during the turmoil caused by the collapse of the schemes about 2,000 people were killed.[65]

Vacuum in legal scholarship

We must not forget about the dearth of legal scholarship and the linked problems researchers may face when opting to write on this topic. It is surprising, first, that notwithstanding the availability of a growing pool of empirical data and the myriad historic cases virtually from many corners of the globe adequately showing that the fall of pyramid and Ponzi schemes could be devastating, economically and otherwise negatively affecting often tens and thousands of vulnerable and other classes of consumers, there is a considerable vacuum in legal scholarship as far as multi-jurisdictional works are concerned. Although the US literature clearly overshadows the rest of the world in this domain, it typically remains limited to US soil. In Europe, the literature, meaning conventional secondary sources of law, is truly scarce, save the writings devoted to two pet topics of the EU: unfair commercial practices[66] extending to pyramid (but not Ponzi) schemes and pyramids-cums-MLMs segment closely resembling the US approaches.

Juxtaposition of the available literature then conspicuously displays that while US law reviews and journals quite willingly publish articles on Ponzi schemes, and in fact quite a number of such articles have been published by now,[67] the attitude is exactly

63 For a detailed account of the case, see Tibor Tajti, 'Central European Contribution to the American Debate on the Definition of "Securities" or Why does the Definition of "Security" Matter?: The Fiasco of the Hungarian Real Estate Investment Cooperatives, Pyramiding, and Why Emerging Capital Markets should be Equipped to "Act" rather than "React"' (Fall 2005) 15(1) Transnational Law and Contemporary Problem 111–216. [Tajti Pyramid Cooperatives 2005].
64 See 2009 Kenyan Taskforce Report, note 29 supra, at 93.
65 Jarvis Paper 2000, note 15 supra, at 1.
66 Pyramid schemes are banned commercial practices in the EU if "*compensation … is derived primarily from the introduction of other consumers into the scheme rather than from the sale or consumption of products.*" *See* Commission Staff Working Document, *Guidance on the Implementation/Application of Directive 2005/29/Ec on Unfair Commercial Practices* (SWD[2016] 163 final (25 May 2016), banned commercial practice No. 14, at 80.
67 Besides the more recent law review articles mentioned herein, one could also add Joseph P. Whitford, 'Pyramid Scheme Regulation: the Evolution of Investment Contracts as a Security under the Federal Securities Law' (1974)25 Syracuse Law Review 690; Mark A. McDermott, 'Ponzi Schemes and the Law of Fraudulent and Preferential Transfer' (Spring 1998) 72 American Bankruptcy Law Journal 157 ; Miriam A. Cherry and Jarrod Wong, 'Clawbacks: Prospective Contract Measures in an Era of Excessive Executive Compensation

the opposite in Europe. In Europe, many think that Ponzi schemes are not really in the bailiwick of lawyers. This deficiency, the lack of sources, a problem the intensity of which varies from jurisdiction to jurisdiction, is inherently reflected upon in this paper as well. It should be conspicuous, for example, that the balance as far as the quantity and depth of sources on Ponzi schemes is clearly tilted toward the US as opposed to Europe and the rest of the globe.

A related problem is that whoever wants to research the topic should also reckon with the scarcity of conventional sources of law. Codes and statutes normally play a modest role in this domain. Consequently, publicized cases – court or agency decisions – would be most welcome as sources that would enlighten the essence of various schemes and help us better grasp the phenomena in our focus herein. Unfortunately, texts of such cases are very few – especially outside the US and a few other jurisdictions that look on the US as a source of inspiration led by Canada (and the Canadian provinces) as well as the Philippines and a few other common law systems. Newspaper articles, agency and industry communications, and blogs should be consulted as well. The same applies to some publications produced by economists, accountants, and finance experts as pyramid and Ponzi schemes increasingly come within their purview as well.[68]

For these reasons, this seminal paper is a modest attempt to change such state of affairs not only by focusing on vulnerable consumers for the study of the troubles of whom very limited (if any) research funding is available but also by offering insight into developments in frontier markets.

Typology of pyramid and Ponzi schemes: the perspective of vulnerable consumers

Why is classification of schemes of utmost importance?

The clothes in which pyramid and especially Ponzi schemes, the chameleons of finance, appear are extremely varied. Their many-facedness is what generates, for both investors and regulators alike, a major cognitive problem manifested in the extreme hardship their perception and identification

---

and Ponzi Schemes' (December 2009) 94 Minnesota Law Review 368 ; Tsai Miranda, 'Rampant Ponzimonium: A Guide to Surfing the Wave of Ponzi Scheme Litigation' (June 2009) 15(3) Bankruptcy Litigation 1–14; Jerry J. Campos, 'Avoiding the Discretionary Function Rule in the Madoff Case' (Fall 2009) 55 Loyola Law Review 587; Robert J. Rhee, The Madoff Scandal, 'Market Regulatory Failure and the Business Education of Lawyers' (Winter 2009) 35 Journal of Corporation Law 363; Jayne W. Barnard, 'Evolutionary Enforcement at the Securities and Exchange Commission' (Spring 2010) 71 University of Pittsburgh Law Review 403 [focused on SEC revamping after Madoff]; Kenneth C. Johnston, Kellie M. Johnson, and Joseph A. Hummel, 'Ponzi Schemes and Litigation Risks: What Every Financial Services Company Should Know' (14 March 2010) North Carolina Banking Institute 29 ; Corey Mathews, 'Using a Hybrid Securities Test to Tackle the Problem of Pyramid Fraud' (April 2020) 88 Fordham Law Review 2045.

68 See Accounting Lies 2019, note 42 supra.

require. As Lewis stressed: "The problem is that, as simple as they are, Ponzi schemes are not easy to identify;" a wisdom that applies with closely equal force to pyramids as well. The hardships with identification then make timely reactions by regulatory agencies often impossible even if the agencies in charge are staffed by experts knowledgeable in finance. A typology of schemes, shedding light on them from different angles, is a tool for grappling with these challenges.

An exacerbating factor, as Kathy Bazoian Phelps, a Ponzi expert validly stressed, is that "not all Ponzis are wacky schemes" of the type offering investments into gold mines and emu chick breeding programs.[69] The correlation is rather that the more realistic they look, the harder it is to detect their true nature. The list of examples with lifelike images or hard-to-unmask complex structures hardly could be limited to Madoff and the few more widely spoken of scams; many more remain topics only within narrower circles of enthusiast scholars and investigative journalists.[70]

Two further aspects of this sector-specific cognitive problem need to be considered. One relates to the fact that the degree to which their outward image, the façade, differs from one another may lead to the mistaken conclusion that there is nothing common to the various classes. For example, it may be hard to realize that there is something common between a gifting and an MLM plan, though historically both have already been ample times used and abused to build up a disguised pyramid or Ponzi scheme. The other is that notwithstanding what the camouflage is, a gifting arrangement, MLM, a nonprofit charity, or a co-operative, each is simultaneously also a form of investment. This fact inevitably links our central topic to the world capital markets and securities; an approach characteristic to the US but foreign not just to emerging systems without deep capital markets but also to the EU. In much of Europe, while pyramids and MLMs are perceived to be topics primarily for consumer protection lawyers, Ponzis are thought to be nothing else but fraud, or crimes falling within the bailiwick of criminal lawyers and without any major linkages to "investment" proper and financial regulations. Yet it should be realized that consumers must "invest" to be eligible to join irrespective of the fact that often they do not

---

69 Michelle Celarier, 'How a Massive Ponzi Scheme Fleeced RIAs, Religious Groups, and Retirees' (13 August 2019), RIA INTEL at (https://www.riaintel.com/article/b1gph3426nl9mn/how-a-massive-ponzi-scheme-fleeced-rias-religious-groups-and-retirees) accessed 25 March 2020. [Hereafter: Celarier – Corinthian 2019].

70 A good example is the Corinthian College & Aequitas Management case that involved a for-profit college (Corinthians), the Aequitas holding company with more subsidiaries and financial firms (also Aequitas affiliated investment advisors), a "convoluted corporate structure" that allowed for intracompany loans, issuance of promissory notes backed by receivables (including student loans purchased from Corinthian), and other transactions that made the scheme nontransparent even for experts. See Celarier – Corinthian 2019.

perceive their contributions as investments and having anything in common with shares or bonds.

There is no country in the world that has not had at least a few fiascos of the sort, but little attention has been paid to their classification. The heightened attention afforded typically to affinity and MLM schemes did not incentivize scholars to typologize either. The focus is rather on high-profile cases and rarely from the angle of vulnerable consumers – a feature attributable to the US as well.[71] Hence, it should not come as a surprise that the legitimate question of whether some classes of schemes are particularly susceptible to lure in specifically vulnerable consumer-investors has not been answered firmly yet either. As will be demonstrated, there seems to be a distinguishable correlation in some cases.

The ensuing classification should figure as an important tool for the understanding of the fraudulent mechanics and unmasking of schemes. Classifications based on other criteria are obviously also possible like the legal bases relied on to criminally prosecute the schemes[72] yet from the perspective of vulnerable consumers and the problems with detection, the one based on their outward appearance seems to be useful.

Schemes normally devoid of vulnerable classes of consumer-investors

Rich people's schemes versus vulnerable consumer-investors' schemes

The view that investors in pyramid and Ponzi schemes are not only individuals who are gullible and greedy but also who have money to invest and therefore are not vulnerable consumers deserving regulatory protections seems

---

71 The Ponzitracker, run by Jordan Maglich, a Florida attorney, listing Ponzi scheme year-by-year, focuses on top reported schemes. The website is at https://www.ponzitracker.com/ accessed 17 May 2020. It is indicative that one could hardly find similar databases in other countries. However, gathering, analysing and making public Ponzi schemes-related empirical evidences could serve as invaluable tool for educating the citizenry on the risks corollary to these forms of fraud. Existence of such databases, furthermore, would also be useful to regulators to better assess their nature and dimensions when formulating the policies aimed at protecting investors and the integrity of markets from them.

72 For example, in Florida, the criminal statutes relied on to combat securities scams include the sector-specific offenses regulated by the Florida Securities and Investors Protection Act (F.S. Ch. 517) of Selling Unregistered Securities–F.S. §517.07, Selling Securities Without a License–F.S. §517.12, Securities Fraud–F.S. §517.301, and the general ones of FLA. STAT. §812.014 (theft); FLA. STAT. §895.03 (racketeering); FLA. STAT. §817.034 (organized scheme to defraud); FLA. STAT. §775.0844 (aggravated white-collar crime). The starting point in all cases is that what is being offered must satisfy the definition of "security" (F.S. §517.021) of the Act. The tests known from federal securities laws have been adopted in this respect in Florida, notably the Reves test for determining whether certain promissory notes qualify as such (Reves v. Ernst & Young, 494 U.S. 56 (1990)) and in particular the Howey test of "investment contracts" [Securities & Exchange Commission v. W.J. Howey Co., 328 U.S. 293 (1946)]. See Judge Tom Barber, 79-FEB Fla. B.J. 8 (February 2005), at 9–10.

to be changing and to be supplanted by a more balanced understanding.[73] Many of the concrete country reports in this paper are living proofs of the changing attitudes realizing how exposed large classes of vulnerable consumers are.

This, however, does not mean that stratagems that are the exclusivity of the most well-off do not exist. The US Madoff scandal seems to be the best recent example.[74] The still unfolding German Infinus scam, involving "soccer greats Franz Beckenbauer and Oliver Kahn, and ice-skating legend Katharina Witt,"[75] could also be added to the list. Who else was among the victims is not known from publicly available sources. These were a sort of restricted-access clubs only to elites, extra rich individuals irrespective of what the US system's reactions have not remained limited to incarceration of Madoff.

Fallen schemes having plundered hundreds (if not thousands) of consumers are known even in such high welfare states with populace knowledgeable in finance as Finland or Austria. In Finland, the WinCapita internet-based Ponzi scheme, having managed to collect about 100 million Euros from more than 10,000 people roughly between 2005 and 2008, ought to be mentioned as the largest ever fraudulent scheme of the country.[76] The sequence of post-collapse events was typical of Ponzi schemes detected *ex post facto*, where the paraphernalia of the high rule of law system were sufficient only to incarcerate the main promoter but not to track down and make the organizers disgorge the illicitly obtained funds. In Austria, an equally well-off country with high rule of law index, the more recent online investment vehicle "Optioment" drew some media attention for collecting about 100 million Euros from roughly 10,000 people by luring them into Bitcoin investments.[77]

73 Given the importance attributed to the 2009 Madoff case, perhaps the words of the trustee express this best. As Floyd Norris, columnist of the *New York Times*, summarized: "*These days 'caveat emptor' — let the buyer beware — is staging a comeback. The trustee in the Bernie Madoff case argues that some people invested with Mr. Madoff deserve to lose not only the fictitious profits they received but should also lose their original investment. Why? Because they were sophisticated investors who should have known that Mr. Madoff was running a Ponzi scheme. It is an interesting concept. If you should have known you were being defrauded, you do not deserve the same protection as those who were not sophisticated. [...].*" See 'Floyd Norris, Victims Who Deserve Their Fate' *NYTimes* (10 February 2011) <https://www.nytimes.com/2011/02/11/business/11norris.html > accessed 17 May 2020.

74 See, e.g., "Bernard Madoff" and the "Mother of all Ponzi Schemes" in Mervyn K. Lewis, *Understanding Ponzi Schemes – Can Better Financial Regulation Prevent Investors from being Defrauded?* (Edward Elgar, 2015) 40–60.

75 Gertrud Hussla and Volker Votsmeier, 'Jail Time for German Ponzi Schemers in the Infinus Scam' *Handelsblatt* (Düsseldorf, 10 July 2018) at https://www.handelsblatt.com/today/finance/punishing-greed-jail-time-for-german-ponzi-schemers-in-the-infinus-scam/23582684.html?ticket=ST-5321593-OvOfsf5jn3o4OLnyC2ZN-ap4 accessed 17 May 2020.

76 See, e.g., *Helsinki Times*, 'Over 700 criminal complaints on WinCapita' (August 13, 2008) and *UUTISET*, 'WinCapita Case Reaches Court' (2 February 2011) https://yle.fi/uutiset/osasto/news/wincapita_case_reaches_court/5315714 accessed on 12 February 2020 when the *Helsinki Times* was not accessible anymore.

77 See, e.g., Mathias Benz, 'Ein Schneeballsystem im Bitcoin-Mäntelchen' [Ponzi Scheme in

The truly translational Lyoness discount-sales-based system established in 2003 in Austria[78] could rather be mentioned as a mixed model, in which one could assume that the proportion of vulnerable consumers is changing depending on which country of operations is at stake. Namely, Lyoness has expanded its operations not only to the countries neighboring Austria – including many of the considerably poorer former socialist countries of Central and Eastern Europe – but it reached as far as Australia; altogether, more than forty countries were affected. In some, Lyoness still faces investigations and trials for it is suspected that the system is a problematic pyramid scheme,[79] and yet in others it has been freed from such allegations.[80]

What needs to be stressed here forcefully is, however, that as opposed to such "posh" schemes, especially in emerging economies, many clearly have been dominated by vulnerable classes of consumers, some unbanked or living at the level of subsistence. It suffices to point to the schemes still unfolding in quite a number of African countries[81] today or the hundreds of thousands of defrauded consumer-investors that fell prey to the Central and Eastern European ones in the 1990s. The number of vulnerable consumers, in other words, changes parallel with the changed socioeconomic environment; a factor always has to be reckoned with in this domain even in the lack of empirical studies, statistics, or direct quantitative data. As a rule of thumb, the lower the living standards in

---

Bitcoin Clothing] *Neuer Zürcher Zeitung* (19 February 2018) available at https://www.nzz.ch/wirtschaft/ein-schneeballsystem-im-bitcoin-maentelchen-ld.1358753 accessed 17 May 2020.

78 The website of the LYONESS headquarters is at https://www.lyoness-corporate.com/de/ accessed 17 May 2020.

79 For example, some lower-level Austrian courts have declared the scheme to be a pyramid, leading to parliamentary investigations. See parliamentary questions as of 27 August 2014 at <https://www.parlament.gv.at/PAKT/VHG/XXV/J/J_02315/fname_362303.pdf > accessed 26 March 2020. It seems that the Norwegian Gaming Authority went the farthest as it prohibited all activities of Lyoness in Norway on 31 March 2018. The text of the decision (in Norwegian) is available at file:///E:/13%20Copenhagen%20access%20to%20finance%20Sept%202019/23%20Norway%202018/1%20Lyoness-Lyconet-Cashback-World-myWorld-vedtak-med-pålegg-om-stans.pdf and the related press release at https://lottstift.no/en/om-oss/aktuelt/lyoness-must-stop-illegal-pyramid-activtiy-in-norway/. Both accessed 5 May 2020.

80 In Australia, the Competition and Consumer Commission did not prove that Lyoness operates a pyramid scheme as it failed to establish that *"such participation payments as were made were induced by the prospect held out that new participants would receive a benefit 'in relation to the introduction of the scheme of further new participants' for the purposes of s 45(1) (b) of the Australian Consumer Law."* See the judgment in Australian Competition and Consumer Commission v. Lyoness Australia Pty Ltd. [2015] FCA 1129 (file number: NSD 884 of 2014). Text available at https://www.judgments.fedcourt.gov.au/judgments/Judgments/fca/single/2015/2015fca1129 accessed 5 May 2020.

81 In Ghana, through four major Ponzi schemes, nearly 119,300 people lost their investments (totaling GHC 59,568,000). See *Business News,* 'Over 119 thousand Ghanaians duped in Ponzi schemes in 2018' (1 April 2019) at https://www.pulse.com.gh/bi/finance/more-than-119000-ghanaians-duped-in-ponzi-schemes-in-2018/dej3n6s accessed 5 May 2020.

a country are in a given historic moment, the higher the number of vulnerable consumers is. This simplistic rule is legitimate irrespective of the exceptions, context-specificity, and the fact that vulnerable consumers exist even in the richest countries of our times.

In case, for example, of the already mentioned Albanian pyramid schemes, more than half of the populace – numbering about 3.5 million – had invested in 1 of the 11 shadow banks (having either the form of foundation or "renting association"). This occurred in a country which, until the fall of communism somewhere in 1990, had been a completely isolated enclave economically depending on communist China, without industry but with about 173,000 concrete military bunkers and most citizens living in poverty and knowing very little about finances, especially capital markets.[82] These circumstances per se made the overwhelming part of the citizenry vulnerable consumers.

The same reasons justify inclusion of the most renowned Russian scheme, called MMM after the first letters of the given names of the three founders, into our elaboration. MMM emerged in a similar environment and had its heyday during the first half of the transitory decade of the 1990s. In one of the largest countries of the world, the estimated figure of involved citizens, a large portion of which did qualify as vulnerable consumers, was about 10 million.[83] How consumer-centered MMM was could perfectly be deducted from the fact that its key marketing figure was indeed the prototype of the average citizen of those years: the Golubkov family.[84] The professional advertisements, in the form of short films, had reached the overwhelming part of the populace thanks to being projected onto TV screens, which were presumably the most important source of information back then besides the few leading newspapers. They had a simple message: anyone can make it and acquire everything they want, from fancy boots and FUR-COAT for a wife to a new apartment and nice cars – just as the Golubkovs. The scheme, in other words, specifically targeted consumer-investors of those times. One does not have to understand Russian to understand the ads. If these desires qualify as greedy, then MMM could be taken as a paradigm for schemes dominated by "greedy and gullible" consumers. The MMM consumer-investors could be looked upon as not (or the least) deserving regulatory protections because MMM openly admitted that it is a pyramid.

82 See Jarvid Paper 2000, note 15 supra.
83 See, e.g., Yuliya Guseva and Oleksiy Kononov, Contract Enforcement in Russia – Positive Developments and Persistent Dilemmas, in: Stefan Messmann and Tibor Tajti (eds.), *The Case Law of Central and Eastern Europe – Enforcement of Contracts,* vol. II (European University Press, Bochum-Germany, 2009), note 9 at 767 referring to 'Russian Investors Learn Tough Lesson' *USA Today* (1 August 1994) and Roger Barrett James, 'Information – the Key to Fair Privatization: British Successes and Russian Pitfalls' (1998) 20 Loyola of Los Angeles International and Comparative Law Journal 837 .
84 See the MMM ads on the Golubkovs on Youtube at https://www.youtube.com/watch?v=DGGSHibJ8BE accessed 5 May 2020.

Yet based on the above, the ultimate lesson one has to draw is that pyramid and Ponzi schemes are definitively not the exclusivities of rich people only.

No-consumer Ponzi schemes

Typical pyramid and Ponzi, as well as MLM, schemes involve individuals in the shoes of consumer-investors. Yet scams involving, or even being dominated by juridical entities, could also be found. The Balsam AG (named after its founder Mr. Friedel Balsam) affair is one of the largest German financial crimes from more recent times by German sources.[85] The complot allegedly involved only fictitious individuals acting as foreign investors plus banks and a factoring company – besides Balsam itself. The saga otherwise could also comfortably be listed under the heading of turned-rogue schemes as for almost 20 years the joint-stock company operated as a completely legitimate business.

The originally small-scale company, established in 1965 with mere 7,000 German Marks capital, managed to develop into a genuine global leader in sports floor manufacturing by the 1980s. This was paralleled with the acquisition of more than 20 market competitors and, unfortunately, also with growing financial problems resulting in questionable practices on the advice of the company's accountant. To raise ever more capital, they began to "pledge" their receivables (invoices) with a factoring company (Procedo).[86] While initially this was nothing unusual and the "price" they paid to the factoring company was based on regular discount rates on the market, later they were forced to offer these at ever larger discounts and ended up issuing completely fictitious invoices to get hold of capital. Allegedly, in the last phase, invoices and other documents with receivables were issued in the name of fictitious Asian and Arab clients. This was the period when the scheme turned into a Ponzi scheme, or an avalanche if the prevailing German term is metaphrased. The scheme collapsed in 1994, leading to liquidation proceedings where no assets were essentially left to creditors. In total, 45 banks lost about 1.7 billion German Marks.[87]

---

85 See, e.g., Spiegel, Nur zum Abheften, issue No. 38/1994, pp. 119–122 available at https://magazin.spiegel.de/EpubDelivery/spiegel/pdf/13686237 accessed 5 May 2020.
86 German literature speaks of this type of factoring as "non-paradigm," "non-true" ("*un-echtes*") factoring as opposed to "true factoring." The key difference is that in case of true factoring, the receivables are sold to the factoring company (or purchaser of receivables) and thus the risk of non-payment (that the invoice-debtor will not pay) is transferred onto the buyer. As opposed to that, in non-paradigm factoring, which is essentially a credit contract, the risk does not pass. Hence, if the factoring company cannot collect the receivables, it may turn back to the transferor of the invoice to get compensation. See, e.g., BGH VIII.Senate *U.GmbH (def) v. G. KG (pl), Judgment of 19 September 1977, 69 BGHZ 254 (1978)*. Translated to and commented upon in English in Stefan A. Riesenfeld & Walter J. Pakter, *Comparative Law Casebook*, Chapter 8 'Retained and Granted Security Interests' (Transnational Publishers, New York, 2001), at 446.
87 See, e.g., Von Nicole Conath, Akte Balsam non geschlossen, in: Neue Westfälische, issue of

Schemes with vulnerable classes of consumer-investors

Potentially all the ensuing types of schemes may involve vulnerable consumer-investors. This obviously depends on wherefrom they stem, which niche of the world with level of welfare and social-security system, among others. Yet it seems that especially affinity schemes and schemes camouflaged as MLMs stand out in that respect though the online variants seem to catch up. Let's take a closer look at them.

Affinity schemes

The class of affinity schemes is spoken of by the US SEC as "investment scams that prey upon members of identifiable groups, such as religious or ethnic communities, the elderly, or professional groups."[88] In fact, as Button and Cross noted in their book on cyber frauds: "A common selection technique of Ponzi […] schemes is to target affinity groups […] [to] leverage the established levels of trust that group members have with each other as well as the social capital in existence."[89]

Some of these affinity groups undoubtedly qualify as vulnerable. For example, as per a recent study working with data on 376 schemes investigated by the US SEC between 1988 and 2012, about 17% of the victims were elderly, 11% family members or friends, 10% belonged to the same religious groups, and 7% shared common ethnicity.[90] Cases of this sort could also be found, like the 2014 case *SEC v. Eadgear, Inc.* (et al.),[91] which was a pyramid schemes offering "memberships" or "business packages" principally to Chinese investors, in the US and abroad.

As Jordan Maglich, running the Ponzitracker website in the US, based primarily on its database containing the list of annually detected US schemes, noted: "Whether it's a church, a religious group, an ethnic group, just a common organization, the schemers use that common link with these people to give the scheme an aura of trust and legitimacy."[92]

The role affinity plays in establishing and running schemes may be especially

---

7 March 2020, available at https://www.nw.de/nachrichten/wirtschaft/10646076_Akte-Balsam-nun-geschlossen.html accessed 5 May 2020.
88 SEC, *Affinity Fraud: How to Avoid Investment Scams That Target Group* (9 October 2013) available at https://www.sec.gov/investor/pubs/affinity.htm accessed 5 May 2020.
89 Mark Button and Cassandra Cross, *Cyber Frauds, Scams and Their Victims* (Routledge, 2017), at 67.
90 See Accounting Lies 2018, note 43 supra, at 14, referring to R.M. Titus, F. Heinzelmann, and J.M. Boyle, 'Victimization of Persons by Fraud' (1995) 41(1) Crime and Delinquency 54–72. The first version of the paper *Who gets Swindled in Ponzi Schemes?* is available at https://www0.gsb.columbia.edu/mygsb/faculty/research/pubfiles/12962/ponzi%20draft%20may%2013%202015.pdf accessed 17 May 2020.
91 *SEC v. Eadgear, Inc.* (et al.). Complaint filed on 24 September 2014, Case: 14-cv-04294, amended and superseded by complaint of SEC 2015 WL 11578507. About $129 m was raised from tens of thousands of investors through 66,000 accounts.
92 Cited by Michelle Celarier, 'How a Massive Ponzi Scheme Fleeced RIAs, Religious Groups, and Retirees' (13 August 2019) RIA INTEL https://www.riaintel.com/article/

fruitful in emerging systems, with populace un- or less educated in finance. In Kenya, where pyramid schemes mushroomed in 2006 and 2007, some of the major schemes involved only Christian consumers because Muslims are prohibited from earning money as "interest" due to the concept of Riba (i.e., prohibition of gambling, meaning also prohibition to charge and pay interest) of Islamic law. As it was found, "the schemes took advantage of the 'prosperity gospel' by the Pentecostal/Evangelical churches. Many investors were duped into joining the schemes after being convinced by their religious leaders that they would prosper."[93]

Affinity groups, "be they religious groups, investment clubs, and employees of larger organizations,"[94] represent particularly fertile grounds for schemers as "[t]hese groups are vulnerable because their members are in close and frequent contacts with each other; among them news travel fast, they share values and tastes, and they trust each other."[95] Notwithstanding these common traits, the structure, characteristics, and the behavior of various affinity group members is not the same. Yet if one is looking for distinct examples of collapsed schemes involving larger numbers of vulnerable consumer-investors, then these should be primarily considered. This should, however, not lead to the conclusion that all members of such affinity groups losing their investments are inevitably vulnerable.

Manifest, disclosed and semi-disclosed schemes

Gifting schemes, chain letters, and similar schemes – genuinely being nothing else but games but often with monetary implications – are the best examples of manifest schemes. In their case, one could presume that even the financially least knowledgeable should foresee that there is an end to the chain at some point in time. Yet even these are within the purview of law.

Besides these game-lookalikes, however, known are also historic schemes that made use of investment tools well-known on the capital markets and yet openly proclaimed that they are pyramid schemes, or made public announcements to that effect. The above-mentioned Russian MMM was, at least at some earlier phases of its long existence, an "animal" of that kind. In the case of MMM, the schemers did not even bother to make proclamations to the effect that the profits stem from specific investment or economic activities. Their public statements openly spoke of the risk of losing everything. As the MMM Global's advertisement pronounced:

> "There are no guarantees and promises! Neither explicit nor implicit. There are neither investments nor business! Participants help each other, sending each other

---

b1gph3426nl9mn/how-a-massive-ponzi-scheme-fleeced-rias-religious-groups-and-retirees accessed 17 May 2020.

93 See 2009 Kenyan Taskforce Report, note 29 supra, at 41.

94 See Statement of Professor Tamar Frankel before the US House of Representative, 111th Congress, First Session, Committee on Financial Services, *Meeting on Assessing the Madoff Ponzi Scheme and the Need for Regulatory Reform* (5 January 2009), at 89.

95 Id.

money directly and without intermediaries. That's all! There's nothing more.

There are no securities transactions, no relationship with the professional participants of the securities market; you do not acquire any securities. (Do you need them?:-)

There are no rules. In principle! The only rule is no rules. At all! Even if you follow all of the instructions, you still may "lose." "Win" might not be paid. Without any reasons or explanations.

And in general, you can lose all your money. Always remember about this and participate only with spare money. Or do not participate at all! Amen.:-)"[96]

Besides acknowledging the existence of this class of schemes, the crucial question is how should these be perceived by regulators? Should they be taken as the paradigms in the sense of whether the law should place these in the center of observations to determine wether to regulate or not, and if yes, then with which tools of law? Compare, for example, Hungarian and US regulations: for Hungary, at least at the beginning of the transition toward market economies in the first years of the 1990s, the schemes were perceived to be "games." In the US, pyramid and Ponzi schemes have always been rather disguised investments or camouflaged businesses to be fought against by an unprecedentedly rich repository of legal tools. In other words, US law does not leave vulnerable consumers on their own and provides for more than "mere" criminalization of these practices; a pattern followed only by few globally today.

Schemes camouflaged as multi-level-marketing plans

Perhaps the most glaring example of schemes typically involving large numbers of vulnerable consumers, even in economies that are at the very beginning of their road toward a working market economy, are the ones clothed in the façade of MLMs. While naked pyramids not involving any products and living exclusively from recruitment of new members are illegal wherever they are in the purview of regulators, MLMs as a form of direct marketing and a distinct business model are prohibited only in a few countries. Which is best exemplified by most recent developments from China or Myanmar. In the EU, the US, and in most developed economies, therefore, legitimate MLMs operate often with significant market shares. The reason why MLMs are nonetheless within the purview of regulators is that "MLM companies and illegal pyramid schemes both use a similarly tiered

---

96 See Sara Hess and Eugene Sotes, 'Russia's greatest Ponzi mastermind is dead, but his legacy lives on in the crypto world' *Quartz* (25 April 2018), available at https://qz.com/1259524/mmm-and-bitcoin-russian-ponzi-mastermind-sergei-mavrodi-is-dead-but-his-legacy-lives-on-in-crypto/ accessed 17 May 2020.

organizational structure."[97] This is also why the MLM-mask can be exploited to build up a pyramid, dupe consumer-investors into joining and investing, and escape the scrutiny of regulators. It was thus legitimately noted by John Oliver in his show devoted specifically to MLMs, titled "Multilevel Marketing: Last Week Tonight with John Oliver:" "[Multi-level marketing schemes] hold up the hope that if you work hard, you can take control of your life, start your own business, and help your family ... but how real is the opportunity?"[98] As MLMs also presume investment of money, often they are confused with Ponzi schemes as well.[99]

From the perspective of unsophisticated vulnerable consumers, the outward image of MLMs might look remote from investments and the capital markets and the addition of real products or services from illicit pyramids as well. What and how MLMs advertise themselves is thus far from being irrelevant as often it is not limited to the "get-rich-quickly" message. Often what consumers will see is an opportunity to join a tested business model paralleled with a job-like position promising stable income; moreover, with a relatively small starting capital. It is not without reason that the US FTC's "Consumer Sentinel Network" includes also "business opportunities and work-at-house" schemes.[100] The prospect not only of a solid livelihood and of rising to affluence blinds many who are often struggling to make ends meet. Indeed, as experts of direct marketing noted, the attractiveness and growth of these business forms in developing economies could be explained by more factors, from "lack of retain infrastructure present in developed economies," to indeed "high levels of unemployment as people seek ways to earn additional money or gain added income security."[101]

In India, Myanmar, and Sri Lanka, such dilemmas that had been faced in the US as the birthplace of MLM decades earlier, routinely get repeated in frontier markets where MLM as a new business model has spread to more recently. What differs is that while these surfaced in the US in the 1970s when the country already possessed one of the most developed consumer protection and securities regulatory systems in the world, in frontier markets they emerge in a vacuum lacking not only experts and properly empowered enforcement agencies but also first generation regulatory responses. Given the low level of financial literacy, the

---

97 See Adam Epstein, 'Multi-Level Marketing and Its Brethren: The Legal and Regulatory Environment in the Down Economy,' (2010) 12 Atlantic Law Journal 91, at 92.

98 John Oliver, 'Multilevel Marketing: Last Week Tonight with John Oliver' https://www.youtube.com/watch?v=s6MwGeOm8iI accessed 17 May 2020.

99 Id.

100 The Consumer Sentinel Network is described as a "*unique investigative cyber tool that provides members [of the Network with] access to millions of consumer complaints,*" besides "business opportunities and work-at-home schemes," also on, among others identity theft, advance-fee loans and credit scores, debt collection, credit reports, and financial matters. See https://www.ftc.gov/enforcement/consumer-sentinel-network accessed 17 May 2020.

101 Timothy J. Wilkinson, Anna McAlister, and Scott Widmier, 'Reaching the International Consumer – An Assessment of the International Direct Marketing Environment,' (2007) 1(1) Direct Marketing: An International Journal 17–37, at 23.

risk that these may threaten the livelihoods of thousands and even the entire economic and governmental system, the regulatory responses often are complete bans of MLM schemes.

In the more developed part of the world, led by the US as the cradle of MLM and the EU as a follower, sophisticated tests have been forged by courts and agencies whereby only those MLMs that either completely, or predominantly, source their income from recruitment of new members are eliminated. In other words, only these are deemed to be pyramid schemes that are to be weeded out from the system. The tests notwithstanding, pyramids disguised as MLM schemes continue to surface, showing that besides the law, a properly staffed, financed, and activist independent regulatory agency is also a must to rigorously investigate novel cases, like the most recent US AdvoCare business model.[102] This scheme built its campaign exactly on the prospects of "unlimited income" and "financial freedom" making quitting one's job possible.

With some delay, a test resembling the US approach was introduced in the EU with respect to MLM schemes, with application in the Member States as well.[103] The test enshrined into the "4finance" UAB decision of the Luxembourg court from 2014,[104] similarly to the US patterns, also requires a case-by-case scrutiny of what has been ongoing behind the façade to determine whether the income earned within the pyramid was only, or predominantly, stemming from recruiting new members. If the recruitment, and not the sales or other economic-activity aspects, dominate, the scheme will be illegitimate. It ought to be stressed that such

---

102 The Texas-based AdvoCare International was in the business of marketing energy drinks, shakes, and supplements and claimed that "*people could earn unlimited income, quit their day jobs, and gain financial freedom by selling its products and recruiting other people to sell them too.*" The FTC was of the opinion that AdvoCare was a pyramid scheme, swindling hundreds of thousands of consumers by "*rewarding distributors not for selling product but for recruiting other distributors to spend large sums of money pursuing the business opportunity.*" As per the FTC, 72% of distributors lost money and earned nothing and only about 18% earned between a penny and $250 a year. The FTC made a settlement with three top executives; while the CEO agreed to pay $150 million for consumer refunds, the other two top executives are to refund $4 million. All were banned from all MLMs. The settlement foresees also a 100% refund for unused products to all members who want to leave the business. See Seena Gressin (attorney of the FTC Division of Consumer and Business Education), *FTC: AdvoCare business model was pyramid scheme* (2 October 2019), at https://www.consumer.ftc.gov/blog/2019/10/ftc-advocare-business-model-was-pyramid-scheme accessed 17 May 2020.
103 For Hungary, see the decision of the Hungarian Competition Authority's in the case against CIG Pannónia Életbiztosító Nyrt. Vj/102/2013 (19 December 2014).
104 See the judgment in the case "4Finance UAB" C-515/12 - ECLI:EU:C:2014:211. The test formulated by the court interpreting the Unfair Commercial Practice Directive 2005/29/EC (of 11 May 2005) concerning unfair business-to-consumer commercial practice in the internal market was that "*a pyramid promotional scheme constitutes an unfair commercial practice only where such a scheme requires the consumer to give financial consideration, regardless of its amount, for the opportunity to receive compensation that is derived primarily from the introduction of other consumers into the scheme rather than from the sale or consumption of products.*"

close resemblance of EU and US laws exists solely in case of MLMs and not of Ponzi schemes. This detail must be paid utmost attention to because – as it has been stressed above – in many European languages no, or no such intense, differentiation is made between pyramid and Ponzi schemes. MLMs deserve special attention, however, not only because of such strong cross-fertilization of laws on the two sides of the Atlantic. Rather, because they look more like jobs and stable income opportunities than investments. As such, they are most capable of attracting vulnerable consumers who could the least be accused of being greedy and gullible.

Disguised service-providers and disguised securities

Albeit MLMs are also operated by duly established business vehicles, some pyramid and Ponzi schemes have managed to come into being and survive for some time because they were hidden behind the façade of legitimate-looking companies, having nothing in common with MLMs, licensed to provide financial services. This was the case not only with the investment company of Madoff – *Bernard L. Madoff Investment Securities LLC*[105] – but also with the *Aman Futures Group* of the Philippines, the *Saxon Capital Ltd* from Myanmar, or the Albanian shadow banks which were named either as "renting associations" or "foundations." In case of these, the proper legal form has undoubtedly played a key role in motivating consumers to invest.

An even more telling example is the official designation of the more recent Romanian complot known as FNI ("Fondului Național de Investiții"), or National Investment Fund, the designation of which suggests involvement of the state and thus stability of investments. That this behemoth Ponzi scheme could have emerged in Romania after the devastating consequences of the charity-clothed *Caritas* of the 1990s – to be synoptically chronicled in the next subsection – obviously must be ascribed to the fact that the scheme excelled in appearing in gowns perfectly displaying the "legitimate business" image. This included also the endorsement of a state-owned retail bank (CEC), which guaranteed the investments into FNI. Needless to say, the collapse of FNI in 2000 brought to the knees many Romanian families,[106] or thousands of vulnerable consumer-investors. The main figure, Mr. Sorin Ovidiu Vîntu, for years one of the richest tycoons of the country, was eventually sentenced to more years in prison and on more accounts,

---

105 On the Madoff saga, see Chapter 20, *Madoff and the World's Largest Ponzi Scheme in:* David E.Y. Sarna, *History of Greed – Financial Fraud from Tulip Mania to Bernie Madoff* (Wiley, 2010), note 31 supra, at 146 et seq.

106 The damage was estimated to amount to almost 7% of Romania's then-GDP of $4.3 billion and was around $300 million. See Romanian Corruption Watch, *What's Ponzi scheme in Romanian? Sorin Ovidiu Vintu* (2 August 2017) https://medium.com/romania-corruption-watch/whats-ponzi-scheme-in-romanian-sorin-ovidiu-v%C3%AEntu-2897cc47a21f accessed 17 May 2020.

not only for his deeds connected to FNI.[107] He was released on probation during April 2020.

The legitimate business form is often coupled with offering of securities, or other more or less known financial products that as well look "real" to consumers. Hence, it should not come as a surprise that consumers buying such products may not realize that actually they are turning into investors in the eyes of the law. The Hungarian real property investment cooperatives,[108] for example, besides being clothed in the widely known business vehicle form of "cooperatives" ("szövetkezet") and describing themselves as experts in real property markets, raised consumer money by selling equity stakes in the cooperatives in the form of *memberships*. However, as these were sold to investors subject to repurchase by the cooperatives within one, three, or six months at a fixed price, the advertisements containing these offerings closely resembled those of commercial banks on savings account deposits. Even the financial supervisory authority was not capable of seeing anything problematic in the offerings, otherwise publicly displayed on advertisement pillars in the streets and in various newspapers.[109]

Given that due-time detection of what is really happening behind the veils and prevention of the escalation of the schemes to the point of collapse requires not only piercing of the corporate veil known to company law but also providing efficient tools to a powerful agency filled with experts, undoubtedly it is US law that has developed the most potent repository for combating pyramid and Ponzi schemes. A regulation that is blind to these realities and relies on static formalism in the name of some drafting dogmas suited for the whereabouts of the 19th or early 20th century is inherently doomed to remain ineffective in this domain. The problems surrounding the chameleons of finance presume, indeed, a regulation that is capable of and expects functional thinking, and which looks at the economy underlying the schemes in lieu of the labels.

Schemes disguised as charities

This category of schemes deserves separate mention because the "bait," the marketing tactics, employed by them, is relying on their charitable nature. The fake message they radiate is that they are nonprofit organizations of the vulnerable and for the vulnerable. The MMM scheme that originated in Russia expanded to some African and Asian frontier markets exactly by converting into charitable organizations with advertisements stressing their charitable nature.[110]

---

107 See, e.g., Ana Maria Luca, 'Romanian Tycoon Receives Third Graft Sentence' *Balkan Insight* (26 April 2018), available at https://balkaninsight.com/2018/04/26/romanian-tycoon-sentenced-in-second-graft-case-04-26-2018/ accessed 17 May 2020.
108 For a detailed account of the case, see Tajti Pyramid Cooperatives 2005, note 63 supra, at 111–216.
109 See Tajti Pyramid Cooperatives 2005, note 63 supra.
110 MMM Nigeria was advertised as a sort of mutual aid fund. See, e.g., Ejike Kanife, 'StreetTech: Loopers, Twinkas and Other Active Ponzi Schemes You May Want to Avoid'

As the recent empirical evidences from Africa amply demonstrate, the formula has worked. Nonprofits are normally subject to much more lenient regulatory oversight compared to for-profits even in developed legal systems. The charitable nature of the scheme must not, however, be linked to and exploited through opting for the not-for-profit operational form.

The Romanian Caritas launched in 1992, right at the outset of the transition from communism to a market economy, could also be a good example.[111] The venture, formally a limited liability company but in reality a Ponzi scheme, hid behind the label *Caritas*, which even to laymen inherently suggested charitable activities. And indeed, as the *Oxford Dictionary* defines, "caritas" means "Christian love of humankind; charity." The scheme, however, did not survive for about two years only because politicians and state officials were given privileges in the form of faster-return investments. The Romanian National Bank estimated that the scheme held about one-third of the country's bank notes. Even the National Bank could hardly disregard this. In those days, debit and credit cards were not in wide circulation (to say that least). Caritas circulated between 1 and 5 billion USD.

Turned-rogue (metamorphosed) schemes

Schemes that after foundation and the initial period of their existence metamorphosed into Ponzis could also be found. The shift may occur intentionally, pressed by the circumstances, or a combination of the two. The initial realistic facet makes detection particularly challenging even for experts, let alone vulnerable consumers.

A suitable example may be the collapse of the Canadian "Golden Oaks Enterprise,"[112] which operated a two-legged venture between 2009 and 2013. This company was designed to exploit the relatively novel "Rent2own" business model borrowed from the US to make the dream of home acquisition possible for those "who did not qualify for a mortgage to buy a home."[113] The formula was simple: in return for a down payment and slightly inflated rent, clients could occupy one of the properties owned or managed by Golden Oaks. After three or five years, occupants had the option to purchase the property. Contrary to paradigm Ponzis, Golden Oaks had on the eve of its bankruptcy 68 properties on its books, out of which only 31 were occupied.

The other prong of the Golden Oaks venture was a pure investment scheme,

(9 August 2019) https://technext.ng/2019/08/09/streettech-loom-twinkas-other-active-ponzi-schemes-you-may-want-to-avoid/ accessed 5 May 2020.

111 On the Caritas saga, see Ileana M. Smeureanu and Florentin Giurgea, 'Enforcement of Contract in Romania' in: Stefan Messmann and Tibor Tajti (eds.), *The Case Law of Central and Eastern Europe: Enforcement of Contracts*, vol. II (European University Press, Bochum – Germany, 2009), note 1, at 680.

112 Doyle *Salewski Inc. v. Scott* (2019) ONSC 5108. (Salewski is the appointed bankruptcy trustee in the case.)

113 Id. para 3.

not as forcefully advertised publicly. Here, short-term promissory notes were sold to investors. While initially the interest rates were merely "attractive," later as the financial situation of the venture worsened, with ever higher rates, rates eventually ended above the criminal rate as defined by criminal laws.

To recap, the business model was premised on the two interlinked prongs supplementing each other though the total costs of the mortgage prong reached more than the double of the income already in the first few years.[115] As the data suggest, the complex enterprise must have metamorphosed into a genuine Ponzi scheme somewhere in mid-2011. As the judge deciding the case noted:

> "Whatever [the single shareholder] Lacasse's original intentions may have been when he founded Golden Oaks, it became a classic Ponzi scheme. [Though] [t]he Rent2Own scheme was never viable."[114]

Apart from proving the legitimacy of the class of turned-rogue schemes, this synopsis of the case, especially the quoted words of the judge deciding the case, should remind us of the fact that detection of pyramid and Ponzi schemes is far from being easy. Indeed, while the judge in the case did declare that the "Rent2own" business model was never viable, he failed to unequivocally declare that the venture was a Ponzi scheme from day one even though he had all the accessible documents, data, and information before him. Contrary to judges, the agencies entrusted with the task of early detection of the schemes, gathering the related evidences and taking action against them are not in such a favorable position and thus one should be more understanding of their occasional failures. It is especially hard to detect a scheme at initial stages of the life of the enterprise that is ab initio a Ponzi scheme, or later turns-into it. Yet if this line of argumentation deserves merit, the quintessential question one ought to formulate is: How much should be expected from uneducated vulnerable consumers?

Postmodern Ponzi schemes: blockchain-based schemes, digital currencies, and other schemes exploiting new technologies

In the new, technology-dependent era featured by cryptocurrencies, blockchain, and algorithms, besides the continued emergence of offline Ponzi schemes, online versions of Ponzi schemes increasingly appear as well. Valuable research results have already been reported by computer scientists and accountants rather than legal scholars. Some of the newly coined designations like "postmodern Ponzi schemes" or the more innocent-sounding "high-yield investment programs"[116] (HYIPs)

---

115 As the court summarized: "From March 1st, 2012 to February 28, 2013, only 3% of the monies deposited into Golden Oaks' bank accounts were rental payments by prospective home-buyers. Over 90% of the money it collected came from investors."

114 Id. para 6.

116 See, e.g., Tyler Moore, Jie Han, and Richard Clayton, *The Postmodern Ponzi Scheme:*

perfectly fit the novel phenomena many of which likewise offer unrealistically high returns and then collapse just like their offline kin yet differ primarily with respect to the milieu in which all this occurs: the online world, the "ether."

Being in the position to join this stratosphere presumes not only some elevated level of technological expertise but also being more well-off to be in the position to purchase, or have access to, the needed equipment and services. No exact data seem to be available yet one could legitimately suspect that a different class of consumer-investors are involved in such offerings compared to the clients, for example, of pyramid schemes disguised as MLM platforms.[117] Still, projecting that no vulnerable consumers fall victims of postmodern pyramid and Ponzi schemes and that the ensuing analysis is completely inapplicable to them would be mistaken. As Button and Cross noted:

> "There is a common perception that victims [of cyber fraud, including cyber Ponzi schemes] must be gullible, greedy, stupid or a combination of these. [...] However, [...] the reality of cyber fraud victimization paints a very different picture compared to the common misconception and false assumptions that currently exist. The reality is that anyone can become a victim of a cyber fraud or scam, if targeted in the right way at the right time by a highly skilled offender."[118]

In fact, as the available data suggest, the recently fallen OneCoin cryptocurrency originating in Bulgaria, but having grown to a genuine international venture thanks to the online world and having been in existence between 2014 and 2019, must have attracted a large number of vulnerable consumers as well.[119] The cautionary language is advisable here because no such empirical evidences have surfaced so far that would allow for more exact claims on the structure of "investors." The case desires formulation of many questions of relevance here and again we may not necessarily get to a clear, unequivocal answer on whether the consumer-investors of this technology scheme should be entirely blamed for

---

Empirical Analysis of High-Yield Investment Programmes https://core.ac.uk/display/ 22577837 accessed 17 May 2020. The research paper found, *first,* that the same rule applies, and the longer-lasting programs offer lower interest rates and longer mandatory investment terms, *second,* only a handful of digital currencies support HYIPs, and *third,* in the authors' estimate about $6 million per month is the turnover by the criminal versions of the schemes.

117 Mark Button and Cassandra Cross, *Cyber Frauds, Scams and Their Victims* (Routledge, 2017), at 62.

118 The methodology applied in the Moore-Han and Clayton study is not clear as far as their conclusions are concerned. The study states that *all* investors in postmodern schemes are aware of the fraudulent nature of these, yet they join believing that they will be in the position to withdraw their investments before the collapse of the schemes. [Note: The emphasis is on the word "all."]

119 See Kerin Hope, 'Crypto Scam Offers Modern Twist on Classic Pyramid Fraud' *Financial Times* (19 December 2020), at 4. [Hereafter: Hope – Crypto Scam FT]

what engulfed them. The conservatively inclined opinionated could, with some dose of legitimacy, note that what is painful in this saga is that the presumably large number of Bulgarian (and other Eastern European) citizens having invested in OneCoin have not learned from the misfortunes brought upon earlier generations by the many smaller and larger pyramid and Ponzi schemes that engulfed the post-socialist (communist) Eastern Europe in the 1990s. It is fair to presume that the larger fiascos must have remained part of common remembrance notwithstanding the change of generations.

Those more sympathetic and understanding of consumer-investors of this and similar online schemes may, on the other hand, readily counter by stating that the big question in these contexts is whether it is justified to presume that the online versions of these scams could so easily be perceived as being merely two appearance forms of the one and same phenomenon. Moreover, both are emerging and unfolding without the interventions of governmental agencies entrusted with monitoring the markets. In other words, it is justified to add a streak of skepticism to New York County District Attorney Cyrus Vance's characterization that this was merely "an old-school pyramid scheme on a new-school platform,"[120] a characterization that became clear to him e*x post facto*, only once the system had collapsed and investigations into the true nature of things were given a green light to proceed. What is offered in the online world additionally is not only unprecedentedly new, typically much less transparent than its offline kin, and thus not understandable to many, but also unprecedentedly fast changing.

Still, although greed, herd behavior, and being lured into the system by the "illusion of affluence"[121] reappear and take a toll in the "crypto-contexts" as well, the technology clothing as supplemented by the hype corollary to new technologies did play undoubtedly a major role in "persuading" individuals to invest in the scheme. The regulatory agencies' lukewarm reactions[122] being

---

120 See Andrew Fenton, True Story of $4 Billion OneCoin Ponzi to Become TV Drama at https://micky.com.au/true-story-of-4b-one-coin-ponzi-to-become-tv-drama/ accessed 23 March 2020. See also the related BBC podcast at https://www.bbc.co.uk/sounds/play/p07sz990. The podcast was not accessible anymore on 23 March 2020.

121 The key figure of the scheme was Ms Ruja Ignatova, who performed "inspirational online talks and live appearances, including at Wembley Stadium in London," but obviously this was definitively not a one-man show. She purchased historic buildings in Sofia, the capital of Bulgaria, and kept a luxurious motor yacht moored at a marina on the Black Sea coast. She disappeared in 2017 as she has failed to show up at the Lisbon meeting of OneCoin promoters scheduled to take the next big step of opening a private online exchange where investors could convert their OneCoins to Euros. See Hope – Crypto Scam FT, note 111 supra.

122 It should not come as a surprise that German and US prosecutors which took the most far-reaching steps in the OneCoin case. The Bulgarian SEC did issue warnings in 2015 specifically related to OneCoin. Ms Ignatova is facing charges of securities fraud, wire fraud, and conspiracy to commit money laundering in the US. It is not known whether and what she was charged with in Bulgaria, if at all.

276 Tibor Tajti (Thaythy)

limited to warnings, and the commonly known fact that Bitcoin and some other cryptocurrencies survive up until today in most countries as legitimate, have hardly been of help either in making the citizenry understand what is what. Especially as OneCoin was, indeed, a "crypto-cum-multi-level-marketing-scheme" as many of its offline predecessors.[123]

Schemes involving governments and their agencies

A distinct category of schemes must be spoken of separately from all the other types: scams that manifestly involved politicians or various prongs and agencies of the government. Although the detailed analysis of these ought to be left for yet another study, the "greedy and gullible" assumption leaves us with no option but to cast a word on them. The rationale is very simple: the more intensely the government, or its agents, are involved in any scheme, the more the strength of the assumption decreases. Put simply, schemes that involve governmental in-volvement besides omission or refusal to enact sector-specific laws inevitably make from such schemes a different kind of "animal." This is so because the appearance or a public statement of a politician, or agency related to a scheme, normally sends out the message that what is being offered can be trusted. Therefore, the promoters of schemes look for contacts with leading political figures to shake hands and to circulate the related photo in the media. It is also known that some schemes benefited politicians in the form of faster returns or higher interest rates.

The most tragic, however, is when it is the government that organizes, overtly or covertly, schemes to plunder people. It is little known, or long forgotten, that during the first Balkan wars of the early 1990s, Milosevich's rump Yugoslavia did organize a pyramid-bank exactly to allure citizens to pull their last foreign currency reserves from under pillows and to invest them with the then brand new Dafiment Bank (named after its founder and CEO, Mrs. Dafina Milanović) to finance the war.[124] Mrs. Dafina was just a puppet figure of the regime yet her bank, fully supported by the government (including the National Bank of Serbia), managed to raise more than a billion German Marks and thereby to ruin tens of thousands of Serbian families. True, an extraordinary story in extra-ordinary times, yet eventually the Dafina Bank saga deserves a gloss.

---

123 Id.
124 See, e.g., Miša Brkić, Kako je natala i propala Dafiment banka: Pipci i konci svemoćnog gazde [The Emergence and Fall of the Dafiment Bank: All the Tentacles and Trumps of the Allmighty Boss], in: Vreme 536 (12 April 2001) at https://www.vreme.com/cms/view.php?id=96130 accessed 17 May 2020.

What has been learnt and what should be given a second thought to?

Filling the scholarly vacuum

The primary reason that made me accept the challenge of researching and writing on the relatively narrow topic of how the collapse of pyramid and Ponzi schemes affect vulnerable consumers was the dearth of pertinent legal scholarship. More precisely, if the scarcity of publications devoted to all classes of consumer-investors of collapsed schemes is apostrophized as grave, then the vacuum applies exponentially to the vulnerable classes. It is not only that the number of sectoral publications is low and one has to grapple with the hardships of extrapolating the relevant information from materials that go much broader, are focused on other aspects of these phenomena, or are hidden in less orthodox sources of law. The lack of empirical studies with statistical and other quantitative data specifically on the number, proportion, and status of vulnerable consumers of collapsed schemes is, as one could presuppose, the major hardship.

Yet the vacuum is most expressed with respect to emerging markets because scholars from the leading legal systems, even the comparatists, tend to remain parochial and captured by the local mainstream narratives. In Europe, for example, while some attention has been devoted to pyramids-cum-MLMs from the angle of the existent legislation, there is barely anything on Ponzi schemes. Yet if the UK found it important to create a special agency – the Serious Fraud Office[125] – for combating white-collar crime, making Ponzi schemes one of the targets,[126] then the neglect is questionable given that Europe is not devoid of them either. Brexit is hardly of any relevance here and as the above-mentioned examples from the countries with less-developed capital markets suggest, although there is a correlation between the number of (detected) Ponzi schemes and the maturity of a Member State's capital markets, the less developed ones are not devoid of them either. The issue is rather whether they are exposed by media,

---

125 https://sfo.gov.uk accessed 17 May 2020.
126 See, e.g., the speech of Sara Lawson, General Counsel of SFO, at Cambridge Symposium on Economic Crime (3 September 2019) https://www.sfo.gov.uk/2019/09/03/sara-lawson-qc-speaking-at-cambridge-symposium-on-economic-crime-2019/ accessed 17 May 2020. As she put it: "*The risks we face include ever-more convoluted schemes by which to tell lies and steal money … from individuals (such as our investor witnesses who have lost their life savings) right up to multi-national businesses who have lost out on valuable contracts because of bribery and corruption. And when Governments are defrauded those who have lost are, of course, widespread too. [SFOs] caseload displays all flavours of fraud and corruption. We see pension fraud schemes, we see Ponzi schemes and we see money laundering. You will know that investment scams fall in and out of fashion. There was a time when wine investment frauds were common. More recently we've been investigating allegations that some green investment schemes – solar panels, biofuels, forestry planting – are not always the win-win propositions they seem.*" [Emphasis added]

or ideally by critical legal scholarship, instead of sweeping the related information under the carpet.

What to do with the "greedy and gullible" narrative?

This chapter set out, and must end, with the alpha and omega of any discussion aimed at answering whether a class (or more classes) of vulnerable consumer-investors ought to be recognized among the victims of collapsed pyramid and Ponzi schemes. As we have seen above, not all, but some specific types of schemes are especially susceptible to attract vulnerable consumer-investors, the best examples being affinity-based schemes and pyramids hiding behind the MLM veil. That consumer-investors deserve closer attention also in some peculiar historic moments, transitory or turbulent eras, is a fact that also speaks against instinctive application of the assumption. Rethinking is needed in case of schemes in emerging economies, or regions with thousands of unbanked people joining. Asserting that *all* consumer-investors of *any of the schemes* a priori are greedy and gullible simply does not stand.

The million-dollar policy question is then which classes of investors deserve extra regulatory protections and in which cases? If the European framework on unfair commercial practices is observed in isolation, the answer is clear, notwithstanding the ongoing debates: all consumers deserve the heeling hands of the system if naked, or pyramids dominated by the recruitment aspect and disguised as MLMs are at stake. The more vulnerable deserve heightened attention though why and in which situations has not been answered as of yet. Not only the US, but the positions of Myanmar, India, or the Philippines resemble' the European one in respect of pyramids, and schemes masked as MLMs.

The bigger challenge therefore concerns Ponzi schemes where the approaches significantly differ. Most European systems entrust this task to criminal law exclusively, or predominantly. Mobilization of the mechanisms of the criminal system, from incarceration or fining of promoters, however, is not equal with compensation of the victims. Criminal law may have deterrent effects and may also provide some sort of moral satisfaction to rebuild trust in the markets; however, none of these is sufficient, either to prevent the emergence of ever-newer schemes, nor to compensate the victims. The utilization of the additional tools of consumer-protection law, or as the US experiences suggest, of the securities (financial) regulatory system are for these reasons needed.

Complete denial of the 'greedy and gullible' narrative, however, would clearly be mistaken, as several examples from around the world could easily show. The Colombian DRFE scheme even advertising itself by the telltale slogan of '*Dinero Rapido Facil y en Efectivo*' [Quick and Easy Money in Cash] is obviously an "animal" different from many schemes appearing in MLM clothes. The latter might have been perceived as a promising new legitimate business format, tested and validly functioning in source jurisdictions, and most importantly – offering the prospects of income and a job-like position. This empirical fact should not be swept under the table.

Indeed, Jean Braucher rightly vouched for avoiding "the pitfall of seeing structural and cultural factors as opposing explanations"[127] when dealing with consumer overindebtedness and bankruptcy because the spectrum of reasons is wide. Instinctive simplification of the extremely variegated spectrum of schemes to a single benchmark that does not fit reality for the sake of scholarly clarity, in other words, is not the pattern to be embraced.

Do Investors of collapsed schemes qualify as vulnerable consumers?

The strength of the argument that many of the victims of fallen schemes are consumer-investors, often vulnerable, significantly increases once examples of fallen schemes and their victims from emerging systems, past, or of more recent vintage, become observable phenomena. The sheer number of people living in a country at subsistence levels and yet being entangled in schemes could be a compelling argument legitimizing the gravity of the problem. The lack of, or underdeveloped, welfare and social-security systems in emerging systems furthermore often make other strata of consumers vulnerable as well.

Yet vulnerable consumers deserving protections exist not only in developing countries. As Tamar Frankel highlighted, in the US as a country with one of the financially most-literate populaces of the world, the schemes may involve not only "people who mimic trustworthiness, who may be self-centered, ruthless narcissists [but also people who] are true victims as well as foolish or fake victims."[128] [Emphasis added] Mervyn K. Lewis, likewise noted in his 2015 book *Understanding Ponzi Schemes* that empirical evidences often refute the "common view [that] the victims of Ponzi schemes have only themselves to blame," as in many cases "many participants (later to become victims) were attracted more by the promise of safety and steady, not remarkable, returns produced by industry icons."[129]

Who to blame and thus who deserves protections is ergo such a complex question that escapes easy answers. Consequently, studies that depart from and treat all victims of schemes as an irrational "herd" may not necessarily take the discourse in the right direction. The insights one may gain from behavioral economics and other disciplines admittedly are important for better understanding these phenomena. Micklitz, analyzing herd behavior and the connected liability issues through three types of historic examples – including pyramid schemes – was therefore right in concluding that "[w]e know that [herding] can

---

127 Braucher – Overindebtedness 2006, at 323, 324.
128 Tamar Frankel, *The Ponzi Scheme Puzzle: A History and Analysis of Con Artists and Victims* (OUP, 2012), at 188. In the book, the author departed from three iconic US Ponzi schemes: those, of Charles Ponzi, Bernard Madoff, and Gregory Bell.
129 See Mervyn 2015, note 2 supra, at 119.

cause dangerous systemic effects, but we still face difficulties identifying the individuals and the institutions that could be held liable."[130]

That the above claims are far more than mere academic questions, however, should not be adjudged solely based on the historical examples canvassed herein or elsewhere. Namely, as history suggests, the number of unearthed (primarily Ponzi) schemes multiplies during major economic or other types of crises due to a sudden shortage of financing and other unexpected anomalies. The demise of the Madoff scheme in the aftermath of the 2008 global financial crisis, commentators agree, is to be ascribed exactly to the Credit Crunch.[131] Whether the Covid-19 pandemic we are faced with as this paper is being written, causing serious distortions in the functioning of the entire financial system locally and globally, is going to act as another catalyst leading to demystification of affinity, charitable, or other types of schemes involving vulnerable consumers remains to be seen. Yet even if the worst happens, the caveat today's regulators must heed is that letting consumer-investors, especially of the vulnerable sort, at their own following the 18th century logic enshrined into the Latin Maxim "Si populous vult decipi, decipiatur"[132] – "If the people wish to be deceived, then they will be deceived!" – is not the one to be heeded.

Bibliography

Hard Laws (Statutory and Sub-Statutory Law)

Austria

Austrian Penal Code 1974 (as amended in 2019) ("Strafgesetzbuch"), Full reference: Bundesgesetz vom 23. Jänner 1974 über die mit gerichtlicher Strafe bedrohten Handlungen (Strafgesetzbuch – StGB), StF: BGBl. Nr. 60/1974 (NR: GP XIII RV 30 AB 959S. 84. BR: S. 326. NR: Einspr. d. BR: Einspr. D. BR: 1000 AB 1011S. 98.).

---

130 Hans-W. Micklitz, 'Herd Behavior and Third Party Impact as a Legal Concept – On Tulips, Pyramid Games, and Asset-Backed Securities' in Stefan Grundmann, Florian Möslein, and Karl Riesenhuber (eds.), *Contract Governance: Dimensions in Law and Interdisciplinary Research* (OUP, 2015), at 146.

131 See Greg Bartalos, 'Madoff is behind Bard. But with Markets Infected by Covid-19, More Ponzi Schemes May Be Unmasked' (7 April 2020) RIAINTEL.

132 As a legal historian noted in his 1938 legal history book on the post-Bubble Act (1720) English company law developments: "[…] in an age in which mercantilism was declining and which was soon to embrace the *laissez-faire* of Adam Smith and the sweet reasonableness of giving free play to the enlightened self-interest of the capitalist, [and after] the tumult of the Bubble period had died down, there was a tendency to let reign supreme that philosophy of finance which was so well satirized by Dean Swift in 1721 as reflecting the view 'Si populous vult decepi, decipiatur.' […]." Armand Budington DuBois, *The English Business Company after the Bubble Act: 1720–1800* (Octagon Books, New York, 1971 reprint), at 438. As a grammatical note, while this source spells the word "decepi" with "e," other sources do that rather with "i" – or "decipi."

European Union

Directive 2005/29/EC of the European Parliament and of the Council of 11 May 2005 concerning unfair business-to-consumer commercial practices in the internal market and amending Council Directive 84/450/EEC, Directives 97/7/EC, 98/27/EC, and 2002/65/EC of the European Parliament and of the Council and Regulation (EC) No 2006/2004 of the European Parliament and of the Council ('Unfair Commercial Practices Directive').

Directive 2014/57/EU of the European Parliament and of the Council of 16 April 2014 on criminal sanctions for market abuse (market abuse directive).

Florida

Florida Securities and Investors Protection Act (F.S. Ch. 517).

Hungary

Hungarian Criminal Code [Law No. 100 of year 2012 on the Criminal Code]. [Full reference: 2012. évi C. törvény a Büntető Törvénykönyvről].

India

Banning of Unregulated Deposit Scheme Ordinance; available in English at https://www.prsindia.org/sites/default/files/bill_files/Banning%20of%20Unregulated%20Deposit%20Schemes%20Ordinance%2C%202019.pdf.

United States (Federal)

Federal Trade Commission Act (15 U.S.C. §§ 45-58, as amended).
Securities Act of 1933 (15 U.S.C. § 77a et seq.).
Securities Exchange Act of 1934 (15 U.S.C. § 78a et seq.).

Sri Lanka

2005 Anti-Pyramid Act is accessible via the website of the US organization Pyramid Scheme Alert web page at https://www.pyramidschemealert.org/PSAMain/news/SriLankaNewLaw.pdf.

Soft Law

EU Commission Staff Working Document, Guidance on the Implementation/Application of Directive 2005/29/Ec on Unfair Commercial Practices SWD [2016] 163 final (25 May 2016), banned commercial practice No. 14, at 80.

ESMA (European Securities and Markets Authority) document ADVICE – Initial Coin Offerings and Crypto-Assets (9 January 2019|ESMA50-157-1391).

Kenyan Ministry for Cooperative Development and Marketing, Report of the Task Force on Pyramid Schemes (2009).

SEC, Affinity Fraud: How to Avoid Investment Scams That Target Group (9 October 2013), available at https://www.sec.gov/investor/pubs/affinity.htm.

Sec. & Exch. Comm'n Office of Investigations, Investigation of Failure of the SEC to Uncover Bernard Madoff's Ponzi Scheme, Public Version 29 (29 September2009), available at https://www.sec.gov/news/studies/2009/oig-509.pdf.

SEC Press Release 2011-234 at http://www.sec.gov/news/press/2011/2011-234.htm.

Statement of Professor Tamar Frankel before the U.S. House of Representative, 111th Congress, First Session, Committee on Financial Services, Meeting on Assessing the Madoff Ponzi Scheme and the Need for Regulatory Reform (5 January 2009).

Court and Agency Cases

Australia

Australian Competition and Consumer Commission v. Lyoness Australia Pty Ltd. [2015] FCA 1129 (file number: NSD 884 of 2014). Text available at https://www.judgments.fedcourt.gov.au/judgments/Judgments/fca/single/2015/2015fca1129.

European Union

C-515/12 ECLI:EU:C:2014:211 ("4Finance UAB").

Hungary

Hungarian Competition Authority Decision in the Case Against CIG Pannónia Életbiztosító Nyrt. Vj/102/2013 (19 December 2014).

Germany

BGH VIII.Senate *U.GmbH (def) v. G. KG (pl)*, Judgment of 19 September 1977, 69 BGHZ 254 (1978).

Ontario (Canada)

Doyle Salewski Inc. v. Scott, 2019 ONSC 5108.

Pacific Coast Coin Exchange of Canada Ltd. v. Ontario Securities Commission (1978), 2 S.C.R. 112 (Ontario Superior Court judgment).

Norway

Norwegian agency decision prohibition activities of Lyoness in Norway (in Norwegian language) as of 31 March 2018 available at file://E:/13%20Copenhagen%20access%20to%20finance%20Sept%202019/23%20Norway%202018/1%20Lyoness-Lyconet-Cashback-World-myWorld-vedtak-med-pålegg-om-stans.pdf.

United States

F.T.C. v. BurnLounge, Inc. 753 F.3d 878 (9th Cir. 2014).
In Re Koscot Interplanetary, Inc. 86 F.T.C. (1974).
In re Amway Corp., 93 F.T.C. 618, 716 (1979).
In Re Bernard L. Madoff LLC 654 F.3d 229, 231 (2nd Cir., 2011).
Reves v. Ernst & Young, 494 U.S. 56 (1990).
Securities & Exchange Commission v. W.J. Howey Co., 328 U.S. 293 (1946).
SEC Complaint, SEC v. Madoff, No. 08-10791 (S.D.N.Y. Dec. 11, 2008).
SEC v. Eadgear, Inc. (et al.). Complaint filed on 24 September 2014, Case: 14-cv-04294, amended and superseded by complaint of SEC 2015 WL 11578507.
Webster v. Omnitrition Int'l, Inc. 79 F3d 776, 781 (9th Cir. 1996).

Books, Monographs, Dictionaries

Armand Budington DuBois, *The English Business Company after the Bubble Act: 1720-1800* (Octagon Books, New York, 1971 reprint).
B.A. Garner (editor-in-chief), *Black's Law Dictionary* (DeLuxe 7th ed., West, 1999).
D.E.Y. Sarna, *History of Greed* (Wiley, 2010).
E. Porras, *Bubbles and Contagion in Financial Markets,* vol 2: Models and Mathematics (1st ed., Palgrave Macmillan, 2017).
F.C. Abrahams, *From Dictatorship to Democracy in Europe* (New York University Press, 2015).
Jacobs, J., *The Death and Life of Great American Cities* (Vintage, New York, 1962).
K.B. Phelps and Hon Steven Rhodes, *The Ponzi Book: A Legal Resource for Unraveling Ponzi Schemes* (LexisNexis, 2012).
M. Button and C. Cross, *Cyber Frauds, Scams and their Victims* (Routledge, 2017).
M. Crouch and T. Lindsey (eds.), *Law, Society and Transition in Myanmar* (Bloomsbury, 2014).
M.K. Lewis, *Understanding Ponzi Schemes – Can better Financial Regulation Prevent Investors from being Defrauded?* (Edward Elgar, 2015).
Putnam, R.D., Bowling Alone: America's Declining Social Capital, in: *Culture and Politics* (pp. 223–234), (Palgrave Macmillan, New York, 2000).
S.A. Riesenfeld & W.J. Pakter, *Comparative Law Casebook, Chapter 8 'Retained and Granted Security Interests'* (Transnational Publishers, New York, 2001).
T. Frankel, *The Ponzi Scheme Puzzle: A History and Analysis of Con Artists and Victims* (OUP 2012).
T.L. Friedman, *The Lexus and the Olive Tree* (Anchor Books, 2000).

Edited Books

A. Gorezi and E. Bashari, 'Enforcement of Contracts in Albania – Overcoming Dilemmas in an Emerging Market' in S. Messmann and T. Tajti (eds), *The Case Law of Central and Eastern Europe – Enforcement of Contracts,* vol I (European University Press, Bochum-Germany 2009).
H.-W. Micklitz, 'Herd Behavior and Third Party Impact as a Legal Concept – On Tulips, Pyramid Games, And Asset-Backed Securities' in S. Grundmann, F.

Möslein, and K. Riesenhuber (eds.), *Contract Governance: Dimensions in Law and Interdisciplinary Research* (OUP, 2015).

I.M. Smeureanu and F. Giurgea, 'Enforcement of Contract in Romania' in: S. Messmann & T. Tajti (eds), *The Case Law of Central and Eastern Europe: Enforcement of Contracts*, vol. II (European University Press, Bochum – Germany, 2009).

J.M. Drew & C. Cross, Fraud and its PREY: Conceptualizing Social Engineering Tactics and Its Impact on Financial Literacy Outcomes, in: T. Harrison (ed.). *Financial Literacy and the Limits of Financial Decision-Making* (Palgrave-Macmillan, 2016).

Y. Guseva & O. Kononov, Contract Enforcement in Russia – Positive Developments and Persistent Dilemmas, in: Stefan Messmann & T. Tajti (eds), *The Case Law of Central and Eastern Europe Enforcement of Contracts*, vol. II (European University Press, Bochum-Germany, 2009).

Journal Articles

A. Epstein, Multi-Level Marketing and Its Brethren: The Legal and Regulatory Environment In The Down Economy (2010) *12 Atlantic Law Journal* 91.

Fukuyama, F., Social Capital and the Modern Capitalist Economy: Creating a High Trust Workplace (1997) *4 Stern Business Magazine* 1–16.

H.L. Pitt and K.L. Shapiro, 'Securities Regulation by Enforcement: A Look ahead at the Next Decade' (Winter 1990) *7 Yale Journal on Regulation* 149.

J. Barnard, Where does the Vulnerable Consumer Fit in? – A Comparative Analysis (Fall 2014) *18 Journal of Consumer & Commercial Law* 2.

J.W. Barnard, 'Evolutionary Enforcement at the Securities and Exchange Commission' (Spring 2010) *71 University of Pittsburgh Law Review* 403.

J. Braucher, 'Theories of Overindebtedness: Interaction of Structure and Culture' (2006) *7(2) Theoretical Inquiries in Law* 323.

J. Stuyck, E. Terryn and T. van Dyck, Confidence through Fairness? The New Directive on Unfair Business-to-Consumer Commercial Practice in the Internal Market, (2006) *43 Common Market Law Review* 107–152.

M. Hofstetter, D. Majía, J.N. Rosas, and M. Urrutia, 'Ponzi Schemes and the Financial Sector: DMG and DRFE in Colombia' (2018) *96 Journal of Banking & Finance* 18–33.

N.K. Mai, 'Analytical Study on the Legality of Multi-Level Marketing' (2019) *XVII (8) Journal of the Myanmar Academy of Arts and Science* 191–204.

R.M. Titus, F. Heinzelmann and J.M. Boyle, 'Victimization of Persons by Fraud' (January 1995) *41(1) Crime & Delinquency* 54–72.

R. Kilian, 'Zur Strafbarkeit von Ponzi-schemes – Der Fall Madoff nach deutschem Wettbewerbs- und Kapitalmarktstrafrecht' (2009) *10(7) Höchstrichterliche Rechtsprechung zum Strafrecht, HRSS* 285–290 <http://www.hrr-strafrecht.de.

R.J. Rhee, 'The Madoff Scandal, Market Regulatory Failure and the Business Education of Lawyers' (Winter 2009) *35 Journal of Corporation Law* 363.

S. Levmore, 'Rethinking Ponzi-Scheme Remedies in and out Bankruptcy (2012) *92 Boston University Law Review* 969–990.

S.A. Bosley, M.F. Bellemare, L. Umwali and J. York, 'Decision-making and

Vulnerability in a Pyramid Scheme Fraud' (2019) *80 Journal of Behavioral and Experimental Economics* 1–13.

T. Tajti, 'Central European Contribution to the American Debate on the Definition of "Securities" or Why does the Definition of "Security" Matter?: The Fiasco of the Hungarian Real Estate Investment Cooperatives, Pyramiding, and Why Emerging Capital Markets should be Equipped to "Act" rather than "React"' (Fall 2005) 15(1) *Transnational Law and Contemporary Problems* 111–216.

T. Tajti, 'Pyramid and Ponzi Schemes and the Price of Inadequate Regulatory Responses: A Comparative Account of the Diverging Regulatory Responses of China, Europe and the United States' (2019) *5 Business & Bankruptcy Law Journal* 19.

T.J. Wilkinson, A. McAlister and S. Widmier, 'Reaching the International Consumer – An Assessment of the International Direct Marketing Environment' (2007) *1(1) Direct Marketing: An International Journal* 17–37.

Titus, R. M., F. Heinzelmann, and J. M. Boyle 'Victimization of Persons by Fraud' (1995) *41 (1) Crime and Delinquency* 54–72.

Newspaper Articles

A.M. Luca, '*Romanian Tycoon Receives Third Graft Sentence*' *Balkan Insight* (26 April 2018) https://balkaninsight.com/2018/04/26/romanian-tycoon-sentenced-in-second-graft-case-04-26-2018/.

Business News, '*Over 119 thousand Ghanaians duped in Ponzi schemes in 2018*' (1 April 2019) https://www.ghanaweb.com/GhanaHomePage/business/Over-119-thousand-Ghanaians-duped-in-Ponzi-schemes-in-2018-734746#.

C. Bohlen, *Hungarians are Thriving, Gloomily The New York Times* (24 June 1991).

F. Norris, *Victims Who Deserve their Fate, NY Times* (10 February 2011) < https://www.nytimes.com/2011/02/11/business/11norris.html.

G. Hussla and V. Votsmeier, '*Jail Time for German Ponzi Schemers in the Infinus Scam*' *Handelsblatt* (Düsseldorf, 10 July 2018) https://www.handelsblatt.com/today/finance/punishing-greed-jail-time-for-german-ponzi-schemers-in-the-infinus-scam/23582684.html?ticket=ST-5321593-OvOfsf5jn3o4OLnyC2ZN-ap4.

Helsinki Times, '*Over 700 criminal complaints on WinCapita*' (August 13, 2008).

K. Hope, '*Crypto Scam Offers Modern Twist on Classic Pyramid Fraud*' *Financial Times* (19 December 2020) 4.

M. Benz '*Ein Schneeballsystem im Bitcoin-Mäntelchen*' *[Ponzi Scheme in Bitcoin Clothing] Neuer Zürcher Zeitung* (19 February 2018) https://www.nzz.ch/wirtschaft/ein-schneeballsystem-im-bitcoin-maentelchen-ld.1358753.

M. Brkić, *Kako je natala i propala Dafiment banka: Pipci i konci svemoćnog gazde [The Emergence and Fall of the Dafiment Bank: Al the Tentacles and Trumps of the Allmighty Boss] Vreme*(12 April 2001) 536 <https://www.vreme.com/cms/view.php?id=96130

S. Hess and E. Sotes, '*Russia's greatest Ponzi mastermind is dead, but his legacy lives on in the crypto world Quartz* (25 April 2018)<https://qz.com/1259524/mmm-and-bitcoin-russian-ponzi-mastermind-sergei-mavrodi-is-dead-but-his-legacy-lives-on-in-crypto/.

Spiegel , '*Nur zum Abheften*' No. 38 (1994) 119–122 https://magazin.spiegel.de/EpubDelivery/spiegel/pdf/13686237

V.N. Conath, '*Akte Balsam non geschlossen*' *Neue Westfälische* (7 March 2020) https://www.nw.de/nachrichten/wirtschaft/10646076_Akte-Balsam-nun-geschlossen.html.

Working Papers, Unpublished Manuscripts

C. Jarvis, 'The Rise and Fall of Pyramid Schemes in Albania,' IMF working paper 99/ 98 (2000)   https://www.imf.org/en/Publications/WP/Issues/2016/12/30/ The-Rise-and-Fall-of-the-Pyramid-Schemes-in-Albania-3161.

J. (Jianqiu) Bai, C. Shang, C. Wan and Y. (Eddie) Zhao, '*Social Capital and Individual Behavior: Evidence from Financial Advisers*' (January 2020).

S. Deason, Shivaram Rajgopal, Gregory Waymire and Roger White, Accounting Lies and Fraud: A Case Where the Two are Separable (12 March 2018), unpublished manuscript. The first version of the paper under the title Who Gets Swindled in Ponzi   Schemes?   https://www0.gsb.columbia.edu/mygsb/faculty/research/ pubfiles/12962/ponzi%20draft%20may%2013%202015.pdf.

Industrial Publications, Command Papers, Law Commission and Other Reports, Conference Papers and Speeches

Anderson, K.B., Federal Trade Commission. *Consumer Fraud in the United States, 2011: The Third FTC Survey* <https://www.ftc.gov/sites/default/files/documents/ reports/consumer-fraud-united-states-2011-third-ftc-survey/130419fraudsurvey_ 0.pdf.

Andrew Ceresney, *Director of the Division of Enforcement given at the UIC-SEC Joint Symposium to Raise Public Awareness: Combating Pyramid Schemes and Affinity Frauds* (March 2, 2016)   https://www.sec.gov/news/speech/ceresney-remarks-joint-symposium-raise-public-awareness-03022016.html.

B. Debroy*Report on Direct Selling Industry in India – Appropriate Regulation is the Key (FICCI and Indicus Analytics)* (April 2013) http://ficci.in/spdocument/ 20237/report-mark.pdf.

Carvajal, A., HunterM., B., Wynter, C.A. Pattillo*Ponzi Schemes in the Caribbean* IMF Working Paper 09-95 (2009).

European Commission, *Consumer Vulnerability across Key Markets in the European Union – A Final Report* (January 2016) https://ec.europa.eu/info/sites/info/ files/consumers-approved-report_en.pdf.

Greg Bartalos, 'Where Crooked Advisers Thrive' (26 November. 2019) *RIA INTEL (Electronic Journal of the Financial Advisory Industry)* <https://www.riaintel.com/ article/b1j68ywn9d31h9/where-crooked-advisors-thrive.

Greg Bartalos, 'Madoff is behind Bard. But with Markets Infected by Covid-19, More Ponzi Schemes may be Unmasked' 7 April 2020) *RIAINTEL.*

Interpellation No. 2315/J XXV.GP filed on 27 August 2014 related to Lyoness International AG (joint-stock company) https://www.parlament.gv.at/PAKT/ VHG/XXV/J/J_02315/fname_362303.pdf.

J.M. Taylor, *The Case (for and) Against Multi-Level Marketing* (Consumer Awareness Institution 2012).

J.T. Barber, 79-FEB Fla. B.J. 8 (February, 2005) 9–10.

M. Celarier, 'How a Massive Ponzi Scheme Fleeced RIAs, Religious Groups, and Retirees' (13 August 2019) *RIA INTEL* https://www.riaintel.com/article/b1gph3426nl9mn/ how-a-massive-ponzi-scheme-fleeced-rias-religious-groups-and-retirees.

NASD (now FINRA) Investor Fraud Study (12 May 2006).

Romanian Corruption Watch, What's Ponzi scheme in Romanian? Sorin Ovidiu

Vintu (2 August 2017) https://medium.com/romania-corruption-watch/whats-ponzi-scheme-in-romanian-sorin-ovidiu-v%C3%AEntu-2897cc47a21f.

S. Gressin (Attorney of the FTC Division of Consumer and Business Education), FTC: AdvoCare business model was pyramid scheme (2 October 2019) https://www.consumer.ftc.gov/blog/2019/10/ftc-advocare-business-model-was-pyramid-scheme.

Special Committee on Ageing, US Senate, Old Scams-New Victims: Breaking the Cycle of Victimization, 109th Congress, 1st Sess. (27 July 2005).

Speech of Sara Lawson, General Counsel of SFO, at Cambridge Symposium on Economic Crime (3 September 2019) at https://www.sfo.gov.uk/2019/09/03/sara-lawson-qc-speaking-at-cambridge-symposium-on-economic-crime-2019/.

[Other] Internet-Based Sources

A. Fenton, 'True Story of $4 Billion OneCoin Ponzi to Become TV Drama' https://micky.com.au/true-story-of-4b-one-coin-ponzi-to-become-tv-drama/ accessed 23 March 2020.

BBC podcast on OneCoin Ponzi at https://www.bbc.co.uk/sounds/play/p07sz990. (The podcast was not accessible anymore on 23 March 2020).

CGAP, A Guide to Regulation and Supervision of Microfinance (CGAP/World Bank 2012) file:///E:/5%20Law%20Growth%20the%20Micro%20Perspective %20HUNG/32%20Microfinance/Microfi-nance-in-Myanmar-Unleashing-the-potential2017The-Business-of-Transition-Law-Reform-Development-and-Economics-in-Myanmar(1).pdf.

E. Kanife, 'StreetTech: Loopers, Twinkas and Other Active Ponzi Schemes You May Want to Avoid' (August 9, 2019) https://technext.ng/2019/08/09/streettech-loom-twinkas-other-active-ponzi-schemes-you-may-want-to-avoid/.

FTC Consumer Sentinel Network https://www.ftc.gov/enforcement/consumer-sentinel-network.

Hungarian Statistical Office (KSH) https://www.ksh.hu/docs/eng/xstadat/xstadat_annual/i_fsp001.html.

Investopedia https://investopedia.com.

J. Oliver, *'Multilevel Marketing: Last Week Tonight with John Oliver'* https://www.youtube.com/watch?v=s6MwGeOm8iI.

LYONESS Headquarters https://www.lyoness-corporate.com/de/.

Madoff Recovery Initiative website https://www.madofftrustee.com/.

MMM ads on the Golubkovs on Youtube at https://www.youtube.com/watch?v=DGGSHibJ8BE.

N. Jentzsch, 'Who Is Targeted? Financial Pyramid Schemes and the Poor' - CGAP Blog Series 'Financial Inclusion and Financial Crime' (18 December 2012) https://www.cgap.org/blog/who-targeted-financial-pyramid-schemes-and-poor.

Ponzitracker (run by Jordan Maglich, a Florida attorney) https://www.ponzitracker.com/.

Pyramid Scheme Alert webpage //www.investor.gov/protect-your-investments/fraud/types-fraud/pyramid-schemes.

T. Moore, J. Han and R. Clayton, the Postmodern Ponzi Scheme: Empirical Analysis of High-Yield Investment Programmes, available electronically https://core.ac.uk/display/22577837.

288   *Tibor Tajti (Thaythy)*

T. Varadarajan, '*The Amazing Madoff Clawback - How two lawyers, Irving Picard and David Sheehan, have recovered 75 cents on the dollar of the stolen money—many times the usual rate in such cases*' Wall Street Journal (30 November 2018), available at http://webreprints.djreprints.com/4482040774476.html.

UK Serious Fraud Office https://www.sfo.gov.uk/?s=ponzi&lang=en.

Index

Printed in Great Britain
by Amazon

38727524R00170